SISTER WIVES, SURROGATES AND SEX WORKERS

Gender in Law, Culture, and Society

Series Editor

Martha Albertson Fineman, Emory University School of Law, USA

Gender in Law, Culture, and Society will address key issues and theoretical debates related to gender, culture, and the law. Its titles will advance understanding of the ways in which a society's cultural and legal approaches to gender intersect, clash, and are reconciled or remain in tension. The series will further examine connections between gender and economic and political systems, as well as various other cultural and societal influences on gender construction and presentation, including social and legal consequences that men and women uniquely or differently encounter. Intended for a scholarly readership as well as for courses, its titles will be a mix of single-authored volumes and collections of original essays that will be both pragmatic and theoretical. It will draw from the perspectives of critical and feminist legal theory, as well as other schools of jurisprudence. Interdisciplinary, and international in scope, the series will offer a range of voices speaking to significant questions arising from the study of law in relation to gender, including the very nature of law itself.

Other titles in the series

Vulnerability: Reflections on a New Ethical Foundation for Law and Politics
Edited by Martha Albertson Fineman and Anna Grear
ISBN 9781472421623

Exploring Masculinities: Feminist Legal Theory Reflections
Edited by Martha Albertson Fineman and Michael Thomson
ISBN 9781472415110

Feminism, Law, and Religion
Edited by Marie A. Failinger, Elizabeth R. Schiltz and Susan J. Stabile
ISBN 9781409444190

Critical Queer Studies: Law, Film, and Fiction in Contemporary American Culture
Casey Charles
ISBN 9781409444060

Sister Wives, Surrogates and Sex Workers
Outlaws by Choice?

ANGELA CAMPBELL
McGill University, Canada

ASHGATE

Published by
Ashgate Publishing Limited
Wey Court East
Union Road
Farnham
Surrey, GU9 7PT
England

Ashgate Publishing Company
110 Cherry Street
Suite 3-1
Burlington, VT 05401-3818
USA

www.ashgate.com

British Library Cataloguing in Publication Data
A catalogue record for this book is available from the British Library

The Library of Congress has cataloged the printed edition as follows:
Campbell, Angela.
Sister wives, surrogates and sex workers : outlaws by choice? / By Angela Campbell.
pages cm. -- (Gender in law, culture, and society)
Includes bibliographical references and index.
ISBN 978-1-4094-3521-1 (hardback) -- ISBN 978-1-4094-3522-8 (ebook) 1. Feminist jurisprudence. 2. Women--Legal status, laws, etc. 3. Women--Social conditions. 4. Feminism. 5. Sex role. 6. Polygamy. 7. Prostitutes. 8. Surrogate motherhood. I. Title.

K349.C36 2013
346.01'6--dc23

2013020320

ISBN 9781409435211 (hbk)
ISBN 9781409435228 (ebk – PDF)
ISBN 9781472430328 (ebk – ePUB)

MIX
Paper from responsible sources
FSC® C013985
FSC www.fsc.org

Printed in the United Kingdom by Henry Ling Limited,
at the Dorset Press, Dorchester, DT1 1HD

Contents

For Maurice, Joshua and Benjamin

Table of Cases

Australia

Black & Black, [2006] FamCA 972.
Chen v Minister for Immigration, Local Government and Ethnic Affairs, [1992] 110 ALR 192.
Coleman v DPP, [2000] NSWSC 275.
Mallet v Mallet, [1984] HCA 21.
Moore v Moore, [2008] FamCA 32.
R v Bonnor (1956), [1957] VR 227.
R v Darnton (1959), [1960] VR 191.
R v Newcombe and Barns, [1996] 1 Qd R 323.
R v Rahme (1993), 70 A Crim R 357.
R v Scarborough (1957), [1959] VR 179.
Re A and B (2000), 26 Fam LR 317.
Re Appln pursuant to the BIRTHS DEATHS AND MARRIAGES REGISTRATION ACT 1997 – BC200002350 (2000), (unreported judgment).
Re Evelyn (1998), 23 Fam LR 53.
Re Mark: an application relating to parental responsibilities, [2003] FamCA 822.
Sibuse Pty Ltd v Shaw, [1988] 13 NSWLR 98.
SL v EHL, [2005] FamCA 132.
Thomas v R, [1937] HCA 83, 59 CLR 279.
Thomas v Thomas (No 2), [1926] VLR 206.
Walsh v Bankstown City Council, [1997] 96 LGERA 62.

Canada

Adoption – 091, 2009 QCCQ 628.
Adoption – 09184, 2009 QCCQ 9058.
Adoption – 09367, 2009 QCCQ 16815.
Adoption – 10329, 2010 QCCQ 18645.
AY v ST, 2010 QCCS 1324.
Bedford v Canada, 2010 ONSC 4264.
Blackmore v British Columbia (Attorney General), 2009 BCSC 1299.
Bruker v Marcovitz, 2007 SCC 54.
Campbell v Campbell, 2007 ABQB 637.
Canada (Attorney General) v Bedford, 2012 ONCA 186.

Canada (Attorney General) v Downtown Eastside Sex Workers United Against Violence Society, 2012 SCC 45.
Canada (Attorney General) v PHS Community Services Society, 2011 SCC 44.
Caron v Caron, [1987] 1 SCR 892.
CL v JLE, 2010 QCCA 2370.
Dans L'affaire du Renvoi fait par le gouvernement du Québec en vertu de la loi sur les renvois à la Cour d'appel, L.R.Q. ch. R-23, relativement à la constitutionnalité des articles 8 à 19, 40 à 53, 60, 61 et 68 de la Loi sur la procréation assistée, L.C. 2004, ch. 2, Procureur Général du Quebec v Procureur Général du Canada, 2008 QCCA 1167.
Ghaznavi v Kashif-Ul-Haque, 2011 ONSC 4062.
Hachey v Dempster, 2003 NBQB 118.
Hartshorne v Hartshorne, 2004 SCC 22.
Hutt v The Queen, [1978] 2 SCR 476.
JR v LH, [2002] OTC 764 (Ont Sup Ct).
Kaddoura v Hammoud, [1998] 168 DLR (4th) 503 (Ont Ct J).
Kerr v Baranow, 2011 SCC 10.
Khan v Khan, 2005 ONCJ 155.
Marshall v Marshall, 2008 NSSC 11.
MB v LL, [2002] 231 DLR 4th 665 (QC CA).
McCulloch v McCulloch, 2003 ABQB 432.
Miglin v Miglin, 2003 SCC 24.
Miron v Trudel, [1995] 2 SCR 418.
Moge v Moge, [1992] 3 SCR 813.
Morris v Morris, [1974] 42 DLR (3d) 550 (MB CA).
Murdoch v Murdoch (1975) 1 SCR 423.
Nova Scotia (Attorney General) v Walsh, 2002 SCC 83.
Pelech v Pelech, [1987] 1 SCR 801.
Quebec (Attorney General) v A, 2013 SCC 5.
R v Barrow (2001), 54 OR (3d) 417 (CA).
R v Big M Drug Mart, [1985] 1 SCR 295.
R v DiPaola (1978), 4 CR (3d) 121 (ON CA).
R v Dudak (1978), 3 CR (3d) 68 (BC CA).
R v Evans (1973), 11 CCC (2d) 130 (ON CA).
R v Grilo (1991), 2 OR (3d) 514 (CA).
R v Harris (1906), 11 CCC 254 (QC SCP).
R v Ikeda (1978), 42 CCC (2d) 195 (ON CA).
R v Jahelka (1987), 79 AR 44 (CA).
R v Kouri, 2005 SCC 81.
R v Labaye, 2005 SCC 80.
R v Lahaie (1990), 55 CCC (3d) 572 (QC CA).
R v Lavallee, [1990] 1 SCR 852.
R v Malott, [1998] 1 S.C.R. 123.
R v McLellan (1980), 55 CCC (2d) 543 (BC CA).

R v Patterson, [1968] SCR 157.
R v Pierce (1982), 37 OR (2d) 721 (CA).
R v Skinner (1987), 35 CCC (3d) 203 (NS SC (AD)).
R v Smith (1989), 49 CCC (3d) 127 (BC CA).
R v Sorko (1969), 4 CCC 241 (BC CA).
R v Whynot (1983), 9 CCC 449 (NS CA).
Rademaker v Rademaker, 2002 NBCA 47.
Re MD, [2008] 52 RFL (6th) 122 (ON Sup Ct).
Reference re Assisted Human Reproduction Act, 2010 SCC 61.
Reference re ss 193 and 195.1(1)(c) of the Criminal Code, [1990] 1 SCR 1123.
Reference re: Section 293 of the Criminal Code of Canada, 2011 BCSC 1588.
Richardson v Richardson, [1987] 1 SCR 857.
Rick v Brandsema, 2009 SCC 10.
Rockert v R, [1978] 2 SCR 704.
Rypkema v HMTQ, 2003 BCSC 1784.
The Queen v Bear's Shin Bone (1899), 3 CCC 329 (NWT SC).
Whitty v Whitty, 2008 NSSC 243.
WJQM v AMA, 2011 SKQB 317.

United Kingdom

A v C (1978), [1985] FLR 445.
Abbott v Smith, [1965] 2 QB 662.
Caldwell v Leech, [1913] 109 LT 188.
Gorman v Standen, [1964] 1 QB 294.
Hyde v Hyde and Woodmansee, [1866] LR 1 P&D 130.
In Re Bethell (1887), [1888] 38 Ch D 220.
Jones and Wood v Director of Public Prosecutions, [1993] 96 Cr App R 130.
Lambert v Lambert, [2003] EWCA 1685.
MacLeod v MacLeod, [2008] UKPC 64.
McFarlane v McFarlane, [2006] UKHL 24.
N v N, [1999] EWHC Fam 838.
R v Ahluwalia, [1992] 4 All ER 889.
R v Duffy, [1949] 1 All ER 932.
R v Massey, [2008] 1 Cr App R 28.
R v Thornton (No.2), [1996] 1 WLR 1174 (CA).
Radmacher v Granatino, [2010] UKSC 42.
RB v United Kingdom, [1992] Application No 19628/92, ECHR.
Re an adoption application (surrogacy), [1987] 2 All ER 826.
Re C (A Minor) (Wardship: Surrogacy), [1985] FLR 846.
Re L (a minor), [2010] EWHC 3146 (Fam).
Re MW (Adoption: Surrogacy) (1994), [1996] 3 FCR 128.
Re S (Parental Order), [2009] EWHC 2977 (Fam), [2010] 1 FLR 1156.

Re X & Y (Foreign Surrogacy), [2008] EWHC 3030 (Fam).
Uddin v Choudhury, [2009] EWCA Civ 1205.
Whiston v Whiston, [1995] Fam 198 (CA).
White v White, [2001] 1 AC 596.
Woolfe v Woolfe, [1931] KB 549.

Table of Legislation

Australia

Assisted Reproductive Technology Act 2007 (NSW).
Assisted Reproductive Treatment Act 2008 (Vic).
Brothels Legislation Amendment Act 2007 (NSW).
Cognate Summary Offences Bill 1979 (NSW).
Crimes Act 1900 (NSW).
Crimes Act 1958 (Vic).
Criminal Code 1902 (WA).
Criminal Code Act 1899 (Qld).
Criminal Code Act 1924 (Tas).
Disorderly Houses Act 1943 (NSW).
Disorderly Houses Amendment Bill 1992 (NSW).
Disorderly Houses Amendment Bill 1995 (NSW).
Family Law Act 1975 (Cth).
Family Relationships Act 1975 (SA).
Infertility Treatment Act 1995 (Vic).
Interpretation Act 1901 (Cth).
Marriage Act 1961 (Cth).
Parentage Act 2004 (ACT).
Police Act 1892 (WA).
Police Offences Act 1935 (Tas).
Prostitution Act 1979 (NSW).
Prostitution Act 1992 (ACT).
Prostitution Act 1999 (Qld).
Prostitution Act 2000 (WA).
Prostitution Amendment Bill 1983 (NSW).
Prostitution Bill 2011 (WA).
Prostitution Control Act 1994 (Vic).
Prostitution Regulation Act 2004 (NT).
Restricted Premises Act 1943 (NSW).
Sex Industry Offences Act 2005 (Tas).
Sex Industry Offences Bill 2005 (Tas).
Sex Industry Regulation Bill 2003 (Tas).
Status of Children Act 1974 (Vic).
Statutes Amendment (Surrogacy) Act 2009 (SA).
Substitute Parents Act 1994 (ACT).

Summary Offences Act 1953 (SA).
Summary Offences Act 1970 (NSW).
Summary Offences Act 1988 (NSW).
Surrogacy Act 2008 (WA).
Surrogacy Act 2010 (NSW).
Surrogacy Act 2010 (Qld).
Surrogacy Bill 2011 (Tas).
Surrogacy Act 2012 (Tas).
Surrogacy Contracts Act 1993 (Tas).
Surrogate Parenthood Act 1988 (Qld).
Vagrancy Act 1902 (NSW).

Canada

An Act for the more speedy and effectual punishment of Persons keeping Disorderly Houses, 1829, 9 & 10 Geo IV, c 8.
An Act further to amend the Criminal Law, SC 1890, c 37.
An Act respecting Offences against Public Morals and Public Convenience, RSC 1886, c 157.
An Act respecting Offences against the Person, SC 1869, c 20.
An Act respecting Offences relating to the Law of Marriage, RSC 1886, c 161.
An Act respecting the Criminal Law, SC 1954, c 51.
An Act respecting the Public Lands of the Dominion, SC 1872, c 23.
An Act respecting Vagrants, SC 1869, c 28.
An Act to amend the Criminal Code in relation to sexual offences and other offences against the person and to amend certain other Acts in relation thereto or in consequence thereof, SC 1980-81-82-83, c 125.
Assisted Human Reproduction Act, RSC 2004, c 2.
Bill 65, *An Act further to amend the Criminal Law*, 4th Sess, 6th Parl, 1890.
Bill C-6, *An act respecting assisted human reproduction and related research*, 3rd Sess, 37th Parl, 2004 (assented to 29 March 2004).
Bill C-13, *An Act respecting assisted human reproduction*, 2nd Sess, 37th Parl, 2002.
Bill C-47, *An Act respecting human reproductive technologies and commercial transactions relating to human reproduction*, 2nd Sess, 35th Parl, 1996.
Bill C-49, *An Act to amend the Criminal Code (prostitution)*, 1st Sess, 33rd Parl, 1985 (assented to 20 December 1985).
Bill C-56, *An Act respecting assisted human reproduction*, 1st Sess, 37th Parl, 2002.
Bill F, *An Act to amend "An Act respecting Offences relating to the Law of Marriage,"* 4th Sess, 6th Parl, 1890.
Birth Registration Regulations made under Section 51 of the Vital Statistics Act, RSNS 1989, C 494 OIC 2007-489, NS Reg 390/2007.

Canadian Bill of Rights, SC 1960, c 44.
Canadian Charter of Rights and Freedoms, Part I of the *Constitution Act, 1982*, being Schedule B to the *Canada Act 1982* (UK), 1982, c 11.
Child and Parental Benefits Regulations, NLR 2009, 43/09.
Civil Code of Québec, SQ 1991, c 64.
Constitution Act, *1867* (UK), 30 & 31 Vict, c 3, reprinted in RSC 1985, App II, No 5.
Criminal Code, 1892, SC 1892, c 29.
Criminal Code, RSC 1970, c C-34.
Criminal Code, RSC 1985, c C-46.
Criminal Code Amendment Act, 1907, SC 1907, c 8.
Criminal Code Amendment Act, 1913, SC 1913, c 13.
Criminal Code Amendment Act, 1915, SC 1915, c 12.
Criminal Law Amendment Act, 1972, SC 1972, c 13.
Divorce Act, RSC 1985, c 3 (2nd supp).
Estate Administration Act, RSBC 1996, c 122.
Family Law Act, RSO 1990, c F3.
Family Law Act, SA 2003, c F-4.5.
Family Law Act, SBC 2011, c 25.
Family Relations Act, RSBC 1996, c 128.*Vital Statistics Act*, SNL 2009, c V-6.01.

United Kingdom

Adoption Act 1976 (UK), c 36.
Bill 75, *Welfare Reform Bill*, 2010-2011 sess, 2011.
City of London Police Act 1839 (UK), 2 & 3 Vict, c 94.
Coroners and Justice Act 2009 (UK), c 25.
Criminal Law Amendment Act 1885 (UK), 48 & 49 Vict, c 69.
Disorderly Houses Act 1751 (UK), 25 Geo II, c 36.
Divorce (Religious Marriages) Act 2002 (UK), c 27.
Human Fertilisation and Embryology Act 1990 (UK), c 37.
Human Fertilisation and Embryology Act 2008 (UK), c 22.
Immigration Act 1988 (UK), c 14.
Matrimonial Causes Act 1973 (UK), c 18.
Metropolitan Police Act 1839 (UK), 2 & 3 Vict, c 47.
Offences Against the Person Act, 1861 (UK), 24 & 25 Vict, c 100.
Policing and Crime Act 2009 (UK), c 26.
Private International Law (Miscellaneous Provisions) Act 1995 (UK), c 42.
Sexual Offences Act 1956 (UK), c 69.
Sexual Offences Act 1985 (UK), c 44.
Sexual Offences Act 2003 (UK), c 42.
Street Offences Act 1959 (UK), c 57.
Surrogacy Arrangements Act 1985 (UK), c 49.

Town Police Clauses Act 1847 (UK), 10 & 11 Vict, c 89.
Welfare Reform Act 2012 (UK), c 5.

Acknowledgements

My interest in the subject of this book was sparked by field research on women in polygamy undertaken in the community of Bountiful, British Columbia. Although they live within what many would consider a deeply patriarchal faith community and under an ongoing threat of state-imposed legal sanctions for their way life, women in Bountiful emphatically resisted the label of "victim." They insisted upon their choice-making capacities while recognizing that the normative orders in which they operated imposed serious social and economic limits. Discussions in Bountiful brought home the way in which socially and legally maligned women can muster agency, resilience, pragmatism and, most importantly, opportunities for choice. These discussions also underscored the damage that the state does when it criminalizes contested and controversial choices in the name of protecting "vulnerable" people. Seeing as this fieldwork represents this book's genesis, it seems fitting to begin by thanking the women who took part in it, particularly in view of the risks that participating in this project carried for them.

I have been granted a number of important opportunities to share the ideas in this book as they developed. In such settings, I received enormously helpful feedback that brought to light gaps and inconsistencies in my research and reasoning, which I hope I have since filled and resolved. In early 2013, I spent a short time as a visiting scholar at Emory Law School's Vulnerability and the Human Condition Initiative—Feminist Legal Theory Project, as well as at the Australian National University (ANU)'s College of Law. Both settings provided extraordinary sites for sharing and advancing this work, and I am grateful to Martha Fineman and Desmond Manderson, who were my hosts at Emory and ANU respectively. I also wish to thank the participants at Emory's Vulnerability and the Human Condition Initiative seminar, who read and reflected critically on my draft chapter related to sex work. Furthermore, I am immensely grateful to colleagues and students at ANU's Gender Institute and College of Law who attended and engaged with my work at seminars I led in those two settings on polygamy, sex work and choice.

The Feminist Legal Theory Collaborative Research Network (FLT-CRN) has afforded terrific opportunities for disseminating and discussing this work with productive and bright feminist colleagues. The FLT-CRN allowed me to present two chapters at separate workshops in 2012, where I encountered tremendous support and enthusiasm for this project, as well as critical feedback that prompted me to refine what I had to say about law's engagement with women's tough choices. I acknowledge Suzanne Kim and Laurie Kohn specifically, my commentators on draft chapters at FLT-CRN workshops, who provided important insights and reflections.

A number of generous colleagues and students read drafts of various parts of this book, and I owe them a huge intellectual and moral debt for thoughtful, rich comments and conversations, which heightened this book's quality and instilled my confidence in it: Pascale Cornut St-Pierre, Bethany Hastie, Nicholas Kasirer, Lisa Kelly, Lisa Kerr, Kyle Kirkup, Robert Leckey, Rod Macdonald, Stu Marvel, Anne Sanders, Ruth Sefton-Green, Cristina Toteda, and Shauna Van Praagh. I also thank Pascale Fournier and Rod Macdonald for instructive comments on this manuscript's draft proposal prior to its submission to Ashgate Publishing.

At Ashgate, my series publisher, Alison Kirk, has been enthusiastic about this project from my very first email contact with her in early 2011. I am appreciative of her patience and thoroughness in collaborating with me throughout this book's development. I am also indebted to the editor of Ashgate's Gender in Law, Culture and Society Series, Martha Fineman, for encouraging this project, for her feedback on the manuscript and for allowing me to visit with her and her colleagues and students working within her Vulnerability and the Human Condition Initiative.

This book benefited from financial support from the Social Science and Humanities Research Council, Canada's Foundation for Legal Research, and the Faculty of Law at McGill University. Funding from these institutions supported the research assistance work of an assembly of eminently competent, intellectually curious, reliable and industrious students. Lainie Basman, Sarah Berger Richardson and Mairi Springate were involved in preparing for, carrying out, transcribing and analyzing interviews carried out in Bountiful. In so doing, they displayed superb intellectual integrity and maturity. Stefanie Carsley, Bethany Hastie and Cristina Toteda combed through a virtual mountain of primary and secondary materials, with a view to discerning relevant and instructive authorities for this book. They carried out this formidable feat with rigour, skill, insightfulness and indefatigable energy!

The Deans of McGill Law during the period of this book's conception, research and writing, Nicholas Kasirer and Daniel Jutras, have encouraged this scholarship, and I recognize and value what their support has meant from institutional, intellectual and personal perspectives.

The encouragement and emotional support that I received while writing this book cannot be overstated. I thank my parents, Ron and Rosa Campbell, for their meaningful and loving presence in my life, and for looking forward to reading this book. My niece, Josephine Campbell, and my "Onichino nieces" consistently inquire about my work, and we have had inspiring discussions about what it means for girls to grow, learn, and choose.

While writing this book, my husband, Maurice Onichino, taught me much about resilience, perseverance and tough choices in the face of unexpected hurdles and limits. I thank him for demonstrating how to identify, seize and cherish the beauty of the silver lining and for supporting my work in all the ways that count. And finally, I am grateful to our clever and dynamic boys, Josh and Ben Onichino, for the gifts of entertainment and laughter delivered via their puzzling questions and riddles, discoveries and challenges, quirky turns of phrase, and monkey business! While writing this book, they were known to ask, "When are you going to be finished, Mom?" or "How many words are you at now?" I thank my boys for putting up with the distraction that this book sometimes caused, and I thank my husband for taking up the helm when that was so (and even when it wasn't). This book is dedicated to the three of them.

Montreal
March 2013

Introduction

When my grandmother was 88 years old, she moved into a residential facility for "semi-autonomous" seniors. The facility provided three meals daily and the managers organized a range of recreational activities and outings for residents. My grandmother ate breakfast, lunch and dinner alone in her apartment unit, and participated in none of the activities. This was partly because she was a generally discontented and difficult person. It was partly that she was Italian-speaking and had difficulty communicating with other residents. And, it was partly a form of protest. She was not happy about being "put in a home" and so, despite the urging of her children and grandchildren to eat and engage with others, my grandmother passed her days alone in her flat watching game shows on television, and eating Special K. She insisted that she had few choices left to make in her life, but whom she talked to, what she ate, and whether she participated in the "Grandmas in Motion" exercise class each morning were her business. She consistently followed these assertions with reminders that she was *sempre da solo* and wanted to be visited more often.

One hot June morning, my grandmother suffered a stroke in her apartment. Given her infrequent interactions with other building residents, no one took note of not seeing her throughout that day or into the next. By the time she received medical attention, her brain's blood supply had been cut off for too long to regain speech or mobility. Her will to continue on in this world dissipated, and she died four months later.

I lamented my grandmother's death. It was not the fact that she had died, but the way her life ended, that was so perturbing. Had my grandmother not been so stubborn in refusing to mingle with others in her residence, someone would have noticed her absence and found her sooner than 36 hours after her stroke. The end of her life would not have been so morally crushing.

It is difficult to resist feeling that my grandmother's choice to isolate herself was a mistake that we should have tried harder to correct. Decisions that seem illogical, inexplicable or perversely counter to the interests of the decision-maker are often chalked up to poor judgment, misunderstanding, duress or depravity. Instinctively, such choices are not appreciated as reflecting the chooser's own ambitions and values, nor are they typically understood as a form of resistance.

Although not having much to do with what we formally see as "law" my grandmother's story here is offered as an example of the difficulty legal actors encounter in responding to controversial or puzzling choices. This is especially the case when such choices are made by individuals whom we classically perceive as vulnerable and when these choices carry far-reaching social and moral implications.

This book explores the meaning, relevance and perils of the concept of choice, particularly in connection with legal approaches to women's morally ambiguous lifestyles. It makes two central claims. First, this book argues that women exercise resilience, resistance and agency, and make reasoned and deliberated choices, even when they live and work within oppressive or patriarchal contexts. Second, this book maintains that the mere fact of recognizing women's ability to make choices in the face of imposing constraints must not serve to justify the state's abdication of responsibility for addressing gender-based discrimination. In other words, this book emphasizes the importance of acknowledging women's choices and strength in the context of constricting and difficult life circumstances. Yet it advances this position cautiously to avoid assuming a dogmatic liberal outlook, pursuant to which emphasizing women's agency might support challenges to legislative and policy measures aimed at reducing risk and broadening women's options and opportunities.

Although this book centralizes the concept and language of choice, it does not argue for a constrained state presence in women's lives. Nonetheless, it contends that such presence in the particular manifestation of criminal law can be profoundly problematic. Criminalizing choices on the grounds of preventing self-harm or social morality evacuates seemingly inopportune decisions of agency, and often exacerbates the harm it purports to prevent. Moreover, criminal law commonly disregards the plurality of influences shaping and giving meaning and value to socially impugned choices. Consequently, this book argues that state law must be informed by the experiential knowledge of those who make such choices, on whose lives this law is most directly brought to bear.

This analysis is developed through a study of three incendiary issues. Polygamy, surrogacy and sex work are subject to intense legal scrutiny and debate. These practices, or those closely associated with them, are generally criminalized on the ground that they tend to corrupt the imagined purity of marriage, reproduction and sexual intimacy while imperiling women. Preeminent legal narratives resist the notion that polygamous wives, surrogates and sex workers make informed and reasoned choices. These women are more likely to be viewed as compelled by dominating, typically male, forces beyond their control.

At the same time, law crafted by the state exhibits a parallel, seemingly paradoxical, inclination to hold any perceived exercise of agency or choice against the chooser herself. That is, although women are cast as exploited victims in conversations circulating around polygamy, surrogacy and sex work, they are also vulnerable to the sanction and stigma of the criminal law. Accordingly, state approaches to these practices set up an incoherent binary with respect to women's choices in morally and socially contested settings. Women are at once understood as weakened and victimized by the oppressive and sometimes violent forces that surround them, while also morally depraved and indifferent, and worthy of punishment. Capacity for choice is either denied, or potentially recriminatory.

This book argues for a renewed and more textured understanding of choice in the evaluation of criminalized and morally challenging activities. It emphasizes that empirical research, which communicates the lived experiences of those most deeply affected by state law, is critical to identifying the way in which individuals can muster power and agency even when they operate within onerous and important constraints. Such research further highlights how ostensibly self-injurious choices might hold critical meaning and value for those making such choices. Finally, this book demonstrates how state law, especially in the form of criminal proscription, curbs rather than optimizes choice-making opportunities for those who encounter social and economic marginalization.

These premises are developed in Chapter 1, which sets out an analytical framework for juridical evaluations of choice in connection with unsettling or thorny issues. This framework is in turn deployed in subsequent chapters, with a view to examining how choice and agency figure within the experiences of sister wives in polygamy, surrogates and sex workers. Chapter 1 demonstrates how feminist legal theorists have rightly criticized the idea of choice as potentially damaging to gender equality and women's interests. Using the examples of women's decisions in relation to domestic violence, domestic work and domestic contracts, this chapter explores the limits and challenges associated with the concept and lexicon of choice. Perfunctory analyses premised on choice bear important risks: they are inclined to obscure constraints on options; they can lead to the ascription of responsibility for morally involuntary outcomes; and they offer monolithic and flat representations of those presumed capable or incapable of making meaningful decisions.

Yet, despite its troublesome features, choice should remain fundamental to feminist discourse and theory, particularly for jurists charged with assessing morally opaque decisions. Chapter 1 develops an analytical framework premised upon an inquiry that lends itself to studying and evaluating choice within juridical inquiry. This framework moves beyond a simplistic investigation based upon whether a woman has either chosen or been coerced in taking up a controversial lifestyle. Such a rudimentary question, which rests on crude choice/coercion and agent/victim binaries, is often central to legal analyses even though it does little to advance understandings of women's experiences and state law's engagement with them. The analytical framework that Chapter 1 develops strives to construct a more robust line of inquiry with respect to choice. It rests upon an investigation of three factors: the presumptions on which relevant state laws rest; the intersection between these laws and informal norms; and state laws' effects on women's options and decisions. Central to this investigation is a reliance on empirical evidence illuminating how women live and experience choices that carry critical tradeoffs.

The analytical framework that Chapter 1 establishes is applied in the ensuing three chapters, each one contemplating the notion of choice in connection with three separate practices that arguably undermine women's interests. Legal narratives circulating around polygamy, surrogacy and sex work predominantly cast women as vulnerable and helpless. These narratives further question and challenge the possibility that women could ever engage or remain in such activities following an independent and informed choice.

Chapters 2, 3 and 4 explore the presence of and limits on women's choices regarding, respectively, polygamy, surrogacy and sex work. Each of these chapters considers the narratives of women involved in such practices as communicated through empirical scholarship, and compares these accounts with relevant legal rules designed by the state. More specifically, each chapter contrasts women's experiences with the presumptions and objectives that drive formal laws grounded in prohibition. Juxtaposing narratives derived from women engaged in these controversial social practices with narratives offered by those involved in the design, interpretation and enforcement of state law illuminates the tacit, informal norms at work in shaping women's difficult decisions affecting family life, reproduction, sex and labour.

Polygamy, surrogacy and sex work bear the further matched trait of being subject to criminal law's scrutiny and sanction in most Western jurisdictions. As elaborated in Chapters 2, 3 and 4, however, criminal law does not bear an identical presence in each of these domains. For example, trading sex for money is not itself criminalized in the jurisdictions considered here, but activities associated with this form of exchange might be, thus making it virtually impossible to engage in sex work without criminal liability. Comparably, polygamy's status under the criminal law is not consistently clear. In some jurisdictions, state law defines this as a distinctly prohibited act, whereas in others, the state explicitly outlaws bigamy while remaining silent as to polygamy. Where this is so, the legal status of polygamy—that is, being party to a conjugal relationship involving plural partners in the absence of formal marriage—remains nebulous.

There are two ways of interpreting the criminalization of the acts of—or acts associated with—polygamy, surrogacy and sex work. According to one view, prohibition is said to be justified by the harm these acts inflict upon vulnerable individuals and groups. This claim usually implies concerns about women and children; the focus of this book, however, is on women of full age. Thus, a first way of understanding criminal law's application in these contexts is to see the practices at issue as so injurious to women's interests that prohibition is necessary for their own protection. The state steps in to deliver women from their own misjudgment or from irresistible external pressures that compel their wrongful behaviour. This line of thinking posits that women have become entangled in problematic practices as victims of necessity or duress, rather than as a result of their own choices.

A second position is that sister wives, surrogates and sex workers have options and opportunities for choice, but have made bad decisions. Such decisions cannot be readily explained away as the unavoidable outcomes of coercive forces. Rather, according to this depiction, women are complicit in carrying out socially and legally impugned acts. Thus understood as morally blameworthy, they are perceived to merit criminal sanction and stigma.

These interpretive strands, although seemingly contradictory, course through state law's principal narrative about women involved in practices like polygamy, surrogacy and sex work. This book argues that neither of these strands invokes choice in an instructive or useful manner, nor do they recognize effectively or appropriately the resistance women can muster in perilous social and economic circumstances. The presumptions and aspirations that drive formal, state-made rules on polygamy, surrogacy and sex work construct a binary through which women are understood as passive victims or independent agents. Sometimes, they are viewed as both victims and agents simultaneously. Yet each of these portrayals undermines women's interests and deprives jurists of the critical ability to discern women's capacity for making choices in the face of affliction, the meaning and value they may ascribe to such choices, and state law's influence on constricting the choices of those whom it claims to protect.

Women's narratives, recorded through empirical scholarship, often contradict the suppositions and aspirations driving the formal governance of polygamy, surrogacy and sex work. These narratives illuminate the normative forces beyond state law that influence women's understanding, evaluation and decisions in regard to morally fraught practices like those considered here. Moreover, empirically drawn experiential knowledge furnishes insights into the potentially oppressive force that state law has in women's lives, particularly those who are poor, racialized, geographically isolated or living within patriarchal family and community structures.

Experiential knowledge brings to light the multiple, often tacit, normative forces at work in women's most difficult decisions. It further reveals the detrimental impact that state law can have in the lives and wellbeing of these individuals. These observations about informal norms and state law are central to this book's effort in enriching juridical understandings of women's lifestyles and choices, which appear to undermine their own interests. This book encourages a move away from reliance on criminal laws premised on simplistic and often inaccurate dichotomies of women as either desperate victims or morally wanton actors toward initiatives that would account more fully for women's lived experiences.

As such, this work is grounded in feminist legal theory and critical legal pluralist approaches. With regard to its feminist strand, the book bears the three elements that Halley (2006: 17) defines as essential to any feminist undertaking: it perceives distinctions as being drawn between women and men; it accepts that women have historically been, and continue to be, subordinated to male interests; and it seeks to counter such subordination while improving women's justice outcomes.

This book fulfills Halley's three criteria through efforts to open legal inquiry and analysis to an unconventional juridical authority—empirical, qualitative, narrative-based research—to inform legal thinking. It adheres to feminist calls for research that departs from the "situated knowledge" (Matsuda 1990: 1764) of those who articulate and enforce formal legal rules to consider the perspectives of individuals most directly affected by these rules. The book aspires to be shaped by the experiences and perspectives of those who live under, construe and contest law (Kim 1993: 55, Harding, S. 1987: 7), and thereby deepen law's engagement with the lives of women whose accounts and knowledge have not traditionally formed part of law's canon. It does so by postulating that personal narrative and experience offered by those historically deprived of access to formal justice institutions can enrich perspectives on complex legal and social problems (Bartlett 1990).

While assuming this position, this book remains mindful of the potential perils of empirical research. As argued elsewhere, there is a danger in assuming the generalizability of qualitative studies and experience-based stories shared with academic or policy-based researchers. Such research gathers individuals' stories at one point in their lives, and it is risky to assume that such accounts statically represent their "truth" either in the past or going forward. Moreover, storytellers willing to take part in field studies might not represent the views of silent or secluded constituents of a community whose beliefs and experiences differ but are not drawn to the surface through empirical inquiry (Campbell 2008). A critical and introspective feminist approach thus requires awareness of the potential for research that asks the "woman question" to isolate and disenfranchise women (Bartlett 1990). It also urges heed to be taken of the political, historical and cultural factors that can alleviate or deepen subordinations caused by zeroing in on gender alone (Bunting 1993). The ensuing chapters of this book aim to signal how the forces of race, sexual identity, class and culture intersect with gender to shape experiences in and choices about practices such as polygamy, surrogacy and sex work.

Beyond feminism, it is possible to study the issues explored in this book through additional conceptual frameworks and perspectives without "*losing access to feminist theory*" (Halley 2006: 8, emphasis in original). Indeed, the view advanced here is that an analysis integrative of other, complementary theoretical approaches enriches this work's feminist credentials. The book draws on critical legal pluralism as an additional perspective from which to analyze the notion of choice. In doing so, its commitment to feminist inquiry is not diluted, but nourished. That is, critical legal pluralism invites the study of law's engagement at the social level in a way that complicates and enriches feminist theory in its most orthodox form.

Critical legal pluralism builds on the philosophy and "ethos" of pluralism, which "enshrines an attitude that embraces multiplicity and diversity in the law" and sees the influence of varied legal orders, both state-based and non-state-based, on human behaviours and decisions (Davies 2005: 93). Accepting this view, this book deploys the term "law" to denote rules formed and interpreted within government institutions, as well as norms that hold persuasion and clout that emanate from social settings outside of the state. Yet a "critical" legal pluralism moves beyond the recognition of heterogeneous normative orders to dislodge the centrality of these orders. It urges the construal of the legal subject as bearing "transformative capacity" that allows her to interpret, avoid, transgress and tolerate formal rules designed by the state (referred to throughout this book as "state law"). At the same time, this legal subject, according to critical legal pluralist thought, constructs, abides by and withstands the requirements and expectations of her other normative contexts, such as those of her family, work environment or cultural community (referred to throughout this book as "non-state law") (Kleinhans and Macdonald

1997). In this way, critical legal pluralism moves the legal subject to the core of law-making and interpreting, positioning her as essential to the jurist's understanding of what law is, what law is not, what law does, and what law fails to do.

The feminist and critical legal pluralist theoretical strands of this work dovetail. Feminism underlies the book's emphasis on deploying empiricism to learn how women encounter and experience controversial choices and acts. Simultaneously, critical legal pluralism rationalizes the effort made here to centralize the accounts of "narrating subjects" in regard to how they understand and respond to socially and legally impugned practices (Kleinhans and Macdonald 1997: 46).

This fusion of feminism and critical legal pluralism is not original. In her work on women in Chasidism, Shauna Van Praagh (1996) persuasively demonstrates the complementarity of these two theoretical rubrics for understanding how women muster and surrender power in the face of competing normative dynamics. Her project illuminates the relevance of identifying the multiple systems of law—formal and informal, state and non-state—that govern women's beliefs, choices and behaviour. Van Praagh further demonstrates (1996: 205) how these legal systems "may be alternatively oppressive and protective," such that women constantly negotiate competing normative influences in their daily decisions.

Van Praagh's analysis demonstrates how layering feminist and critical legal pluralist lenses lends itself to identifying the contradictions and fluidity in women's experiences. Recognizing that women can occupy the twin, seemingly incompatible, roles of agent and victim suggests "room for contradictions" and thus aligns with what some have identified as a feminist "third wave" (Reed 1997: 132, see also Whelehan 2007, Stone, A. 2007). While refraining from situating itself firmly within any particular feminist branch or generation, this book embraces the view that women's lived realities can both constitute and be constricted by multiple legal systems and norms. They can at once be subordinated and stifled by cultural and social patriarchy, economic oppression and the criminal law, while also assembling resistance and power in the face of such forces. In a word, regardless of the law—whatever its source and degree of formalism—contouring women's deliberations and conduct, they can and do make relevant choices. Yet, identifying such choice must not in turn serve as a ground for reducing women to liberalism's rational, free agent who does not need or want the state's attention and support. That move would run counter to a feminist and critical legal pluralist project tethered to aspirations of gender equality and empowerment.

The goal, rather, is to turn to informal norms and obscured sites of power, which throw into relief the authority that those living in ostensibly compromising or damaging circumstances may yield, especially those leading criminally proscribed lifestyles. This line of inquiry also shows how law crafted by the state coexists and collides with non-state rules and expectations; in many instances different normative systems impose conflicting demands on their subjects. In consequence, individuals will often aim to harmonize conceptually the legal orders to which they have an allegiance. Where this is not possible, they will adhere to the norms they see as most meaningful and valuable, even if this entails disobedience of state law. Such efforts at normative reconciliation and ordering are made evident by analyses informed by feminist legal theory and critical legal pluralism.

While critical of "law" as conventionally understood, and "without exaggerating law's importance," empirical narratives and "everyday experience" indicate that state law matters and makes a difference (Valverde 2012: 6). Formal governance is therefore fundamental to the analytical framework for understanding choice that this book develops. In considering the law of the state, the focal points are the jurisdictions of Canada, the United Kingdom and Australia. In choosing to study these three counties in particular, the analysis does not purport to be comparative in an "instrumental" sense; the aim is not to consider how state laws in these places compare, influence or may be harmonized with each other (Valcke 2004: 715). Rather, these jurisdictions have been selected with a view to providing examples of and insight into how Western, multicultural, democratic states, which share a common legal tradition, regulate and respond to women's morally charged lifestyle choices. Each case study sets out relevant historical and contemporary legal approaches in Canada, the United Kingdom and Australia. This analysis reveals overlapping themes and aspirations in the state laws in place in these jurisdictions, which are contrasted, in each case study, with women's empirically derived narratives. This allows for an interrogation into the way in which the formal law of the state reflects accurately, if at all, women's views, values and experiences.

The accounts of "sister wives" considered in Chapter 2 illuminate law's gaps in understanding how these women may give meaning and value to being married polygamously. Polygamous sister wives' marriages are often entered with a view to adhering to tenets of faith or cultural expectations. They may accept polygamy knowing that it falls within the purview of the criminal law, feeling an obligation to community that surpasses their sense of obligation to the state. Comparably, Chapter 3 demonstrates how decisions regarding surrogacy made against the backdrop of the risk of penal sanction may be fueled by a desire to contribute or belong socially or to meet family and community expectations. And sex workers, considered in Chapter 4, hone skills to identify and negotiate the physical, emotional and financial risks of their work. Their narratives illustrate how risk-management strategies, pragmatism and efforts to optimize labour conditions compel movement within and around the boundaries of state law as well as the norms and culture of street-based and indoor sex work sites.

Each of these case studies incorporate experiential narratives recorded through field studies to consider how women navigate multiple sites of normativity. They demonstrate how the presumptions and goals underpinning state laws often miss, quite sharply, the lived realities of those most affected by these laws. Most notably, state law in the areas considered here typically hinges upon an absolute, unhelpful narrative about women and choices fraught with moral ambiguity, which either deems choice inexistent or invokes choice as a basis for holding ostensible choosers responsible for adverse outcomes. Prior to developing the case studies announced regarding polygamy, surrogacy and sex work, Chapter 1 aims to theorize choice within feminist legal thinking and develop a method for examining this concept in a way that avoids the pitfalls of liberalism's conventional understanding of choice, rationalism, agency and responsibility. The analysis mounted in Chapter 1 should bear as much pertinence to matters as socially significant and challenging as those central to this book as to ordinary, everyday issues such as whether to respect the decisions of an elderly person who self-isolates and refuses to socialize. With this aspiration in mind, this book sets out to inform juridical thinking on choice in a way that will bear meaning and instructive value across issues and controversies, regardless of the breadth of their perceived social stakes and import.

Chapter 1
Complicating Choices

The language and concept of choice often divides feminists. Choice might be viewed as fostering women's empowerment and opportunities. This viewpoint, which is often associated with abortion debates (Michelman 2005, Jackson 2001), presumes the chooser's autonomy and the ability to control or govern one's physical and moral self. It also presumes agency, a concept understood here as incorporating autonomy "plus options" to allow for viable choices (Showden 2011: 1). The exercise of agency through choice is presumed to spur change that is typically consistent with the chooser's objectives (Sen 1999). These empowering images stand in contrast to a more skeptical view of choice. For many feminists, the concept invites intense scrutiny, especially in circumstances that seem constraining or coercive, or when outcomes appear hostile to the chooser's interests. In these situations, many feminists would see the failure to interrogate and critique choice as irresponsible (Gill 2007, Williams 1991, Majury 2009).

Substantive debates over choice are complicated by its relationship with the concept of consent. Choice is often seen as overlapping with or as encompassing consent. Making a choice, like giving consent, is conceptually associated with individual autonomy or self-governance and is understood as an action that reflects the chooser's or consenter's identity, preferences, and values. Choice and consent also connote acquiescence to or an adoption of a particular result. But choice and consent are not synonymous, and their distinctiveness is best retained even though their relationship is "complex" (Biggs 2007: 142) and even though the terms circulate through feminist writings without extensive attention to their individual meanings and distinctions (West 1995, Hunter and Cowan 2007). This book's deliberate focus on choice, rather than consent, is based on a specific understanding of these two concepts. "Choice" is appreciated here as linked to agency and is thus viewed as a selection made in the face of multiple possibilities. In contrast, "consent" is perceived as an acceptance or allowance of a particular action or situation that affects the consenter's person or well-being (Hanna 2010: 136). This book also understands choice as involving more than a single, discrete moment of consent-giving, and instead incorporates a prolonged mental state and process. That being said, this mental state and process embedded in choice need not be emotionally unequivocal or static for the chooser. One may regret or revisit a difficult choice, and may feel more positively or negatively about it at different moments in time (Wiegers 1992: 192). The understanding of choice advanced in this book thus accepts that ambivalence or lament should not, by itself, be interpreted as a signal that one's choice was coerced or unauthentic. Moreover, choice and consent need not coexist, and a choice may or may not include consent to the circumstances surrounding a decision (Peters 2004: 3-4). For example, as discussed in Chapter 3, a woman may choose to become a surrogate, but she may object (and not consent) to the social, economic and political factors (e.g., anxiety about attachment to the fetus, her financial state and needs, the demands of the "intending parents") that may operate to shape her decision and the way that she manages its outcome. This understanding of choice as an extended cognitive state and process is critical for this book, which explores the factors that precede and explain a choice, as well as the consequences that cascade from it and their management by the chooser. Furthermore, appreciating choice as a selection from an array of possibilities—as distinct from consent, which involves accepting or rejecting a proposed intervention or change in circumstance—allows for a contemplation of the options at the chooser's disposal. This understanding is central to this book, which aims to understand difficult choices against the backdrop of options women identify as available to them, as shaped both by non-state law—that is, norms grounded in social, economic, political and cultural forces—and state law.

Feminist discussions illuminating the intricacies of choice surface in a range of contexts. A rich body of work has assessed women's choices in relation to heterosexual sex (Dworkin 1987), pornography (MacKinnon 1985, MacKinnon 1989, Dworkin 1991), cosmetic surgery (Chambers 2008), religious divorce (Fournier 2012b, Bakht 2007), or conservative religious dress (Sloan 2011, Bakht 2012). This literature reflects two trends in feminist debates on choice. First, these debates are generally polarized and because of this, feminists risk oversimplifying or making mistakes about women's realities, and their possible vulnerabilities and strengths. Choice advocates run the risk of playing too little heed to the factors that may seriously constrain women's options and impair their well-being and happiness (West 1987). Meanwhile choice skeptics may overlook women's abilities to exercise agency and autonomy even where these are subject to constraints (Minow 1992).

A second feature of feminist debates on choice is their level of abstraction, and this is a particular problem for jurists. Discussions do not indicate how state law and policy should deal with critiques of choices made by women or members of other equality-seeking groups. Current analyses do not guide jurists as to whether and when to take at face value women's choices that seem self-defeating, when and how to interrogate such choices, or when the state—through formal legal rules—is justified in overriding choice because of vitiating circumstances or in the interests of pressing public objectives or concerns. Moreover, there is no defined sense as to when such a choice is so poor that it merits state intervention in the form of penalizing, through criminal law, the chooser herself.

This book seeks to takes up this challenge. This first chapter explores contemporary perceptions of choice contemplated within legal authorities and feminist theory. It further develops an analytical framework premised upon a series of questions aimed at enriching juridical study of difficult and controversial choices.

Part 1 examines the ways in which state law broaches three distinct issues that trigger debates on women's choices as they pertain to family and intimate relationships: domestic violence, domestic work and domestic contracts. In each of these contexts, women are often understood as victims who require the state's support and protection. In this way, they are unlike the polygamous sister wives, surrogates and sex workers studied in later chapters, whose questionable choices cause them to be viewed as social and legal offenders.

Part 2 engages in an analysis of the limits and challenges associated with the concept and lexicon of choice in connection with the difficult decisions about family and intimate life women often make. Discussions about choice obscure constraints on women's options, cause women to be held morally and legally responsible for outcomes that they might not have willed, foreseen or controlled, and offer a uniform and un-textured representation of the type of women capable of making authentic choices. These difficulties underscore the importance of scrutinizing the language and ideology of choice.

Nevertheless, an outright and simplistic rejection of choice remains problematic. Part 3 of this chapter explains why, despite its troublesome features, choice should remain fundamental to feminist discourse and theory, particularly for assessing the legal implications of morally ambiguous decisions made in the face of severe constraints. The discussion here examines feminist work that offers different conceptual paradigms through which we might assess women's supposedly poor choices. While helpful, these texts are restricted in their guidance for jurists who seek to examine women's choices through a feminist, critical legal pluralist lens. Specifically, these texts do not engage with particular formal state law and policy instruments that seek to govern women's tough choices, nor do they seek to identify the informal governance tools that do not emanate from the state, such as family, labour and community norms, with which women engage when making such choices. Moreover, these texts do not examine how women's controversial choices engage with state and non-state law through the use of empiricism and experiential narratives.

Part 4 develops a framework for the analysis of choice through a legal lens. It identifies questions that will further juridical appreciations of women's controversial choices. It thus calls for an analysis of such choices themselves, as well as the way in which they are regulated by the state. Three lines of investigation in relation to state and non-state law form the focus of analysis, namely: the presumptions on which such state laws rest; state law's interaction with non-state normative forces; and state laws' effects on women's options and decisions. Moreover, this book maintains that women's experiential knowledge as derived from empirical study will inform the study of these questions. Empirical data yield rich insights that are not otherwise accessible to jurists, bearing the potential to further the analyses of legal scholars, practitioners and decision-makers called upon to assess choices that appear adverse to the decision-maker's interests.

Prior to initiating this discussion, a preliminary word about the case studies that figure in this book is in order. The reader may query why Chapter 1 draws upon three issues distinct from the book's primary case studies, which are also commonly tethered to juridical analyses of women's choices. The logic behind an exploration in this first chapter of women's choices in relation to domestic violence, domestic work and domestic contracts, when these are not developed in the remainder of the book, may not be readily apparent. The purpose of using these examples, rather than those at the centre of the upcoming case study chapters, is to ground an analysis that focuses specifically on issues of choice, without the distraction and complication that might be triggered by introducing at this point the complex legal and social issues associated with polygamy, surrogacy and sex work. In addition, the goal is to ground this initial chapter within social and legal contexts that are more familiar to and frequent than the three principal case study topics. The "everyday" nature of challenges associated with domestic violence, domestic work and domestic contracts facilitates the laying of conceptual foundations for this book, given the importance to a critical legal pluralist project of appreciating law's pervasive social presence and relevance (Macdonald 2002, Van Praagh 1996). Moreover, leaving aside for the moment issues of polygamy, surrogacy and sex work allows for this foundational chapter to develop without delving into the intricate legislation and policy designed to govern these practices, which are described in ample detail in ensuing chapters. The present chapter could not do justice to explaining and analyzing these rules while simultaneously crafting a theoretical framework for plumbing law's engagement with women's choices. As such, other pertinent examples are selected for their social and legal commonness, and because legal approaches in such contexts are amenable to discussion within this single chapter. Like the case studies discussed in subsequent chapters, examples deployed here reflect dilemmas associated with valuing, while remaining critical about, precarious and morally equivocal decisions that may compromise women's interests and autonomy. In later chapters, this inquiry is nuanced by focusing directly on juridically prohibited choices that put women at risk of criminal penalty and stigma.

Part 1: Choice, Family Life and Law

Women's abilities to make self-protecting choices are often viewed as compromised when the decisions in question affect family or intimate relationships. In such contexts, women's choices may be governed by an interest in protecting and preserving relationships with intimate partners and dependents instead of their own preferences (Gilligan 1982, West, 1987). Economic constraints may also operate to circumscribe the options that a woman has at her disposal (McRae 2003: 317, 334, Barrett and St. Pierre 2011: 50). Finally, a cultural commitment to family cohesion may obstruct efforts to terminate unhappy or threatening relationships (Weitzman 2000, Moss et al. 1997: 442, 449, LaViolette and Barnett 2000: 17-18, 36-38). These factors may fuel choices that result in bigger concessions than personal gains for the chooser. This proposition has important ramifications for assessing women's choices about domestic violence, domestic work and domestic contracts. The discussion in this Part explores state law's treatment of these three issues, focusing on developments in Canada, Britain and Australia. It illuminates the way in which state law understands choice, laying the foundation for a critique of choice-based reasoning that is subsequently developed in Part 2.

Domestic Violence

Formal laws crafted by the state address the issue of domestic violence in a number of different ways. Most obviously, the prosecution of individuals charged with physically harming a family member will trigger the rules of criminal law. State law is also preoccupied with outcomes for children who are exposed to domestic violence, and may require or allow the state to intervene in family settings through applicable child welfare legislation.[1] Legislation might also direct courts to consider past domestic violence in child custody and access determinations.[2]

Possibly the most morally and intellectually challenging issue for jurists in relation to domestic violence is whether a woman who uses force preemptively to prevent an anticipated attack from a violent partner is justified in her conduct and thus exempt from liability for her actions. This issue is particularly acute where the force in question proves deadly, yielding the possibility of homicide charges (Dalton et al. 2001). Legal developments in multiple jurisdictions have resulted in recognizing a potential viable defense to criminal prosecutions in these circumstances. These developments were sparked by a perception of domestic violence as potentially cultivating, in the mind of an abused woman, the sense of

---

1 In Canada, see e.g., Quebec's *Youth Protection Act*, RSQ c P-34.1, s. 38 which includes "exposure to conjugal or domestic violence" in its definition of "ill-treatment," subjection to which may be a ground to consider a child's security or development in danger. In the United Kingdom, the *Children Act 2004* has been construed as imposing on police, health authorities and social workers a responsibility of taking steps necessary to ensure the protection of children in violent living conditions (United Kingdom, Quality Protects Program, H. Cleaver et al., *Child Protection, Domestic Violence and Parental Substance Misuse: Family Experiences and Effective Practice – Executive Summary*. Available at: http://dera.ioe.ac.uk/8820/1/child-protection-domesticviolence-parentalsubstance-misuse-2.pdf [accessed: 8 June 2013]).

2 In Canada, see e.g., *Family Law Act*, SBC 2011, c 25 and Ontario's *Children's Law Reform Act*, R.S.O. 1990, c. C. 12, s. 24(4). In Australia, see s. 60CG of the *Family Law Act 1975*, which requires that the court consider when deciding what order to make the risk of exposing a person to an unacceptable risk of family violence, to the extent that it is possible to do so consistently with the child's best interest. In determining what a child's best interests are, s. 60CC(2) of the *Act* states that one of the primary considerations is "the need to protect the child from physical or psychological harm from being subjected to, or exposed to" family violence. An additional consideration in determining the best interests of the child, set out at s. 60CC(3)(j) is whether there has been any family violence involving the child or a member of the child's family (Powell and Murray 2008).

lacking any real means of self-preservation other than the use of extreme force against a violent intimate partner. This understanding of the possible result of domestic violence on a woman's mental state has come to the attention of courts through expert evidence explaining "Battered Woman's Syndrome" (BWS), a diagnostic developed within feminist psychology in the late 1970s and early 1980s. Evidence about BWS was adduced for the purpose of explaining the distinct mind frame of an abused woman, demonstrating how a woman might reasonably fear for her life at the hands of her spouse, even while not in the throes of assault.

BWS was central to the Supreme Court of Canada's reasons for judgment in *R. v. Lavallee*. In this landmark ruling, the Court upheld the trial judge's decision to admit expert testimony explaining BWS and to allow the jury—which ultimately rendered an acquittal verdict—to consider this evidence in assessing the culpability of an accused charged with the murder of her abusive spouse. Testimony as to BWS was deemed necessary to assess the reasonableness of Lavallee's claim that she did not perceive herself to have any reasonable alternative but to shoot her spouse even though a physical assault was not underway or imminent when she killed him.

British law has similarly shifted to make space for defense claims recognizing the realities of battered women. Initially, a woman in the United Kingdom who faced a charge of murdering her violent spouse was barred from relying on the provocation defense because of the Common law's requirement that a provocation cause a "sudden and temporary" loss of self-control leading to a homicide (*R. v. Duffy*). This requirement of "suddenness," similar to the imminence requirement in Canadian self-defense law pre-*Lavallee*, placed serious limits on a battered woman's ability to invoke the provocation defense where time had elapsed between her spouse's last violent act and her own homicidal response (see e.g., *R. v. Ahluwalia*, *R. v. Whynot*).[3] However, public criticism and advocacy as well as a Law Commission report on the topic (Cmnd. 304 2006: ss. 5.19, 5.24, 5.29, 5.50-5.57) prompted the British Parliament to revise the law of provocation in 2009 to remove the "sudden and temporary" requirement. In doing so, the government enabled a woman abused by her intimate partner to rely on this defense even where her reaction was not an immediate response to an assault (*Coroners and Justice Act* 2009: ss. 54(1)(a), 54(2)). Similarly, 1982 legislative amendments in New South Wales, Australia removed the "suddenness" element of the provocation defense, with a view to rendering the defense available to

3 But see *R. v. Thornton (No. 2)*, where even though the court affirmed the "sudden and temporary loss of control" requirement for provocation in a case involving the homicide of an abusive man by his wife, fresh evidence of "abuse over a period upon [the accused's] mental make-up" was considered relevant enough to warrant the granting of appeal from conviction for murder. According to the reporter's note, the accused was convicted of manslaughter and sentenced to five years' imprisonment at her new trial.

women charged with murder in domestic violence contexts.[4] The State of Victoria introduced a comparative legislative amendment to its *Crimes Act 1958* to include a provision governing the specific context of family violence. This provision allows for criminal law defenses—particularly, self-defense and provocation—to be invoked where the actor uses force to respond even to a non-immediate threat, and permits a court to consider evidence of family relationships and dynamics, and the psychological effects of these, in its assessment of criminal responsibility (*Crimes Act* 1958: s. 9AH).

Law's openness to justifying—at least partially in the case of provocation—a homicide carried out by a battered woman reflects a perception of this woman as having little control or choice as to her conduct. The *Lavallee* narrative is illustrative. There, the Canadian Supreme Court centred its decision on expert testimony that described the accused as feeling "terrorized," "vulnerable," "worthless" and "unable to escape" (859). The Court found such evidence essential for a trier of fact to appreciate why a battered woman would reasonably perceive herself to lack any means of leaving a violent relationship (871-872) and a reasonable fear that her life was endangered by spouse even outside the context of an imminent assault (882-883). *Lavallee* also recognized that this psychological state can be exacerbated by fear of her spouse, by economic dependence on him, by concern for her children, or by familial or cultural expectations related to marriage and family stability, any of which may serve to truncate opportunities for exit from a violent household or relationship (887).

These legal developments understand choice in connection with domestic violence in a way that parallels the "dominant cultural script" in social work and domestic violence advocacy, which rejects staying or returning to an abusive relationship as a viable strategy (Baker 1997: 56). Where a woman remains in or resumes cohabitation with a violent partner, she is viewed as compelled by fear of reprisal by her spouse, or by her economic dependence on him. Alternatively, it may be understood as a mistake, an abdication of agency, and a basis for attributing to her own poor judgment any subsequent abuse that she encounters (Dunn and Powell-Williams 2007, Thapar-Bjökert and Morgan 2010). Part 2 of this chapter illuminates how these perceptions of women in domestic violence reflect key shortcomings in attributing to choice poor outcomes for women in connection with their intimate and family relationships.

Domestic Work

Concerns about choice rhetoric and ideology also surface in analyses of the transitions some women make from the paid workforce to homemaking. These discussions zero in on the circumstances of the most socially and economically resourced women; they generally have sterling educational backgrounds and

4 Austl, New South Wales, L. Roth, *Provocation and Self-Defence in Intimate Partner and Homophobic Homicides* (Briefing Paper No 3/07) (2007) at 10.

career prospects, and husbands successful enough in their own careers to take on, unilaterally, the role of family provider. Feminist preoccupations pertain to decisions by such women to replace their professional lives with unpaid caregiving work, thereby becoming economically dependent on their spouses.

This phenomenon—broadly known as the "Opt-Out Revolution" (Belkin 2003)—broaches legal concerns in less obvious ways than do the two other case studies studied in this chapter (domestic violence and domestic contracts) or the three main case studies considered in this book (polygamy, surrogacy and sex work). Engaging as it does questions about why women—even those with outstanding professional training and aptitude—adopt the role of homemaker and primary caregiver to children, freeing up their husbands' time to thrive in their own careers, the Opt-Out Revolution seems to raise issues that are more plainly social than legal. Nevertheless, state law plays a tacit role both in shaping and responding to the Opt-Out Revolution. State law may be viewed as an impetus driving this phenomenon, which is commonly perceived as triggered by an absence of accessible quality care for preschool-aged children and for children with special needs (Albiston 2005, Stone, P. 2007, Williams 2010). Thus, the state's failure, to deliver affordable and appropriate care to children can be an important factor in a woman's decision to leave a paid job to take up personally the work of childcare. The same is true where maternity and parental leave entitlements crafted by legal rules and policies are limited or difficult to take up. These burdens are compounded by rigid workplace policies and schedules. Even in places where the state has developed relatively generous leave entitlements and subsidized preschool care, some parents continue to face challenges that may preclude their ability to balance work and domestic responsibilities effectively (Campbell 2006, Thörnqvist 2006).

Apart from potentially contributing to decisions by parents, especially women, to leave the paid workforce, state law responds to the Opt-Out Revolution when it addresses the value of domestic and care-giving work at the time of spousal union dissolution. A typical scenario involves a female spouse's claim for maintenance or property division in recognition of her contribution to the family and her spouse's career through her domestic and care labour. The claim might also extend to a woman's unpaid work in a husband's business (e.g., *Hachey v. Dempster*, *Rademaker v. Rademaker*, *Marshall v. Marshall*, *Whitty v. Whitty*). While this type of claim did not historically encounter much success (see e.g., *Murdoch v. Murdoch*), courts now frequently consider, in assessing claims for spousal support, "the effect of the marriage in either impairing or improving each party's economic prospects" (*Moge v. Moge*: 848-849). The power to consider and compensate a spouse for non-material contributions to a family and for adverse effects on earning potential resulting from homemaking work is often grounded in statutory jurisdiction.[5] Apart from support, family property rules might allow for a sharing of assets acquired over a spousal relationship despite uneven material

5 In Canada, see e.g., *Divorce Act*, RSC, 1985, c 3(2nd Supp), ss. 15(4)(b) and 15(6) as interpreted in *Moge v. Moge*, and Ontario's *Family Law Act*, RSO 1990, c. F-3, s. 33(9)

contributions.[6] Australia's High Court, however, has ruled against a presumption of equal division in family property, opting instead for a regime that measures each spouse's contributions to the family, whether material or through the work of homemaking and parenting (*Mallet v. Mallet*). The House of Lords took a similar position in *White v. White*, directing courts to consider spouses' contribution to the "welfare of the family"—rather than family wealth—in assessing spouses' contributions, and thus their property entitlements, on marriage breakdown. This approach fuels analyses that evaluate homemaking work, as well as lost past and future wage-earning opportunities, in property calculation and division (e.g., *Campbell v. Campbell*, *McCulloch v. McCulloch*, *McFarlane v. McFarlane*, *Lambert v. Lambert*, *Moore v. Moore*, *S.L. v. E.H.L.*).

While praiseworthy for their recognition of the value of caregiving and domestic labour, these legal developments are not comprehensive. Many women who opt out may find themselves without a statutory basis of their claims for relief. In such cases, a court's jurisdiction to award spousal support or a proportion of the matrimonial property is narrow. For example, the Province of Quebec does not recognize a right to spousal support or property division for unmarried spouses. While courts occasionally use alternative legislative tools to circumvent this barrier (e.g., *C.L. v. J.L.E.*, *M.B. v. L.L.*), cohabiting partners in Quebec have generally been viewed as legal strangers to one another, with no statutorily-imposed rights or obligations at the end of their relationship (*Quebec (Attorney General) v. A.*). Comparably, courts in common law jurisdictions may invoke equitable remedies, such as unjust enrichment, to award property sharing for unmarried partners when such relief is not granted by statute. The Canadian Supreme Court recently ruled that such a remedy is justified where the claimant shows a "joint family venture" such that her contributions resulted in an accumulation of wealth disproportionately shared by the parties at the time of relationship breakdown (*Kerr v. Baranow*).

While some legal instruments may allow courts to palliate the economic fallout for women who participate in the Opt-Out Revolution, state law's remedial power should not be exaggerated or romanticized. The legal mechanisms just explained are unlikely to restore the woman who opts out to the economic status she would have enjoyed had she never left the workforce. That woman, being the claimant for spousal support or property sharing, will bear the burden of proof in relation to her needs and entitlement and her former spouse's ability and obligation to pay. Apart from the time, energy and expense associated with this onus, it might prove difficult to convince a judge of her right to a material award that either restores her indefinitely to the economic position she enjoyed during the spousal relationship, or that compensates fully for her domestic contributions and professional

(ii), (v), (vi). In the United Kingdom, see *Matrimonial Causes Act 1973*, s. 25(2)(a), (f). In Australia, see *Family Law Act 1975*, s. 75(2k) and s. 90SF(3)(j), (k).

6 In Canada, see e.g., the Ontario *Family Law Act*, s. 5(7). In the United Kingdom, see *Matrimonial Causes Act 1973*, s. 25(2)(a), (f). In Australia, see *Family Law Act 1975*, s. 79(4) and s. 90SM(4)(a)(b)(c).

sacrifices. She may be aided by showing that a decision to leave the workforce was a "joint family venture" as opposed to something she chose by herself, for her own self-fulfillment (*Kerr v. Baranow*, cf. *Radmacher v. Granatino*). This effort might be complicated, however, if choice language and imagery are invoked, as this might cast a decision to leave the workforce as a unilateral decision rather than a shared spousal or family undertaking. Moreover, given that a court is charged with goals other than compensating the economically weaker spouse when ordering support—one of which may be to encourage that spouse to obtain economic self-sufficiency (e.g., *Divorce Act*: s. 15.2(6)(d))—alimony awards might come with a termination date and an expectation that this spouse eventually return to waged work. The latter objective may be unrealistic when a woman has spent an extensive period away from the workforce and when she retains important childcare and custody responsibilities (Waldfogel 1998).

Domestic Contracts

Domestic contracts governing spousal or family relationships—which include prenuptial agreements, contracts made during marriage or cohabitation, or separation agreements—stand apart from the preceding case studies for two principal reasons. First, as contracts, they engage more obviously with issues of consent than choice. Second, they seem to fall squarely within law's purview, whereas domestic violence and domestic work simultaneously tackle social and economic questions. It is worth looking at these points more deeply before taking up a discussion of how choice and constraints figure in this context.

As indicated, this book disentangles the concepts of choice and consent, retaining the former as its object of study. In contemplating domestic contracts, consent seems to be the pertinent consideration, as this is a vital component for any legally enforceable agreement (*Rick v. Brandsema*: para. 48). One might even characterize consent as the foundational organizing concept underpinning contracts (Barnett 2012, Hadfield 1997). Just the same, conventional contract theory also sees choice as constitutive of obligations; one is indebted to another because one chose this to be so. This is unlike other areas of law where obligations may be created and enforced pursuant to statute or by legal doctrines (e.g., tort), regardless of whether one desires, intends or chooses to be subject to these obligations (Hadfield 1997). Moreover, this book understands choice as encompassing the process of contemplating, making and living with a decision. It is thus broader than a singular moment or act of consent-giving or of executing a juridical act. Applying this mode of reasoning to domestic contracts permits an analysis of the parties' negotiations, deliberations, decision-making, and management of contractual consequences.

The second point that sets domestic contracts apart from the two other case studies considered above relates to law's explicit role in their regard. As instruments that create juridical rights and obligations between parties, contracts clearly fall within law's domain. Yet domestic contracts attract unique and heightened scrutiny for a multiplicity of reasons. To begin, these contracts were historically legally suspect, given concerns about their propensity to incite the dissolution of marriage or at least facilitate such a process (Peaslee 1902). Moreover, in at least the English legal tradition, domestic contracts did not square with the unity theory, according to which spouses upon marriage formed one juridical person. Given that the contract, by definition, requires at least two separate parties, an agreement between husband and wife (legally one and the same person) seemed incongruent to a conventional common law appreciation of marriage. Contracts between spouses were also rendered void by virtue of the doctrine of coverture, which evacuated the married woman of her own separate civil existence and rendered her incapable of contracting independently (Pateman 1988: 155-156).

Most of these concerns that could serve to invalidate domestic contracts have been quelled by legal developments that produce a more modern view of marriage and of women's entitlements within this institution. Nevertheless, domestic contracts continue to attract scrutiny, primarily on account of concerns related to the emotional climate of family and spousal negotiations, and awareness that spouses' disparate bargaining powers can foster unfair results. These concerns have generated varied legal analyses as to whether and in what circumstances domestic contracts set between spouses should be upheld and enforced.

Early analyses of the issue in Canada drew on the concept of unconscionability. In three companion judgments rendered in 1987—known as the "*Pelech* trilogy" (*Pelech v. Pelech*, *Richardson v. Richardson*, *Caron v. Caron*)—the Supreme Court held that an application to vary spousal support arrangements determined by a negotiated separation agreement could succeed only where the claimant demonstrated "a radical change in circumstances flowing from an economic pattern of dependency engendered by the marriage," and that the agreement was "unconscionable in the substantive law sense" (*Pelech v. Pelech*: para. 83). As explored below, the Supreme Court has, since the *Pelech* trilogy, established a less onerous standard for judicial intervention in domestic agreements. Yet recent Canadian cases continue to allude to the doctrine of unconscionability. For example, in *Khan v. Khan*, a trial court refused to hold the parties to a marital contract signed in Pakistan (a "*Nikah-Nama*") that barred the wife from claiming spousal support. While evidence was led as to the *Nikah-Nama*'s binding character under Islamic law, Clark J. set the agreement aside, underscoring the wife's "lack of choice" in signing the document which was attributed to "the cultural traditions and social customs of her community" (para. 51). The judge further found that the wife did not understand the contract's nature or "unconscionable consequences" (paras. 53-57). Both of these findings would have justified the decision to set aside the contract under the applicable family law statute (*Ontario Family Law Act*: ss. 33(4)(a), 56(4)).

Canada's Supreme Court also recently relied on unconscionability to set aside a separation agreement in *Rick v. Brandsema*. The case involved a husband who misrepresented the scope of his assets and exploited his wife's precarious medical condition during their negotiations. Unconscionability's centrality in *Rick* is curious since the Court had at its disposal a less stringent test for reviewing domestic contracts (see discussion of *Miglin* below), as well as applicable statutory language (*British Columbia Family Relations Act*: s. 65(1)) that permitted review of the contract on the less onerous "fairness" standard (Leckey 2009: 273).

The Supreme Court invoked this statutory "fairness" threshold in *Hartshorne v. Hartshorne* to assess a prenuptial agreement signed on the parties' wedding day. The parties' agreement departed from the legislative presumption of equal partition of family assets (*British Columbia Family Relations Act*: s. 56). It stipulated that the couple would remain separate as to property throughout the marriage with the exception of an interest the wife would accumulate in the family home over the marriage. At divorce, the wife petitioned to set aside the agreement on the grounds of "unfairness," a contention that the Supreme Court majority ultimately rejected. Examining the parties' economic situations at the time of marriage breakdown and finding that the spouses had both accurately predicted at the time of contract formation their personal and economic situation, and had "truly considered the impact of their choices," the majority found an insufficient basis for characterizing the agreement as "unfair" (para. 46).

The Supreme Court of the United Kingdom also deployed a "fairness" standard of review in a decision recognizing, for the first time in that jurisdiction, the validity of prenuptial agreements. The Court held in *Radmacher v. Granatino* that an agreement "freely entered into by each party with a full appreciation of its implications" should not be subject to judicial interference unless upholding the agreement would "not be fair" in the circumstances (para. 75). In declining to intervene in the impugned contract the majority stressed the relevance of "respect for individual autonomy" (para. 78) and the propriety of recognizing the claimant's choices and preferences affecting his financial interests. Things might have differed had the claimant—the husband—made out a claim for compensatory support. Although he had left a high-earning career during the marriage, the court found that his choice to do so "was not motivated by the demands of his family, but reflected his own preference" (para. 121).

Comparable allusions to autonomy, choice and preference figure in Canadian jurisprudence developing a third standard—apart from unconscionability and fairness—for judicial intervention in domestic contracts. *Miglin v. Miglin* considered the validity of a mutual spousal support waiver within a detailed separation agreement negotiated with independent legal advice over 15 months. Approximately four years after the agreement's execution, the wife applied for spousal support. The Supreme Court majority rejected her claim. In doing so, it held that *Pelech*'s narrow test for judicial intervention in domestic contracts was no longer applicable, and should be replaced with a new standard for intervention. This standard was articulated as a two-part inquiry. The first part involved examining circumstances surrounding the agreement's negotiation and execution, and the agreement's substance, to ensure compatibility with the objectives of the *Divorce Act*. At this stage, factors amounting to less than "unconscionability" in ordinary contract terms may be considered, but imbalances of power are not to be assumed. The second stage called upon courts to investigate whether, at the time of the judicial application, the agreement continued to reflect the parties' intentions and complied substantially with the objectives of the *Divorce Act*. Applying this framework to the facts of *Miglin*, the majority concluded that the separation agreement should be given "significant and determinative weight." It emphasized that the release from spousal support in the contract was the product of a rigorous and informed negotiation. The court further considered the support waiver against the backdrop of all of the financial arrangements crafted by the parties upon separation, which aimed to compensate the parties for disadvantage arising from the marriage breakdown while striving to "facilitate a disentanglement of their economic lives and promote their self-sufficiency" (para. 98).

For some feminists, courts' apparent privileging of "contractual liberty" in spousal relationships is "*dépassé*" and questionable (Langevin 2009). Nevertheless, judicial approaches to domestic contracts also exhibit some sensitivity to the vulnerabilities of parties to such agreements, and suggest that these should not be treated as ordinary commercial contracts. This sensitivity is prominent in cases involving agreements that incorporate obligations rooted in religious doctrine. Such obligations most often surface in cases where a husband has promised to grant his wife the *get* (a Jewish divorce granted by a husband allowing his wife to subsequently marry and have legitimate children under Jewish law) or to give his wife the *Mahr* (a gift that a man makes under Islamic law to his fiancée, which is often partially paid before marriage with the remainder deferred) (Fournier 2012a: 8-9). In Canada, courts have in the past exhibited some discomfort with the religious tenor of such obligations and have refused to enforce them in some cases (*Morris v. Morris*, *Kaddoura v. Hammoud*). Since 1990, however, federal divorce legislation grants courts jurisdiction to sanction the failure to remove obstacles to a religious divorce, which can incite a reluctant husband to give a *get* (*Divorce Act*: s. 21.1). Moreover, although the reach of the Supreme Court's decision in *Bruker v. Marcovitz* may be more limited than it first appears (Fournier 2012b: 7), it implies judicial authority to award damages where the *get* was withheld in breach of a contractual promise. In the United Kingdom, legislation enacted in 2002 allows a court to "require" the dissolution of a religious marriage before granting a civil divorce (*Divorce (Religious Marriages) Act*). Even prior to this statute's creation, there were intimations of judicial discretion to intervene in domestic arrangements with a view to compelling the granting of the *get* (*N. v. N.*: paras. 68-74).

While these developments indicate that religious domestic contracts remain justiciable, they do not pronounce on courts' jurisdiction to relieve women whose interests are undermined by such contracts. *Bruker* and cases that followed saw courts enforcing religious obligations that operated to the wives' benefit, particularly in cases involving enforcement of the *Mahr* (see e.g., *Ghaznavi v. Kashif-Ul-Haque*, *A.Y. v. S.T.*, *Uddin v. Choudhury*, and Brown 2010). But what if a court were petitioned to evaluate a domestic agreement, post-*Bruker*, which resembled the terms of the *Nikah-Nama* in *Khan*, pursuant to which a woman lost her right to claim spousal maintenance? While the court arguably retains its jurisdiction to set the agreement aside under contract law or applicable statutory provisions, a more obscure issue is whether religious contexts might affect a court's perception of a woman's choices about family and intimate life. Discussions about religious arbitration in family law suggest that such cases would be marked by accentuated scrutiny of women's choices and by a perceived imperative to protect women from adverse outcomes engendered by patriarchal cultural and religious values (Bakht 2007).

Western law's commitment to conventional liberal underpinnings of contract, emphasizing choice, autonomy and free will, is punctuated in the realm of domestic agreements by concern for injustices yielded by parties' uneven strengths and vulnerabilities. This dynamic justifies heightened legal oversight of such agreements, typically with a view to safeguarding women's interests. Intervention occurs according to three identifiable standards: unconscionability, fairness and the more intricate two-step inquiry developed by the Canadian Supreme Court in *Miglin*. It is noteworthy, too, that the presence of a religious dimension in domestic contracts tends to complicate legal analyses, and renders courts generally more prone to override an agreement in the name of women's protection. This observation foreshadows developments discussed in Chapter 2 regarding law's engagement with polygamy. In that context, the reader will detect reliance on principles of gender equality and protection, ostensibly undermined by the religious doctrines and beliefs underlying polygamy, to justify legal actors' prompt and blunt interventions in women's intimate and family choices.

The discussion that follows in the present chapter draws on the three examples discussed here to highlight the difficulties for feminists of accepting choice ideology uncritically. At the same time, the analysis demonstrates the ongoing value of retaining some relevance for choice in legal frameworks that seek to appreciate the rationales and values of women whose choices and lifestyles generate controversy, particularly from a gender equality perspective.

Part 2: The Trouble with Choice

Choice-based analyses of women's morally ambiguous decisions and lifestyles can be severely problematic. An uncritical acceptance of choice renders opaque the constraints that limit viable options for women in challenging social and economic situations. Attributing outcomes to choice further cultivates problematic links between choice and responsibility. Finally, discussions about women and choice reflect a proclivity to draw stark divisions between women who are presumed to bear agency and choice-making capacity, and women who are not.

Illusory

Discussions premised on choice often fail to consider fully the social and economic constraints under which many decisions are made. This critique resists a market analysis premised on presumptions of the chooser's neutrality, voluntariness and autonomy. It urges a contextual contemplation that references the chooser's relationships and responsibilities (Wiegers 1992). It further finds choice troublesome even when it is not "coerced" in the classical liberal sense in that it is tainted by duress or fraud (see contra Hurd 1996: 125, 144). Pursuant to this reasoning, "seductive offers" (Yuracko 2003: 64-65) without a feasible alternative may be enough to raise a red flag in connection with the authenticity and validity of a choice (Minow 1992: 2107).

Domestic violence, domestic work and domestic contracts each reflect the potential of constraints to severely curtail women's options, such that any apparent "choice" is in fact a compelled, possibly undesired, outcome. The predominant legal and social narratives surrounding domestic violence stress the absence of control and choice in the lives of women. Reliance on Battered Women's Syndrome to understand the effects of intimate partner violence results in the depiction of woman as snared, pathologized and disempowered, and it is this psychological state—rather than any free choice or manifestation of agency—that is perceived to underlie decisions to return to or remain with a violent partner (Shaffer 1997, Martinson et al. 1991: 53-54). While some feminist accounts seek to underscore women's potential agency and resistance in the face of intimate partner violence, most reject the idea that women's choices in these circumstances are unhindered. Frye (1985: 215), for example, characterizes women who stay with abusive partners as "making a choice among evils in a severely constrained situation," and rejects the idea of voluntary decision-making in such a context. Other work emphasizes that mothers in violent relationships are at a deeper disadvantage, fearing a partner's retaliation against a child or operating in reaction to a partner's threats of abduction or fierce custody litigation tactics (Davies et al. 1998: 33). Such factors undergird feminist resistance to "easy assumptions" about choice for women who encounter intimate partner violence, and call attention to the serious constraints that curb or eliminate their options (Stubbs 2002: 45).

Similarly, feminist commentary on the Opt-Out Revolution examines the role and relevance of constraints on choice. It underscores that serious pressures motivate women to leave professional life for domestic work. Childcare costs, inflexible workplace and family leave policies, and political and social attitudes that perpetuate expectations of mothers retaining primary responsibility over household affairs combine to shrink the professional mother's options. Although she may resist seeing herself as "constrained between a rock and hard place," a feminist analysis of her circumstances can reveal that she is actually caught in a double-bind, with multiple forces propelling her to pack up her office to take up care of her house, husband and children (Stone, P. 2007: 105, 112, 114). The critique sees the career-to-homemaking move not as the fruit of the women's preferences, desires or ambitions, but as driven by overpowering social and economic forces. Viewed this way, choice discourse seems misplaced here; rather than empowering women it obscures gender inequality as regards work within and outside the home, and causes a woman's sacrifice to be mistakenly understood as a reflection of her "personal priorities" (Williams 1991: 1607).

Finally, feminist concerns about domestic contracts—whether incorporating religious obligations or not—are grounded in an identification of constraints in this context. Acknowledging the "unique emotional dynamics" at play in spousal negotiations (Shaffer 2004: 281) and women's frequent economic reliance on husbands (Rogerson 1991: 249, Martin 1998), feminists resist the application of a "market methodology" to domestic contracts that would presume partners' equal bargaining power and ability to maximize preferences (Wiegers 1992: 191-192). Legal interventions are necessary to foster substantive equality between the spouses (Langevin 2009). Where a domestic contract is overlain with faith-based obligations, additional worries arise about whether women could negotiate freely in the face of patriarchal cultural requirements (Fournier 2001, Bakht 2007). These economic, psychological and cultural factors can truncate women's ability to make shrewd, self-promoting choices in contracts with domestic partners (Cossman 1990: 345).

Beyond the substantive content of domestic contracts, procedural constraints might also dilute choice. Family mediation and private settlement are inconsistently amenable to fair spousal bargaining (Wiegers and Keet 2008: 737, Shaffer 1988: 188), especially where a history of family violence exists (Grillo 1991: 1605) or where religious communities may exert pressure to accept terms delineated by faith (Bakht 2007: 125-126). Family negotiations are further characterized by a "settlement culture" (Hunter 2007: 166) and "harmony agenda" (Macfarlane 2005: 35) that might compound a woman's inequalities in domestic contract negotiations and pressure her to relinquish valid claims and accept concessions that run counter to her own interests (Wiegers and Keet 2008: 746-747). Quick settlement at the expense of advancing meritorious claims might also be prompted by a lack of resources to bargain vigorously and by a desire to "buy peace" (Hunter 2007: 165), thus avoiding protracted contact with a former spouse (Rogerson 1991: 249-250). Last, such negotiations happen in private where there is typically no judicial oversight of processes and thus no external mechanism to account for or to recalibrate parties' bargaining powers.[7]

Feminist analyses of domestic violence, domestic work and domestic contracts compel critical questions about the breadth of choice available to women who negotiate family dynamics and outcomes with their intimate partners. These analyses illuminate the pressures and constraints that may shape and confine decision-making ability. Although formal legal interventions in these domains reflect sensitivity to women's potential risks, they do not elaborate on the scope and influence of the constraints that operate on tough decisions, which may render illusory any appearance of choice or agency in these settings. Feminist scholarship

7 The potential risks of private family settlement procedures, specifically in relation to religious arbitration, were spelled out in submissions made to the Boyd Commission on Religious Arbitration in Ontario (Canada, Ontario, Marion Boyd, *Dispute Resolution in Family Law: Protecting Choice, Promoting Inclusion* [Toronto: Ministry of the Attorney General, 2004] at 29-34).

fills this gap by emphasizing the necessity of considering the contexts in which choices are made. This feminist work helps to ensure that social, economic and cultural forces driving choices and outcomes are brought to light. This in turn helps to dissipate the tendency of choice-based analyses to hold responsible and to penalize individuals who are deemed to have controlled, foreseen and accepted the adverse results of their choices.

Responsibilizing

The legal and moral link between the individual who chooses and responsibility for the results of her choice is generally axiomatic (Kaufman 2004). Moreover, assignments of responsibility are based on an understanding of power and the capacity to determine outcomes (Wendell 1990: 15). As such, choice and power are elements that justify the individuation of moral and legal culpability and the imposition of the costs of adverse consequences.

An analysis of choice that assumes the chooser's freedom and voluntariness and fails to identify and account for the constraints and pressures under which she acts creates risks that feminists should find troubling. This mode of reasoning unrealistically abstracts the chooser and her choices, contemplating these "in a vacuum" without reference to context (Majury 2009). Our choices, especially those most ethically nebulous or involving onerous tradeoffs, are often grounded in relational settings essential to consider in assessing where responsibility for managing and correcting poor outcomes should rest. A central feminist critique of the liberal legal subject as "abstracted from its social context, including the context of its own body" (Lacey 1995: 8) thus stresses the relevance of considering an individual's connections to and interdependence with others as a platform for exercising autonomy and making choices (Nedelsky 1993, Williams 1991: 1561). It also calls for assessments that recognize the possibility that women make choices with a view to maintaining relationships, if not to "serve the needs and satiate the desires of others" (West 1987: 97). Acknowledging that women may act on others' demands and desires creates space to recognize the potential responsibility of other actors, especially those exerting dominating forces, for the harms women incur (Eichner 2009: 4).

From this perspective, attributing responsibility by mapping outcomes to an individual decision-maker is too simple and possibly inequitable (Minow 1992: 2107). Ignoring context and the reality that many of women's most difficult choices reflect a selection from a range of equally untenable options, this approach furthers a pattern of "victim-blaming," a phenomenon that feminists have long strived to combat (Wendell 1990: 20). Instead, a feminist effort to localize responsibility would consider the relational dynamics and context that prompted apparent choices. This in turn may diffuse legal responsibility for restoring or reducing losses caused by difficult choices. Refraining from deploying choice as a simple catalyst for responsibility could also halt the invocation of choice as a shield for public actors and private citizens against financial claims (Albiston 2005: 43-44), equality claims (Majury 2009) or even claims for physical protection advanced by women who require support (Baker 1997: 68-69). In other words, it would not be a defense to such claims to argue that a woman "chose" a particular path and must therefore live with her encountered outcomes, however unfortunate.

Case studies examined in Part 1 exhibit choice discussions' tendency to trigger assignments of responsibility. Women who retaliate with force against an abusive partner are held to be justified in their actions and exempt from criminal liability if they are viewed as having no choice in relation to their conduct. A woman who has options, then, may be infused with legal and moral responsibility for the costs that result from her decisions (see *R. v. Whynot*, *R. v. Malott*). The social advocacy context surrounding domestic violence also sets up paradoxical imagery in relation to choice and responsibility. Although the battered woman is a trapped victim without real options, she is also viewed as bearing control over whether she stays or leaves her violent partner. This fosters a culture in which she may be blamed for violence she encounters when she stays in or returns to an abusive relationship (Thapar-Björkert and Morgan 2010, Dunn and Powell-Williams 2007). She is simultaneously the target of social and legal interventions that aim to separate her from her spouse (see Acorn 2005, Suk 2006). Little effort is made to reform or engage with the abuser or with family and community members whose support a woman may need to leave or improve her relationship (Baker 1997: 71).

The narrative that surrounds the Opt-Out Revolution reflects a comparable potential to shift responsibility for penalizing consequences to women ostensibly making choices in this domain. The label of the Opt-Out Revolution itself suggests the existence of choice and options. While perhaps this initially conveys an empowering image of women taking control over their professional and family lives, a woman might also see this move as a failure, reflecting an inability to cope simultaneously with the multiple demands in each of these spheres (Stone, P. 2007: 128-189). For some, this failure extends to affect not only the individual mother opting out but women in general, as it undermines and retreats from feminists' hard-fought gains in relation to workplace equality and jeopardizes women's intellectual and moral development (Yuracko 2003: 120-121, Hirshman 2005: 23, 26). Whether celebrated or not, opting out creates financial risks that a woman may be forced to bear individually if these are viewed as the product of autonomous choice in furtherance of self-actualization. The discussion of the Opt-Out Revolution in Part 1 highlights how the full weight of such risks is brought to bear at the end of a spousal union, when the woman who apparently opted out is left suddenly without the support of a providing husband (Cossman 2009: 460-461, Williams 1996, Williams 1991: 1603-1604). Apart from their potential financial liabilities, women seen as having chosen homemaking over professional life may be saddled with sole responsibility for mediating work–family tensions. If women's move away from career for domestic life is viewed as aligned with self-interest, this alleviates pressures on employers to think creatively about workplace policies that would accommodate employees with care responsibilities who wish to remain in the paid workforce (Albiston 2005: 44). Similarly, there will be minimal burden on men to adjust their own career goals and patterns if their wives are seen as wanting and choosing to devote their lives to domestic work (Williams 1991: 1630-1631). Cast as a preference, opting out can dilute a claim that domestic work should be as highly valued as paid labour as a family contribution, since it may be understood as cultivating personal goals rather than a sacrifice made as part of a shared project to benefit the entire family unit. Choice-based discourse here thus does not readily contemplate extending responsibility for the move from career to home-life to husbands, employers or the state since these actors do not figure as decision-makers in this individualized account of domestic work (Albiston 2005: 44, Cossman 2009: 473-474). If women are viewed as the sole actors involved in opting out, they are likely to shoulder the burden of any economic fallout that results from this presumed individual choice (Cossman 2009: 472).

An analogous situation occurs when viewing domestic contracts through the prism of choice. Some feminists argue that assuming autonomy and choice drive domestic contracts risks privatizing the costs of any negative results they yield. This indictment, particularly targeted in Canada at the Supreme Court's *Pelech* decision (see Cossman 1990: 338), is rooted in a concern that arranging family affairs by contract shields them from state oversight and intervention, and facilitates abuse and manipulation of the weaker party to the bargain (Langevin 2009: 24). In her comment on *Hartshorne*, Martha Shaffer (2004: 284-285) critiques the Supreme Court majority's perception of the prenuptial agreement as resulting from Mrs. Hartshorne's "choosing to enter an agreement," and argues that the majority's analysis "allows the stronger party to impose his or her will on the weaker." Moreover, where a spouse is left, by virtue of a domestic agreement, without adequate resources and in a situation of need, she will bear the burden of coping with this outcome; the state is not clearly obliged to make up for any shortfall (Mossman 2004). This can be especially disconcerting for feminists, seeing as marriage or spousal union breakdown can contribute to women's impoverishment, even where there are no unbalanced or oppressive contracts in issue (Avellar and Smock 2005, McLanahan and Kelly 2006, Holden 1991). Although one reading of *Pelech* suggests that the Court's willingness to uphold a contract and thereby limit intra-familial support obligations reflects an ethos of state welfarism over libertarianism (Leckey 2008b: 115), a focus on "choice" lends itself to assumptions about responsibility, such that the "chooser" must accept and live with the consequences she selects. This line of reasoning would support the view that a woman who ostensibly chooses to end her spousal relationship by settlement and contract is responsible for managing the results of that process and generally is not justified in seeking a bailout from a third party, whether a state or private actor.

Ultimately, a weak analysis of choice, which fails to consider context and which assumes that personal interests primarily motivate the chooser, carries risks. It overlooks the constraints that shape the hard choices women make about intimate life and leaves a slim margin for legal interventions in such choices or their results. This approach also neglects the risks of "responsibilizing" the chooser. Simple causal links drawn between choice and responsibility hold accountable those who ostensibly chose in an ill-advised fashion. Thus, the woman who returns to an abusive partner, who leaves a career for unpaid domestic work, or whose domestic settlement dilutes her economic interests is, within this rubric, solely responsible for absorbing costs engendered by what is perceived to be her own choice.

Essentializing

Narratives that both rely on and critique choice do not give a consistent sense of whether women are competent or impotent to make real choices in the face of difficult and constraining life circumstances. While the dominant feminist critique of women who return to violent households, opt out of careers, or give up rights through domestic contracts is that their choices are illusory and shaped by constraints rather than preference or self-interest, some critical work suggests that women can exercise autonomy even in complex, emotional and challenging situations. This point is taken up more fully in Part 3 below. The wrinkle, however, is that space for identifying women as autonomous choosers has been acknowledged only for those who are not cast as victims or disempowered. In other words, choice narratives depict the woman who chooses in a meaningful and authentic way as someone who holds social and economic privilege and forms part of a dominant cultural group. As just explored, a woman viewed as having the autonomy to make active choices may be held responsible for the results of her choices. The counter-paradigm is the woman precluded from making real choices as a result of disempowerment and victimization by family, community or state actors. Focusing unitarily on her weakness and vulnerability, choice discussions may miss indicia of agency in her relationships and life patterns. State law and policy often exhibit resistance to holding this woman responsible for poor outcomes. This may be appropriate if the choices in question were extracted by coercion or subject to significant constraint. Yet rudimentary assumptions about when and which women can make authentic choices set up blunt and unhelpful divisions between the concepts of choice and agency on one hand, and constraint and victimization on the other. These assumptions fail to recognize how the same woman may simultaneously see herself as bold and empowered in relation to some choices, but oppressed in connection with others (Abrams 1995: 375).

Legal and social analyses of domestic violence, domestic work and domestic contracts reflect the predisposition of choice debates to generate essentializing assumptions about women. Conventional accounts of women in abusive intimate relationships build on a perception of these women as helpless, trapped and induced into mental illness by their partner's violence (Dunn and Powell-Williams 2007, Martinson et al. 1991: 53-54, Shaffer 1997).[8] Battered women are thus understood as unable to make appropriate choices for themselves

8 Austl, New South Wales, L. Roth, *Provocation and Self-Defence in Intimate Partner and Homophobic Homicides* (Briefing Paper No 3/07) (2007).

and this in turn justifies the involvement of social and legal actors who either choose on their behalf or attempt to reorganize the effects of their decisions. The dominant narrative does not address the experiences of women who are physically, intellectually or economically stronger than their partners. Someone who does not fit "the stereotype of a victimized, passive, helpless, dependent, battered woman" will not necessarily be capable of claiming she had no option but to stay with a violent partner or use violence to escape the relationship (*R. v. Malott*: para. 40). Excluded from the "homogenization of intimate violence," battered women who do not harmonize with the victim paradigm may be misunderstood as fully in control of their circumstances and thus accountable for the outcomes they are viewed as having chosen (Peled et al. 2000: 17). Moreover, a failure to account for the diversity of factors that cause and aggravate intimate partner violence and the varied concerns and experiences of women in such circumstances yields ineffective and often insensitive or inappropriate state-based responses to this dilemma. The point has been compellingly made by scholars reflecting on legal approaches to domestic violence in Aboriginal (McGillivray and Comaskey 1999), African-American (Ruttenberg 1994) and immigrant (Suk 2006) communities. Finally, and in a related vein, the essentializing dynamic of choice ignores the issue of intersectionality, which should prompt an analysis of domestic violence that moves beyond gender to consider features such as race, class and sexual orientation as factors salient to the understanding of domestic power differentials and marginalization (Sokoloff and Dupont 2005, Crenshaw 1994, Bograd 1999).

The main storyline developed in relation to the Opt-Out Revolution similarly presents a monolithic view of women capable of making choices. Unlike the women central to legal and social accounts of domestic violence, women who opt out are presumed to possess control over their lives and the ability to choose homemaking over career. "[Assuming] a particular family structure, and a particular class privilege" (Albiston 2005: 46, Cossman 2009: 463), the Opt-Out Revolution is driven by the tale of predominantly white professional women supported by their husbands' income once they leave their paid jobs. These women may themselves see their ability to morph into homemakers as a function of their "privilege" or as a "status symbol," and may perhaps take pride in what they perceive to be a free decision (Stone, P. 2007: 125). Thus, although admittedly not unequivocal (McDonald, Bradley and Guthrie 2006: 486-487), the Opt-Out Revolution indicates that it is married, monied and educated women who have these choices. Excluded from the core of this phenomenon are the experiences of racialized, single or working-class women. For them, a decision to leave paid labour is impossible or perceived as a moral failing and social problem justifying public scrutiny and critique, rather than a laudable choice (Gavigan and Chunn 2007, Reese 2005).

Finally, feminist discussions surrounding domestic contracts also develop a unidimensional representation of women and choice. Here again, economically disadvantaged women are presumed generally incapable of choosing rationally and cleverly. Legal interventions in domestic contracts typically respond to women's assumed vulnerabilities and seek to protect their interests. However this approach risks slipping into a passive acceptance of gender stereotypes that, as Cossman (1990: 367) notes, cannot be generalized across all spousal relationships. It would be a mistake to presume that educated, white women who negotiate domestic contracts make choices meriting full recognition while women with limited education or economic resources, or whose contracts bear religious dimensions, are inherently and distinctly vulnerable and consequently compelled to accept outcomes that counter their own interests.

These examples reflect presumptions embedded in discussions about choice which essentialize the women deemed to bear agency and those, by contrast, victimized by constraints. Wealthy and educated women with private social and economic support networks may be seen to have real options. This may be problematic where constraints and pressures on choice are ignored and responsibility for outcomes over which they lacked control is foisted upon them. In contrast, socially and economically marginalized and cultural minority women are often relegated to the paradigms of victimhood. This may absolve such women of responsibility for poor outcomes and may mobilize public support for feminist "causes" (Doezema 1998). Yet it may simultaneously deny power, capacity and agency (Dunn and Powell-Williams 2007: 92).

Such a monolithic image misses the heterogeneity of women's experiences in relation to choice as well as the instances of agency that women can negotiate for themselves within confining or onerous parameters. While underscoring the mistake that state law makes when it accords "responsibility for results not chosen," Minow (1992: 2096) observes that identifying choices that people can make in the face of stark adversity "can accord them dignity while highlighting the sources and shapes of their constraints." From this perspective, we might be positioned to understand ostensibly vulnerable women as capable of negotiating and making choices that align with goals and interests, and as being empowered by doing so. At the same time, the essentializing quality of current choice ideology and debates can make the equally problematic mistake of assuming choices are free of constraints that propel particular outcomes. Contemporary discourse that presumes the availability of choice only for a set group of women thus clouds the role and relevance of pressures that stifle choice, potentially attributing too much or too little weight to their influence on decision-making.

The absolutism bound up in choice discussions positions women either as rational, responsible agents or as coerced, innocent victims. This dyad is challenged in the discussion that follows in Part 4, which develops a framework for juridical analyses of women's controversial choices. Before embarking on that discussion, the ongoing relevance of choice to feminist discourse and reasoning is worth contemplating, particularly through existent conceptual paradigms pertinent to women's controversial choices and lifestyles.

Part 3: Choice, Agency and Feminist Paradigms

Despite its shortcomings, choice remains a fundamental concept for feminism. Its retention as a focal point of discussion is necessary since, even where impressive constraints exist, women may still display agency and resistance and may remain capable of making choices worthy of social and legal respect. Moreover, principles of responsibility and obligation that connect to choice and agency cannot be understood as universally burdensome. Where coupled with sensitivity to an individual's social and moral context, notions of responsibility and obligation may in fact nourish her citizenship and agency (Campbell et al. 2011).

The discussion that ensues begins with an analysis as to how agency and choice might exist even in the face of impressive social, economic and cultural pressures. This is developed as a basis for the argument that agency and choice should remain central to feminist conversations and legal strategies. In advancing an argument about the pertinence of choice, guidance is sought from recent feminist work, which identifies criteria for state involvement in choices made by historically disadvantaged persons, particularly women. As explained below, this work makes valuable conceptual contributions, however, it does not robustly address questions regarding how women understand the multiple normative influences—including those that state law exerts—on their choices, nor does it contemplate when state action in women's choices is warranted, or what form that action should take. Finally, this Part identifies what it argues are central questions for juridical assessments of women's controversial choices.

Agency and Choice in the Face of Constraint

A feminist juridical approach to choice that acknowledges the potential for agency even where women's lives are constricted by important social, cultural and economic forces is imaginable. Rather than casting choice and constraint as diametrically opposed and mutually exclusive, this approach recognizes that although in tension, self-determination and "systematic gender-based oppression" may co-exist (Abrams 1995: 333). This approach also departs from a "dominance feminism" account on the ground that this tells an "incomplete and misleading story," chalking up women's intimate practices to coercion rather than seeing these as potential instantiations of agency (Eichner 2009: 312). Viewed through this prism, state law's responses to morally ambiguous decisions must do more than seek to outlaw choices that seem self-victimizing, while simultaneously retreating and remaining inactive when women appear to bear agency (Abrams 1995: 375). More equitable and effective legislation and policy would devote minimal effort to halting controversial practices. They would instead aim to identify and mitigate constraints on options while recognizing instances of resistance and supporting decision-makers as they navigate outcomes.

An emphasis on constraints, which overlooks the human capacity for resourcefulness and for appropriating authority even in oppressive settings, obscures the persistence of women's agency. For example, a focus on the fearful, vulnerable and compelled status of a battered woman limits opportunities for assessing whether and in what circumstances she might feel that remaining with or returning to her violent intimate partner is a viable and desirable strategy. This choice might not be optimal or readily explicable, but it can still be the product of rational deliberation. Recognizing this allows for the development of a thicker domestic violence narrative that accounts for the varied reasons women give for maintaining commitments to partners who have exhibited violence, and supports efforts to negotiate the outcomes of such choices (Peled et al. 2000: 19-20). It also creates room to account for the intricate emotions inherent to intimate and interdependent relationships that can prompt conflicting and evolving choices over time even in contexts afflicted by abuse (Baker 2001, Hanna 2010: 139).

The dominant feminist critique of the Opt-Out Revolution also largely neglects the possibility of seeing a woman's decision to leave her career as a form of resistance to unacceptable work conditions and an effort to manage her life and family as she deems appropriate. Viewed this way, opting out may be seen as motivated by interests a woman prioritizes or prefers, and not just as the unavoidable result of compelling external forces (Williams 1996: 757). Just as a battered woman who remains with her partner may consciously and carefully navigate multiple social, economic and emotional constraints, so too might the woman who opts out as a project of "self-governance" that pushes back against her subjection to the demands of balancing labour and familial demands (Cossman 2009). Thus to attribute the transition from high-powered career to homemaking solely to the constraints that contour this move, or to call this an impoverished, un-feminist choice, undermines the agency and contribution of women who might in fact want and choose domestic over professional life (Cossman 2009: 470, Williams 1991: 1626-1629). This can only have the effect of deepening the marginalization of women's unpaid caregiving work.

Last, traditional accounts of domestic contracts tend to overlook the fact that a woman might use such agreements to negotiate for more than what she would receive materially under statutory support or property division regimes (Rogerson 1991: 164, 252). A valid contractual relationship plainly requires at least two willing partners. A desire or choice to negotiate will thus be frustrated if one's partner refuses to engage in this process; the point has been made in Canadian jurisprudence regarding the "choice" to marry (*Nova Scotia (Attorney General) v. Walsh*: paras. 141ff., *Miron v. Trudel*: para. 22, *Quebec (Attorney General) v. A.*).

Where domestic contracts are reached between the parties, presuming that these invariably subvert women's interests raises difficulties. Some women might want to craft support and property arrangements by contract rather than leaving these matters to be determined by statute or by judicial discretion (Fehlberg and Smyth 2002: 134). Others may be willing to relinquish their claims with a view to showing their commitment to a faith community or to avoiding ongoing contact with a spouse. Women might value either of these goals more than the material sacrifice in question (Fournier 2012a: 27-28, Rogerson 1991: 249-250). However, they risk seeing their economic and social lives destabilized by legal regimes that neglect context and facilitate the override of private settlements. Thus, while state law recognizes the emotional climate of domestic contract negotiations, this alone is not a sufficiently plausible basis for discounting such agreements as valid expressions of human will. This is true regardless of whether such a claim is advanced by a woman or her husband (*Black v. Black* (2006): para. 149). Fair, self-protective deals can be reached even in emotional circumstances (Leckey 2007: 14). Emotion might even empower in domestic contract negotiation; women's presumed connections to "the children and the home in which [family members] live" might weigh against the concerns of a male spouse seeking custody or generous access and might be seen as a bargaining chip (*MacLeod v. MacLeod*: 42). This observation problematically reinforces traditional perceptions about gender roles in marriage. Nonetheless, it illuminates how power in family law might not be connected only to wealth and property and it creates space for taking account of women's potential strengths and advantage in domestic contract negotiations.

Such examples illustrate the value of a feminist interpretation of choice premised on openness to recognizing agency despite the presence of constraints. It also acknowledges choice's fluidity. Difficult decisions, like the ones considered in this book, are rarely made without a sense of normative ambiguity and without considerable tradeoffs (Stone, P. 2007: 122). In the process of choosing, the chooser might not feel wholly or consistently free or coerced, and she may second-guess or even regret her choice as she makes it and as she manages its results. Yet even a "deeply imperfect" choice can reflect autonomy and agency (Hanna 2010: 138-139).

This point is essential for feminist legal thinking, as it aims to avoid legislation and policy that mistakenly presume women's victimization or attribute responsibility, and that react by revoking—rather than fostering—opportunities. But while feminists may need to accept the possibility of choice, resistance and agency, even in problematic and constraining contexts, a couple of questions for jurists remain outstanding. A first relates to the process through which such dynamics can be identified. How is a lawyer, judge or legal scholar to know whether a woman's decision is compelled or reflective of her own interests and goals? A second question links to the interactions between state law and women's choices on particular issues. This question calls for: identifying and critiquing the conceptual premises on which state law is based, exploring the interaction between such law and non-state laws and norms that shape decision-making; and appreciating the effect of state law on constricting or expanding options for women and on driving choice outcomes. These questions are taken up in the final part of this chapter. Before turning to that analysis, however, an examination of current feminist literature that explores choice and that proposes criteria for public involvement in women's choices will be helpful.

Feminist Paradigms for Evaluating Choice

Recent feminist scholarship presents different angles from which women's controversial choices might be logically critiqued. This scholarship offers different rationales for state intervention either to prevent women from making particular choices or to rearrange the outcomes of their choices. The discussion here sets out models presented in three particular feminist texts. A discussion of their distinct contributions foregrounds the limits of these texts for jurists seeking to understand women's choices against the backdrop of state law and policy.

Yuracko's (2003: 27) thesis rests on perfectionist theory, which both describes "how people should live" and drives "social policies and structures that promote individual flourishing." More broadly, perfectionism is understood as a moral theory predicated on promoting the development of the individual's human nature, in its "best concept" (Hurka 1996: 9). Yuracko argues that although feminist critiques of women's choices are often couched in neutral terminology and focus on the constraining modalities under which women make decisions, these critiques ultimately rely on perfectionist theory. For Yuracko, the seemingly objective, process-focused language of feminist criticisms thinly veils the perfectionist reasoning that actually lies at the heart of feminist preoccupations. She posits that although feminists use neutral, liberal language to scrutinize choice, they are in fact concerned with substantive outcomes and the correctness of women's decisions. Other feminist philosophers, while not mounting arguments within the frame of perfectionism, have comparably questioned process-focused reasoning. This work suggests that assessing choice by focusing on procedure while remaining neutral as to content risks presuming as autonomous choices that are in fact influenced by women's internalization of "oppressive norms of femininity" (Stoljar 2000: 95). For Yuracko (2003: 104), feminist scrutiny of choice ultimately aims to shelter women from "excessive risk of certain kinds of harms, regardless of whether these choices are made by clueless women who do not know what their choices entail or knowledgeable women aware of the risks involved."

Building on this premise, Yuracko sets forth her own theory of "pragmatic perfectionism," which aims to provide a more functional, transparent and justifiable basis for identifying and criticizing women's bad choices. She sets out four principles—sexual non-commodification, intellectual and moral development, self-love, and self-sufficiency—and proposes their use as a barometer for testing the "goodness" or "perfectness" of a woman's choice. Yuracko develops the workability of these principles through their application to three "hard choices" women face, relating to: sex work, sexual objectification and full-time homemaking. She argues that drawing on her four principles will allow feminism to be explicit about the perfectionist values it already embraces but currently keeps hidden in its "liberal closet." This will ultimately, according to Yuracko (2003: 132-135), channel a feminist vision of the good life into political debates affecting women's lives and status.

While Yuracko resists feminist entanglements in liberalism, Chambers (2008) engages with liberal theory by exploring how it should operate when accounting for "a feminist awareness of social construction and gender inequality." She further draws on liberal theory to assess how the notion of "free choice" cannot, by itself, surmount gender equality's entrenchment in social norms (Chambers 2008: 8). Chambers (2008: 43-44) accepts liberalism's focus on autonomy, yet argues that its privileging of choice is flawed in three ways: its focus on individuals' intellectualism and ideologies to understand choice without exploring their "physical, practical, and everyday experiences"; its study of the individual to the neglect of her broader social context; and its conceptualization of power as a "negative, repressive force" without acknowledging its liberating and creative potential. As such, Chambers maintains that respect for choice and autonomy must be accompanied by a careful study of the social context in which choices are made, so as to understand those choices more fully. An appreciation of social context also yields important insights about gender equality, which are subject to neglect when choice is considered through a conventional liberal lens.

Drawing on case studies that include genital cutting, aesthetic plastic surgery and wearing high-heeled shoes, Chambers unpacks the relationship between social and cultural expectations and women's choices that risk physical harm. She perceives state intervention in such choices, even when they are apparently freely made, as justified when two factors are discernible, namely, "the disadvantage factor" and "the influence factor." She explains the former as the diminished advantage that "differently choosing groups receive" and warns that the greater the difference in disadvantage and the more irreversible it is, the greater the grounds for public concern (Chambers 2008: 121). The "influence factor" is explained as "identifiable processes by which one group is encouraged to make a disadvantageous choice" (Chambers 2008: 123). For Chambers (2008: 132), the confluence of disadvantage and influence substantiates an inference of injustice and would rationalize state interference with the choice and outcome. Specifically, the state should be capable of devising measures that aim to affect both formal laws and informal norms within social and cultural groups, such as workplaces or religious communities.

A third recent text wrestles with the concept of agency in feminist theory in connection with women's choices that appear confined by "discursive forms of juridical and social power" (Showden 2011: xii). Like Chambers, Showden focuses on factors that constrain women's options and practices. Showden refrains from engaging in efforts to locate the objectively "correct" decision in different circumstances and instead seeks to uncover the multiple norms at work that drive women's choices. Moreover, Showden's sophisticated analysis of agency grounds her argument that possibilities for control over the self and for making choices exist despite "the weight of the cross-cutting axes of dominating power within an individual's situation" (Showden 2011: 33).

Showden develops her theory of agency through a study of domestic violence, assisted reproduction and sex work. Drawing on these contexts, she challenges conventional "binary conceptions of women as 'victims' or 'heroes'." She thus argues that agency, "in all its messy, complicated, and compromised inglorious drudgery," can exist even when women face real limits on choice (Showden 2011: xv). Showden explores both the processes surrounding choice while also alluding to feminists' role in evaluating the substance of women's tough decisions. Showden further considers what ameliorative law and policy schemes might look like in relation to each of her three examples. This discussion acknowledges simultaneously law's transformative potential for fostering agency as well as its generalizing inclinations that focus on formal equality and ignore context (Showden 2011: 31-32). Although Showden's work contemplates regulatory options that would affect choice, her project—like Yuracko's and Chambers'—is a political one, aiming to enhance opportunities for women to recognize and express agency. State-originating legal rules and norms, particularly those that confer rights recognition, are thus viewed as tools for furthering political cohesion and empowerment in "[opening] up vistas of possibility" and in "facilitating the collective development of agency" (Showden 2011: 216).

Yuracko, Chambers and Showden advance feminist discussions on choice in a vital way. Each tackles choice from a unique angle, namely through: perfectionism, a feminist critique of liberalism and scrutinizing the bridge between agency and choice. Their analyses offer nuanced frameworks for understanding and assessing the most difficult and controversial choices women might make. They also propose distinct and thoughtful bases upon which intervention in such choices might be warranted. For Yuracko, state involvement may be justified where the choice in question compromises perfectionist theories of a "meaningful human life," particularly where the choice threatens the principle of "non-commodification" of personhood. Chambers sees such intervention as called for when a choice is characterized by disadvantage on the chooser's (or the choosing group's) part and the chooser (or choosing group) is influenced or encouraged to make poor choices. Last, for Showden, state intervention through legislation and policy is sensible where this recognizes and enhances agency even in extremely harsh life circumstances.

These feminist approaches analyze choice through the lens of political philosophy, thereby offering rich bases for uncovering multiple, often hidden, sites of power that might limit women's opportunities. This scholarship also develops a range of metrics for evaluating the justice implications of women's choices, and further contemplates various grounds upon which state intervention in choice can be rationalized. This feminist work is thus crucial to jurists seeking to understand the role of state and non-state law in choices that yield ostensibly poor results for women. However, those interested in thinking about the way in which the state and society engage with women's choices, particularly through formal legal rules, can get only so far by relying on these feminist theories of choice that have been developed within the sphere of political philosophy. It is true that legal and political reasoning will at some points overlap and rich legal analysis typically requires the legal scholar to venture into the domain of political theory to appreciate the underpinnings of legal rules and standards in view of their larger political and institutional contexts (Waldron 2002). Nevertheless, an analysis of political theory alone is incomplete in the domain of assessing controversial choices by women, as this work does not yield normative or precise insight into pertinent legal rules. This is understandable; political philosophy's mandate does not typically include a fine-grained analysis of discrete laws or policies, or of doctrines such as *stare decisis*, judicial review or the rule of law (Leckey 2008a: 272). It is also not generally concerned with the questions of remedies and who is best suited to redress outcomes that yield harm, particularly when such outcomes are connected to fault or other wrongful conduct. These issues fall squarely within the jurist's ken. As explained in the discussion that ensues, a juristic study of law's engagement with divisive choices is enriched and rendered more concrete through reference to specific and relevant legal rules and their engagement with choice. This engagement between rules and choice is relevant both at the moment of assessing options that women may have and when examining whether and how to remedy adverse outcomes that appear tethered to their own choosing.

This analysis of choice that this book develops seeks to further this existent feminist scholarship through an approach aimed at improving juridical understandings of complex choices fraught with moral uncertainty. It encourages the integration of empirical evidence that illuminates women's lived experiences in connection with choices that fall subject to social and legal scrutiny. The analysis proposed here thus aims to prompt legal actors to consider more robustly whether and how women ascribe meaning and value to impugned choices and lifestyles, and how they respond to normative forces exerted by state and non-state institutions and rules.

Part 4: Toward a Juridical Analysis of Choice

The political theory analyses presented above are essential to theorizing choice from a feminist perspective. This project builds on this existent literature through its development of a juridical approach to women's controversial choices that will have particular relevance for legal scholars, practitioners, reformers and adjudicators. While the analysis here pays heed to the social contexts in which women's choices are made (Waldron 2002), it seeks to understand these choices not only in relation to these contexts but also through an analysis of relevant formal and informal legal rules, remedies, standards and institutions. The juridical dimension of this analysis is further cultivated by its efforts to identify "the structural and ideological underpinnings" of current legal rules and to assess their social value (Rhode 2002: 1338). Thus, while this framework ultimately considers the political theory—particularly feminist political theory—that advances arguments about the way law "ought to be regarded" (Waldron 2002: 357), and while it may have relevance for policy development in relation to various topics and places (Rhode

2002: 1338), it forms part of a project committed to legal scholarship through its assessment of formal, state-crafted rules that affect women's choices.

A jurist interested in understanding difficult choices in the lives of women will typically be preoccupied with three central questions, which are essential to the analytical framework for choice developed in this book. The first question pertains to the choice itself and prompts the jurist to ask—as do the political philosophers discussed in Part 3—whether the controversial choice is reflective of the chooser's own interests or is a product of external pressures and constraints. A second line of inquiry is more obviously connected to the discipline of law. It calls for an identification of the state's legal approaches to the choice in question; for example: How does state law address the choices of women who remain with or return to abusive intimate partnerships? A third investigation critically evaluates state law through analyses of: its assumptions and goals; the way in which it engages and intersects with non-state norms; and its effects on shaping, expanding or constricting women's options. The discussion that follows explains each of these questions essential to the juridical analysis of choice proposed here. It concludes with some remarks regarding the essential nature of empirically derived knowledge to developing compelling responses to the questions raised.

Juridical Assessments of Choice "on the Merits"

A jurist who seeks to understand and assess the substance or merits of a woman's controversial choice, particularly one that appears nefarious to her interests or her well-being, will typically pursue such inquiry with a view to understanding whether and how legal actors ought to engage with that choice. For example, in contemplating the decisions of women who partake in the Opt-Out Revolution, a jurist may be interested in assessing whether and how state and non-state law drive a professional women's move to homemaking. Alternatively, a legal scholar, practitioner, lawmaker or judge may study women's choices in connection with the Opt-Out Revolution with a view to assessing how state law ought to respond to or remedy such choices. One might consider here the family law developments discussed in Part 1, which accord value to women's domestic and childcare contributions in assessments of their family property and maintenance entitlements on the breakdown of a spousal union.

Efforts to understand the substance of a difficult choice will be furthered by an examination of the meaning (that is, the explanation or motivation) and value (that is, the subjective importance) women ascribe to their choices. As discussed more fully below, this inquiry is aided by reliance on empirical study that illuminates women's experiences in relation to their choices. Consider the example of a woman who signs a separation agreement pursuant to which she receives considerably less spousal support than she would likely have been granted by a judicial ruling. She accepts the agreement knowing that it will dissuade her spouse from seeking custody of their children. An inquiry rooted in empiricism would expose her own understanding of the agreement and why she accepted its terms.

This connects to the *meaning* she gives the contract. Such analysis would also permit an appreciation of the normative importance she gives the agreement, that is, whether she sees it as a good and desirable thing, and on what basis. This point connects to the *value* she attributes to her choice.

Having said this, it should be underscored that simply because a woman can make sense of (give meaning to) and claim that she appreciates or desires (gives value to) her choice, that choice should not prompt passive social or political acceptance of her circumstances. Claims about meaning and value merit scrutiny, and this does not preclude studying such claims with a view to understanding the forces that drive women's decisions and lifestyles (Campbell 2008: 130). Moreover, the distinction between desire and choice should be borne in mind in analyzing the meaning and value of choices that affect women's intimate relationships. Hanna's work on this front is insightful, demonstrating how consent and autonomy can persist even in the face of tightly constrained options (Hanna 2010: 136). While perhaps sometimes associated with practices or outcomes that are not fully desired, choice may subsist and remain relevant to one's happiness about particular arrangements (Hunter 2007: 165). Conversely, a chooser might reject or choose against things she desires (Hurd 1996: 126). Efforts to demarcate the line between desire and choice will be complicated by the inherent ambivalence of much of our decision-making, particularly as related to intimate relationships (Brett 1998: 80).

Although efforts to discern the meaning and value women ascribe to choice might be difficult or yield results that should be subject to analysis and scrutiny, the exercise is a worthy one for jurists. It allows for insight into the way that state law can foster, facilitate or complicate difficult choices. Additionally, an inquiry into the meaning and value women attribute to their choices may reveal the unobvious benefits of legally and socially impugned practices.

State Law's Approaches to Choice

Apart from understanding the difficult and controversial choices women make, jurists will be concerned with a second line of analysis pertaining to state law's approach to such choices. It prompts the identification and critical evaluation of legislation and policy that govern choice in a given context.

Feminist political philosophers who explore choice propose various options through which the state might reasonably be called upon to contemplate and evaluate practices and decisions that ostensibly harm women. Chambers, for example, develops the concept of an "equality tribunal." Modeled on the structure and function of labour tribunals, Chambers imagines the equality tribunal as a state institution serving to adjudicate claims advanced by women in relation to events of discrimination or oppression occurring within particular cultural settings. Chambers (2008: 132) sees the tribunal as a place where women can assert their views and voices, and where the state can intervene to comment normatively on, and try to change, practices rooted in gender inequality. Showden's (2011: 82-85) evaluation of public domestic violence initiatives also exhibits insightful reflection on the way in which legal action can benefit women whose options are seriously constrained by social and economic power dynamics.

While instructive to jurists studying choice through a feminist lens, these discussions do not analyze the various tools that the state deploys to intervene in women's choices. Such an analysis seems critical for a textured understanding of choice from a juridical stance. This analysis would illuminate whether and how a government has acted to govern issues on which women must make difficult choices. It would further facilitate reflections on the efficacy of such government action or inaction in broadening meaningful options for women. Domestic violence may be taken as an example. A host of state governance initiatives would be relevant to investigate in order to appreciate fully women's options in this realm. Policies affecting women's shelters and their accessibility, criminal law provisions that force the separation of spouses, criminal law defenses that might pertain where women use physical force to protect themselves, and developments in family law affecting child custody and access in cases of intimate partner violence might all be relevant to evaluate the range of choices available to women in abusive relationships. Equally relevant to this study is a contemplation of the absence of state initiatives that might empower these women, for example, by shifting accountability for their wellness and that of their children to their violent partners or, more broadly, to government actors (Miccio 2005).

Law and policy strategies developed by the state to address situations where a woman's presumed choice compromises her interests might have one of three orientations. They may be *facilitative*, seeking to widen the range of options at a woman's disposal before she makes a choice, or supporting her as she manages the outcomes of a choice after it is made. Examples include initiatives oriented toward preventing domestic violence, supporting women who remain with violent intimate partners, or counseling violent partners themselves. Similarly, strategies that assist women who seek a return to paid work after having committed themselves to homemaking and care work would be properly characterized as facilitative in nature. Alternatively, strategies can be *remedial*, such that a state institution—most typically a tribunal or court—could be called upon to correct the outcomes of unjust circumstances leading to inappropriate choices. This approach would be manifest in a legislative or judicial approach allowing an individual to claim that her domestic contract was negotiated under coercive or unfair circumstances, resulting in material losses. Finally, formal governance strategies may be premised upon a *punitive* approach when it sees a woman's choice as harmful to herself or others. As discussed in Part 2, choice discourse has the result of casting many women as victims of constraints that constrict their opportunities. This image is incongruent with envisaging women who make bad choices as responsible offenders. Yet where a woman is viewed as having control over her decisions, criminal law might target her if her choice is so unpalatable and reprehensible that it calls for a penal sanction.

Legal approaches grounded in prohibition are central to discussions in the chapters that follow, which focus on women's choices connected to polygamy, surrogacy and sex work. Although this first chapter has concentrated on other, non-criminalized choices, its examples are an instructive platform from which to launch an analysis of polygamy, surrogacy and sex work. Like the choices discussed in this chapter (domestic violence, domestic work and domestic contracts), those at issue in the ensuing chapters are made in contexts in which women appear to be at risk, primarily because of presumed power dimensions in their intimate and sexual relationships. Moreover, the choices studied above, which are not criminalized, and those taken up in the following parts of this book, all trigger state involvement in decision-making by focusing on the woman chooser. Rather than exploring the contexts surrounding decision-making and the factors that might propel particular outcomes, formal governance responses to choices connected with domestic violence, domestic work and domestic contracts, like those associated with polygamy, surrogacy and sex work, cast a woman's adverse outcomes as emanating from her own individual ignorance, impotence and moral shortcomings. In consequence, state law's remedial efforts target single choosers and single choices—for example, allowing courts to hear self-defense evidence led by a battered woman, or placing at risk for prosecution the woman who opts to marry a polygamist—instead of striving to ameliorate conditions that might expand the chooser's real options.

Evaluating State Law Governing Choice

In any given context, a number of formal laws and policies might seek to regulate a practice that raises controversies over women's choices. In the context of women's decision-making affecting intimate life and relationships, legal instruments typically fall within the ambit of family law. Yet the three case studies explored in Part 1 show that employment law, contract law and criminal law might also be engaged by such complex choices. Beyond identifying such relevant state governance tools, juridical analyses will benefit from understanding state law's objectives, its points of convergence with non-state norms, and its effects on options and choices.

An investigation into and critique of the objectives of a formal legal rule will illuminate the premises that ground state approaches to choice in a given domain and the extent to which these premises reflect the experiences of those whom the rules in question affect. Relevant sites of information for this inquiry include the text of legislation and policy statements, law commission reports, and debates surrounding such legislation and policy. Moreover, as explored below, relying on empirical research may enable an assessment as to whether the claimed purpose of state law bears out in the actual lives and experiences of women affected by such rules. A study of mandatory arrest and protection orders for battered women is instructive. Although well-intentioned, when such initiatives neglect women's lived experiences and social and economic contexts, they risk backfiring and imposing significant costs on the women they purport to protect. As such, women might suffer economically and lose control and privacy over family life, factors they might prioritize over protection (Suk 2006: 63, Acorn 2005: 345, 364). Such initiatives can be especially threatening for minority and immigrant families who may have difficult relationships with law enforcement actors and institutions and, in the latter case, may be threatened with deportation (Haviland et al. 2001, Loke 1997).

A juridical study of women's choices is further aided by identifying the points of intersection between state and non-state law that shape choices and outcomes. Here again, empirical research and experiential accounts will be valuable in generating an informed and relevant analysis, as they should illuminate the varied sources of motivation and normativity that may account for women's choices in difficult circumstances. For example, a woman's decision to arrange her family affairs by a contract that integrates religious-based obligations can be understood only partially by studying how state law treats such juridical acts. A fuller appreciation requires contemplating the woman's economic and social commitments. It also calls for examining the way she views and values relationships with and obligations to family and community, and the norms arising in these social contexts (Fournier 2012a).

Last, juridical analyses should contemplate the effects of state laws governing choices made in controversial contexts, particularly when these laws take the form of criminal prohibitions. Questions in this respect will centre on the ways in which state law's presence or absence in a given domain affects (or not) the options that women have and the choices they make. Where a legal intervention is facilitative or remedial, the inquiry may investigate the extent to which women are aware of and rely on this. A helpful example is state-subsidized childcare law and policy initiatives. Analyses can illuminate how such initiatives may broaden options and facilitate meaningful choices about work and care for some families, but not others (Campbell 2006). Where punitive, legal interventions tend to force practices out of social view, with the result of compromising decision-makers' personal security and integrity (*Canada (Attorney General) v. PHS Community Services Society*, *Bedford v. Canada*). A study of state law's effects on choice, similar to a study of state law's underlying premises and engagement with non-state norms, will benefit from empirical research that speaks to the lived experiences of women who make controversial and presumably deleterious choices.

The Role and Relevance of Empiricism

Prior to concluding, reference should be made to the place of empirical research within the analytical framework proposed here for interrogating and understanding choice. This book argues that empiricism will enrich a juridical feminist study of choice grounded in particular contexts. Rather than relying solely on accounts in political and formal legal spheres, it advocates building on experiential knowledge offered by women about how they perceive their own options and how they see law, in its various forms, engaging with their choices. This approach centres the voices, experiences and ideas of individuals and groups most deeply affected by the legal rules under scrutiny. Previously, I have argued that such a strategy may yield a critical counter-narrative to state law and policies, and it holds particular relevance for women who are seen, or who see themselves, as subordinated by patriarchal influences at the level of family, community or state (Campbell 2008). Moreover, empirical research can illuminate the gaps between social perceptions of law and the actual content and impact of state-made legal rules. This exploration of the way in which state laws are interpreted, understood, misunderstood and resisted within various social constituencies, each having their own set of norms that guide expectations and conduct, reflects the critical legal pluralist thrust of this book (Webber 2006).

Gathering experiential knowledge from women requires reliance upon empiricism. This would involve the collection of women's stories through research methods that provide opportunities for women to articulate their own narratives. Experiential knowledge in relation to choice is not evident in political theorists' accounts considered in Part 2. Yet this would prove valuable to the legal analysis of choice that the present text proposes. Specifically, experiential knowledge and narrative derived through empiricism may offer insights into the way in which women ascribe meaning and value to their choices and how they choose in response to or in defiance of, or perhaps even without accurate knowledge about, formal governance initiatives. This in turn may illuminate how women's understandings of their choices either collapse or compete with social and political assumptions about choice in a given domain. It can further expose the multiple normative systems—formal and informal, state and non-state—that drive women's most difficult choices and outcomes.

Recognizing the promise of empiricism is not meant to eclipse the relevance of other research tools and strategies in appreciating choice through a jural lens. This book turns to empiricism as one source of knowledge, but women's choices are studied here also through reference to traditional legal research sources and authorities such as judicial decisions, legislation and policy, and government documents and debates. At the same time, the reliance on empiricism is cautious, given its inherent challenges. It is never clear that the results of an empirical study, especially one that is qualitative in nature, will be generalizable across or even within social constituencies. Moreover, particularly where controversial and sensitive issues are broached through empirical and narrative-based methodologies, queries will arise in relation to whether a participant is recounting a full and accurate story. Further, what "counts" as experience often is not easy to discern given that narratives are historicized, politicized and commonly contested (Scott 1991). Responding to such concerns and questions with confidence is difficult, if not impossible. Studies involving individuals who make seemingly illogical or inexplicable choices tend to trigger concerns about research participants' "false consciousness" that clouds their narratives and hinders their truth-telling abilities (Campbell 2008).

A further potential drawback of empirical scholarship lies in its potential to recreate the problem its use seeks to avoid. Empiricism is invoked here with the intention of nuancing polarized debates about choice, however its value might be questioned if accumulated narratives are varied or contradictory. This book maintains that empirical knowledge remains relevant even where it yields inconsistent accounts of experiences in relation to difficult choices. Variances might themselves be telling. Specifically, the monolithic image that state law often yields of women whose choices are controversial and suspicious—as vulnerable, as victimized or even as potentially threatening—can be evaluated, critiqued and textured through a study of lived experience that reveals multiplicity and diversity within individual accounts (Whelehan: 2007). Furthermore, this work posits that it is not only the results of such research that bears relevance for jurists, but also the task of seeking out, listening to and taking seriously the stories of individuals who are usually uninvolved in formal rule-making processes. Empiricism's methodology is therefore as important and valuable as its results.

While empirical research will never produce perfect, certain or even necessarily replicable results, it is one of the few strategies that allows for recording first-hand accounts that can illuminate the motivations driving socially and legally impugned choices and laws' relevance and effects in the lives of the relevant choosers. Clearly, empiricism's contribution reaches beyond law's disciplinary boundaries. For jurists, however, it has a distinct relevance because, if done well, it can have a "practical impact" (Posner 2002: 1326) by drawing the attention of law reformers, judges and legal scholars to knowledge that would not be acquired or advanced through conventional doctrinal scholarship (Heise 2002). Empiricism, interdisciplinary research, narrative and personal experience—again, scrupulously developed and applied—can help legal scholarship avoid being "out of touch with fundamental social problems" (Rhode 2002: 1341-1342). In connection with the present book, the information gleaned from empirical research is considered with reference to concrete examples of challenging, contentious choices that some women make, with a view garnering a fuller understanding of these choices, state law's responses to them, and women's engagement with state and non-state law. In the case studies that follow, empirical insights reveal the shortcomings of state law responses premised on the criminalization of morally ambiguous choices. Narratives offered by women who make such choices show how the criminal law, although advanced in the name of delivering these women from their own misjudgment and from external coercion, heightens the risk of harm and loss to which they are exposed.

In the final analysis, then, empiricism as drawn on here is not intended as a foundation for revising or recreating, at a systemic level, regimes regulating controversial practices and choices. Rather, it is intended to inform and foster a richer appreciation of law's social relevance and impact in connection with complex choices that carry gender-equality implications. Legal analyses that refer to empirical evidence can guide jurists called upon to design rules or adjudicate outcomes in a manner that pays attention to individual social circumstances and needs and is thus potentially more just.

Conclusion

This first chapter develops an analytical framework for the juridical study of morally ambiguous choices. Drawing on the examples of domestic violence, domestic work and domestic contracts, it explores three chief pitfalls of choice lexicon and ideology. An uncritical acceptance of choice undermines the constraints that may operate to compel particular outcomes, rendering choice more apparent than real. Furthermore, it can lead to holding women liable for outcomes shaped by a range of forces outside their control or influence. Finally, it can essentialize women's experiences, neglecting the relevance of contextual factors on a woman's ability in any given situation to exercise agency and make meaningful choices.

While feminists should remain critical of choice-based reasoning, dismissing the possibility of choice in the face of seemingly inimical circumstances risks abandoning analyses of women's difficult situations to notions of duress and disempowerment. This is risky for women. Without intending to devalue the need to identify and redress gender-based coercion and oppression where it exists, chalking up any and all poor outcomes for women to these concepts without further inquiry is too simplistic. It fails to account for the potential that women may make even thorny or seemingly harmful choices because these align with what they see as best for them. Accounting for this possibility complicates the binaries that conventional discussions set up between agency and victimization, and between choice and coercion.

Seeking to depart from the limits of this dyadic reasoning, this book relies on the juridical mode of analysis developed in this chapter to recognize the possibility for agency and constraint to exist simultaneously, each exerting a different amount of influence at different moments. It advocates an understanding of women's experiences in relation to difficult choices, and an understanding of law's approaches to such choices, by drawing on knowledge developed through empirical study. These principles frame the questions developed in Part 4 as essential to a juridical assessment of controversial choices.

This discussion sets the groundwork for the analysis that develops in the remainder of this book, which contemplates choice with reference to three new case studies: polygamy, surrogacy and sex work. Although not discussed in this opening chapter, these case studies remain germane to its discussion. Like the three scenarios explored in this chapter (domestic violence, domestic work and domestic contracts), polygamy, surrogacy and sex work are characterized by moral ambiguity and raise questions about women making ostensibly self-injurious choices. Moreover, similar to the contexts studied so far, polygamy, surrogacy and sex work elicit particular scrutiny of women's decisions linked to family, reproduction and sex.

What sets these three new case studies apart, however, is that they are subject to governance tools that, in most Western jurisdictions, criminalize the chooser. Feminist discussions on choice have by and large not focused on the use of criminal law to stigmatize and punish women's poor choices. Yet there is critical relevance to assessing whether a woman can and would make a choice that both looks contrary to her own interests and would trigger the possibility of criminal prosecution. The acute risks of choice in such circumstances prompt questions about whether a woman would ever deliberately and independently make that choice. We might presume women in these scenarios are coerced. But the questions for juridical assessment developed in this chapter underscore the relevance of exploring the meaning and value that women might attribute to, and the plural normative forces that shape, even criminally-sanctioned choices that result in intense tradeoffs. These questions also call for critical examination of relevant state law by drawing on the experiential knowledge of the women who are directly affected by this law.

The discussions that unfold in the remainder of this book highlight the relevance of a juridical awareness of women's agency that remains sensitive to constraints thwarting the possibility of choice. This includes attention to the coercion that may be engendered by state law and policy themselves. The objective, then, is to engage with state-crafted legal rules in a way that avoids obscuring pressures, individualizing and privatizing responsibility for harsh outcomes, and generalizing about women's experiences while recognizing and trying to cultivate opportunities for meaningful choice even in unexpected and un-obliging contexts.

Chapter 2
Polygamy: The Myths of Multiple Marriage[1]

By definition, polygamy—sometimes also termed "plural marriage"—involves the marriage, or conjugal union, of one individual simultaneously to two or more people. Polygyny refers to this practice when a man has two or more female spouses or "sister wives," and polyandry is the term used to describe a woman's taking of two or more male spouses. Where polygamy exists, it almost always takes the form of polygyny rather than polyandry (Levine and Silk 1997: 376), and the term "polygamy" thus is typically used in both social and academic parlance to denote polygynous relationships. In keeping with this semantic convention, references to polygamy and plural marriage throughout this book shall describe relationships between one man and at least two female spouses. These terms will also be used distinctly from polyamory, an arrangement of intimate partnerships between one person and multiple partners. Polyamory is briefly considered here and, as shown, it may involve a woman with plural male partners.

Polygamy's place in legal analyses is unique and stands apart from the two other practices considered in this text in some important respects. Polygamy, like surrogacy and sex work, raises concerns about the authenticity of women's choices given their ostensible vulnerability within these practices and the compromise they appear to impose on women's interests. Polygamy, however, is distinguished by its perception in the West as a "foreign" or "imported" social phenomenon. A practice conjuring associations with cultish, patriarchal, undereducated or geographically isolated communities, plural marriage is met with steep legal and social skepticism and resistance. Juridical risks for those associated with polygamy include prosecution under criminal law, removal orders made pursuant to immigration and refugee regulatory regimes, or the apprehension of children by youth protection authorities.

These potential legal ramifications for women in polygamy render the acquisition of empirical data about their experiences exceedingly difficult. While a considerable amount of research has been undertaken on the experiences of women in countries where polygamy is permitted by the state (see e.g., Al-Krenawi 2001, Al-Krenawi and Graham 2001, Al-Krenawi and Lev-Weisel 2002, Al-Krenawi et al. 2001, Elbedour et al. 2002), studies that set forth sister wives' narratives deriving from jurisdictions that prohibit the practice are scarce. This chapter focuses on scientific data obtained from the latter contexts, that is, settings

1 Parts of this chapter draw and build on the author's prior publications, namely: Campbell 2013a, Campbell 2013b, Campbell 2010 and Campbell 2009b.

where polygamy is criminalized, and where it also falls under intense scrutiny by immigration and child welfare public agencies.

This chapter also draws principally on literature that has studied women's experiences in polygamy within Western secular states. Literature from jurisdictions governed by religious or customary law, or where polygamy is legally accepted, would not yield results generalizable to an analysis of plural wives' experiences in Canada, the United Kingdom and Australia. Furthermore, while some compelling research contemplates the experiences of men and boys in polygamy even in settings pertinent to this book (Billie 2008), these studies are peripheral to the present discussion, which aims to develop a fuller understanding of women's decisions about plural marriage.

This chapter follows the analytical framework for juridical understandings of choice announced and defined in Chapter 1. It thus investigates empirical and juridical narratives with a view to understanding how accurately and effectively state law reacts, reflects and responds to the life circumstances of women in plural marriage families and communities. Part 1 draws on women's narratives pertaining to polygamy to illuminate how women ascribe meaning and value to their lives in polygamy. Part 2 explains how state law and policy respond to plural marriage in Canada, the United Kingdom and Australia. Part 3 develops a critical appraisal of the governance of polygamy, reflecting on the presumptions and objectives that drive state law, the interface between state law and non-state law—that is, expectations and rules that wield normative force emanating from social sites such as families, religious communities, schools or the workplace—pertinent to polygamy, and state law's adverse effects on the choices and experiences of women in polygamy.

Part 1: Plural Narratives about Choice

This section presents narratives offered by women in polygamy, as recounted through field-based research. As indicated, polygamy's severe legal implications generate a great deal of resistance among women to share their experiences as plural wives or as members of plural marriage communities. As such, polygamous women's experiential knowledge is not widely disseminated, and this is an important impediment to understanding their encounters with this practice. It results in a limited number of empirical studies, particularly from jurisdictions where polygamy carries the risk of onerous legal sanctions, and further raises questions about the significance and generalizability of the research that has been conducted.[2]

Empirical scholarship on women in plural marriage in the West derives primarily from studies within American and Canadian polygamous communities. This can

2 See e.g., Bauman CJSC's discussion questioning my own research in *Reference re: Section 293 of the Criminal Code of Canada*: paras. 757-758.

be explained by the concentration of fundamentalist Mormon societies within these jurisdictions. As set out below, a key tenet of fundamentalist Mormonism is adherence to polygamy. The relevance of literature deriving from American communities within the present project may be questioned, given that the United States is not one of the three main jurisdictions considered here. Yet historical and contemporary alliances between Canadian and American fundamentalist Mormon communities, which are explicated in the ensuing discussion, and comparable legal approaches to polygamy in these jurisdictions substantiate reliance on empirical studies developed in American settings.

Elsewhere in the West, polygamy is taken up primarily within Muslim communities.[3] Even within Islamic societies, however, polygamy appears controversial and anomalous. In the result, relevant empirical research on polygamy in Islam is, unsurprisingly, nearly non-existent. Finding participants willing to take part in interview studies about a practice that places them at risk of prosecution is a challenge. When risks of participation broaden to include potential deportation and removal orders, the implications for sharing one's experiences with a researcher are more onerous.

Locating and identifying polygamists can also be difficult. Communities known for polygamy, where a concentration of practitioners can be found, offer an identifiable space for carrying out empirical research. In other communities, polygamy may not be a core principle or practice, and instances of it will be sporadic and geographically dispersed. These factors can frustrate, or at least deeply complicate, empirical inquiry.

Some of the literature contemplated here draws on past research I have undertaken with polygamous women in a Canadian plural marriage community. This community, known as Bountiful, is located in British Columbia and is home to about 1,000 followers of fundamentalist Mormonism, also known as the Fundamentalist Church of Jesus Christ of Latter Day Saints (FLDS). In 2008 and 2009 I formally interviewed 22 women who were then living, or who had at one time lived, in Bountiful. I also met other women who refused to speak on the record due to fear of legal ramifications. In designing my research on polygamy in Canada, I chose to concentrate on Bountiful. This community has garnered extensive public and legal attention as a known locus of polygamy. The preoccupation with Bountiful gave rise to Canadian discussions about polygamy riddled with untested assumptions about the practice's disastrous impact on women. Some commercial texts have also emerged in the last decade (Bramham 2008, Jessop and Palmer 2007, Palmer and Perrin 2004) to offer horrific accounts of life in communities like Bountiful. While worthy of contemplation, the weight ascribed to these texts must account for the fact that they were released by commercial publishers for a lay readership that do not represent the fruit of empirical research. Moreover, these texts are not grounded in a study of how women in polygamy view their lives and

3 See e.g., in Canada, Javed 2008; in England, Serck 2012; in Australia, Anonymous 2012a.

choices in relation to the law of the state and the norms of their communities and families. My own research aimed to tackle these distinct issues through qualitative research with women in Bountiful. Although a number of women in Bountiful declined to be interviewed as part of my study, this community proved to be a rich site for gathering the narratives of women in polygamy.

While my Bountiful project and other studies on polygamy in fundamentalist Mormonism (e.g., Bennion 1998, 2008, 2011, Pelland 2007, Boehmer 2010) provide insight into women's experiential knowledge, this scholarship cannot be wholly generalized across jurisdictions or across cultural groups. Recognizing the relevance of an empirical study's focus and scope, it is clear that women who live polygamously pursuant to the tenets of Islamic or indigenous customary law will not share in full the experiences of plural wives in Bountiful or other fundamentalist Christian communities. Wherever feasible, then, references are made here to polygamy research outside the fundamentalist Mormon context. Yet the pool of available research remains admittedly unbalanced, with a preponderance of studies on polygamy in the West concentrated on the experiences of fundamentalist Mormon women. The paucity of empirical literature on women's experiences in polygamy in other contexts presents an important challenge to the development of nuanced academic inquiry in this area. Furthermore, even within FLDS societies, women's experiences will be heterogeneous and blanket extrapolations of findings within a single community are impossible.

The state of polygamy scholarship is essential to bear in mind in analyses of the topic, and remains vulnerable to critique. At the same time, like the two other case studies taken up in this book, the shortcomings of empiricism involving "hidden" (Heckathorn 1997) women should not justify outright abandonment or disregard of empirical work that does exist. Instead, the empirics merit integration within this analysis of women's controversial choices, accounting for the weight attributable to the varying studies from which they derive.

The Meaning Women Ascribe to Engaging in Polygamy

As explained in Chapter 1, the analytical framework for studying choice from a juridical perspective should begin with an interrogation of the way in which women ascribe meaning and value to the impugned choice at issue. While meaning refers to the explanation or rationale women convey for making a choice, value relates to the way in which they normatively assess their experiences as a result of that choice. Empirical studies identify three principal rationales for women's engagement with polygamy. The first, most obvious, motivator is faith. Many women consent to plural marriage pursuant to their religious views. Second, some women indicate that their choices about polygamy are anchored to a perception that plural marriage will yield social and economic benefits. A third explanation for women's association with polygamy relates to compulsion rather than choice. For some, entry into plural marriage is the consequence of fear, duress or coercion rather than an informed and deliberate decision. In such circumstances, one might link the "meaning" of polygamy to the constraints that narrow or eliminate women's alternatives in regard to family life.

Religious beliefs Religion is the dominant theme within women's explanations as to why they or members of their community take up plural marriage. In the context of fundamentalist Mormonism this stems from marriage's primordial importance as a social and religious institution; marriage is perceived as essential to realizing the promise of resurrection after death, and of exaltation, or becoming close to, or like, God (Daynes 2001: 4-5). Mormon theology posits that, after life on earth, there are three levels of glory or exaltation, each bearing a closer proximity to God: telestial, terrestrial and celestial. Although it is believed that most people will, after their time on earth, inherit one of these kingdoms of heaven, the most virtuous will attain the highest level of glory, that is, celestial exaltation, where the spirit becomes a god itself (Bushman 2008: 75-76). The necessity of marriage for achieving celestial existence is made explicit in the Doctrine and Covenants of the Church of Jesus Christ of Latter-Day Saints (131: 1-3), which forms part of the canon of the Mormon Church and contains early revelations to the Church's founders.

Plural marriage was instated in Mormonism in 1831 by the religion's founder, Joseph Smith, pursuant to revelations from God, which he claimed commanded this practice (Ryan 1991: 218-221, Bushman 2008: 86). Over time, polygamy came to generate extensive controversy and critique within the United States, resulting in the enactment of legislation aimed at depriving polygamists of civil liberties and at financially debilitating the Mormon Church (White 2009). American anti-polygamy laws were engendered by the perception of polygamy as a foreign and barbaric practice, and inconsistent with the prevailing supremacist attitudes of the day (Ertman 2010). This is consistent with the impetus underlying state law elsewhere in the Western world, as discussed below (Part 3, "State Law's Presumptions and Objectives in Relation to Polygamy, Women and Choice"). Mormon Church leaders consequently issued manifestos calling for the cessation of plural marriage (Bushman 2008: 89), and followers who subsequently engaged in polygamy were threatened with excommunication (Bushman 2008: 98-99. See also Campbell 2001, Forbes 2003, Ward 2004, Embry 1984: 57).

Fundamentalist Mormons broke away from the mainstream Church and despite grouping themselves within different sects, shared the view that plural marriage remained essential to Mormon theology (Bushman 2008: 91). They have thus continued to adhere to the original Mormon view that the celestial kingdom is attainable only through a man's taking of multiple wives through the "Law of Sarah," that is, the requirement of a first wife giving her consent to her husband's taking of subsequent wives. This belief, along with the view of the Gospel as eternal and unchanging, led fundamentalist Mormons to cling to the original teachings of Mormonism, pursuant to which polygamy is central (Bennion 2008: 30, Musser 1944: 14).

Although the Fundamentalist Church of Jesus Christ of Latter Day Saints (FLDS) community of Bountiful is widely known as a site of polygamy, many of its constituents today marry monogamously. Just the same, female constituents indicate that the practice still retains a sacred place in their community. They suggest that more relevant than the actual practice of plural marriage is one's openness to it as a possibility during one's lifetime or upon entering a kingdom of heaven. Some participants in my research therefore explained their views on marriage in terms such as: "I was always taught, 'Live your life planning not to be a polygamist but leave that open,'" and "[I]n our beliefs, this isn't the end of our life, right? We go on, and on. And, if you're open enough in your heart, then maybe the next life or the next life you'll have the opportunity to live [polygamy]" (Campbell 2013a).

This view was not, however, shared by all participants I interviewed in Bountiful. One woman made clear her perception that a failure to live polygamously would carry moral consequences:

> [We] believe that in order to, um, get to the highest kingdom of heaven, [it's necessary] not only to have more than one wife … but to be honourable and to treat the ladies fairly and kindly. … And that's not the case in every situation, even in our religion. But I, I believe that anybody that doesn't live up to it is going to be accountable for that. (Campbell 2009b: 198)

Other scholars who have carried out empirical work with polygamous wives affirm that women explain their involvement in plural marriage primarily as an effort in "pursuit of the Kingdom of God" (Bennion 1998: 8-9). Several women in Boehmer's doctoral study affirmed that plural marriage is not merely a social or lifestyle choice, but a cornerstone of their faith. They expressed the belief that God expects them to adopt this form of marriage and that this would enable them to attain "eternal exaltation" (Boehmer 2010: 175).

Women's spiritual commitment to polygamy may be so ingrained that they are willing to absorb its juridical consequences. Most plural wives in the West generally are aware that their marital relationships generate acute legal suspicion. Yet they may defend their marriage practices as essential to their faith and their identity as constituents of their religious communities. They thus emphasize that plural marriage is not lightly chosen or undertaken, particularly in view of its legal implications. Rather, it is a family structure adopted pursuant to deliberation and as an expression of their commitment to a set of faith tenets (Pelland and Casoni 2010: 62-63).

Legal consequences aside, plural wives may see their willingness to endure polygamy's adverse social and psychological outcomes as a marker of their devoutness and "an ideological statement" (Zeitzen 2013). Even women who embrace plural marriage acknowledge its challenges and its requirement of "both spiritual commitment and emotional suffering" (Zeitzen 2008: 104). Despite the "pain and suffering" motif that marks some women's narratives, polygamy is considered a worthwhile endeavour, as it yields hope of attaining "goddesshood" and a righteous afterlife in heaven (Bennion 1998: 51-52). Thus, although these women acknowledge their sacrifices as plural wives, they may see their marriages as resulting from active decisions that allow them to self-identify as "victors rather than victims" (Boehmer 2010: 178).

Faith tenets serve to explain decisions about polygamy primarily for fundamentalist Mormon women. The same does not seem to be true, at least from what is discernible from existent literature, for women within other polygamous contexts. As discussed below, polyamory may be viewed as a form of polygamy. These relationships might not involve plural wives, but plural partners. That is, it is not uncommon for polyamory to be characterized by a woman at the hub of the relational network with multiple male partners. Polyamorous partnerships are not systemically formed pursuant to religious doctrine.

Even where faith is relevant to polygamy, it might not be central to the meaning women ascribe to this practice. Within Islam, polygamy is understood as permissible for men, but it is not a requirement. Pursuant to a traditional interpretation of Shari'a law, a man may marry up to four wives simultaneously provided he treats each of them equally (Mir-Hosseini 2003: 7, *Reference re: Section 293 of the Criminal Code of Canada*: paras. 242-249). In jurisdictions that recognize Shari'a law for matters of family and successions, polygamous marriages will be recognized. Yet, most legislation enacted in these jurisdictions stipulates specific conditions that must be met before a plural union will be recognized by the state (Campbell 2005: 22ff.).

Social and economic solidarity Beyond faith doctrines and beliefs, a second factor may explain women's involvement in polygamy. Many attribute this choice to the social and economic support they derive from sharing a household or family with sister wives (Altman and Ginat 1996: 91, White 2009: 451, Sigman 2006: 172-173).[4] This family structure offers an "'instant' support group" for many women, particularly for those "in precarious social, financial and interpersonal circumstances" (Altman and Ginat 1996: 440). Sister wives will often represent "companions to socialize with, friends who will help you cope with an often hostile outside world, and co-workers who will help you run the household" (Zeitzen 2008: 104). These social connections lend critical value to polygamous life for women and commonly constitute a reason for their entry into a plural marriage.

For some women, polygamous marriage also offers reprieve from poverty and isolation, and is viewed as a vehicle for upward social and economic mobility (Zeitzen 2008: 104). Women may convert to fundamentalist Mormonism and choose polygamous life because of their marginalization within the mainstream FLDS Church and within society more generally, wherein they might feel that they have "lost their way" (Altman and Ginat 1996: 440). These women have often

4 In some cases, sister wives who share a husband live in the same home, but in other cases different households are established for different wives and their children.

encountered social and economic deprivation. They may be divorced, widowed, have never married or raise their children as single mothers and lack strong support networks. Plural marriage and the FLDS community may be viewed as offering some response to a search for a more fulfilling and facilitated existence. Beyond religious doctrine, then, women may be drawn to the stability and solidarity they expect to find within polygamous life (Bennion 1998: 9, 15), and by the access polygamy may offer to otherwise unavailable social and material resources (Bennion 2008: 11, 46, 153).

Lack of viable alternatives In any society where polygamy exists, some women take up the practice as the sole viable path to follow. Marrying monogamously, or not marrying at all, may not figure as a possibility given family and community expectations. In these circumstances, the social and economic tradeoffs of deviating from polygamy might be too significant to sustain.

Accounts of coerced polygamous marriages, specifically those targeting young women or adolescent girls, have long circulated about FLDS communities (Palmer and Perrin 2004, Ward 2004: 149, Peters 1994: 86-87). A group of unidentified women produced a report on plural marriage in Bountiful, which was commissioned by the Government of British Columbia. This report maintains that residents of the community have conventionally been deprived of freedom of thought and choice, which translated into a lack of options in regard to marriage, particularly for women.[5] A scholar contemplating plural marriage in American FLDS communities endorses this view (Ward 2004). She challenges the idea of women in polygamous societies actively choosing plural marriage given the social isolation and religious indoctrination to which they are subject. For this author, plural wives are victims of "religious coercion" depriving them of the ability to make choices about marriage, about sex once married, or about leaving a polygamous marriage (Ward 2004: 145-147).

My research within Bountiful indicates that while many women currently believe that a person should reach adulthood before marrying, traditionally it was routine for a girl to wed in her teens, often to much older men who had one or more existing wives. Even today girls might not heed contemporary advice to delay marriage until the age of majority; one mother in Bountiful described her daughter as succumbing to "peer pressure" to marry at the age of 16 (Campbell 2009b: 201). It is difficult to discern whether real choice can be operative where a parent aims to dissuade a child from marrying within a community that historically encouraged girls to become wives during adolescence. The anecdote is illustrative of the normative plurality shaping decisions about polygamous marriage, in which state law may sometimes bear negligible influence.

My fieldwork further highlighted evolving norms in Bountiful related to marriage choices. A number of women indicated that, at least within more liberal

5 Canada, British Columbia, Anonymous, *Life in Bountiful: A Report in the Lifestyle of a Polygamous Community* (Committee on Polygamous Issues, 1993).

strands of the FLDS Church, women and men make mutual decisions about whether and when to marry and whether their union should become polygamous. Moreover, where a woman marries a man who already has a wife, she is said to bear some control over the processes of "courting" and marrying that man and his existent spouse(s) (Campbell 2009b: 194-196). The second subsection of Part 3, which explores the interface between state and non-state norms pertinent to polygamy, discusses this point in fuller detail. For the moment, it is sufficient to recognize emergent possibilities and options connected with marriage for some women in plural marriage societies.

These possibilities and options were far more circumscribed in Bountiful as recently as a decade ago. At that time, community patriarchs arranged marriages, and individuals wed the person(s) to whom they were assigned. One participant in my research explained this convention in the following terms:

> Well, at this point, in ... the community it's much different than it was when I was growing up. So for part of the community, at this point, it appears like the young people are having more of a choice. When I was married, the marriages were arranged. ... [I]t was my experience at the time. [U]ntil the last five years, there ... really hadn't been a consideration to the requests of the females. ... I'm seeing that, it's somewhat different for a part of the community. (Campbell 2009b: 195)

Another participant described her marriage as set by her father. Although she at first resisted his decision, she ultimately acceded to it. As she explained, "he was just so disappointed and that was it. I had that choice, I didn't have to. Then I decided that I didn't want to disappoint him. I really respected him" (Campbell 2009b: 195). While recognizing herself as having "choice," this woman also identified her desire to avoid falling short of her father's expectations as the central factor governing her decision. Her articulations in relation to choice are perhaps communicated with more absoluteness than can be realized in a patriarchal religious community, where resisting "the demands of tradition" can present difficulties for women (Kaganas and Murray 1991: 133).

Zeitzen's study of Christian polygamy in America recognizes that while some contemporary Mormon women support and actively choose plural marriage, others will enter such relationships involuntarily (2008: 104). Furthermore, a few biographical and autobiographical accounts suggest devastating circumstances for plural wives and emphasize that polygamy imposes a complete bar on choice for women in relation to all aspects of intimate life (Bramham 2008, Jessop and Palmer 2007, Palmer and Perrin 2004). As indicated, these commercial texts offer relevant stories about life in polygamy, but they are individual narratives and are not grounded in scientific study.

In a rare empirical study examining polygamy among American Muslim women, Hassouneh-Phillips found that women entered plural marriage with reticence, anxiety and unhappiness, particularly in view of the uncertainty and instability that this family form tended to foster. Participants in this project generally equated polygamy as a form of spousal abuse (Hassouneh-Phillips 2001). It is difficult to imagine that these women saw the rationale underlying their involvement in polygamy as linked to agency or choice. Instead, the meaning ascribed to their respective identities as plural wives appears more plainly connected to fear, duress or the absence of realistic alternatives. This being said, it should be noted that Hassouneh-Phillips' study focused specifically on domestic violence, not polygamy, among Islamic families in the United States. Thus all of the women she interviewed, including those who had been in monogamous relationships, had experienced difficult spousal relationships and this would likely have affected their reporting on polygamy.

Even accounting for the challenges to the empirical literature setting out women's encounters with polygamy, it is apparent that the practice engenders circumstances that attenuate opportunities for choice about marriage. A woman might have difficulty ascribing any meaning to her involvement with polygamy other than a desire to avoid untenable adverse outcomes. That being said, at least some women have, through empirical narratives, conveyed distinct rationales for becoming plural wives, which suggest their deliberation and decision in that regard. Most women in FLDS communities draw upon religious doctrine to explain their motivations. Many also refer to the social benefits (companionship and support from sister wives) and economic gains (pooled family resources) that they anticipated from living polygamously. Having discussed the various facets of polygamy that lend meaning to this practice, the discussion now turns to an analysis of the factors that figure within women's evaluations of plural marriage.

The Value Women Ascribe to Engaging in Polygamy

As shown here and in the two subsequent chapters on surrogacy and sex work, the meaning and value women ascribe to controversial choices are distinct things. While a choice's meaning pertains to its underlying explanations, rationales or motivations, its value is associated with the way in which women see themselves as gaining or losing from the choice. In this way, a study of the value ascribed to particular decisions illuminates why a particular practice may be perceived as important and beneficial or, conversely, as impairing individual or collective welfare.

In evaluating their experiences within polygamy, women's narratives circulate around two principal themes, namely, the moral fulfillment and pragmatic benefits that they see plural marriage as yielding. The discussion below explores each of these aspects in turn. It concludes with an analysis of features that might detract from women's evaluations of their experiences in plural marriage.

Moral fulfillment Sister wives who characterize themselves as happy and satisfied within polygamy commonly refer to the moral fulfillment they associate with this way of life. This sense of personal or moral satisfaction derives from two separate dimensions, spiritual and social, both occupying a prominent place within plural wives' narratives.

The spiritualism that engenders moral fulfillment for women in polygamy is comprehensible, given the centrality of religion and scripture to the motivations of polygamous wives' choices about marriage and family. Plural marriage is undertaken against the spectre of promised exaltation. Many women, at least within fundamentalist Mormonism, consequently see their marriages as "sav[ing] their souls" (Bennion 1998: 17) and as fulfilling a religious commandment that serves as a "prelude to a celestial existence in the hereafter" (Altman and Ginat 1996: 171, Altman 1993: 17). Moreover, women's ability to endure polygamy's hardships may be perceived to emblemize the intensity of their faith and affirm their membership within a community of believers. Some women also saw their encounters with struggles in polygamy as a route toward self-improvement and toward enriching their moral and spiritual constitution (Altman and Ginat 1996: 171).

While polygamy's spiritual dimension undoubtedly accounts largely for the moral fulfillment a woman may experience as a sister wife, social relationships within plural families can also be morally and emotionally elevating. During my field research in Bountiful, women who shared a husband were often described as bonded by a deep-seated sense of sorority and solidarity. They referred to their sister wives as their "best friends," "life partners," and spoke of not being able "to imagine life without them." Participants acknowledged that they typically spend more time and have closer relationships with their sister wives than with their husbands. The moral and emotional support that relationships among sister wives can foster is illuminated by comments offered by two participants in my research. A first woman indicated:

> My sister wives are like my very best friends. … I do more things with my sister wives than I do with my husband. I'm with my sister wives 24/7. … Sometimes I feel like I'm more married to my co-wives than I am to him!

A second noted:

> It's [My relationship with my sister wife is] kind of like in a monogamous relationship where you and your husband are really close. Well, a lot of us actually get that closeness with each other that you would have with your husband. … We know everything about the other person. Feel what they feel; we think what they think. (Campbell 2009b: 214)

Similar reflections surface in other studies of women in polygamy. In her work on Christian polygamy in the United States, Zeitzen underscores that a woman's bonds with her sister-wives and other female relatives proved frequently to "constitute a more critical relationship than that with her husband for her productive, reproductive and personal achievements" (2008: 127). Other scholars of polygamy in the United States (Chambers 1997: 73-74, Forbes 2003: 1542-

1543) and even in non-Western settings (Anderson 2000) also indicate that women benefit from the female companionship and friendship that polygamy may afford. These personal networks can foster women's independence and interdependence, reducing the need to rely on husbands for moral fulfillment and, as discussed below, for social and financial support (Bennion 2008: 72).

Plural conjugality might not always emanate from religious beliefs. Polyamorous relationships involve a plurality of intimate partnerships, often within a shared household. Polyamorists usually do not take up their family structure according to faith tenets. Rather, this secular form of plural conjugality is linked to values of "caring, intimacy, honesty, equality, non-exclusivity and relational autonomy" (Haritaworn et al. 2006: 518). In Canada, evidence about polyamory was adduced in the recent reference trial regarding the constitutionality of polygamy's criminal prohibition. Evidence given by a woman who maintained plural conjugal partnerships with men echoes religious plural wives' narratives with respect to the moral rewards of her lifestyle:

> Our family believes a non-monogamous lifestyle choice facilitates us all to grow to more complete, supported and aware selves. We encourage one another to pursue additional safe and healthy relationships that may have a romantic or sexual aspect to them. (*Reference re: Section 293 of the Criminal Code of Canada*: para. 458)

Although the ideological contexts of religious plural marriage and polyamory differ, this evidence suggests the transversal relevance of moral enrichment as a valued feature of plural unions, whether faith-based or secular.

Polygamy's pragmatic benefits Beyond moral fulfillment, women's social networks in plural marriage families might also bear practical relevance and value. Most notably, sister wives can relieve each other in taking up the extensive childcare and domestic responsibilities often associated with polygamous life. They commonly care for each other's children, allowing them to pursue other interests and goals (Bennion 1998: 50-51). This can be particularly helpful if a woman works or studies outside the home (Campbell 2009b: 212-214). One participant in my research, enrolled in a college program, indicated:

> I couldn't do it without them. … [M]y sister wives help me with my children and I help them with their children, and if I need them, they are always willing to help me out. (Campbell 2009b: 212)

Another woman, also pursuing postsecondary studies, described a similar arrangement with her sister wives:

> I go to school and I've got a babysitter, right there at home. He [my son] doesn't have to go anywhere. They're already home. They're in their own environment.

> And they are already cared for by their own family. You know and, myself, I can stay home and babysit for someone else who has to go to work. (Campbell 2009b: 213)

Support from sister wives is especially valuable in moments where physical capacities are limited. Sister wives might coach one another through labour and childbirth. They might also provide an opportunity for respite when a woman is unwell or has just given birth. For example, women in Bountiful spoke about getting a "month off" from their ordinary domestic duties postpartum, receiving help from sister wives and other women in the community during this period.

Views expressed by a woman in a polyamorous family comparably highlighted how multiple adult partnerships within a household could produce more efficient outcomes. She stated, "[t]ime cannot be expanded upon, but simultaneous activities increase nurturing of multiple goals at a time" (*Reference re: Section 293 of the Criminal Code of Canada*: para. 458). Like plural wives, this polyamorist underlines the benefits of multiple domestic caregivers and parental figures. She remarked in the following terms on the ways in which her family reflected historical and multicultural family structures that integrate plural parental figures:

> I have heard a First Nation's elder speak about family, with more broad definitions, like our own. My grandmother spoke about all the women in her neighbourhood helping to care for children (1950s) as they travelled between yards. I believe our present family has incorporated many of the benefits of widening the concept of nuclear family. (*Reference re: Section 293 of the Criminal Code of Canada*: para. 458)

As indicated, caution must be exercised in comparing the narratives of polyamorists and religious plural wives, given their particular cultural and social contexts that affect issues of choice in connection with intimate life and conjugality. At the same time, analyses must refrain from presuming the moral superiority or heightened credibility of polyamorous women on the grounds that their choices are not "tainted" by religious doctrine or by the differing gender dynamics at play in these contexts. This point is developed further in the second subsection of Part 3 below ("Interface between State and Non-State Law").

Beyond relief from family and household responsibilities, solidarity among polygamous wives may take the form of a common front against a shared husband. This can allow women to assume substantial control over family decision-making. As one woman in Bountiful reported:

> When we want something [it's] pretty hard for him to stand up to two of us so, if we could afford it, we can make it happen. And if it's something you know we want to do to the house. We say, honey, we're doin' this, right, okay. And so, it happens. (Campbell 2009b: 214)

Sister wives thus might enjoy enhanced autonomy and freedom through the network they develop with each other, particularly in challenges or confrontations with a husband (Bennion 2011: 172, Bennion 1998: 50-51).

Networks formed among wives also provide a "built-in" structure for support that may ease polygamy's economic hardships (Bennion 1998: 109). Women may pool their financial resources or earnings, usually pursuant to a household or family understanding as to how labour within and outside of the home will be shared. Facing and surmounting economic challenges as a family can solidify women's commitments to each other (Bennion 1998: 130). Economic networks among women may also cultivate their social influence, allowing them to assume the administrative helm of a household to determine domestic schedules, budgets and divisions of labour (Campbell 2009b: 213, Sigman 2006: 143). They may also play decisive roles in the management of community welfare and governance, serving as vocal and visible decision-makers (Bennion 1998: 9, 16).

The authority women muster in solidarity with each other indicates that while they must confront and tolerate a faith community's patriarchal norms, they may simultaneously develop a parallel, women-centric ideology that boosts morale as well as their social and economic status. This ideology, which manipulates and reshapes conventional patriarchal dogma, culls elements of doctrine focused on feminine divinity to foster a glorified image of women as central religious and social actors (Bennion 1998: 50, 52, 60). This phenomenon thus underlines the possibility for women's agency to emerge in sites that state law presumes oppressive to women. Failure to engage with and appreciate the multiple normative influences shaping the meaning and value women ascribe to their choices prompts oversight of the opportunities women identify and channel for their own empowerment within ostensibly patriarchal settings.

Pernicious encounters debasing women's experiences The moral and pragmatic value that women might associate with polygamous life emanates largely from positive relationships with sister wives. Yet relationships premised upon sharing domestic space, economic resources and husbands may predictably generate strife injurious to a plural wife's moral, social and material wellbeing. Empirical research shows that sororal life in polygamy can spawn frustration, loneliness and jealousy, particularly when a new wife joins a family (Campbell 2009b: 215). In some international contexts, these adverse sentiments have at times caused women to experience deep emotional harms and physical abuse at the hands of one another (Starr and Brilmayer 2003, Bala 2009: 195).

Even in the absence of animosity among plural wives, women in polygamy face the complicated and arduous task of managing the conflicting emotional dimensions of their family structures. While camaraderie among wives may be expected and common, polygamy simultaneously fosters competition. A woman in Bountiful remarked, in describing her relationship with her sister wives: "[T]here's more to it than just the support system. There's a lot of work on your part, too. You have to give and take" (Campbell 2009b: 215). Participants in another empirical study described plural marriage as an "unending struggle" to overcome rivalry and conflict (Altman and Ginat 1996: 436-437). Others acknowledged tensions between their religious obligations and feelings of romantic love. While the latter shaped their desires, they recognized the former as appropriately governing choices about marriage (Jankowiak and Allen 1995: 285).

Polygamous wives may acknowledge these emotional hurdles as they concurrently articulate a steadfast commitment to polygamy as an indicium of faith, personal strength and sacrifice. They recognize pressures from an "outside world" that rejects and outlaws polygamy, and from "internal stresses" within their own families and communities. Plural wives are prepared to endure these challenges "because they believe in the religious righteousness of their lifestyle" (Altman and Ginat 1996: 439). Moreover, they see their choices as projecting a sense of family and community solidarity (Boehmer 2010: 174). As such, many women experience polygamy as "a paradox" (White 2009: 451) that carries markedly nuanced social value. The practice integrates the "highs and lows" (Boehmer 2010: 67) of the complex relationships in plural families. This is especially true of connections among sister wives who, sharing many facets of day-to-day life, develop profound and intricate bonds while simultaneously navigating the inevitable challenges that ensue from sharing scarce material resources, physical space and a husband's intimacy and sexual attention. Such complexity among sister wives' inter-relationships likely explains one empirical researcher's finding that, "fundamentalist women often live a 'split' existence of exalted love and suppressed contempt of their sister wives" (Bennion 1998: 39).

Ultimately, although women may cite religion as the key motivator for their decisions to live polygamously, an analysis of the factors that generate satisfaction or distress for plural wives indicates a reality of value pluralism. Various attributes of polygamy, which include but are not limited to its centrality to particular religious philosophies, lead women to encounter fulfillment and happiness, or alternatively, frustration and discontent. To this end, it must be underscored that the empirical literature on polygamy, though it may be scant and focused on one particular religious group, emphasizes women's diversity of experiences as plural wives and resists drawing generalized conclusions about polygamy's implications for women's autonomy (e.g., Bennion 1998, 2008, 2011, Campbell 2005, 2009b, 2010, Sigman 2006).

The following sections of this chapter canvass and critique the legislative history of polygamy in three Western jurisdictions, each having its own particular encounter with this phenomenon. This discussion elucidates governance efforts premised on a portrayal of polygamy as an aberrant, unorthodox marital and family structure, wholly at odds with contemporary social and sexual mores. Debates surrounding the development of these regulatory frameworks are also, at times, flagrant in their reference to polygamy's transgression of dominant—that is, Christian—religious ideals, rendering it a morally unacceptable practice. Finally, state laws crafted in response to polygamy are, much like the rules that formally govern surrogacy and sex work, publicly and politically touted as protective of women's interests. This is the case even though the state's governance structure accounts minimally for the array of lived experiences of those involved with plural marriage, or for the meaning and value they may ascribe to it.

Part 2: State Law's Approach to Polygamy in Canada, the United Kingdom and Australia

This Part sets out the regulatory frameworks governing polygamy in Canada, the United Kingdom and Australia. Legal approaches reflect Western encounters with this practice through colonial contact or through immigration. The focus here is on criminal law responses to polygamy given this book's engagement with the proscription of women's controversial life choices. At the same time, because the issue is addressed in legislative debates and initiatives in the domains of family and immigration law and policy, these topics are also canvassed within this discussion.

Canada

State regulation of polygamy has attracted acute political and public attention in Canada at different moments throughout the country's colonial and postcolonial history. Canada's confederation coincided with American developments in the mid- to late nineteenth century that sought to eradicate polygamy through efforts targeting the Mormon Church and individual practitioners. Fundamentalist believers who remained committed to polygamy in the face of these efforts either continued the practice clandestinely, in remote and secluded settlements, or immigrated north to territories that would ultimately join Canada. Drawing the attention of Canadian lawmakers, this phenomenon prompted regulatory initiatives that "fell under the influence of American law" and were designed to quash polygamy among Mormon settlers through the use of prohibitions and the threat of criminal sanction.[6] Thus, as discussed below, polygamy was included as an offence within the Canadian *Criminal Code* in 1892.

While the public historical record on polygamy would leave the impression that legislative efforts were focused exclusively on Mormon immigrants from the United States, a second concern underlay efforts to control this practice. Politicians and missionaries struggled with what they perceived as the fluid, indulgent and cavalier nature of Aboriginal customary marriage, and in particular, with the Aboriginal acceptance of—in colonizers' terms—"polygamy" and "divorce" (Carter 2008, Campbell 2009a). These practices were viewed as a deep threat to nation-building efforts in the Canadian West, which was premised in part on a

6 Canada, Law Reform Commission of Canada, *Working Paper 42* (Ottawa: Law Reform Commission of Canada, 1985) at 22. See also Pelland 2007: 65, Beaman 2004: 24, and Canada, British Columbia, Anonymous, *Life in Bountiful: A Report in the Lifestyle of a Polygamous Community* (Committee on Polygamous Issues, 1993) at 24.

homestead policy that rewarded white settlers through free land grants (*An Act respecting the Public Lands of the Dominion*: s. 33). Thus, while polygamy's criminalization was spurred by concern over the Western Mormon presence, only two convictions for this offence have ever been entered in Canada, both at the turn of the twentieth century, both resulting from the prosecution of Aboriginal men (*The Queen v. Bear's Shin Bone*, *R. v. Harris*).

Over time, the preoccupation with Aboriginal polygamy in Canada waned, only to be replaced by disquiet regarding plural marriage settlements in the West, particularly the one that became known as Bountiful. Ultimately, attention on Bountiful became so focused that it led to prosecutorial attempts within the community and a landmark judicial ruling on polygamy. These developments are explained more fully in the ensuing analysis.

Polygamy's early criminalization Before polygamy became an explicit focus of legislative activity in Canada, a statute was in place prescribing norms relating chiefly to the procedural dimensions of marriage. *An Act respecting Offences relating to the Law of Marriage* established four distinct offences: unlawfully solemnizing or procuring the unlawful solemnization of marriage; procuring a feigned marriage; solemnizing marriage in violation of provincial law; and bigamy. As noted by Chief Justice Bauman in *Reference re: Section 293 of the Criminal Code of Canada*—a judgment that is considered in detail below—it is unclear that any prohibition in this early statute could have captured polygamy as practiced by Mormons, Aboriginal persons or Muslims in Canada. That is, the bigamy offence required the sequential entry into a formal, state-sanctioned marriage, with two or more persons. Because religious and cultural communities often formed polygamous bonds through "spiritual" or private celebrations, they could well have fallen outside the ambit of the prohibition (*Reference re: Section 293 of the Criminal Code of Canada*: paras. 854-856).

This uncertainty was eliminated by subsequent legislative action related to polygamy. Bill F, *An Act to amend "An Act respecting Offences relating to the Law of Marriage,"* introduced in the Canadian Senate in 1890, would have added polygamy to the offences contained in the *Act respecting Offences relating to the Law of Marriage* (*Reference re: Section 293 of the Criminal Code of Canada*: para. 860). It explicitly referenced Mormon plural marriage as included within the prohibition while simultaneously excluding its application to Aboriginal practitioners for whom polygamy was consistent with the customary law of their respective nations (Bill F, *An Act to amend "An Act respecting Offences relating to the Law of Marriage"*: ss. 5(c), 5(4)). This exemption for Aboriginal persons generated some dissent in Senate (*Reference re: Section 293 of the Criminal Code of Canada*: para. 862).[7]

7 Canada, *Debates of the Senate*, 6th Parl, 4th Sess, Vol 29 (25 February 1890) at 142 (Hon Mr Dickey).

When a criminal law amendment bill was introduced a month later, Bill F was withdrawn. In February 1890, Canada's Minister of Justice introduced Bill 65, *An Act further to amend the Criminal Law*, which proposed adding a specific prohibition against polygamy within the *Act respecting Offences relating to the Law of Marriage*. This new amendment did not stipulate an exclusion in its application to indigenous persons, although like its predecessor, it did incorporate a particular reference to Mormon plural marriage (Bill 65, *An Act further to amend the Criminal Law*: s. 5(c)). Bill 65 received royal assent and came into effect in May 1890. Within two years, however, this legislation was replaced through an initiative that consolidated most of Canada's existing criminal offences within a single statute. With some rewording, *Criminal Code, 1892* imported both the bigamy and polygamy prohibitions from the prior statute (*Reference re: Section 293 of the Criminal Code of Canada*: paras. 867-868).

Twentieth- and twenty-first-century criminal law reform and enforcement The *Criminal Code* provisions on bigamy and polygamy were subject only to minor revisions in the years that immediately followed their enactment. Significant reform occurred, however, in 1955, pursuant to a legislative initiative aimed at revising the country's *Criminal Code*. The most notable amendment involved excising the reference to Mormons within the polygamy provision. Although early iterations of the polygamy ban had included a subsection to ensure the inclusion of Mormon "spiritual" or "plural" marriage, the 1955 revisions eliminated this reference without substantive comment, identifying these as merely formal amendments. A briefing note from the Department of Justice indicated that these amendments to the provision were intended to simplify it. Ultimately, the reform to the polygamy prohibition within the *Code* passed without amendment or comment, receiving royal assent and entering into force on 1 April 1955 (*Reference re: Section 293 of the Criminal Code of Canada*: paras. 872-875). The provision, which has since remained unchanged, defined polygamy in broad terms:

> Every one who
>
> (a) practises or enters into or in any manner agrees or consents to practise or enter into
>
> (i) any form of polygamy, or
>
> (ii) any kind of conjugal union with more than one person at the same time, whether or not it is by law recognized as a binding form of marriage; or
>
> (b) celebrates, assists or is a party to a rite, ceremony, contract or consent that purports to sanction a relationship mentioned in subparagraph (i) or (ii) of paragraph (a),

is guilty of an indictable offence and is liable to imprisonment for five years.

While legislative records suggest that this reform to the Canadian provision outlawing polygamy was intended only as a formal, drafting change, some commentators have suggested that it reflects a redirection in policy and legislative purpose. Whereas the ban's original animus appears to have been rooted in stamping out Mormon and other religious or cultural forms of polygamy, in its newer incantation it purported to prevent harm to women and children. This point merits attention given the "no shifting purpose" doctrine within Canadian constitutional law (Drummond 2009: 360, Bailey et al. 2005: 23). The doctrine prevents a legislature called upon to justify a statute that compromises a constitutionally guaranteed right or freedom from arguing that, while the statute's original purpose was invalid, its original goal has since the time of legislative enactment been replaced by another, more compelling purpose (Hogg 2012: 38-26, *R. v. Big M Drug Mart*: 335).

The *Criminal Code* prohibition against polygamy, now found at section 293, remained an inert provision for decades. Two Canadian law commissions questioned its utility and retention within the corpus of the country's criminal law. In 1985, the Law Reform Commission of Canada (LRCC) issued a working paper arguing that a ban on bigamy (the practice of being simultaneously married formally to more than one spouse) remained justified, whereas the ban pertaining to polygamy (the practice of simultaneous conjugal unions, without the necessity of formal marriage) should be lifted. The LRCC described polygamy as "a marginal practice which corresponds to no meaningful legal or sociological reality in Canada."[8] Decriminalizing polygamy would thus signal "confidence" in the prominence and viability of monogamous marriage, and "evidence of moderation" within the country's criminal justice framework.[9] These recommendations encountered some academic critique (Kaufman 2005: 337, Bala et al. 2005: 3) and were not subsequently adopted by Canadian lawmakers.

More recently, the Law Commission of Canada (LCC) emphasized the relevance of wider legal recognition for diverse family relationships and structures. Although the LCC did not consider polygamy extensively, its general advocacy for broadening Canadian family law's imagination of the relationships that should generate legal rights and obligations raised questions about plural spouses' juridical claims and entitlements. Moreover, the LCC questioned directly the efficacy of criminal law for addressing any inequalities in polygamy, and noted the LRCC's prior recommendation of repealing its prohibition.[10]

8 Canada, Law Reform Commission of Canada, *Working Paper 42* (Ottawa: Law Reform Commission of Canada, 1985) at 23.

9 Canada, Law Reform Commission of Canada, *Working Paper 42* (Ottawa: Law Reform Commission of Canada, 1985) at 29.

10 Canada, Law Commission of Canada, *Beyond Conjugality: Recognizing and Supporting Close Personal Adult Relationships* (Ottawa: Law Commission of Canada,

Polygamy's prohibition within section 293 of the *Criminal Code* was subject to more concentrated scrutiny within the context of various reports produced by special prosecutors appointed by the Province of British Columbia. These reports issued recommendations as to the viability of prosecuting residents of Bountiful suspected of polygamy, in view of the prohibition's apparent constitutional vulnerabilities.[11] Various recommendations were issued leading ultimately to the laying of charges against two male religious leaders in Bountiful early in 2009. These charges were subsequently quashed on the grounds that the acting provincial Attorney General had exceeded his jurisdiction in pursuing these prosecutions (*Blackmore v. British Columbia (Attorney General)*).

The Attorneys General of Canada and British Columbia thereafter initiated constitutional reference proceedings before the British Columbia Supreme Court. That court was asked to determine whether Canada's criminal prohibition of polygamy infringed various rights protected by the *Canadian Charter of Rights and Freedoms*. If an interference with any such right was shown, the court was asked to assess whether this could be reasonably justified in a "free and democratic society."[12]

Reference re: Section 293 of the Criminal Code of Canada affirmed section 293's constitutional validity. Bauman CJSC found the provision to infringe on none of the fundamental liberties protected by the Canadian constitution, with two exceptions. First, its application to minors was held to be overbroad and a violation of liberty as protected by section 7 of the *Charter*. Section 293 was consequently read down to exclude its application to persons under the age of 18. Second, Chief

---

2001) at n 32.

11 Canada, British Columbia, R.C.C. Peck Q.C., *Report of the Special Prosecutor for Allegations of Misconduct Associated with Bountiful, BC: Summary of Conclusions* (Victoria: Criminal Justice Branch HQ, Ministry of Attorney General, 2007); Canada, Criminal Justice Branch of the Ministry of the Attorney General of British Columbia, Media Release, 07-08, *Special Prosecutor Recommends Reference Question on Constitutionality of Polygamy Law* (1 August 2007). Available at: http://www.ag.gov.bc.ca/prosecution-service/media-statements/pdf/07-08_Bountiful-SpProsReport-1Aug2007.pdf [accessed: 11 November 2012]; Canada, Criminal Justice Branch of the Ministry of the Attorney General of British Columbia, Media Release, 08-10, *Leonard Doust, Q.C., Confirms Findings and Recommendations of Special Prosecutor* (7 April 2008). Available at: http://www.ag.gov.bc.ca/prosecution-service/media-statements/pdf/08-10_Bountiful-LDoustQC_ConfirmsSpProsRecomm-7Apr2008.pdf [accessed: 11 November 2012]; and Canada, Criminal Justice Branch of the Ministry of the Attorney General of British Columbia, Media Release, 08-11, *Special Prosecutor Appointed in Bountiful* (2 June 2008). Available at: http://www.ag.gov.bc.ca/prosecution-service/media-statements/pdf/08-11_Bountiful-SpProsApptd-2Jun2008.pdf [accessed: 11 November 2012].

12 This language derives from the constitutional justificatory provision in the *Charter*. Section 1 of the *Charter* provides: "[t]he *Canadian Charter of Rights and Freedoms* guarantees the rights and freedoms set out in it subject only to such reasonable limits prescribed by law as can be demonstrably justified in a free and democratic society."

Justice Bauman held that, for at least some practitioners of polygamy, the practice had religious meaning and its legal prohibition interfered with religious freedom. Nevertheless, he found that this limitation was justified given the harm the court deemed inherent to polygamy, which threatened women, children, society and "the institution of monogamous marriage" (para. 5).

Although this was a trial level decision with direct application only within the province of British Columbia, the amicus counsel appointed to respond to the Attorneys General opted against appealing Bauman CJSC's ruling. The Attorneys General also refrained from referring the matter to a higher court, which they might have done to obtain a judgment of wider application in Canada. In the result, polygamy's prohibition remains in place, subject only to a restriction—again, explicitly applicable only within British Columbia—respecting minors. Thus, despite the extensive legal attention and activity that polygamy has generated in recent years, the juridical status quo remains. The decision in *Reference re: Section 293 of the Criminal Code of Canada* offers some clarification and a useful precedent as to the ban's constitutionality, but its reach seems limited. Moreover, while this state of affairs might have prompted law enforcement officials to reinitiate charges against suspected polygamists in Canada, this has not occurred. Following the judgment, another special prosecutor was appointed to investigate criminal activity in Bountiful. Initially, this inquiry did not include polygamy-related offences, however, the prosecutor's mandate was subsequently broadened to incorporate investigations and the potential laying of charges pertaining to polygamy. As of the time of writing no such charges have been laid (Anonymous 2012b, Stueck 2012).

The United Kingdom

Compared to Canada, polygamy has occupied a less prominent place on British political and legal landscapes. Contemporary discussions about polygamy have arisen almost exclusively in policy debates related to immigration whereas historically, the matter was confronted through Britain's colonial efforts. In both contexts, polygamy has been treated unequivocally as an "alien" practice, unknown domestically until its import by foreign nationals through migration processes (Shah 2003: 392). This perception is explored and critiqued in Part 3.

Under British law, it is clear that bigamy is a criminal offence and bigamous marriages are unrecognized, triggering no legal effects, rights or obligations. Bigamy has been prohibited in England and Wales since 1604, when the Parliament of James I took action to restrain "evil persons" marrying more than one wife. Anyone found guilty of the crime would be sentenced to death (Chapman 2001: 26, Capp 2009). The *Offences Against the Person Act, 1861*, which consolidated the criminal laws of England, also explicitly cited bigamy as a criminal offence, providing:

> Whosoever, being married, shall marry any other person during the life of the former husband or wife, whether the second marriage shall have taken place in England or Ireland or elsewhere, shall be guilty of felony, and being convicted thereof shall be liable ... to be kept in penal servitude for any term not exceeding seven years. (s. 57)

This provision renders illegal the celebration of a sequential marriage when a person is already married. Apparently excluded from the prohibition are references to polygamous unions, that is, concurrent conjugal relationships that have not been officiated as marriages. The *Offences Against the Person Act, 1861* thus establishes a more restricted ban on plural marriage than does Canada's *Criminal Code*, which outlaws "any form of polygamy" or a "conjugal union" with more than one person regardless of whether that union is "by law recognized as a binding form of marriage" (s. 293).

British law's focus on bigamy therefore raises a question as to whether a person who lives polygamously, without having celebrated formally more than one marriage, would fall within the prohibition's parameters. This ambiguity is accentuated if one interprets bigamy to include an element of fraud or deception. British courts have understood the prohibition as designed to protect against the degradation of "fundamental notions of monogamous marriage" and the marriage ceremony, with a view to promoting public morals (*Whiston v. Whiston*, Chapman 2001: 95-97). As such, consensual plural unions that have not been celebrated through a formal, state-recognized process may fall beyond the ambit of the criminalized practice.

Beyond the criminal law, it is worth considering—because British legal thinking about polygamy has occurred primarily within the frameworks of immigration and colonial policy—how the matter has been approached with respect to migrant and foreign practitioners. Until the twentieth century, colonizers viewed polygamy as a practice inimical to Christianity and civilization (Seuffert 2003, Martin 1994: 421, Shah 2003: 374-375, Esplugues 1984: 303-305) and courts traditionally refused to recognize polygamous marriages formed in foreign jurisdictions (*Hyde v. Hyde and Woodmansee*, *In Re Bethell*). From the 1930s onward, English courts adapted this position to meet the realities of a country hosting an influx of migrants from many countries, some of which permitted polygamy (Shah 2003: 375, Esplugues 1984: 306). To temper the harsh effect of earlier judgments refusing recognition of plural marriages, courts found that a "potentially" polygamous marriage—that is, one formed in a jurisdiction where polygamy is recognized, but that has not yet become polygamous—could "convert" to monogamy. Such marriages could thus be recognized as valid, permitting spouses to apply for matrimonial relief in the United Kingdom (Shah 2003: 375, Esplugues 1984: 307, Marasinghe 1978: 398). Ultimately, legislation was passed to grant marital relief to polygamous spouses whose marriages were valid where celebrated (*Matrimonial Causes Act 1973*: s. 47, *Private International Law (Miscellaneous Provisions) Act 1995*: ss. 5, 7, Martin 1994: 427, 443).

Entry by polygamous wives into the United Kingdom was considerably restricted by the introduction of the *Immigration Act 1988* (Shah 2003: 383ff., Chapman 2001: 50-51). This statute barred the admission of a wife where another wife or widow of the same man had previously been admitted into the country (Shah 2003: 391). Although these immigration restrictions have been challenged as a human rights violation, the European Commission has found that a state may justifiably limit the entry of polygamous families to preserve "the Christian based monogamous culture" dominant in the United Kingdom. As such, the restrictions are deemed justifiable under the *European Convention on Human Rights* (*R.B. v. United Kingdom*).

As British law stands, bigamy is explicitly proscribed, yet there is ambiguity about whether this prohibition includes polygamy that does not involve formalized plural marriages. Moreover, while polygamous marriages are void, there is some room for giving effect to these marriages if they were formed by foreign domiciliaries in jurisdictions that permit the celebration of plural unions. As explored below, British approaches to polygamy and bigamy are rooted in the understanding of this practice as foreign and as corruptive of conventional marriage ideals. Little attention is given to the experiences and choices of women associated with polygamy. This is the case even when legislative efforts clearly target women, such as the immigration restrictions just discussed, which may bar entry of a plural wife whose husband has migrated to the United Kingdom. Neglect of women's experiential knowledge has also occurred in the development of a recent proposal before the House of Lords to terminate the practice of allowing polygamous wives to claim public benefits (Bill 75, *Welfare Reform Bill*, ss. 1-2).

Australia

Australian public policy has approached polygamy as a matter arising nearly exclusively within its immigrant and indigenous communities. Relevant political discussions have thus typically occurred within broader contexts pertaining to multiculturalism and religious accommodation. To a lesser extent, polygamy has also drawn some attention within Australian debates pertaining to family law reform.

Polygamy has not, however, been a major preoccupation for Australian political and legal actors as a matter of criminal law. Although individual states have jurisdiction to regulate polygamy, the practice has been governed at the Commonwealth level since the passing of the *Marriage Act 1961*. Prior to this statute's enactment, individual states and territories legislated in this area. The *Marriage Act 1961* was deemed necessary "in order to facilitate prosecution for such an offence and to obviate difficulties which might now arise if reliance in this respect was placed upon the State laws."[13] The goal thus was to achieve harmony across Australia in regard to regulatory approaches to polygamy.

Like relevant British legislation, the *Marriage Act 1961* concentrates on bigamy, that is, the act of marrying when one already has a legally-recognized spouse, usually without the latter's knowledge or consent. The statute qualifies bigamy as a criminal offence (ss. 94(1), (4)), and further provides that bigamous marriages celebrated in the country are void (ss. 23(1)(a), 23B(1)(a)). The status of polygamy, however, is ambiguous. Given that it is not an offence in Australia to cohabit as a *de facto* partner or to live as though married with more than one person, plural marriages that are celebrated only religiously and do not receive state sanction or civil recognition are arguably exempt from prohibition.

Indeed, reported judicial decisions would indicate that the crime of bigamy is limited to circumstances involving multiple state-sanctioned marriages. Justice Dixon qualified the essence of Australia's bigamy prohibition in *Thomas v. R.* as follows:

> It is only because of the wrong done by the wickedness of going through a form of marriage with the knowledge of the impediment of a prior marriage that the subsequent marriage merits punishment.

It appears, then, that although bigamy is not regularly prosecuted in Australia, where charges for this offence have been laid, the relevant circumstances match the definition of bigamy, and not polygamy. Cases typically involve an accused who was not carrying on plural conjugal relationships, but instead had ceased cohabitation with a married spouse and subsequently married another person without first obtaining a divorce (*Thomas v. Thomas*, *Thomas v. R.*, *R. v. Bonnor*, *R. v. Scarborough*, *R. v. Darnton*, Jeanes 2005).

As noted, polygamy has been treated in Australian public policy primarily as a topic linked to immigration and family law rather than criminal law. Following a review in 1978 of its policy priorities, the Commonwealth government articulated nine guiding principles. One of these stated that: "[e]ligibility and suitability standards for migrants should reflect Australian social mores."[14] Pursuant to this principle, polygamous unions were deemed unacceptable and immigration law thereby allowed for the sponsoring of not more than one married or *de facto* spouse (*Chen v. Minister for Immigration, Local Government and Ethnic Affairs*, Parkinson 1996: 321). Therefore, while Australian law theoretically recognizes polygamous marriages legally celebrated abroad (*Family Law Act 1975*: s. 6, *Marriage Act 1961*: s. 88C(1)(a)), immigration policy aims to ensure "no possibility of an actually

13 Austl, Commonwealth, House of Representatives, *Parliamentary Debates* (19 May 1960) at 2006 (Sir Garfield Barwick).

14 Austl, Commonwealth, John Gardiner-Garden, *The Multiculturalism and Immigration Debate 1973-1993*, Background Paper No 8 (Canberra: Parliamentary Research Service, 1993) at 9.

polygamous relationship existing in Australia" given the stipulation that only one legal spouse may enter the country (Parkinson 1994: 498).

Similar to developments in Canada, Australia's Law Reform Commission has contemplated and commented on legal approaches to polygamy. In 1989, Australia's Law Reform Commission (LRCA) was called upon to report on whether family law, criminal law and contract law in the country were adequate and appropriate in view of the country's multicultural realities. The LRCA adopted the view that state law should embrace, recognize and protect "the relationships people choose for themselves."[15] This principle was viewed as a viable basis for a regulatory design that would "take into account the diversity of family arrangements in Australian society," and respect "differently defined" relationships.[16]

In view of this conclusion a submission was made that the LRCA should, according to its own goal of acknowledging family diversity, craft a recommendation for the legal recognition of polygamy. The LRCA rejected this proposition without equivocation. Although it conceded that the legal recognition of polygamy could benefit some members of plural marriage communities, it characterized the practice as "alien to mainstream Australian culture and to the Western European culture from which it derives."[17] The LRCA further underscored its view of polygamy as compromising the country's commitment to gender equality (Parkinson 1994: 499). Similar concerns were expressed in a 2011 Inquiry into Multiculturalism, which created a forum for the discussion of various issues, including polygamy. Opinions expressed during public hearings conveyed a resounding opposition to plural marriage, urging legislators to resist its formal acceptance and recognition.[18]

The LRCA's report and the 2011 Inquiry reflect considerable resistance to polygamy, although the LRCA did recommend the reconsideration of Australia's criminalization of bigamy.[19] In this way, the LRCA's approach is comparable to that taken by Canadian law reform inquiry bodies, which have suggested decriminalization while remaining skeptical about and resistant to the legal recognition of polygamous spousal relationships.

Australia's legal engagement with polygamy has occurred also through governmental encounters with Aboriginal customary law. Early approaches to the issue suggested that applying a sudden prohibition against bigamy to indigenous

---

15 Austl, Commonwealth, Law Reform Commission, *Multiculturalism: Family Law* (Discussion Paper No 46) (Canberra: Australian Government Publishing Service, 1991) at para. 3.28.

16 Austl, Commonwealth, Law Reform Commission, *Multiculturalism and the Law* (Report No 57) (Canberra: Australian Government Publishing Service, 1992) at para. 4.7.

17 Austl, Commonwealth, Law Reform Commission, *Multiculturalism: Family Law* (Discussion Paper No 46) (Canberra: Australian Government Publishing Service, 1991) at para. 3.43.

18 See discussion at *infra*, notes 46-47.

19 Austl, Commonwealth, Law Reform Commission, *Multiculturalism and the Law* (Report No 57) (Canberra: Australian Government Publishing Service, 1992) at para. 5.11.

populations would be both impractical and could "cause destruction."[20] Later, the Law Reform Commissions of both the Commonwealth and New South Wales issued reports identifying polygamous marriage under indigenous customary law as a matter of juridical concern.[21] Little has come of this observation, however, as federal and state governments have opted against articulating a distinct policy approach, or contemplating law reform, in regard to customary marriage. On this topic, the LRCA described the issue of polygamy as "a matter for Aborigines themselves to decide."[22]

Insofar as Australian criminal law has addressed polygamy, the juridical status of this practice is uncertain. Bigamy is clearly outlawed, whereas consensual polygamy is not a clear focus of Australian criminal law. Nevertheless, Australian conversations about polygamy remain instructive, as these illuminate the way in which state lawmakers tend to envisage women involved in plural marriage. The following section explores critically the ideology driving state law in this domain. It further investigates state law's engagement with non-state norms, as well as state law's influence on decisions women make in connection with polygamous life.

Part 3: Evaluating State Law

Having explored the way in which state law approaches polygamy, the current section assesses juridical stances on polygamy, specifically evaluating the extent to which they grapple meaningfully with women's choices about plural marriage. This analysis draws on the empirical evidence canvassed in Part 1 to identify whether and how women in polygamy see themselves as making decisions and exercising agency. The discussion begins by exploring suppositions and objectives that drive state law in this realm. It then contrasts these suppositions and objectives with non-state norms underlying women's choices about polygamous life. Finally, the way in which state law, especially criminal law, impairs women's outcomes is explored through an investigation of the way in which this law affects their choices in relation to plural marriage.

---

20 Austl, Commonwealth, House of Representatives, *Parliamentary Debates* (29 March 1960) at 671 (Mr Anderson). See also the later comments of Senator McKenna, Austl, Commonwealth, Senate, *Parliamentary Debates* (11 April 1961) at 417.

21 Austl, Commonwealth, Law Reform Commission, *The Recognition of Aboriginal Customary Laws* (Report No 31) (Canberra: Australian Government Publishing Service, 1986); Austl, New South Wales, New South Wales Law Reform Commission, *Uniform Succession Laws: Intestacy* (Issues Paper No 26) (Sydney: New South Wales Law Reform Commission, 2005).

22 Austl, Commonwealth, Law Reform Commission, *The Recognition of Aboriginal Customary Laws* (Report No 31) (Canberra: Australian Government Publishing Service, 1986) at paras. 258-260.

State Law's Presumptions and Objectives in Relation to Polygamy, Women and Choice

Within legislative and policy debates surrounding the state's governance of polygamy, there are few explicit reflections on the issue of whether women choose to engage with this practice. This is particularly evident when one compares the discourse on polygamy with that pertaining to surrogacy and prostitution. Conversations circulating around the latter two topics have considered far more frequently and directly the capacity of women to make deliberate and valued decisions about engaging with these practices. In the context of polygamy, however, two main concerns shape relevant state law. The first takes the form of resistance to foreign practices deemed inconsistent with the tenets of Christianity. The second relates to concerns about gender oppression. This concern is framed in human rights language, presupposing that women in polygamy invariably see their equality rights damaged by this practice.

As shown here, these two concerns pertaining to culture and gender are intertwined in political discussions. Specifically, although the nature of the public rhetoric on polygamy has shifted over time such that its explicit focus has transitioned from cultural preservation to women's rights and gender equality, conversations have consistently reflected ethnocentric assumptions about the minimal capacity for agency exercisable by women within minority religious and cultural groups.

Historical political narrative Contemporary discussions on polygamy are wrapped up in concerns about this practice's apparent threats to women's dignity. Historically, polygamy debates focused on preoccupations about achieving cultural and social solidarity. Whether practiced by immigrant settlers or indigenous inhabitants of a territory, polygamy in the Western world has been viewed as a social and moral threat. The state's mission has historically been to halt, or at least seriously impede, its practice. This outcome was presumed to be a means of fostering greater political and social stability for the territory in question, and of elevating the moral pedigree of its inhabitants. This being state law's focus, early polygamy debates devote minimal attention to its implications for women or questions about whether women take up this practice willfully.

The perceived link between polygamy and social instability emerges prominently in Canadian political debates at the turn of the twentieth century. As indicated, this period was marked by the confluence of Mormon immigration, confederation initiatives, and political efforts to settle territories populated by indigenous nations. A practice accepted by many Mormon settlers and by some Aboriginal groups, polygamy was associated with constituencies who came to personify a threat to the political objectives of European occupation and settlement in the Canadian West. Polygamy was politically labeled a "serious moral and national ulcer,"[23] a "very bad seed grain,"[24] "heathenish,"[25] an "abomination,"[26] and a "nefarious practice."[27] Legal efforts to eradicate it were directly targeted at Mormons and, less explicitly, at Aboriginal persons. Their objective was to ensure compliance with Canadian law, without exception for cultural or religious deviations. In delivering this message to Parliament, Sir John A. Macdonald—Canada's first Prime Minister—did not equivocate:

> Her Majesty has a good many British subjects who are Mohammedans, and if they came here we would be obliged to receive them; but whether they are Mohammedans or Mormons, when they come here they must obey the laws of Canada.[28]

Early political distaste for polygamy was thus generated primarily not by gender equality concerns, but by its possible effects on social cohesion on the Western plains, territory that was at that time marked by political uncertainty and demographic diversity.

Having said this, reflections on gender moved to the foreground occasionally even in these early discussions characterizing polygamy as an exotic cultural practice presumably unknown to Christianity, and lacking in civility and modernism. For example, "concubinage" in China was referenced in 1886 Canadian Sessional Papers as deplorable for women given the "oppression" and the "tyrannies and jealousies" that it fostered between a legally recognized wife—"the lady who is supreme in the household"—and a man's "supernumerary 'wives.'" The latter were, allegedly, at risk of being "discarded; sold and made the slaves of keepers of houses of prostitution."[29]

Sessional Paper references to Aboriginal polygamous wives reflected less overt concern about their wellbeing. These women were understood as being used by men to accumulate government benefits. Characterizing plural marriage as a "transgression," Indian Agents were instructed to prevent husbands from drawing

---

23 Canada, *House of Commons Debates*, 6th Parl, 4th Sess, No 30 (10 April 1890) at 3177 (Mr Mulock).

24 Canada, *House of Commons Debates*, 6th Parl, 3rd Sess, No 28 (3 April 1889) at 980 (Mr Doyon).

25 Canada, *House of Commons Debates*, 5th Parl, 3rd Sess, No 19 (26 May 1885) at 2127 (Mr Paterson).

26 Canada, *House of Commons Debates*, 6th Parl, 4th Sess, No 30 (10 April 1890) at 3178 (Mr McMullen).

27 Canada, *Debates of the Senate*, 6th Parl, 4th Sess, No 29 (25 April 1890) at 584 (Hon Mr Power).

28 Canada, *House of Commons Debates*, 6th Parl, 4th Sess, No 30 (10 April 1890) at 3180 (Sir John A. Macdonald).

29 Canada, Parliament, "Transmitting Report of Royal Commission on Chinese Immigration" in *Sessional Papers*, No 54a (1885) at iii.

annuities for any spouse save for the woman recognized as a "legal" wife.[30] While these commentaries on Aboriginal and Chinese polygamy each has a different orientation, they are consistent in their representation of the women involved as passive and vulnerable, lacking agency or authority within their marriages.

Similar trends are notable in early British political commentary on polygamy. Initial resistance to the practice was rooted in "doctrinal presuppositions of Christianity" and a rejection of "'alien' customs and cultures" (Shah 2003: 392). British experiences with colonialism and immigration fostered encounters with polygamy that spawned public repugnance and an appreciation of the practice as "othered" and as leading to the "decay" of the cultures and communities in which it was accepted.[31] Some scattered references to polygamy's implications for women were bundled within this discourse of civilization and culture. Lord Penzance's decision in *Hyde v. Hyde and Woodmansee*, which crafted the common law definition of marriage as "the voluntary union for life of one man and one woman, to the exclusion of all others," is illustrative. His Lordship refused recognition of a potentially plural marriage, noting its incompatibility with the notion of marriage "as understood in Christendom" and its character as "revolting to the ideas we entertain of the social position to be accorded to the weaker sex" (136).

Polygamy did not figure prominently in Australian political debates prior to the introduction of the country's *Marriage Act 1961*. Nevertheless, sporadic historical references are altogether in line with the ideology of civilization and cultural unity explicit within Canadian and British discussions. In 1905, a member of Australia's House of Representatives aligned polygamy with slavery, war and cannibalism as phenomena "regarded with horror,"[32] and as "inseparable from a low state of civilization."[33] His view was endorsed in parliamentary debates more than a half-century later when divorce was likened to "chronological polygamy" and a "return to the jungle."[34]

Such references to polygamy within historical Australian legislative debates are fleeting and incidental. The marginal attention polygamy received seems attributable to a view of the practice as fundamentally inconsistent with national mores in that period, and thus as unfathomable as a common occurrence. One legislator referred casually to the legalization of polygamy as one of "all sorts of silly things" the legislature could, constitutionally, enact. Yet he recognized

30 Canada, Parliament, "Indian Affairs, Annual Report" in *Sessional Papers*, No 6 (1882) at 88.

31 UK, HL, *Parliamentary Debates*, vol 305, col 1802 (24 May 1886) (Duke of Argyll).

32 Austl, Commonwealth, House of Representatives, *Parliamentary Debates* (19 September 1905) (King O'Malley).

33 Austl, Commonwealth, House of Representatives, *Parliamentary Debates* (26 October 1905) at 4188, *Estimates* (King O'Malley).

34 Austl, Commonwealth, House of Representatives, *Parliamentary Debates* (12 November 1959) at 2697 (Mr Caldwell).

that such a legislative initiative would lack social support and that "no Parliament which passed such laws could live."[35] More than 25 years later, precisely the same views were articulated in the House of Representatives:

> The Minister for Information referred earlier to the fact that though the Australian Government has the constitutional power to legislate to make polygamy legal in Australia, no government would dare to enact such legislation because, if it did, it would not last long. I agree![36]

In all three jurisdictions contemplated in this book, historical political narratives related to polygamy centre on preoccupations with ethnicity. These accounts consistently cast polygamy as derogating from the civility that political actors sought to establish and protect in the face of encounters with cultural otherness through imperialism and immigration. Moreover, polygamy's threats to cultural unity and enlightenment were viewed as significant enough to justify the use of criminal law to eradicate its presence.

Contemporary reflections on culture, gender and polygamy The religious and cultural animus that marked historical debates about polygamy is muted within contemporary discussions on this topic. These concerns have "metamorphosed" such that they are presently articulated in terms of "the unacceptability of the custom on grounds of 'community relations' or the norms of gender equality and human rights" (Shah 2003: 392). Current conversations draw heavily on a rhetorical commitment to women's interests. This being said, the transformation of the discourse has not obliterated anxieties over cultural identity. These preoccupations continue to surface within modern conversations, however they are now laced through articulations that focus on polygamy's gender implications.

The preeminent contemporary narrative on polygamy's repugnance casts plural wives as ensnared and enslaved by their cultural norms. These women are portrayed as living in "fundamentally unequal relationship[s]" (Javed 2008) that facilitate their "treat[ment] as chattels and allocated as concubines into harems" (O'Malley 2007). Canadian politicians commenting on circumstances in Bountiful have called for "action to support women and children trapped in this polygamist cult,"[37] urging for measures "to protect those women and children from potential

35 Austl, Commonwealth, House of Representatives, *Parliamentary Debates* (5 December 1912) at 6514 (J.H. Catts).

36 Austl, Commonwealth, House of Representatives, *Parliamentary Debates* (25 November 1948) at 3532 (Mr Thompson). See also Austl, Commonwealth, House of Representatives, *Parliamentary Debates* (25 November 1948) at 3520 (Mr Caldwell).

37 Canada, British Columbia, Legislative Assembly, *Official Report of Debates (Hansard)*, 38th Parl, 4th Sess, Vol 32, No 9 (8 May 2008) at 12183 (Bill Bennett).

abuse and human rights violations."[38] Comparable ideas emerged in Chief Justice Bauman's decision in *Reference re: Section 293 of the Criminal Code of Canada*, particularly in his reasons as to why polygamy's criminal prohibition in Canada constitutes justified state action. He concluded that Canadian law rightfully rejects polygamy because of polygamy's propensity to reduce women to "slaves," "servants" and "'mere instrument[s] of pleasure and propagation' for her husband" (paras. 199, 214). Modernity, he wrote, has favoured monogamous marriage because of its ability to foster "mutuality and equality between husband and wife" (para. 199), in apparent contrast to polygamy (Campbell 2013c).

British political debates bear similar intonations. Law reform efforts aimed at allowing women to terminate polygamous marriages and claim matrimonial relief emphasized the impropriety of a legal regime that prevented a woman, "who by Christian standards had never been a wife at all," from dissolving her marriage "however cruelly or badly [she] was treated."[39] Cast as protecting women's welfare and equality,[40] while at the same time resisting an endorsement of polygamy, this initiative was viewed as "acceptable to the Christian conscience."[41]

In Australia, gender concerns emerged vociferously in a debate triggered by a call from two senior Islamic community leaders for the recognition of plural unions. Reactions emphasized that polygamy countered the "core value" (Anonymous 2008a) of gender equality, and could generate subordinate relationships that "necessarily make women the underlings of men" (Bolt 2008). Commentators further emphasized that recognizing polygamy would erode the requirement of mutual informed consent in marriage and "destablise and alter society for the worse" (Anonymous 2008b).

While contemporary discourse on polygamy is focused primarily on concerns about women, these preoccupations remain linked to national identity and culture. Perceived as revoking women's autonomy and equality, polygamy has been characterized as inconsistent with, and threatening to, "unifying" national values (Mayeda 2009, Ferretti 2009).[42] Canadian members of Parliament have repeatedly emphasized that the practice "has no place in modern Canadian society," with this

38 Canada, British Columbia, Legislative Assembly, *Official Report of Debates (Hansard)*, 38th Parl, 4th Sess, Vol 30, No 5 (10 April 2008) at 11212 (Leonard Krog).

39 UK, HL, *Parliamentary Debates*, vol 321, col 1223 (9 July 1971) (Lord Chancellor).

40 UK, HC, *Parliamentary Debates*, vol 836, cols 409W-410W (11 May 1972) (Mr Maudling).

41 UK, HL, *Parliamentary Debates*, vol 321, col 1218 (9 July 1971) (Lord Bishop of Lichfield).

42 Austl, Commonwealth, Joint Standing Committee on Migration, *Submission No 299 (Family Council of Victoria)* (2011).

pronouncement linked to the view that polygamy "leads to the exploitation of"[43] and is "harmful" to women.[44]

In the British Parliament, polygamy has been characterized as "wholly at odds with what the European Court of Human Rights has said about the equality of women."[45] Thus, members supporting legislation to restrict the immigration of plural wives emphasized that the initiative harmonized with "acceptable social custom,"[46] local "traditions" and "civilized society."[47] A view of polygamy as invariably exploiting women (Kennedy 2007) also predicates Britain's 2012 *Welfare Reform Act*, which seeks to end the practice of paying public benefits to plural wives as married claimants.

In Australia, various submissions advanced within the 2011 Inquiry into Multiculturalism viewed polygamy as colliding with the values of equality and democracy. Pitched as an immigrant practice, these submissions called for affirmations from Muslims recognizing polygamy as degrading to women.[48] Other reactions characterized polygamy as a phenomenon that could "violently seek to change [Australian] culture."[49]

Gender-based discourse pertaining to polygamy is thus doubly problematic. It surfaces as a paramount theme in modern debates, shifting the narrative about cultural preservation to the background. In so doing, discussions about women's interests might be viewed as a decoy for the core political interest driving regulatory regimes. Focusing on gender is a distraction and neutralizer for the otherwise blatantly xenophobic and ethnocentric pronouncements on polygamy that figured in historical debates. A second, equally troubling feature of ostensible preoccupations with women's interests relates to the fact that although gender has taken centre stage in contemporary discussions, this has not resulted in enriched perspectives on women's experiences. According to the dominant public narrative, women do not take up polygamy actively, but are instead taken up by it according

---

43 Canada, *House of Commons Debates*, 41st Parl, 1st Sess, Vol 146, No 51 (22 November 2011) at 1410 (Mr Pierre Lemieux); Canada, *House of Commons Debates*, 41st Parl, 1st Sess, Vol 146, No 52 (23 November 2011) at 1450 (Mr Kyle Seeback).

44 Canada, *House of Commons Debates*, 41st Parl, 1st Sess, Vol 146, No 52 (23 November 2011) at 1450 (Mr Rob Nicholson); Canada, *House of Commons Debates*, 41st Parl, 1st Sess, Vol 146, No 54 (25 November 2011) at 1100 (Mr Maurice Vellacott).

45 UK, HC, *Parliamentary Debates*, vol 122, col 826 (16 November 1987) (Anne Widdecombe).

46 UK, HC, *Parliamentary Debates*, vol 122, col 785 (16 November 1987) (Douglas Hurd).

47 UK, HL, *Parliamentary Debates*, vol 495, col 49 (21 March 1988) (Lord Renton).

48 Austl, Commonwealth, Joint Standing Committee on Migration, *Submission No 205 (Endeavour Forum)* (7 April 2011); Austl, Commonwealth, Joint Standing Committee on Migration, *Submission No 277 (B M)* (2011).

49 Austl, Commonwealth, Joint Standing Committee on Migration, *Submission No 48 (name withheld)* (2011). See also Austl, Commonwealth, Joint Standing Committee on Migration, *Submission No 299 (Family Council of Victoria)* (2011).

to foreign patriarchal norms. The prospect of women choosing polygamous life or exercising agency within it is absent from discussions driving state law and policy. This stands in contrast to empirical data explored in Part 1, which illuminates the factors that infuse polygamy with meaning and value for at least some women. This data is further indicative of the range of norms that influence women's decision-making. These norms, and their engagement with state law governing polygamy, are the subject of the discussion that follows.

Interface between State and Non-State Law

Juxtaposing the empirical literature on women's experiences in polygamy against the presumptions on which state law in this domain rests reveals three sites of convergence between state and non-state norms affecting women's choices in relation to this practice. These nexus points highlight the contrast between state law's suppositions about polygamy and the range of normative forces beyond formal state regulation that affect women's decisions about polygamous life. The three junctions at which state and non-state law intersect pertain to: understandings of women's opportunities for dissent; appreciations of and approaches to marriage as a social institution; and the definition of polygamy as a foreign or "othered" practice. Each of these points is examined in turn.

Women's opportunities for dissent in polygamy The formal governance of polygamy in Canada, the United Kingdom and Australia presumes that life within plural marriage families or societies leaves women with no opportunity to convey dissent with respect to this way of life. Viewing plural wives as "trapped,"[50] "exploited" (Kennedy 2007) and "socially isolated" (*Reference re: Section 293 of the Criminal Code of Canada*: para. 230) within patriarchal communities, state actors presume that these women require rescue from an existence where they have no voice or authority.

An examination of polygamous life for women "on the ground" nuances this imagery underpinning state law. While some evidence suggests that plural wives may lack opportunities for independent choice, particularly about marriage (e.g. Bala 2009: 192-195) other research indicates that the plurality of norms at work within plural marriage communities can invest women with the authority and obligation to contribute to and improve community life. As discussed in Part 1, polygamous wives might capitalize on dimensions of religious doctrine that emphasize feminine authority and control. In so doing, they reveal an ability to appropriate religious norms despite their patriarchal premises. This process increases women's agency and leadership within their families and communities, and contributes to their spiritual fulfillment.

50 Canada, British Columbia, Legislative Assembly, *Official Report of Debates (Hansard)*, 38th Parl, 4th Sess, Vol 32, No 9 (8 May 2008) at 12183 (Bill Bennett).

Social dynamics within some plural marriage communities also may allow for women to take the reins of family and community life, assuming roles as key administrators in those contexts. Relationships among plural wives can offer women emotional and pragmatic support. Consequently, women often qualify their relationships with one another as more relevant than relationships with their husbands, suggesting the latter's decreased moral and social relevance in family life. Moreover, solidarity among plural wives can foster their governance over domestic, childcare and financial affairs within a family or community. The claim, then, is not that polygamous life offers full gender equality or parity. Rather, it is that state laws fail to identify and account accurately for the sources of women's authority and command within their familial and cultural settings.

On a larger scale, political mobility may also be possible for women in polygamy. In 1993, a group of women prepared a publicly-funded report setting out the severe difficulties they experienced within a Canadian polygamous community.[51] While detailing the challenges that many women faced as plural wives, the report itself demonstrates women's ability to communicate beyond their community's boundaries and advocate for legal and social change in that setting. This text has received considerable attention from academics[52] and was considered by Chief Justice Bauman in *Reference re: Section 293 of the Criminal Code of Canada*.

Women in Bountiful have also engaged in political outreach efforts by holding media conferences aimed at sharing their experiences with "outsiders" to foster a fuller public understanding of their choices about polygamy (Pelland 2007: 113, 125, 90). Some women used such opportunities to call upon the state for statutory reform that would increase the age of consent to sexual contact from 14 to 16 years of age (Anonymous 2005). These instances complicate, if not challenge, the view that polygamous life quashes women's opportunities for dissent, affording them "very little room to instigate change or increase equality within the community" (Alberta Civil Liberties Research Centre 2005: 23).

Voicing opposition and seeking cultural change is one manner in which a woman might exercise autonomy within her community. Another is to leave that setting (Newman 2007). This latter option, exiting polygamous life, merits comment given presumptions that polygamy is a "trap" for women.[53] Leaving a plural marriage inevitably carries significant tradeoffs. This is particularly so where a woman's contact with the world outside her community has been minimal

51 Canada, British Columbia, Anonymous, *Life in Bountiful: A Report in the Lifestyle of a Polygamous Community* (Committee on Polygamous Issues, 1993).

52 See Campbell 2005, Bala et al. 2005, and Canada, Department of Justice, R. Cook and L. Kelly, *Polygyny and Canada's Obligations under International Human Rights Law* (Ottawa: Department of Justice, 2006). Available at: http://www.justice.gc.ca/eng/dept-min/pub/poly/poly.pdf [accessed: 11 November 2012].

53 Canada, British Columbia, Legislative Assembly, *Official Report of Debates (Hansard)*, 38th Parl, 4th Sess, Vol 32, No 9 (8 May 2008) at 12183 (Bill Bennett).

and where leaving her spouse would entail total "disengagement" from her family or community (Bennion 2008: 46-47). Exit is also complicated when a woman lacks employment or independent sources of income, or where she is not her husband's legal spouse and cannot claim spousal support or property division (Bennion 1998: 17, 66-67). Anxieties about child custody could further inhibit a woman from leaving her marriage. Leaving polygamy can be especially daunting within immigrant communities. Where a woman lacks citizenship or residency status, the risks of departure from her marriage or her community rise above social isolation and impoverishment. It will encompass also the risk of falling under the scrutiny of immigration authorities, which may in turn trigger the initiation of removal proceedings (Starr and Brilmayer 2003).

While potentially imposing a serious onus, leaving polygamy remains possible for at least some women. Instances of exit are sometimes self-described as surreptitious and daring "escapes" from deplorable living conditions (Jessop and Palmer 2007). Yet some women express emotional ambiguity about the prospect of leaving one's marriage, family and community. I interviewed two women in Bountiful who, dissatisfied with their marriages, had terminated them. Their stories shed light on the complex implications of that decision. Even though several participants suggested a woman could remain in this community after leaving her husband and opting not to remarry polygamously, the two women I met in that situation had, after ending their marriages, left Bountiful's geographic boundaries (Campbell 2010: 357). That being said, they retained social and emotional ties with community members, especially with relatives and former sister wives, and while they no longer lived in Bountiful, they were still welcomed in that setting (Campbell 2010: 357-358).

The issue of exit from polygamy is thus layered and rendered complex by the multiple connections that a woman has with her family and community members. Some accounts suggest that leaving is a dangerous proposition that puts women in emotional and physical jeopardy. Other narratives are more nuanced, suggesting that although exiting a polygamous marriage imposes challenges and life changes, it remains possible for at least some women. This conclusion textures state law's representation of plural wives as invariably and involuntarily caught in oppressive and degrading marital structures.

None of these observations seems curious when contemplated against the usual hardships even monogamously married women face in dissolving their spousal unions (Malik 2006: 216, Shachar 1999: 100). A woman in Bountiful underscored this point when I asked her, within a focus group discussion, what a woman's alternatives would look like if she opted to leave her polygamous marriage. She returned the question to me, asking: "Well, what would your alternatives be?" I noted that my options would be generally undesirable, citing concerns about the consequences for my children and about leaving that which was familiar. This participant responded, "Everything you said, it's exactly the same for us" (Campbell 2009b: 203).

As I have previously noted (Campbell 2009b: 203), it is probably inaccurate to suggest that the consequences of ending my marriage would be "exactly the same" as those resulting from such a choice in Bountiful. Imagining that a monogamously married Canadian law professor shares a parallel universe with a plural wife in a fundamentalist religious society overlooks the class, geographic and cultural factors that broaden and constrict options for women in regard to intimate and family relationships. Just the same, the exchange highlights the difficulties of relationship termination that can transcend intersectional boundaries. It further warns against hastily assuming that secular and religious women face wholly distinct liabilities and opportunities in seeking reform of or in exiting their families and communities.

Marriage's centrality as a social institution State law assumes that monogamous marriage as reflected in Christian mores fosters women's equality and dignity, whereas polygamy undermines these values. This understanding of marriage rests on two premises. The first is that the institution of marriage and the virtues presumed to be inherent to it are unimportant to polygamists and therefore, legitimizing polygamy would undermine women's equality and dignity. A second premise underlying state law's approach to polygamy is that monogamous marriage is a gender equality-producing institution that benefits women. Both of these propositions merit scrutiny.

Investigating the understanding of marriage in polygamous communities illuminates the centrality of this institution according to both religious and social norms. In fundamentalist Mormon communities, marriage is viewed as a sacrament that signifies a commitment between a couple enduring throughout terrestrial life and after death, in the afterworld. This is true even when the marriage is polygamous. The fundamental marriage commitment remains between a husband and wife who exchange vows to express publicly their mutual obligations. Where a marriage is polygamous, existing wives may be brought into the marriage celebration with a view to signifying their consent to their husband's taking of a new spouse and so that all participants communicate their commitments to and bonds with each other, as a family (Campbell 2013a).

Empirical research on polygamy also illuminates social expectations about the critical value of marriage and of remaining virtuous as a spouse. Although a man might have more than one wife, the standards of his faith and community demand that he remain committed and loyal to these women. Women I interviewed in Bountiful emphasized this point. One participant, when asked about what she would teach her son about marriage, stated:

> I will teach [him], to find one woman and, in his heart, if there's another that wants to come then accept that but don't you ever go looking! [chuckle] It's not his right to look. (Campbell 2009b: 201)

Other participants affirmed the view that it would be improper for a man to scout for additional wives, and that women are meant instead to seek out a family to join if they wish to become a plural wife. On this point, another participant stated:

> The biggest lie anyone could ever make, is to intentionally break a marriage vow. When people make commitments with each other, they should keep them. To me, it would seem like cheating on your wife to be out looking for another wife. (Campbell 2009b: 197)

Such remarks suggest that polygamy may be less about satiating men's sexual desires than the manifestation of a commitment to marriage, albeit not in its conventional binary form. Drawing from this observation, it may be possible also to discern the way women envisage marriage within their own conceptual frameworks informed by religious tenets and by social relationships and expectations. This analysis facilitates a departure from state law's simple understanding of polygamy as a vehicle for objectifying women and their sexuality. Instead, contemplating the range of normative forces that influence choices about polygamy permits a fuller appreciation of these decisions and of the centrality of marriage underpinning them.

Beyond adhering to and reinforcing community-based perceptions of marriage, some women may be capable also of remolding understandings of this institution within their polygamous families and communities. In Bountiful, I met a pair of women who were "celestially" married to the same husband. As neither had a formally recognized marriage to this male spouse, and because they shared most aspects of their domestic lives, these women solemnized their relationship through a civil marriage ceremony, making theirs the first open same-sex union in Bountiful.[54] While they indicated that their marriage surprised many community members, some of whom disapproved of it, they described their marriage to each other as symbolizing and confirming the intimate and lifelong commitment they had already undertaken to one another and to each other's children. To this end, one of the spouses stated in a joint interview with the couple:

> I go to work and support her and she tends my kids. And we really and truly and honestly are partners. … Honestly there's not any [*sic*] two ladies that live as a couple as we do.

While making this assertion, these women remained part of their polygamous marriages to a shared husband, and part of their polygamous community. They thus appeared to value marriage according to both its conventional ideal as a steadfast dyadic partnership, and according to unorthodox manifestations, namely polygamy and same-sex relationships.

Women in polygamy therefore might resist multiple normative pressures at once. On one hand, they elide the state law rules regarding polygamy, opting

54 This relationship is described in detail in Campbell 2010: 354ff.

for plural marriage where they see this as critical to expressing their faith or meeting their social and economic needs. On the other hand, they may push back against the nuptial rules of their community. Same-sex marriage in a community unequivocally committed to heteronormative ideals is one example. Perhaps less dramatic is the instance of the young woman whose mother I interviewed, who opted to marry at 16 despite her mother's wishes and contemporary community views that marriage should not happen prior to adulthood (Campbell 2009b: 201).

Beyond assumptions about the centrality of marriage and spousal commitment, state law's insistence on monogamy relates to a presumed correlation between marriage and gender equality. State law understands monogamous partners as arriving at and experiencing marriage as equal partners who give "full consent" to this arrangement (Anonymous 2008b). This proposition, touted repeatedly by Chief Justice Bauman in *Reference re: Section 293 of the Criminal Code of Canada*, served to rationalize a decision to maintain polygamy's criminalization (paras. 208, 217, 884). Bauman CJ's reasons focused sharply on the goal of protecting monogamous marriage as a stabilizing and enriching social institution. He thus concluded that Canada's ban on polygamy applies only when "a marriage ceremony or other sanctioning event" had transpired, but did not extend to conjugal cohabitation relationships (para. 939).

Like other juridical authorities that eschew polygamy by proclaiming a need to preserve monogamy's sanctity, the decision in *Reference re: Section 293 of the Criminal Code of Canada* neglects the drawbacks that a woman may encounter even when she is her husband's only wife (Zylan 2012: 2, 10-11). One need not scratch too deeply beyond the surface of the monogamous ideal to appreciate the thrust of this critique. Feminists have long contemplated marriage's pernicious implications for women. Becoming a wife has historically entailed the complete absorption of a woman's legal identity and economic wealth. Contemporary wives and mothers continue to make sizable sacrifices resulting in foregone educational and career opportunities and in reduced economic independence (see Boyd 2004, Eichler 1997, Sheppard 1995, Williams 1994: 2246ff., Hill Kay 2003, Post 1997).

Observations about what women may lose even in monogamous marriage contexts tests assumptions of liberty and equality in monogamy. Rather, a host of factors may converge to prompt or compel women to marry in any setting. A critical appraisal of monogamy that looks at the institution beyond its idealization within state law indicates that it is not necessarily an extreme that stands opposed to polygamy in terms of its gender implications. Rather, both forms of marriage can yield mixed and complicated experiences for women that might be actively chosen by its female participants despite their potential adverse outcomes.

Polygamy as othered and foreign A third point of intersection between state and non-state law invites reflection on Western law's vision of polygamy as a practice assumed by foreign or indigenous cultural groups. It further calls for juxtaposing this perspective against actual conjugal practices adopted and accepted within Western settings. This analysis reveals that the sharp criticism Western legal traditions direct at polygamy seems reserved for religiously-rooted forms of this practice. In contrast, what might be viewed as secular polygamy bears some immunity from the state's scorn for plural conjugal partnerships.

State law's presumption of polygamy as a practice that differs from and potentially threatens that which is known, local and stable comes across through myriad historical and contemporary references. Termed a practice that would "violently seek to change"[55] domestic marriage norms and "put the nation on a slippery slope toward surrendering its identity and traditions" (Anonymous 2008b) polygamy is cast as absolutely external and challenging to "unifying values" in Western secular societies (Mayeda 2009).[56]

This perspective is intertwined with the understanding of the practice as un-Christian and, consequently, unenlightened. Legislative debates have labeled polygamy as "heathenish"[57] and "repugnant,"[58] while emphasizing the objective of aligning state law's approach with "doctrinal presuppositions of Christianity" (Shah 2003: 392). This approach aimed to protect marriage as "informed by centuries of Judeo Christian tradition" (Anonymous 2008b) and to uphold a "Christian based monogamous culture" (*R.B. v. United Kingdom*).

Legal and political discourse within states like Canada, the United Kingdom and Australia thus represent polygamy as an exotic and foreign phenomenon, imported by outsiders unfamiliar with and potentially hostile to local norms and traditions. Even when polygamy occurs within populations that follow faith tenets rooted in Christianity, the practice remains staunchly characterized as the product of aberrant doctrines upheld by a "polygamist cult."[59] Within the dominant political narrative, minority religious and cultural traditions are presented as the sole sources of non-state norms prompting polygamy. These norms are held out as challenging accepted and orthodox marriage practices, especially heterosexual monogamy, which Western law parallels with progress and equality.

Yet the essence of polygamy—that is, the partnering by one person with more than one conjugal spouse—exists well within the parameters of Western secular society. Examples abound. The Canadian Supreme Court has held that consensual collective sex and "swinging" do not constrain public autonomy and liberty and thus do not merit criminalization (*R. v. Labaye*). Adultery is understood as the pursuit of coexistent sexual relationships without conjugality, and may

55 Austl, Commonwealth, Joint Standing Committee on Migration, *Submission No 48 (name withheld)* (2011).

56 See also Ferretti 2009, who suggests that accepting polygamy and other practices rooted in religious norms threatens a shared history and culture.

57 Canada, *House of Common Debates*, 6th Parl, 4th Sess, No 30 (10 April 1890) at 3177 (Mr Blake).

58 UK, HC, *Parliamentary Debates*, vol 183, col 302 (2 May 1866) (Mr Knatchbull-Hugessen).

59 Canada, British Columbia, Legislative Assembly, *Official Report of Debates (Hansard)*, 38th Parl, 4th Sess, Vol 32, No 9 (8 May 2008) at 12183 (Bill Bennett).

appear easily distinguishable from polygamy. The delineation between these two practices becomes more obscure, however, when an adulterous relationship takes on a level of permanence or domesticity. Moreover, an individual may cohabit with a partner after separating from, but not divorcing, her married spouse. That individual formally has two conjugal partners and may be caught in Canadian law's definition of polygamy (Drummond 2008). Last, the practice of polyamory calls for contemplation. In *Reference re: Section 293 of the Criminal Code of Canada*, the Canadian Polyamory Advocacy Association acted as an interested party. Its interventions emphasized the presence of plural conjugality in Canada—citing at least 112 polyamorous households in the country—and noted the potential virtues of this lifestyle (para. 447).[60]

Despite their proximity to polygamy as traditionally understood, legal actors seem to interpret the foregoing "secular" practices as eliding criminal law's reach. Even polyamory, seemingly encompassed by the Canadian *Criminal Code*'s definition of polygamy as a "conjugal union with more than one person at the same time" even when formally unmarried, appears to have been read out of the ban by Chief Justice Bauman in *Reference re: Section 293 of the Criminal Code of Canada*. The Chief Justice reasoned that a conjugal relationship was distinct from a conjugal union, the latter marked by a "marriage ceremony or other sanctioning event" that rendered it subject to s. 293 (para. 939). Because polyamorous relationships are not normally initiated by such a ceremony—usually one according to religious or spiritual rites—they are not conjugal "unions" and are therefore shielded from prosecution.

State law thus fails to account for the plurality of factors beyond religion and culture that might prompt plural conjugality and polygamy. Characterizing polygamy as an irregular practice, "foreign in every sense" to local traditions[61] and situated exclusively within minority faith and ethnic groups facilitates polygamy's exclusion from the boundaries of tolerable intimate activities and relationships. This characterization also has the effect of centralizing monogamous marriage, particularly between heterosexual partners, within the ambit of acceptable conjugal partnerships. Yet analyses of factors that may imbue polygamy with meaning and value for many women, and of choices individuals in secular society make about marriage and intimacy, challenge state law's polarized theory about polygamy, which casts the practice as devious, aberrational and altogether absent from secular communities. Such analyses demonstrate how polygamy resembles practices existent and accepted within Western law and society. They further exhibit the unfounded nature of claims about polygamy as an unparalleled threat to monogamous marriage.

---

60 See also Fraser 2012 for insight into the growing social presence and acceptance of polyamory.

61 Austl, Commonwealth, House of Representatives, *Parliamentary Debates* (20 May 1975) at 2484 (Mr Luchetti).

Concluding remarks: interface between state and non-state law Examining the non-state norms that influence how polygamy is practiced brings into relief the gaps in state law's understanding of plural marriage and women's experiences in it. Western law's approach to polygamy is based on an assumption that women face deep inequalities and impaired dignity in plural marriage because they have few or no opportunities for self-determination, for directing family and community life or for leaving plural marriage life if they so wish. These premises overlook instances of agency, resistance and leadership that women can develop within their polygamous families and communities, which are exposed by empirical research.

State law in this area also centres monogamous marriage as an institution that represents venerable commitment, fosters social stability and promotes women's rights. Each of these postulations intersects with non-state norms pertinent to polygamy in a way that illuminates state law's conceptual inaccuracies and apertures. Religious doctrine and social patterns that guide polygamous communities may converge to position marriage and spousal fidelity as equally foundational within plural marriage societies as they are presumed to be within the Western monogamous ideal. Moreover, a critical examination of that monogamous ideal illuminates its potential pitfalls for women, rendering it a more controversial point of reference than state law posits for measuring polygamy's gender-based effects.

A third junction point between state and non-state law relates to perceptions about who practices polygamy and why. State law sees the phenomenon as imported and alien, anchored to regressive and patriarchal cultural worldviews. Yet polygamy and comparable practices are driven not only by religious and cultural norms, but also by social and economic circumstances, human desires and preferences about intimate and sexual life. Polygamy is thus taken up in secular contexts, as well as those governed by faith. In secular sites, however, the state largely ignores the practice or sees it as benign, and non-religious practitioners are shielded from the threat of prosecution.

Exploring points of engagement between state and non-state law reveals plural wives' opportunities for appropriating control and agency in relation to family life while casting questions about whether gender equality and dignity necessarily inhere to monogamy. These instances would remain invisible on a reading of juridical sources pertinent to polygamy alone. Diffusing the study of polygamy so as to incorporate empirical evidence illuminates the shortcomings in juridical understandings of this phenomenon, particularly in relation to women's experiences and the opportunities for choice they might have in this domain. Be this as it may, rules crafted by the state retain some influence over whether and how women become plural wives. The discussion that follows contemplates state law's ongoing impact on these decisions, focusing on the consequences of plural marriage's criminalization.

Criminal Law's Persuasion over Polygamy Choices

When interviewing women in Bountiful, I asked participants how their lives would change if, the following morning, they woke up to learn that polygamy in Canada had been decriminalized. Most suggested that such a development would not wield much practical impact. One woman stated: "I'd still be a mother at home with my children, and it doesn't really affect me." Another asserted: "[I]f it [i.e., polygamy] could be decriminalized tomorrow, I would say, 'Yay!' And then I would carry on with my daily life. It really wouldn't change anything" (Campbell 2009b: 219).

Polygamy's criminalization does not appear to have deterred its practice. Women in Bountiful suggested that this was primarily because they felt a stronger commitment to their religious principles than to the requirements of state law. Their comments reinforce the centrality of religion and culture to individual identity, limiting state law's potential for halting or changing practices and perspectives rooted in religious beliefs (Geertz 1977). Reflections further gesture at the futility of proscriptive rules aimed at enforcing a monolithic vision of family and marriage (Alexandre 2007: 30). One woman remarked in regard to the prospect of polygamy's decriminalization: "I don't feel it would necessarily change it [i.e., polygamy] that much because people are still living it and practicing it and not necessarily because it's against the law or not." Another woman indicated: "I grew up knowing that polygamy was in my life, and it's part of my religion so I mean, there was nothing that was going to stop me from doing what God wanted me to do." In the same vein, a different participant affirmed: "It's not gonna matter if they decriminalize it or not. … I mean, in my mind, that's how I live" (Campbell 2009b: 220).

Criminal law's limited influence over the practice of polygamy might stem in part from a lack of understanding about polygamy's legal status. Some women in Bountiful did not recognize polygamy as an offence until the issue became a matter of intense media concern. One community member reported: "I honestly was not aware it was criminal until a couple of years ago. … Because, you know, they had a raid, they gave the kids back so you just said, 'Okay, it must have been okay'" (Campbell 2009b: 220). This comment referred to government interventions in FLDS societies, involving the mass apprehension of children and removal of parental custody rights. The most notable of these were raids in Short Creek, Arizona and El Dorado, Texas occurring in 1955 and 2008 respectively (Bradley Evans 2011). Although occurring in American FLDS settlements, these events generated worry and concern among women in Bountiful (Campbell 2009b: 222-223).

Other empirical observations suggest confusion between the implications of decriminalization and legalization, with some women in Canada incorrectly presuming that the former entailed the latter. They maintained that the ban on polygamy should be struck down such that plural wives could become "legal" spouses, with all of the obligations and rights associated with that status. These remarks reflected a lack of understanding about the limits of decriminalization, which would alleviate the risk of prosecution but would not, by itself, permit the formal recognition of plural marriages (Campbell 2009b: 220-221).

Whether generated by ignorance or misunderstanding of Canadian law, or by a woman's view that her commitment to faith tenets supersedes her duty to obey state-made rules, women in polygamy have not abandoned this practice on account of criminal law. This point emerges plainly in Bountiful, Canada, and is also apparent in other jurisdictions. In Britain and Australia, political debates discussed in the first subsection of Part 3, above ("State Law's Presumptions and Objectives in Relation to Polygamy, Women and Choice"), highlight the ongoing presence of polygamy despite its non-recognition by the state as a valid conjugal form. And while the criminal status of this particular practice remains unclear, the related practice of bigamy is an offence in both jurisdictions.

While prohibition has not halted polygamy, it has had the foreseeable effect of exporting it to hidden social and geographic contexts. Polygamous societies, wary of the penalty and social stigma that accompany a criminalized lifestyle, are often characterized by physical and social isolation (Pelland 2007: 125, Sigman 2006). This isolation engenders suspicions and social understandings of polygamy premised on presumptions and stereotypes. As one empirical researcher notes:

> There is a sense that the outside world is eager to believe the worst about the [plural marriage] community; but, when women speak out positively about their lives, the larger society is quick to label them as ignorant, uneducated, and brainwashed. It seems that when humans do not understand the choices of others different from them, there is the judgment that oppression and compulsion have driven those choices. (Boehmer 2010: 151)

Aware of these views, polygamous wives may resist contact with broader society (Pelland 2007: 117, Peters 1994: 42), resulting in circumstances of mutual distrust between those living within and outside of polygamous groups (*Reference re: Section 293 of the Criminal Code of Canada*: para. 707). This can significantly affect community members' perceptions of the geographical spaces in which they feel they can safely operate, for example, in seeking employment or health and social services (Altman and Ginat 1996: 199-200). This point is subject to elaboration momentarily.

This being said, such a bifurcation between worlds "inside" and "outside" of polygamy is artificial. As explained earlier, societies known to be "polygamous," such as Bountiful, might in fact be the sites of multiple forms of family life, including monogamy (Campbell 2010). Conversely, the Western world, although presumably founded on the institution of monogamous marriage, has come to accept a range of intimate and sexual practices and relationships, both conventional and unorthodox. The inconsistency between the "high-and-mighty attitude that polygamy is awful" and the plurality of family and marriage types in fact existent and accepted in Western societies has even been suggested to constitute "hypocrisy" for one British Lord.[62] In this connection, one might consider Western law's acknowledgement of polyamory and "swinging" as practices that do not attract prosecution, as noted above. It is also worth underlining state law's recognition of potential simultaneous claims against a spouse for property division or support by two or more concurrently married or unmarried spouses.[63] So while state law conveys a distinction between "polygamous" and "mainstream" societies, it would be a mistake to see this divide as fixed and watertight.

Polygamy's physical and social isolation has the added effect of increasing harm and complicating the prosecution of criminal behaviour. Insulation increases risks of abuse and exploitation (Allred Solomon 2003: 13, Bennion 2008: 177). Offences associated with such harms (sexual assault, sexual exploitation, sexual interference, and fraud) have, by and large, remained unprosecuted (Sigman 2006: 181-182). Perpetrators "fade into the background" with impunity, at the expense of their community's most vulnerable constituents (Bennion 2011: 163). This outcome is both ironic and counterproductive from a criminal justice perspective, leading, at least in the North American context, to "prohibitions and prosecutions when they were otherwise unwarranted, failures of enforcement when it most certainly would have been warranted, and the imposition of a one-size-fits-none behemoth that has left a trail of collateral damage for over one hundred and fifty years" (Sigman 2006: 102).

Additionally, the clandestine practice of polygamy frustrates its effective study. Researchers will face difficulty identifying where polygamy occurs. Even where sites of polygamy are known, earning the trust of community members who will share knowledge about their lifestyles and experiences is a formidable feat, given the steep costs for research participants of falling subject to state scrutiny. This factor played a significant role in circumscribing my own research on polygamy and has also been acknowledged by other researchers in this field (Peters 1994, Bala et al. 2005: 18). It further accounts for the limited number of empirical studies on immigrant polygamy in Western societies.

Beyond threats associated with insularity, legal responses to polygamy engender stigma and anxiety given concerns about prosecutorial, immigration or child welfare interventions. Even though it seems unlikely that women would be criminally charged, this possibility does not lie beyond the realm of imagination. In *Reference re: Section 293 of the Criminal Code of Canada*, Chief Justice Bauman

62 UK, HL, *Parliamentary Debates*, vol 495, col 50 (21 March 1988) (Lord Bonham-Carter).

63 See e.g., in Australia, the *Family Law Act 1975*, s. 4AA(5)(b), which states that, for the Act's purpose: "a de facto relationship can exist even if one of the persons is legally married to someone else or in another de facto relationship," and the *Interpretation Act 1901*, s. 2F(5), which reiterates this principle; in Canada, British Columbia's *Estate Administration Act*, s. 85.1, which states: "For the purposes of section 85, if 2 or more persons are entitled as a spouse they share the spousal share in the estate in the portions determined by the court as the court considers just."

explicitly concluded that women are not exempt from the prospect of prosecution, viewing them as potentially complicit in their polygamous marriages. He held:

> I question whether the capable consenting spouse is a "victim." To the contrary, she can be seen to be facilitating an arrangement which Parliament views as harmful to society generally. (para. 1197)

The threat of criminal sanction thus looms large for women in polygamy, at least in Canada. Beyond this, women are also acutely aware of the possibility that child welfare authorities and, if they lack residency or citizenship, immigration officials may hold their involvement in polygamy against them in the exercise of administrative discretion.

Stigma and fear of legal sanction leads some women to be reticent about seeking out public services they or their children may need. In Bountiful, most women seem to be at ease with running errands or seeking out what might be viewed as morally benign services in nearby neighbourhoods and communities. Yet they suggested that reluctance and shame would accompany an effort to access services related to reproduction, mental health, domestic violence or family counseling (Campbell 2009b: 210-211). Some women in plural marriage communities are also apprehensive about seeking employment in greater society, as they worry they will face poor treatment or discrimination if their polygamous lifestyle becomes known (Bennion 2008: 57-58, Campbell 2009b: 210). Reticence to engage outside of the community for such services or work risks limiting women's opportunities to enhance wellbeing and establish an independent source of income. The latter result can be especially harsh for a woman who may at a later point wish to exit her marriage but feels precluded from doing so by a scarcity of financial resources and an inability to claim support from her spouse. The irony of state law is thus again apparent, as rules formed to protect women in ostensibly precarious situations ultimately may deter or preclude them from obtaining the resources needed to improve or exit those situations (Sigman 2006, Drummond 2009: 362), thereby positioning them as "perpetual victim[s]" (Chan 2011: 26-27).

Consequently, state law, while not halting polygamy outright, influences various dimensions of the lives of women involved in the practice, including the way in which it is taken up. Polygamy's regulatory structures are premised largely on a perceived vulnerability among plural wives and an objective of enhancing their equality and dignity. As shown here, however, the juridical rejection of polygamy, primarily through the vehicle of the criminal law, drives the practice to the shadows of mainstream law and society. Such underground sites present opportunities for abuse and exploitation and exacerbate polygamy's adverse potential outcomes. This situation arises also in connection with the two other practices this book considers (Duncan 2008: 331-332). There is no question, then, that women are made deeply vulnerable by legal regimes that at once "infantilize" them and esteem them incapable of consenting to and choosing plural marriage (Sigman 2006: 172), while holding them accountable as social threats and destabilizers through their acceptance of this way of life (Campbell 2013c). While state law can have this oppressive effect, however, women in polygamy can display remarkable resistance in drawing on the resources around them to give meaning and value to their lives and to "secure acceptable outcomes for themselves" (Shah 2003: 398). In doing so, some of the resources they deploy might in fact stem from state rules, as witnessed by the plural wives who used Canadian law's allowance of same-sex marriage to formalize their relationship of commitment to each other within their own community's religious and social constructs. In this way, one is forced to "question the claims about the dominance of the official legal system" (Shah 2003: 398) and account for the multiplicity of normative influences that can both foster and constrict the agency women exercise in morally ambiguous contexts.

Conclusion

As just discussed, polygamy's criminalization has obscured the practice from public view, making this phenomenon difficult to research. This in turn limits possibilities for informing juridical actors called upon to assess choices about polygamy. While literature based on empirical research in the West is limited, that which exists points to the heterogeneity of women's experiences in plural marriage. This lifestyle imposes constraints and hardships, and some participants clearly become entangled in polygamy against their own will. Empirical research also suggests, however, that some women choose polygamous life and ascribe discernible meaning and value to it.

Empiricism thus offers a counter-narrative to the dominant representation of plural wives in Western societies, particularly as cast by state law. Within the latter paradigm, polygamy is understood as a practice that systematically degrades women's social status, autonomy and wellbeing. The practice is viewed as rooted in cultural norms removed from, and potentially threatening to, the presumably progressive and egalitarian tenets of Western state law.

An evaluation of intersections between state and non-state presumptions and norms shaping decisions about polygamy illuminates state law's weak conceptual grip on this practice and on its potential meaning and value for women. State law's presumption of polygamy as an unequivocally misogynist phenomenon prompts it to overlook the agency, power and mobility that plural wives can muster in construing, resisting and using to their own advantage the norms of family, community and state. Formal rules crafted by the state also miss the central relevance of marriage as an institution within polygamous cultures, while at the same time idealizing monogamy in a way that ignores its historical and ongoing pitfalls for gender equality. It further mistakes polygamy as an exclusively religious and cultural phenomenon, overlooking secular instantiations of the practice.

These oversights prevent state law from engaging meaningfully with women's choices about polygamy. On the one hand, polygamy's criminalization—as shown here—forces the practice to isolated and invisible sites, exacerbating hazards for women with diminished social and economic clout. Women live under the threat of prosecution based on the view that they have chosen polygamy; any constraints under which they operate are unaccounted for. On the other hand, state law deems choices about polygamy invalid, generally refusing to recognize the effects of a plural marriage that might offer them and their children necessary social and economic protection. In this way, state law's failure to grapple and engage with sister wives' lived experiences forces these women to occupy both sides of the responsible agent–innocent victim dyad, but in neither role are their interests acknowledged or protected. The following two chapters explore the emergence of a comparable phenomenon arising from juridical approaches to surrogacy and sex work in Canada, the United Kingdom and Australia.

Chapter 3
Engaging with Surrogates' Choices: Tracing and Proscribing Viable Mothers in Law

Commercial surrogacy can be distinguished, in three key ways, from the two other central case studies taken up in this book. First and most obviously, although the exchange of human reproductive services for money is prohibited in most Western jurisdictions, surrogates themselves are not the object of criminal law in this context. Unlike the sister wife or the sex worker, the surrogate's conduct is often not proscribed and she therefore does not bear the risk of prosecution and sanction. Instead, state law typically criminalizes the acts of brokering or paying for a surrogate's services.

Second, surrogacy's overarching purpose and focus is on reproduction as opposed to intimacy. Use of assisted procreative measures can allow for a child's birth without sexual contact between the surrogate and those who commission her services. Further, she often will have no genetic connection to the child she produces, nor is she intended to have legal or social parental status with respect to that child. Thus, while surrogacy facilitates the creation or expansion of a family, it generally lacks the sexually intimate or physical dimensions present in the relationships at play in polygamy and sex work.

Third, juridical and political discourses on surrogacy gravitate toward issues affecting children. The potential implications of this practice for children are an equal, if not even greater, legislative and policy concern than the risks surrogates themselves assume. Although children remain relevant to discussions regarding polygamy and prostitution, reproduction is surrogacy's direct purpose, explaining the prominence of children's interests within legal and political narratives.

Despite these distinctions, commercial surrogacy retains its place in this analysis of women's criminalized choices linked to family, intimacy and sex, in which state law views women as both victimized and menacing. Commercial surrogacy is perceived as encouraging women to capitalize on their sexual and reproductive capacities while rendering themselves susceptible to coercion in this process. Even when surrogates themselves do not face penal sanction, criminalizing aspects of surrogacy subjects surrogates to stigma, critique and suspicion. As such, surrogacy fits within this project's analysis of state law's engagement with women's morally and politically fraught lifestyles and choices.

Much like the discussions that circulate around women and sex work, money is presumed to be surrogates' key motivator. Surrogates are also similar to other women considered in this book in that they are viewed as disempowered and exploited by those with whom they negotiate and form relationships. This chapter illuminates how these suppositions emerge in legal and policy analyses and how they compare with surrogates' narratives. This analysis enables an investigation into whether and how women make meaningful choices about surrogacy, and the extent to which such choices are influenced by both state and non-state law.

This chapter follows the structure developed in Chapter 1 for interrogating, from a juridical perspective, women's morally complex choices. It begins, in Part 1, by setting out narratives collected through empirical research, which illuminate the experiences of women who have acted as surrogate mothers. Part 2 explains the governance regimes in place regulating surrogacy in the three jurisdictions that this book contemplates: Canada, the United Kingdom and Australia. These two bodies of data—that is, the empirical social science research and the collection of legal rules developed by the state pertinent to surrogacy—are juxtaposed and analyzed in Part 3. There, state law—particularly, the criminalization of commercialized surrogacy—is critically evaluated in light of the lived experiences of surrogates as recounted through empiricism.

Before engaging in this substantive analysis, some brief preliminary points about Chapter 3's scope and terminology are apposite. The focus here is on paid, or commercialized, surrogacy. This term refers to circumstances in which surrogates are remunerated for the services of gestating and giving birth to one or more children for another individual or couple. This practice is distinct from gratuitous surrogacy, in which surrogates are paid nothing or are only reimbursed for reasonable expenses they incur as a result of pregnancy and childbirth. It is also important to note a distinction between "genetic" and "gestational" surrogacy. The former is currently less frequent and involves circumstances in which a surrogate and the child she bears have a genetic connection, typically as a result of the surrogate undergoing artificial insemination. The latter occurs where conception occurs through *in vitro* fertilization such that the surrogate and child are unrelated genetically (Ciccarelli and Beckman 2005: 22). Last, it should be signaled that surrogates might contract with one or more persons, of the same or opposite sex. This chapter refers to those with whom the surrogate contracts as "intending parents," although they are sometimes known in the literature as "commissioning parents."

Part 1: Plural Narratives about Choice

Jurists' understandings of surrogates' choices can be enriched by knowledge of the empirics of surrogacy. Empirical research in this domain stems primarily from the fields of psychology, ethnography, anthropology and sociology. It draws upon methods—notably, fieldwork, qualitative interviews and questionnaires—aimed at studying surrogates' decisions and behaviour. As discussed in Chapter 1, the value of such research lies in its potential to showcase the motivations underlying the choices women make regarding controversial practices tainted by criminalization, like surrogacy. This research further illuminates whether, how and for what reasons a woman's experience as a surrogate might benefit her. Finally, empirically derived narratives expose the ways in which women living seemingly inopportune lifestyles respond to state law as well as normative forces exerted within non-state settings.

As set out in Chapter 1, this project esteems empiricism to be of value for accessing the experiential knowledge of women, particularly those with reduced social and political clout. It argues that this knowledge should inform the state's engagement with these women and their life choices. Nevertheless, there are critical limits to empirical research in the domain of surrogacy, which bear mention here. These limits are not unlike those that circumscribe the value of such research on polygamy and sex work. To begin, the bulk of this scholarship contemplates surrogacy in the American and British contexts. This chapter thus does not consider the narratives of women in the developing world who may become surrogates and whose motivations and outcomes may differ dramatically from those who are the focus of the literature discussed here (see e.g., Rengachary Smerdon 2008). Moreover, even within Western settings, surrogates' experiences may vary, given the distinct legislative contexts operative in different jurisdictions and state's law's potential influence on social practices pertaining to family and reproduction (Leckey 2011, Harvison Young and Wasunna 1998). Encounters with surrogacy will also be shaped by a woman's particular social and economic circumstances. In a connected vein, surrogacy literature typically does not distinguish between remunerated and unremunerated surrogacy, rendering it difficult to discern whether and how payment affects surrogates' experiences.

Additional limits pertain to methodological constraints, such as small and self-selected participant groups and the possibility of surrogates' resistance to interviews or to reporting on adverse events, given the social stigma associated with this practice (van den Akker 2003, 2007: 60, Baslington 2002: 67, Jadva et al. 2003). Furthermore, surrogates willing to participate in research might only be those who encountered positive experiences, resulting in a possibly skewed representation of the practice (Jadva et al. 2003). Alternatively, researchers acknowledge that their participants may succumb to recall bias, reporting only favourable aspects and views of surrogacy (MacCallum et al. 2003: 1340-1341, Jadva et al. 2003: 2203). Other scholars express some skepticism in regard to surrogates' accounts privileging culturally accepted motivations for becoming surrogates, suggesting that surrogates' aim to deliver a socially desirable narrative leads to emphases on reproduction and maternity, while minimizing the proclaimed relevance of financial gain or relationships with intending parents and children (Ciccarelli and Beckman 2005: 30, Ragoné 1996: 354, Jadva et al. 2003: 2203). Last, some surrogates' accounts may have been shaped by the way researchers frame their interview questions; research less firmly rooted in Western assumptions about motherhood might prompt less orthodox accounts from surrogates (Teman 2008).

While these factors might generate cautious reliance on empirical literature pertinent to surrogates' experiences, it would be mistaken to interpret them as a ground for disregarding this research. Methodological hurdles will vex any scholar aiming to gather empirical knowledge about "hidden populations" (Heckathorn 1997), particularly when involvement in research carries criminal implications (Campbell 2008, Tyldum and Brunovskis 2005: 18). Nevertheless, it offers critical insight, likely inaccessible through other means, into the efficacy and equity of state law's methods for dealing with such communities.

The discussion that follows draws on empiricism to explore the meaning and value that women attach to the practice of surrogacy. The distinction between these concepts, although set out in Chapter 1, bears canvassing here. The meaning women ascribe to a practice pertains to the motivations underlying their choices in its regard. By contrast, the value of a choice is intended to convey women's assessments of it *ex post facto*, that is, after the choice is made and they have engaged with the practice concerned. Thus, while "meaning" refers to ways a woman might explain her choice, "value" has a normative connotation, and emanates from her analysis of whether that choice benefited her or not.

The Meaning Women Ascribe to Engaging in Surrogacy

Empirical studies on surrogacy indicate that women rationalize, or give meaning to, the choice to become surrogates by pointing to three different factors: anticipated psychological and emotional benefits, the prospect of financial gain, and family and community expectations.

Psychological and emotional benefits Surrogate mothers often explain their choices in connection with surrogacy as prompted by the prospect of a psychological and emotional benefit. Specifically, surrogates typically expect to develop: (1) a sense that they have engaged in a socially useful project, (2) a sense of accomplishment and identity, (3) enjoyment of pregnancy, or (4) a sense of restoring a prior loss. Each of these factors is discussed in turn.

Surrogates who express an interest in conferring a social benefit commonly describe themselves as having a desire, or "calling" to help childless couples experience parenthood (Busby and Vun 2010: 55-59, Avery 2002, Ruparelia 2007: 34), believing that their role demands "a special type of person" (van den Akker 2007: 55). In one surrogacy study, 91 percent of participants articulated a goal of assisting those who sought to become parents (Jadva et al. 2003: 2199). Empathy with the childless might be especially acute for surrogates who know infertile couples personally (Ragoné 1994: 60). Some may frame their mission as an equality project, referring to a desire to help gay men have children (Kashmeri 2008: 51-52).

Surrogates also commonly expect to derive a sense of accomplishment (Busby and Vun 2010: 57-58, van den Akker 2007: 56, Blyth 1994: 192) or "self-fulfillment" from surrogacy (Jadva et al. 2003: 2199). They might rationalize their choices on the basis of striving to succeed at something that would make them "feel good about themselves" (van den Akker 2003: 150). One surrogate described this view of surrogacy as a means to "do something interesting with [her] life" and feel valued (Blyth 1994: 192). Surrogacy may also be characterized as an episode of adventure, representing an opportunity to "put [one's] mundane life on hold" (Teman 2010: 264). Researchers hypothesize that women might seek to boost their self-esteem by becoming surrogates, perceiving this as a method of pushing and "transcending the limitations of their roles as wives, mothers and homemakers," even when they see these roles as important and gratifying (Ragoné 1996: 357). In a related vein, surrogates may develop a "heroic" persona (Ragoné 1996: 358), viewing themselves as essential to "making people's dreams come true" (Berend 2010: 245). Another researcher theorizes that surrogacy can offer a woman hope of some salvation from a "damaged sense of herself, perhaps linked to abandonment or abuse by a parent" (Kanefield 1999: 12). As discussed momentarily, the accomplishment and meaning women hope to draw from surrogacy signals that their engagement with the practice is best understood as a marker of citizenship and social contribution rather than as an altruistic undertaking, even when they are not remunerated.

Empirical research also documents the inherent enjoyment of pregnancy as a reason cited by women for choosing to become surrogates. Many surrogates report finding a surrogate pregnancy especially enjoyable since it occurs with knowledge that full responsibilities of parenthood will not ensue (Blyth 1994: 192, Jadva et al. 2003: 2199). Interest in pregnancy may also be linked to some women's sense that they are more attractive and more feminine when pregnant, or that pregnancy garners positive attention (Parker 1983: 118).

Last, the literature cites reparation for a past loss as a possible motivation for surrogate motherhood. Surrogates who reflected on this objective indicated an intention to make up for losses inflicted by previous miscarriages or terminated pregnancies, or by a decision to place a child for adoption (Kanefield 1999, Parker 1983: 118, van den Akker 2003: 150). For instance, one participant in a study on surrogacy motivations stated: "I feel guilty about my second abortion. I unconsciously said if I can find a way to pay that back, I would" (Kanefield 1999: 11). Another participant in a different study similarly commented, "I had two abortions. I had twins [surrogate pregnancy] which made up for the two abortions I'd had" (Hohman and Hagan 2001: 77). As explained more fully below, this sentiment may be anchored to a desire to acquire some control over a pregnancy. That is, while previously surrogates may have lacked the ability to carry a pregnancy to term and parent a child, for some women, surrogacy enables them to feel that they possess a firmer grip on processes and outcomes related to pregnancy (Kanefield 1999: 10). At least one scholar, however, has questioned the reparative element of surrogates' narratives, describing this as an attempt by researchers to infuse surrogates' experiences with "morally acceptable content" (Teman 2008: 1107).

Financial gain As discussed below, policy arguments objecting to surrogacy, especially paid surrogacy, commonly point to its potential to "commercialize" or "commodify" children and women's procreative abilities. This language focuses on surrogacy as an exchange of money for gestational services and ultimately, for a child.[1] It implies a perception of surrogacy as an opportunity for financial gain. Exceptionally, surrogates refer to money as the driving force behind their decisions about surrogacy (Einwohner 1989, Baslington 2002). More frequently, however, money is just one among a plurality of other equally or more significant influences (Parker 1983: 118). Most research thus suggests that remuneration is rarely the sole or primary motivator for taking up surrogacy (Busby and Vun 2010: 55, van den Akker 2007: 56, Blyth 1994: 191, Ragoné 1994, Parker 1983: 118). Surrogates typically do not perceive the sum they are paid as significant enough to serve as a pure incentive, noting that remuneration alone could not offset the emotional and physical stress of a pregnancy (Ragoné 1996: 354). One study reported several surrogates affirming the notion that "there are many easier ways to earn some money" (Kanefield 1999: 9-10, see also Ragoné 1996: 354-355, Blyth 1994: 192), although a respondent in a separate study described surrogacy as "an 'easy' way to gain a large sum" (Blyth 1994: 191). Other surrogates claimed that they would have acted "for free," and that surrogacy is "not a job. It's compassion alone" (Kanefield 1999: 10). Accordingly, surrogacy advocates and representatives stress that removing the commercial element from the practice would be unlikely to deter or change most surrogates' choices (Ragoné 1996: 354, 356).

While possibly not the sole or the most important motivator in most cases, money remains relevant for many women who engage in commercial surrogacy. The possibility of being remunerated while also being able, in most cases, to remain home with one's own children (Ragoné 1996: 355, Blyth 1994: 191) or to pursue one's current work or educational path can be an attraction (Gibson 1994: 403, Ragoné 1996: 355). This point is brought home by reports of a broad number of American military wives engaging in surrogacy as a means of gaining income while relocating frequently and living on bases with few employment opportunities (Kessler 2009, Ali 2008). The financial gain associated with becoming a surrogate can also open the door to pursuing educational opportunities that were not before present (Blyth 1994: 191).

Even women who do not see financial benefit as a principal incentive for surrogacy can justify receiving money for this service. Payment can be viewed as a reward to the surrogate and her family for the inconvenience inflicted by pregnancy (Ragoné 1996: 354-355, Kashmeri 2008: 42, Baslington 2002: 63). It can also be rationalized as reimbursement for the expenses, risks, discomfort, travel and lost earnings that might be associated with pregnancy (Blyth 1994: 192, Kashmeri 2008: 43). In a Canadian study, one surrogate likened her role to that of a childcare provider or babysitter, stating: "you would never take your kid to a

1 As indicated, surrogacy may be gratuitous, possibly allowing for the compensation of the surrogate's losses or expenses, or remunerated, that is, integrating a payment beyond such expenses or losses. Remuneration in the early to mid-1990s was reported to be between USD $10,000 and $15,000 (in today's dollars, roughly $15,000 to $22,500) (see Ragoné 1996: 354).

sitter and expect her to watch them for free. Would you? Nobody does anything for free. You don't do things for free" (Kashmeri 2008: 42). Money for surrogacy might also be perceived as a necessary element for allowing women to fulfill their goal of "gifting" a child to another couple (Levine 2003: 180-181, Ragoné 1996: 355). Finally, some women conceive of surrogacy as a "job." Even though most surrogates do not see payment as sufficient to offset surrogacy's inconvenience, risk and labour, viewing surrogacy as work rationalizes remuneration and facilitates emotional distancing from a surrogate pregnancy (Baslington 2002, Ragoné 1996: 356).

Having said all of this, it remains critical to bear in mind the cultural context of research on the relevance of economic gain to surrogates' choices. Stigma attached to receiving payment may affect the extent to which surrogates report money as a motivator. As noted, several researchers remark that surrogates' interview responses might aim to deliver socially palatable narratives about their motivations and experiences. This might explain, at least in part, the reduced weight their accounts give to money as a reason for becoming a surrogate. Where commercial surrogacy is permitted and facilitated by state law, such as in Israel, surrogates might present as "unapologetic, honest, and upfront about money being their primary goal in pursuing surrogacy," while simultaneously describing their choices as prompted by the same psychosocial benefits as those referred to by Western surrogates (Teman 2010: 23).

Family pressures and expectations Most surrogacy literature discussing surrogates' motivations focuses on the prospect of emotional and financial gain associated with this practice. A few studies, however, illuminate how surrogacy might be prompted by family pressure on a woman to provide a child for a relative facing fertility challenges. Ruparelia's (2007) work is illustrative. Although her study focuses on South Asian families, she indicates that family coercion might explain surrogacy in a range of cultural sites. The point is substantiated by literature documenting surrogacy practices involving kin in the West (Connell 2012; Kirkman and Kirkman 2002).[2] The risk of intra-familial pressure in any cultural or political setting thus cannot be discounted. Moreover, Ruparelia's (2007) work underscores that cases of "altruistic" or unremunerated surrogacy may be just as exploitative and morally problematic as some commercial surrogacy arrangements. This point is developed further in Part 3 below.

Moralistic presumptions about the virtues and vices of unpaid and paid surrogacy respectively raise crucial questions about why women would choose to become surrogates without monetary reward. For some, these suppositions reflect patriarchal expectations about what women should strive for and value. That is, they may be rooted in a perception that a noble woman will desire and enthusiastically assume the experiences of gestation, childbirth and mothering, even for another.

2 See also *Adoption – 09184*, involving surrogacy undertaken by an aunt for a niece with fertility challenges.

Where this expectation about maternity exists in a woman's family, it "may be so engulfing that, for all practical purposes, it exacts a reproductive donation from a female source" (Raymond 1990: 10). While subject to some critique (Baker 1996: 42ff.), the point hints at the potential for moral coercion anytime a surrogate knows the intending parents personally, and pressures may be most acute when a familial bond exists between them. It is worthwhile here to consider Israeli legislation, which prohibits surrogacy contracts between blood-related parties, as this is meant to avoid "potential pressure" on surrogates and "subsequent complications" in families (Benshushan and Schenker 1997: 1832).

These pressures illuminate the flaw in presuming the moral superiority of unpaid surrogacy. Economics aside, constraints on decision-making can exist in the form of family and community expectations, which may be sufficiently compelling to drive a woman to become a surrogate particularly if this facilitates retaining important social relationships. The point underlines the multiplicity of norms that might influence and limit choice, and the error in drawing direct equations between payment for surrogacy and coercion on one hand, and gratuitous surrogacy and agency on the other.

The Value Women Ascribe to Engaging in Surrogacy

While the foregoing discussion illuminates the way in which women who act as surrogates might explain, rationalize or give meaning to surrogacy, a second question pertains to the way in which surrogates value their experiences. This latter issue bears a normative dimension of analysis, investigating whether and how surrogates view this practice as enhancing their lives or wellbeing. Surrogates' evaluation of surrogacy is connected to the psychological and emotional outcomes they encounter. Put another way, the "good" derived from surrogacy seems to be strongly correlated to the degree to which a surrogate feels she benefited psychologically and emotionally from this experience. Three particular outcomes seem to wield the greatest influence over surrogates' assessments of their experiences: control over reproduction and maternity, the development of a sense of social contribution and citizenship, and social connections formed with intending parents.

Control over reproduction and maternity Surrogacy is socially and legally understood as twisting natural paths to reproduction and parentage. Surrogates counter this perception by developing narratives that normalize and purify their involvement in surrogacy (Teman 2003: 81). This is accomplished by distinguishing between artificial and natural pregnancy and motherhood, with surrogacy falling into the former category. Surrogates and intending mothers thus may talk about surrogacy as a means of "fooling God" or "fooling nature" (Teman 2003: 89-90). Such rhetoric suggests a sense of surrogacy as a nearly supernatural phenomenon over which surrogates have control, a view that can empower the surrogate even when intending parents cast her as marginal to the reproductive process (Goslinga-Roy 2000). Surrogacy commentators and critics suggest concern about surrogates' "self-alienation" (Gibson 1994: 412) and bodily objectification, noting the disquieting descriptors, such as "hotel"[3] and "incubator," often used to characterize surrogate mothers (van Niekirk and van Zyl 1995: 347). Yet surrogates can appropriate this imagery to make sense of and give a particular purpose to their pregnancies (Kuczynski 2008). Moreover, appreciating their pregnancies as "outside nature" facilitates the acquisition of control over a pregnancy and reinforces emotional disconnection from and "unrelatedness" to the children they carry (Goslinga-Roy 2000: 117-118, Teman 2003: 87). It can further allow the surrogate to create metaphysical distance from her own body during pregnancy and delivery (Phillips 2011: 730). Such attempts to separate one's capacities from one's physical self clearly raise pragmatic and political difficulties. Most obviously they imply that the body can be treated as a detached thing or as property (Pateman 2002: 33; Phillips 2011: 731). Some may view this mode of conceptualization as a means through which surrogates suppress intuitive maternal sentiments (Tieu 2009: 173-174). Just the same, their narratives indicate that a central factor grounding the value many surrogates ascribe to their experiences pertains to control over their pregnancies, which facilitates and substantiates the moral propriety of relinquishing a child to intending parents.

Accordingly, the construal of a surrogate pregnancy as a mechanical process, while often critiqued for demeaning women, may serve surrogates and allow them to derive psychological gain from their experiences. Perceiving themselves as agents who make possible the goal of having children, but not as parents themselves, surrogates can rationalize and extract personal value from their role. This benefit would likely be unrealizable if their understanding of surrogacy were embedded in the usual pregnancy narrative characterized by natural emotion and attachment. A natural–artificial pregnancy binary thus makes sense of a practice that is otherwise "transgressive" for women and mothers (Teman 2003: 81). It also gives women a sense that they are in control of their bodies and their experiences, allowing for reproduction where "naturally" this was not possible. Surrogates may consequently prize this practice on the ground that it enables maternity and parenthood where otherwise, there would be infertility (Gibson 1994: 404-405).

Social contribution and citizenship As indicated, most surrogates rationalize their choices in altruistic terms: they seek to render parenthood possible for those who would otherwise be childless. They may therefore derive satisfaction from using their reproductive capacity to bestow a "gift" on other families (Berend 2010). The lexicon of contribution and gifting are prominent in surrogates' narratives. However, the distinctions between these terms bear attention, even though they are commonly conflated in surrogacy research. The language of contribution-making is more appropriately associated, at least for the purposes of the present

3 Austl, Tasmania, House of Assembly, *Parliamentary Debates* (12 April 2011) (Ms Petrusma).

discussion, with conceptions of citizenship and social belonging, whereas that of gift-giving is tethered to moral norms of altruism and selflessness. It is argued here that surrogacy, whether undertaken for payment or not, should be understood as a contribution rather than a selfless act of giving.

Properly understood, a gift is purely "unconditional" and "unrequited"; there is no *quid pro quo* (Shaw 2008: 17). Surrogacy, however, happens in the context of a relationship where the surrogate—even when unpaid—almost consistently acknowledges that she gets something in return for her services, be it money or not. More specifically, surrogacy is not a project that the surrogate undertakes entirely selflessly for the intending couple. Rather, it is more accurately viewed as a project of self-governance, which allows the surrogate to define, at least in part, her identity and her social relevance (Shaw 2008: 22). These conceptions emerge in surrogates' discussions about their desire to do something "interesting" (Blyth 1994: 192), "transcending" their ordinary or everyday lives (Ragoné 1996: 352, Teman 2010: 264).

In this way, the decision to become a surrogate seems to square more readily with the notion of a social contribution than a private gift to the intending parents. It not only allows the latter to overcome childlessness, it also stakes out the surrogate's place and role within a community and allows her to complete a "mission" or "big achievement" that bears social value. As such, surrogacy is framed by a citizenship norm that encourages the definition of self-identity, self-management and meaningful modes of social engagement (Teman 2009, Shaw 2008: 19-20). This process can lead to claiming a broad sense of social membership or it might solidify a woman's commitment to and place within her family or her cultural community. Thus, where a cultural group places a high premium on procreation and childbirth, surrogates who facilitate that end may be viewed as making a particularly valuable collective contribution. The same situation might arise within families. While intra-familial surrogacy might expose women to risk (Ruparelia 2007: 13), some surrogates who assist relatives see their undertaking as cementing family relationships and improving outcomes for both their immediate and extended families. The following remarks of a woman who acted as her sister's surrogate offer insight in this respect:

> My children wanted siblings, which they were not going to get. Two children were all Jim and I planned to have. A cousin was the next best thing. … The accolades I have received have been fantastic and I have loved receiving them, but that is not why I undertook to gestate Alice. It was the right thing for me to do. There was a place for Alice in our family and I was able to facilitate her taking that place. (Kirkman and Kirkman 2002: 139)

This norm of citizenship that may give value to the choice to become a surrogate also comes to light through references to corrective justice and responsibility that infiltrate their narratives (Weinrib 1992). As noted earlier, for some women, service as a surrogate permits the righting of past pregnancy-related decisions viewed in hindsight as morally flawed, such as terminating a pregnancy or placing a child for adoption. An effort to restore or repay this past loss or injury suggests a sense of social responsibility integral to the essence of citizenship (Campbell et al. 2011). As a corollary to this premise, surrogates might also benefit from surrogacy as a way to reciprocate or pay forward "in kind" their own ability to conceive biologically (Goslinga-Roy 2000: 120-121).

Social connections The quality and tenor of a surrogate's relationship with intending parents, both before and after delivery, will have a significant influence on how she evaluates her surrogacy experience (Ciccarelli and Beckman 2005: 32). Most surrogates expect some post-delivery contact (van den Akker 2007: 57). This may link to surrogates' perception of their investment in the surrogacy process, which emphasizes connection and relationship to the family they helped to create over their instrumental role in reproduction (Goslinga-Roy 2000). Surrogates thus report favourably on their experiences where a positive relationship exists, especially where the parties have common expectations about their respective roles and responsibilities during and following the surrogate's pregnancy (Hohman and Hagan 2001: 44-49). Where surrogates have minimal or no contact with the child or intending parents after birth, they appear to be more likely to face psychological difficulties (van den Akker 2007: 59, Goslinga-Roy 2000: 133-134) and reflect on their experience with dissatisfaction (Ciccarelli and Beckman 2005: 33). This view is supported by at least one study that records some postpartum depression immediately following the surrogate's delivery and "handover" of a child to intending parents (Jadva et al. 2003: 2203, but contrast with van den Akker 2007). In another study, surrogates reported disappointment when intending parents lose touch despite promises to remain in contact (Reame et al. 1998, Ciccarelli and Beckman 2005: 33). Other surrogates fantasized about being reunited with the child they had delivered to the intending parents (Kleinpeter and Hohman 2000: 959). Thus, while many women may reflect fondly on their surrogacy experiences (Ciccarelli 1997) and would repeat the experience if given the chance (van den Akker 2007: 56), others encounter regret or unhappiness where expectations of a postpartum relationship with intending parents and child go unfulfilled.

Surrogacy's value may also be illuminated by an alternate interpretation of loss and regret. Most surrogates recognize the risks that inhere to pregnancy, yet "readily embrace the idea of meaningful suffering, heroism, or sacrifice" (Ragoné 1996: 354). Nevertheless, a surrogate's inability to conceive, miscarriage or stillbirth can engender disappointment, grief and potentially a sense of failure. While these sentiments are, for many, linked to mourning for a lost fetus, they are also connected to an effort to identify with the intending parents' grief, given that they are likely to have bonded more intensely with the "couple they carry for" than with the fetus (Berend 2010: 243-244). For some women, this is translated into a sense of having betrayed the intending parents' trust. Surrogates may recount their experiences following failed conception, miscarriage or stillbirth as a "failure to deliver the promised gift" or as "letting down" the intending parents. These accounts also illuminate surrogates' investment in the idea of contributing to the "dream" (Berend 2010: 245) or "miracle" (Berend 2010: 257) of parenthood. Failed conception and fetal loss will detract from each of the factors identified here as lending value to the practice of surrogacy. That is, not only will such an experience tend to erode relationships with intending parents, it might also challenge the surrogate's sense of identity, contribution and control.

Ultimately, the value surrogates ascribe to their decisions about surrogacy is marked primarily by the way this experience fosters social presence and connection. Surrogates' satisfaction with their experiences appears most pronounced when they appreciate the project as cultivating their own sense of self and of citizenship through a process that they see themselves as directing. Moreover, their evaluations of surrogacy rise when expectations about the social relationships surrogacy will afford play out in the lived reality of their rapports with intending parents and the children produced through the surrogacy arrangement.

Empirical research highlights that surrogates' motivations relate primarily to anticipated psychosocial benefits, and to the financial prospects this practice might offer. Family pressures also are a factor to be accounted for in some cases. Surrogates' descriptions of how they value surrogacy, that is, how they normatively assess their experiences with this practice, indicate that the development of a sense of control, social contribution and social connection are imperative to positive outcomes. These points differ starkly from the perception of surrogacy offered by formal regulatory frameworks created by the state. The discussion now turns to a contemplation of these frameworks as developed in Canada, the United Kingdom and Australia.

Part 2: State Law's Approach to Surrogacy in Canada, the United Kingdom and Australia

This part surveys legislative developments in place in the three jurisdictions under study in this book. Along with Part 1, it sets the groundwork for a critical assessment of state law governing surrogacy. Specifically, it allows for contrasting presumptions about surrogates' choices that course through legal and political discourse with the lived experiences of these women as recorded through empirical study.

Canada

Canada's *Assisted Human Reproduction Act* (AHRA), which received royal assent in March 2004, was drafted in response to concerns raised over a decade earlier in the Royal Commission on New Reproductive Technologies' (Royal Commission)

1993 Report, *Proceed with Care* (Apold 2005: 32).[4] After four years of gathering information on activities related to assisted human reproduction in Canada, the Royal Commission recommended that the federal Parliament take action to ban a number of practices, including payment for surrogacy (Burpee 2009: 325).[5] This recommendation stood in contrast to conclusions drawn by Ontario's Law Reform Commission (OLRC) nearly a decade earlier.[6] The OLRC, which was the first Canadian policy body to study surrogacy, concluded that regulation rather than prohibition would most viably protect the interests of those affected by this practice, notably children conceived through surrogacy (Serratelli 1993: 660). Although the OLRC's report received academic support (Menon 2009: 135, Shewchuk 1993: 157-158), the Royal Commission took an alternate stand on surrogacy. It concluded that the practice in its commercial form merited criminal proscription.[7] It further recommended that all surrogacy contracts be considered null and void and that brokering such an agreement be deemed a criminal offence.[8]

A first bill crafted to address these conclusions died on the Order Paper in 1997 (Bill C-47 1996, Apold 2005: 36). In 2001, Canada's Health Minister again presented draft legislation to the House of Commons' Standing Committee on Health, which in turn submitted recommendations in December of that same year. As several commentators have noted, this process of consultation and debate from 2001 onward led to a more tempered and less "sanctimonious" or "paternalistic" version of the bill on assisted reproduction (Harvison Young 2005: 125, Caulfield 2002: 451, Kashmeri 2008: 23). Bill C-56, introduced in 2002 and later named Bill C-13 represented a shift in public and social sentiment regarding assisted reproductive technologies from fear and skepticism to recognition of their utility and possible benefit (Menon 2009: 13-15, Harvison Young 2005: 128). The Bill passed second and third readings in the House of Commons in 2003.[9] In March 2004 the proposed legislation, by then called Bill C-6, *An Act Respecting Assisted*

4 Canada, Royal Commission on New Reproductive Technologies, *Proceed with Care: Final Report of the Royal Commission on New Reproductive Technologies* (Ottawa: Minister of Government Services, 1993); Canada, House of Commons, Standing Committee on Health, *Assisted Human Reproduction: Building Families* (December 2001) (Chair: Bonnie Brown).

5 Canada, Royal Commission on New Reproductive Technologies, *Proceed with Care: Final Report of the Royal Commission on New Reproductive Technologies* (Ottawa: Minister of Government Services, 1993) at 689-690.

6 Canada, Ontario, Ontario Law Reform Commission, *Report on Human Artificial Reproduction and Related Matters* (Toronto: Ontario Law Reform Commission, 1985).

7 Canada, Royal Commission on New Reproductive Technologies, *Proceed with Care: Final Report of the Royal Commission on New Reproductive Technologies* (Ottawa: Minister of Government Services, 1993) at 683.

8 Canada, Law Reform Commission of Canada, *Working Paper 65* (Ottawa: Minister of Supply and Services Canada, 1992) at 135.

9 Second reading in the House of Commons took place on 9 October 2002. Third reading in the House of Commons took place on 28 October 2003.

Human Reproduction and Related Research, passed through Senate and received royal assent.

Legislative debates surrounding the development of the AHRA illuminate two key objectives driving Canada's juridical treatment of surrogacy. A first is to protect Canadians from the perceived harms of commercial surrogacy; a second is to support Canadians in their choices about building families (Kashmeri 2008: 30-31). The AHRA seeks to achieve these objectives in part by distinguishing commercial from gratuitous surrogacy. The AHRA bans payment for remunerated or "commercial" surrogacy and for its arrangement (s. 6). It excludes unpaid agreements from prohibition, and allows surrogates to be reimbursed for surrogacy-related expenditures and, under certain conditions, work-related income losses related to surrogacy (s. 12). Such reimbursements must be made "in accordance with the regulations and a license," but this provision is not in force and regulations pertaining to it have not yet been promulgated. This renders the juridical status of reimbursed surrogacy arrangements precarious and unpredictable. Theoretically, remunerated surrogacy contracts are punishable by a criminal sanction (s. 6) while gratuitous arrangements that include reimbursements to a surrogate for relevant expenses are excluded from the AHRA's ambit. Yet distinguishing "remunerated" from "reimbursed" surrogacy can prove challenging, and the absence of a regulatory scheme delineating the nature and scope of surrogacy costs subject to compensation renders it impossible to determine whether a surrogacy arrangement is criminal or not (Menon 2009: 19-20, Kashmeri 2008: 26ff., Blackwell 2009, Gazze 2007, Anonymous 2008c). As discussed below, a vacuous legislative framework impedes meaningful choices about contentious social practices like surrogacy.

An even more prominent academic controversy has circulated around the federal government's jurisdiction over surrogacy in Canada. Debates on whether Parliament's efforts to legislate in the domain of assisted procreation are *ultra vires* surfaced even before the AHRA was enacted (Harvison Young and Wasunna 1998, Caulfield 2002, Campbell 2002, Healy 1995). Critics argued that Parliament was relying on its criminal law power (*Constitution Act 1867*: s. 91(27)) disingenuously to appropriate jurisdiction over assisted procreation matters, which ordinarily would be governed by the individual Canadian provinces and territories (*Constitution Act 1867*: s. 92(13)). Ultimately, Quebec referred the matter to the judiciary through a constitutional reference. While the Supreme Court of Canada found that Parliament had encroached upon provincial competence with regard to certain AHRA provisions, it affirmed that prohibiting payment for surrogacy fell properly within federal jurisdiction over criminal law matters (*Reference re Assisted Human Reproduction Act*).

The AHRA's criminalization of the commercial dimension of surrogacy allows Canada's provinces and territories to regulate the private law aspects of the practice, notably, issues of filiation and the enforcement of non-commercialized arrangements. Most provincial and territorial governments have not established explicit regimes, although three provinces have crafted legislative provisions aimed at determining filiation in surrogacy contexts.[10] This legislation has not given rise to reported jurisprudence; throughout common law Canada, most litigation on surrogacy focuses on matters of birth registration and whether and how to avoid naming the surrogate as the child's mother on the latter's birth registration (see e.g., *Rypkema v. H.M.T.Q.*, *W.J.Q.M. v. A.M.A.*, *J.R. v. L.H.*, *Re M.D.* See also Burpee 2009: 330, Apold 2005: 41).

By contrast, Quebec, which is Canada's sole province governed by a civil law tradition, takes a distinct approach to this issue, refusing to recognize any agreement for surrogacy services. The *Civil Code of Québec*'s (CCQ) provision establishing the unenforceability of such agreements makes no exception for gratuitous surrogacy contracts. Article 541 provides that "[a]ny agreement whereby a woman undertakes to procreate or carry a child for another person is absolutely null." Articulated in the language of absolute nullity, article 541 CCQ differs from its original phrasing established in 1994 and enduring until 2002: "Procreation and gestation agreements on behalf of another person are null."[11] The insistence on the absolute nature of the nullity signals that surrogacy—whether for payment or gratuitous—violates public order (Giroux 1997: 539) and that a declaration of nullity protects a general social, rather than private, interest (Baudouin et al. 2005: no 400). Characterizing such contracts as absolutely null further conveys a legislative perception of the contract as having an illegal object (Baudouin et al. 2005: no 423). In the surrogacy context, the perception is rooted in the exclusion of certain objects or services, particularly those involving the human body, from commercialization (Giroux 1997: 537, 539).

While Quebec's legislative scheme on surrogacy suggests a refutation of the practice, surrogacy arrangements are formed and executed within the province. Provided there is no payment, such an agreement is not illegal. However, a difficulty arises if a party contests the agreement, given its unenforceable nature. Challenges also arise with respect to birth registration, given that a birth mother is ordinarily recorded on a newborn child's act of birth as the legal mother. The sole method for the intending mother to replace the surrogate on the birth registration is via adoption. Normally, adoption in Quebec is initiated by the state through youth protection, however, a "special consent" provision in the *Civil Code* allows a parent to give consent to a child's adoption by particular relatives, one of whom is a married or *de facto* union spouse (Article 555). Several special consent adoption applications arising from surrogacy arrangements have proceeded before Quebec

10 Alberta: *Family Law Act*, s. 8.2; Nova Scotia: *Birth Registration Regulations made under Section 51 of the Vital Statistics Act*; and Newfoundland and Labrador: *Vital Statistics Act*, s. 5(6). Note that Newfoundland and Labrador's *Child and Parental Benefits Regulations* in section 9 also suggests some recognition of parentage that occurs through surrogacy arrangements.

11 Article 541 CCQ was implemented pursuant to *Projet de loi no. 84—Loi Instituant l'union civile et* établissant *de nouvelles règles de filiation*, Assemblée Nationale, trente-sixième législature, deuxième session, 2002, art 27.

courts since 2009. These have been initiated by the man registered as the child's legal father and have sought adoption by his spouse on his "special consent" and on consent of the surrogate.

The earliest of this series of cases held that using the *Civil Code*'s special consent adoption provision amounted to a "misappropriation" ("détournement") of this juridical vehicle. Here, Dubois J. seemed particularly perturbed by the exchange of money that had taken place between the parties and by the fact that the surrogate withheld her name from the child's birth registration (*Adoption – 091*). Subsequent judgments on special consent adoption applications exhibit greater openness to the use of this regime in surrogacy contexts. These judgments emphasize that granting the adoption application would, in each case, serve the child's best interests (*Adoption – 09184*, *Adoption – 09367*, Giroux 2011). At least one court has held that such interests should prevail, since the absolute nullity of surrogacy arrangements should affect only the contracting parties without prejudice to the children concerned (*Adoption – 09367*: para. 23). In a related vein, a court may view adoption to be especially appropriate where the intending mother is also the genetic mother, as adoption would grant the child a "true maternal filiation" and would permit that filiation to mirror the child's "reality" (*Adoption – 10329*: para. 24). Moreover, the fact that the *Civil Code* does not explicitly preclude adoption by special consent in surrogacy cases may be interpreted as giving courts latitude to grant such applications (Giroux 1997: 544, 546).

Consequently, surrogacy in Canada becomes a legal preoccupation generally when it is practiced for payment. Federal legislation prohibits remuneration for and brokering of surrogacy agreements. Beyond this, the individual provinces and territories are left to determine for themselves how, if at all, to regulate such arrangements. As noted, most provincial and territorial governments in Canada are silent on the matter. Three provinces have enacted legislative provisions to address determinations of filiation in surrogacy contexts, but by and large, the issue has not been controversial in common law Canada. By contrast, Quebec's juridical approach to surrogacy raises more nuanced questions given the apparent incompatibility between the unenforceability of surrogacy contracts and jurisprudence accepting adoption applications brought forward by parties open about their engagement in surrogacy. As discussed in Part 3 of this chapter, such questions pertain to state law's effects on women's choices about intimacy and reproduction. Prior to engaging in that analysis, however, the discussion turns to an examination of British and Australian legal approaches to surrogacy.

The United Kingdom

As in Canada, British legislation regulating surrogacy was implemented following considerable parliamentary debate and a series of publically commissioned inquiries. In the United Kingdom, however, public attention to surrogacy frequently has been drawn by high-profile judicial disputes highlighting surrogacy's moral ambiguity and the problems arising from legislative silence in this area. The discussion below traces the development of three statutes governing surrogacy: the *Surrogacy Arrangements Act 1985*, the *Human Fertilisation and Embryology Act 1990* and the *Human Fertilisation and Embryology Act 2008*.

The *Surrogacy Arrangements Act 1985* was enacted primarily in reaction to the "Baby Cotton" case (*Re C. (A Minor) (Wardship: Surrogacy)*). The matter arose from reports that a woman was paid £6,500 to serve as a surrogate for a child conceived using her own ova and the sperm of a man whose wife could not conceive. All parties consented to the arrangement and Baby Cotton, as she was known in the press, would have been transferred without conflict to the intending parents but for the intervention of Scotland Yard (Anonymous 2012c). The child was made a ward of the state, with the court ultimately granting the care and custody of the child to the intending parents. In rendering judgment, Justice Latey stressed that "the well-being of children is of paramount importance" and thus commercial aspects of the transaction would have no bearing on the court's wardship jurisdiction (*Re C. (A Minor) (Wardship: Surrogacy)*: 849). The Baby Cotton case sparked a rush to legislate on surrogacy, with the enactment of the *Surrogacy Arrangements Act 1985* occurring within just six months of Justice Latey's ruling.

Even before the Baby Cotton affair became a matter of public concern, however, surrogacy had been the subject of political and legal attention. In 1978, the Court of Appeal rendered the first surrogacy decision in the common law (Stuhmcke 2004: 19). *A. v. C.* (1978) involved a 19-year-old surrogate who refused to relinquish a baby conceived through a commercial surrogacy arrangement. In denying the intending father's application for access, the judges seized of the matter expressed vehement opposition to surrogacy. The arrangement was characterized as "bizarre and unnatural," a "sordid commercial bargain" crafted by individuals with "very grave defects" of character (455), an "unusual, unattractive type of transaction" tantamount to "baby-farming" (459-460), and an "ugly little drama" (461).

Four years later, a Committee of Inquiry into Human Fertilisation and Embryology ("HFE Committee") was convened to study the legal, social and ethical implications of assisted reproduction, including surrogacy. The HFE Committee's report (the "Warnock Report"), underscored the social and moral dilemmas that surrogacy presented. Drafted against the backdrop of *A. v. C.*'s unequivocally harsh stance on surrogacy and a general climate of "conservative morality," the Report was unsurprisingly oriented toward the proscription of the practice (Gamble and Ghevaert 2009a: 223). The HFE Committee recommended legislation criminalizing surrogacy, targeting third parties and surrogacy agencies but not the surrogate herself. On the latter point, the Committee articulated an interest in "avoid[ing] children being born to mothers subject to a 'taint of criminality'" (Horsey and Sheldon 2012: 70). It further advised against regulating surrogacy, expressing a concern that this would encourage the expansion of the practice.[12] The HFE Committee was not, however, unanimous on these points. A dissenting opinion recommended that surrogacy be permitted as a last resort measure for childless couples, and that the practice be scrupulously regulated to safeguard participants' interests.[13]

Although the Warnock Report was the fruit of extensive public inquiry, as indicated, it was the notorious Baby Cotton case of 1985 that proved to be the central catalyst for Britain's first regulatory initiative regarding surrogacy (Serratelli 1993: 641),[14] the *Surrogacy Arrangements Act 1985* (SAA). The SAA prohibits the commercial arrangement of surrogacy, targeting surrogacy agencies and brokers while excluding the main parties to the surrogacy arrangement (the surrogate and intending parents) from the prohibition (Horsey and Sheldon 2012: 70, Apold 2005: 52). The SAA leaves private surrogacy contracts unregulated, remaining silent as to their legality and enforceability (Serratelli 1993: 643). During debates over this statute's drafting, some argued that it was insufficiently comprehensive, remaining silent on gratuitous surrogacy and prohibiting only the criminalization of surrogacy brokering.[15]

Once enacted, the SAA banned commercial negotiations aimed at the formation of a surrogacy arrangement, information-gathering for negotiating or concluding surrogacy arrangements, acts that would cause another to engage in such conduct, and advertising in relation to surrogacy (ss. 2(1), 2(3), 3). The statute did not prohibit private payments from intending parents to surrogates. While the United Kingdom's *Adoption Act 1976* prohibits payment or reward for adoption (s. 57(1)), judicial decisions rendered after the SAA's enactment reflect a willingness to give effect to surrogacy arrangements achieved through adoption, even where consideration was paid to a surrogate (*Re an adoption application (surrogacy)*) or where she was promised payment but withheld her consent to the adoption (*Re MW (Adoption: Surrogacy)*). In this respect, courts stressed the relevance of giving effect to children's best interests without undue emphasis on surrogacy's moral implications and challenges (Stuhmcke 2004).

---

12 UK, HC, "Report of the Committee of Inquiry into Human Fertilisation and Embryology," Cm 9314 in *Sessional Papers* (1984) 1 at 47.

13 UK, HC, "Report of the Committee of Inquiry into Human Fertilisation and Embryology," Cm 9314 in *Sessional Papers* (1984) 1 at 87-88.

14 But see comments of Earl of Caithness, who argued that the Bill was not the result of the Baby Cotton case, but that the government had been concerned for a long time about commercial surrogacy: UK, HL, *Parliamentary Debates*, vol 464, col 1535 (14 June 1985); UK, HL, *Parliamentary Debates*, vol 465, col 925 (28 June 1985).

15 UK, HC, *Parliamentary Debates*, vol 77, col 27 (15 April 1985) (Mr Frank Field); col 28 (Michael Meacher); col 32 (Sir Bernard Braine); col 25 (Peter Bruinvels); col 41 (John Butterfill); UK, HL, *Parliamentary Debates*, vol 464, col 1533 (14 June 1985) (Viscount Sidmouth); UK, HL, *Parliamentary Debates*, vol 464, col 1534 (14 June 1985) (Viscount Brentford); UK, HL, *Parliamentary Debates*, vol 464, col 1532 (14 June 1985) (Viscount Sidmouth).

The SAA's silence on the general enforceability of surrogacy contracts attracted scholarly criticism echoing concerns that had been raised by members of Parliament during legislative debates (Morgan 1986: 365, Harding, L.M. 1987: 52, Sloman 1985: 978, Baggish 1989: 226-227). Public criticism reemerged also in the House of Lords in the form of a *Surrogacy Arrangements (Amendment) Bill*, introduced within months of the SAA's coming into force.[16] The proposed amendments would have addressed surrogacy concerns not covered by the SAA. Although the bill passed third reading, it was not debated in the House of Commons given that, by this time, the British government had reopened the issue of surrogacy's regulation. Specifically, in 1986, it determined a need for more detailed consultations on all matters of human fertilization and embryology. Such consultations resulted in a White Paper published in November 1987, which set out proposals for new legislation.[17] Contemplating the regulation of assisted reproduction in general, the White Paper adopted what it esteemed to be a critical proposal within the *Surrogacy Arrangements (Amendment) Bill*[18] and concluded that all surrogacy contracts should be deemed unenforceable. Yet the White Paper also advised against the criminalization of any aspect of surrogacy, save for the operation of commercial agencies, maintaining that this would run counter to children's best interests.[19]

This White Paper served as a precursor to the *Human Fertilisation and Embryology Bill*, introduced in the House of Lords in November 1989.[20] This draft legislation spurred fiery debates around a host of issues related to genetic science and assisted reproduction, within which surrogacy figured with less prominence than it had in discussions prior to the SAA's enactment in 1985. The bill was passed as the *Human Fertilisation and Embryology Act 1990* (HFEA 1990), which introduced the "parental order," a judicial order made on application recognizing the intending parents' filial connection to a child conceived by surrogacy (s. 54 [1990: s. 30]).[21] The statute stipulated a number of criteria pertaining to factors such as marital status, residency and a genetic connection to the child for a parental order application to succeed (s. 54(1)-(4) [1990: s. 30(1)-(4)]). It further

16 UK, HL, *Parliamentary Debates*, vol 468, col 978 (28 November 1985) (Earl of Halsbury).

17 UK, HC, "Human Fertilisation and Embryology: A Framework for Legislation," Cm 259 (1987) 1 at 1.

18 UK, HL, *Parliamentary Debates*, vol 491, col 1454 (15 January 1988) (Lord Skelmersdale).

19 UK, HC, "Human Fertilisation and Embryology: A Framework for Legislation," Cm 259 (1987) 1 at 12.

20 UK, HL, *Parliamentary Debates*, vol 513, col 21 (22 November 1989) (Lord Mackay of Clashfern); UK, HL, *Parliamentary Debates*, vol 513, col 1003 (7 December 1989) (Lord Mackay of Clashfern).

21 The HFEA 1990 was ultimately updated by the HFEA 2008. References are thus to the current provisions in the HFEA, with the corresponding provisions to the 1990 statute in square parentheses.

required that the surrogate and, if applicable, her spouse consent to the order (s. 54(6) [1990: s. 30(5)]), and that there have been no financial exchange save for the reimbursement of reasonable expenses (s. 54(8) [1990: s. 30(7)]). The HFEA 1990 deemed the surrogate the mother of a child conceived by surrogacy, with full parental rights and obligations, unless and until a parental order was issued (s. 33(1) [1990: s. 27(1)]). Finally, this statute stipulated the unenforceability of surrogacy agreements through an amendment to the SAA of 1985 (s. 1A, HFEA 1990: s. 36(1)).

The creation of the parental order within the HFEA was—much like the SAA—prompted primarily by a highly publicized judicial ruling that arguably triggered undue legislative "panic" (Freeman 1989: 165, Freeman 1999, Anderson 2010: 42). The case in question involved intending parents who used their own genetic material to conceive twins carried and delivered by a surrogate. As their parentage under existing law could be recognized only through adoption, the intending parents petitioned their Member of Parliament in regard to this matter. The latter proposed an amendment to the Solicitor-General that would recognize married couples' filiation by surrogacy without requiring adoption proceedings.[22] This amendment to the proposed bill, which resulted in the articulation of parental orders at section 30 of the HFEA 1990, came into force only in 1994.[23]

In 1997, a "Review Team" was commissioned to consider the propriety of payment to surrogates (without considering the potential for third parties to profit) and whether the practice should be publically regulated.[24] The Review Team's inquiry, while arguably limited to exclude the "cornerstones" of the existent surrogacy regulatory regime (non-enforceable contracts, prohibited commercialization) (Horsey and Sheldon 2012: 71), culminated in the Brazier Report, after the name of its chairman, Professor Margaret Brazier. The Report emphasized that payment to surrogates did not in itself amount to exploitation,[25] but it warned against full commercialization of the practice given its "unknown degree of psychological risk."[26] While the Report resisted the outright prohibition of surrogacy, it identified a series of "unacceptable" potential outcomes to women, children and society in general should payment for gestational services be permitted. In the result, the Brazier Report recommended limiting surrogates'

22 UK, HC, *Parliamentary Debates*, vol 248, col 972 (26 October 1994) (Michael Jopling).

23 UK, HL, *Parliamentary Debates*, vol 558, col 626 (26 October 1994) (Lord Fraser of Carmyllie).

24 UK, HC, "Review for Health Ministers of Current Arrangements for Payments and Regulation," Cm 4068 (1998) 1 at i, 1, 2.

25 UK, HC, "Review for Health Ministers of Current Arrangements for Payments and Regulation," Cm 4068 (1998) 1 at 35.

26 UK, HC, "Review for Health Ministers of Current Arrangements for Payments and Regulation," Cm 4068 (1998) 1 at 35-36.

payment to expenses generated directly by their surrogate pregnancies, and called for tighter regulation of surrogacy.[27]

The Brazier Report's recommendations were never fully enacted and some argue that the challenges it identified persist (Horsey and Sheldon 2012: 68). Nevertheless, some minor amendments to surrogacy regulations occurred in the Report's wake through a *Human Fertilisation and Embryology Bill* introduced in November 2007. This proposed legislation aimed to modernize regulatory approaches to assisted reproduction; surrogacy was a minor focus. The Bill culminated in the *Human Fertilisation and Embryology Act 2008* (HFEA 2008). The HFEA 2008's minimal attention to surrogacy was criticized as offering insufficient protection to women and children (Horsey and Sheldon 2012: 76).[28] The statute did, however, affirm that a surrogate would be considered a child's mother unless a parental order was issued. It also recognized that civil and cohabiting partners could, like married spouses, apply for parental orders (s. 54(2)(b)(c)), whereas single persons were not so entitled (Gamble and Ghavaert 2009b: 731). Finally, the HFEA 2008 reflected ongoing resistance to commercial surrogacy, stipulating that intermediaries between intending parents and surrogates could not operate on a for-profit basis (s. 59(4), SAA 1985: ss. 2A(b), 2C, Gamble 2009: 58).

In a manner that reflects a trend in Quebec's contemporary jurisprudence on surrogacy, judicial decisions in the United Kingdom evince courts' discomfort with giving effect to public policy in a way that would adversely affect children's interests. Where this tension emerges, courts have shown themselves willing, albeit with some hesitance, to give effect to surrogacy arrangements that fall on or outside the margins of what is legally permissible. Such outcomes are rationalized by an effort to protect the needs and interests of the children concerned (*Re: X. & Y. (Foreign Surrogacy)*, *Re S. (Parental Order)*, *Re: L. (a minor)*, *Re an adoption application (surrogacy)*, *Re M.W. (Adoption: Surrogacy)*, Gamble and Ghevaert 2009a: 226, Theis et al. 2009, Horsey and Sheldon 2012: 78ff., Griffith 2011: 258.). These results might be compared with a recent British Child Support Agency determination that a surrogate who decided, before birth, that she would keep the child could not be ordered to honour the terms of a surrogacy agreement. The agency further ordered the intending father, also a genetic parent, to pay maintenance for the child (Eccles 2011, Pearce 2011).

In view of the foregoing, some parallels in the Canadian and British approaches to surrogacy are evident. In both jurisdictions, commercialization and the risk of exploiting surrogates have been central, resulting in a legislative framework that aims to restrict payments to surrogates to "reasonable" disbursements and costs while seeking also to proscribe the brokering and facilitating of surrogacy

27 UK, HC, "Review for Health Ministers of Current Arrangements for Payments and Regulation," Cm 4068 (1998) 1 at i, 40, 46.

28 UK, HC/HL, Joint Committee on the Human Tissue and Embryos (Draft) Bill, "Human Tissues and Embryo (Draft) Bill," HL Paper 169-I/HC Paper 630-I, vol 1 (2007) at para. 289.

arrangements for profit. Distinctions in the jurisdictions' approaches also exist. Most notably, although British legislation sets parameters for determining the filiation of children produced via surrogacy—albeit in a way that has been criticized (Horsey 2010)—the Canadian AHRA could not cover this issue, which falls to the competence of individual provincial and territorial governments. Moreover, criminal law's target in these jurisdictions differs: in Canada the focus is intending parents and brokers whereas this is restricted to intermediaries in the United Kingdom.

Australia

Australia's governance of surrogacy occurs at the state and territorial level.[29] The Commonwealth (federal) Parliament plays a limited role in legislating on surrogacy and assisted reproductive technologies as all pertinent heads of power (health, criminal law and parentage) are excluded from its jurisdictional competence (Snow and Knopff 2012: 15).[30] To prevent forum shopping within the country, some efforts have been undertaken to craft federal surrogacy legislation or to harmonize surrogacy's regulation across states and territories (Johnson 2010: 619, Burpee 2009: 310, Stuhmcke 2004: 8-18). While a formal proposal to this effect released in 2009[31] has not been adopted, a review of regulatory frameworks across Australian states and territories, as well as the debates surrounding their formulation, reveals the influence that various jurisdictions exert on one another through the process of statute reform and the consequential parallels in legislative regimes. The discussion that follows thus describes legislative approaches to surrogacy developed in the six Australian states and the country's two mainland territories.

Queensland Queensland's *Surrogacy Act 2010* came into force on 1 June 2010, repealing the *Surrogate Parenthood Act 1988*, which had criminalized surrogacy arrangements of any kind. Premised primarily on the best interests of children (ss. 5(b)(iii), 6(1), 6(2)), the *Surrogacy Act 2010* allows gratuitous surrogacy contracts while retaining the prohibition on commercial arrangements (ss. 5(a), 56-57). Encompassed by the ban are those who pay or receive "payment, reward

29 Austl, Victoria, Victorian Law Reform Commission, *Assisted Reproductive Technology and Adoption: Final Report* (Melbourne: Victorian Government Printer, 2007) at 18, 44.

30 Jurisdictional competence of Australia's Commonwealth Parliament are set out by the Commonwealth of Australia's *Constitutional Act* (s. 51). Austl, Victoria, Victorian Law Reform Commission, *A.R.T., Surrogacy and Legal Parentage: A Comparative Legislative Review* (Melbourne: Victorian Law Reform Commission, 2004) at 18.

31 Austl, Commonwealth, Standing Committee of Attorneys-General, *A Proposal for a National Model to Harmonise Regulation of Surrogacy* (Sydney: Attorney General's Department, 2009).

or other material benefit or advantage" for surrogacy beyond reimbursement of the birth mother's costs related to the surrogate pregnancy (s. 57). The prohibition further covers the provision of services (technical, professional or medical) to parties known or intending to be involved in a commercial surrogacy agreement (s. 58), as well as diverse aspects of advertising commercial surrogacy (s. 55). The legislation also bans extra-territorial commercial surrogacy, making it an offence for a Queenslander to engage in the practice in another jurisdiction (s. 54(b)).

By contrast, the *Surrogacy Act 2010* does not prohibit unpaid agreements. The latter are considered unenforceable, but not void (s. 15(1)). That being said, an obligation to reimburse the surrogate's costs can be enforced, with the exception of situations in which a child is born from the agreement and the surrogate does not relinquish the child to the intending parents (ss. 15(2)(a), 15(2)(b)(i)(ii)).

The *Surrogacy Act 2010* further clarifies that the surrogate maintains control over her pregnancy during the gestational period and that she is presumed to be the child's mother after birth until a parentage order issues (ss. 16(1)(2), 17). The statute sets up a procedural framework for parentage order applications, which are the means through which intending parents may acquire filial status *vis-à-vis* the child born from a surrogacy plan (ss. 21-32). It requires courts to ascertain that the order would serve the child's best interests and wellbeing and that consent has been given by the intending parent(s), the surrogate and, if she has one, her spouse (s. 23(2)(h)). In this way, the *Surrogacy Act 2010* sets up a scheme that mirrors considerably that created by Britain's HFEA 1990.

As indicated, before the *Surrogacy Act 2010* was in force, surrogacy was governed in Queensland by the *Surrogate Parenthood Act 1988*, which criminalized commercial and gratuitous surrogacy arrangements and rendered void all surrogacy contracts. The *Surrogate Parenthood Act 1988* was subject to review beginning in 2008, when the Queensland Legislative Assembly appointed an Investigation into Altruistic Surrogacy Committee. This body encouraged the decriminalization of altruistic surrogacy. It also supported the recognition of "pre-conception" agreements but took the view that these should remain unenforceable. Queensland's *Surrogacy Bill 2009*, the precursor to the *Surrogacy Act 2010*, embraced these recommendations, now embodied in the 2010 statute.

Victoria Victoria's *Assisted Reproductive Treatment Act 2008* (ARTA) came into force on 1 January 2010, repealing the *Infertility Treatment Act 1995* (ARTA: ss. 2(3), 126). The latter statute permitted assisted reproduction only where a woman was unlikely to become pregnant or was at risk of transferring a genetic abnormality or disease to a child during pregnancy (s. 8(3)(a)(b)). The ARTA, which addresses surrogacy in the larger context of assisted reproduction, removed this as a fixed requirement. The ARTA also instituted the Patient Review Panel (the "Panel") to approve all surrogacy arrangements that meet specified criteria. Such approval is necessary before a registered provider of assisted reproductive technologies can offer services in the context of a surrogacy arrangement (s. 39).

Criteria required for the Panel's approval include evidence that the intending parent is unlikely to become pregnant, endure a pregnancy or successfully give birth (s. 40(1)(a)). The Panel must further ensure that parties have received counseling and legal advice (s. 40(1)(c)(d)) and that they are prepared for the possibility of the agreement proceeding in a way that does not match their intentions (s. 40(1)(e)). The Panel may approve arrangements that do not fulfill these criteria if doing so would be reasonable (s. 41).

Under the ARTA, any agreement that includes terms of payment is void and unenforceable (s. 44(3)), however, the surrogate can be reimbursed for "prescribed costs" linked directly to the surrogacy arrangement (s. 44(2)). Beyond this, the surrogate may not accept material benefit or advantage for surrogacy, on pain of a penalty of up to two years imprisonment (s. 44(1)). Unlike statutes in other jurisdictions considered here, Victoria's ARTA extends this criminal prohibition only to the surrogate, although brokers and intending parents may be caught by broad "publication" bans (s. 45).

Similar to the parentage order scheme in place in Queensland, Victoria's ARTA permits courts to issue a substitute parentage order on application by intending parents (*Status of Children Act*: s. 20). Prior to making such an order, a court must be satisfied of various factors, most notably that this would serve the child's needs and interests, that the appropriate consents are obtained, that the agreement was not a commercial one, and that the Panel approved the arrangement (*Status of Children Act*: ss. 22(1)(a), 22(1)(e), 22(1)(d), 22(1)(b)). Before a substitute parentage order is issued, the surrogate is presumed to be the child's mother (*Status of Children Act*: ss. 13-16).

New South Wales New South Wales' *Assisted Reproductive Technology Act 2007* (ARTA), which came into force 1 January 2010, renders surrogacy agreements void. The ARTA prohibits entry into or arrangement of commercial surrogacy agreements, or the acceptance of any benefit accrued from such an agreement. Advertising or soliciting a commercial surrogacy agreement is further criminalized. These prohibitions are subject to a penalty of two years' imprisonment (ss. 43-44).

Even following the ARTA's enactment, surrogacy remained subject to limited regulation in New South Wales. This fact, and relatively easy access to fertility centres in the state, made New South Wales a popular site in which to practice surrogacy (Johnson 2010: 618). A Standing Committee on Law and Justice was thus charged with investigating whether unremunerated surrogacy should be publically regulated and if so, under what conditions. It concluded that surrogacy agreements should be unenforceable and that commercial surrogacy should not be permitted. These recommendations served as a basis for the *Surrogacy Act 2010*, which sets out a more elaborate regulatory framework on surrogacy than that in place under the ARTA (Dodson and Smith 2011: 27). The *Surrogacy Act 2010* renders surrogacy arrangements unenforceable save for the obligation to reimburse a surrogate's costs as part of a "pre-conception" arrangement (s. 6). It criminalizes any party who enters a commercial surrogacy arrangement (s. 8) or who advertises surrogacy services (s. 10). As in Queensland and the ACT, the legislation also has extraterritorial reach, prohibiting any New South Wales resident from engaging in commercial surrogacy abroad, even in jurisdictions where the practice is permitted by local law (s. 11(1)(2)).

Like legislation in Queensland and Victoria, the New South Wales statute recognizes parentage orders, which permit the transference of parentage from the surrogate to the intending parents through court order (s. 12). Most requirements for such an order compare to those in other states, namely, the existence of consent, prior counseling and legal advice, service to the child's best interests, and the gratuitous nature of the arrangement (ss. 16, 22, 23-24, 35-36).

South Australia A first legislative initiative on surrogacy in South Australia took the form of the *Statutes Amendment (Surrogacy)* Bill 2006, introduced by the Hon. J.S.L. Dawkins pursuant to his work with two female constituents who had encountered fertility challenges.[32] The Bill was debated in the legislature and subsequently referred to a Social Development Committee,[33] which recommended that the government prepare and introduce draft legislation addressing their concerns.[34]

In February 2008, given that the government had yet to follow these recommendations, Dawkins reintroduced the *Statutes Amendment (Surrogacy) Bill 2008*.[35] The Bill passed as the *Statutes Amendment (Surrogacy) Act 2009* (SASA), taking effect on 10 November 2010. The SASA amended the *Family Relationships Act 1975*, adding provisions that distinguish between "surrogacy contracts," "procuration contracts" and "recognized surrogacy contracts" (*Family Relationships Act 1975*: s. 10F). Both surrogacy and procuration contracts are deemed illegal and void (s. 10G), and receiving valuable consideration under a procuration contract constitutes a criminal offence (s. 10H(a)). "Recognized" surrogacy agreements are surrogacy contracts that meet specific requirements, including that parties to the agreement are at least 18 years old and domiciled in the state. The intending parents must be married or have been in a conjugal union for a specified time, and the female partner must face infertility or risk transferring serious illness to a child she conceives. Parties must receive counseling, there cannot be any payment of consideration other than for costs associated with the pregnancy, and parties must have stipulated their intention to the effect that the

---

32 Austl, South Australia, Legislative Council, *Parliamentary Debates* (21 June 2006) at 437 (J.S.L. Dawkins).

33 Austl, South Australia, Legislative Council, *Parliamentary Debates* (27 September 2006) at 764.

34 Austl, South Australia, Legislative Council, *Parliamentary Debates* (2 April 2008) at 2219.

35 Austl, South Australia, Legislative Council, *Parliamentary Debates* (13 February 2008) at 1667 (J.S.L. Dawkins).

intending parents would apply for a parentage order after the child's birth (ss. 10HA(2)(b), (6)).

Tasmania Until 30 August 2012, Tasmania was the sole Australian state that criminalized all forms of surrogacy. The *Surrogacy Contracts Act 1993* prohibited facilitating, arranging or negotiating a surrogacy contract, inducing someone to enter such an agreement (s. 4(1)(2)(3)), advertising or soliciting surrogacy services (s. 6), and the making or receipt of payment or reward for surrogacy (s. 4(4)). Professional services could not be provided to support a pregnancy known to be the object of a surrogacy arrangement (s. 5). The statute further rendered all surrogacy contracts void and unenforceable (s. 7).

In April 2008, the Tasmanian Parliament's Legislative Council appointed a Select Committee on Surrogacy. The Select Committee's report established a position against commercial surrogacy, citing concerns about children's commodification and women's exploitation. In the result, legislation was passed in 2012 revisiting Tasmania's legislative stance on surrogacy. The *Surrogacy Act 2012* allows all individuals, regardless of marital status or sexual orientation, to apply for parentage orders pursuant to a gratuitous surrogacy arrangement. Commercial surrogacy and associated advertising and solicitation activities, however, remain prohibited and any involved party is subject to criminal penalty (ss. 40-41). Moreover, surrogacy agreements remain unenforceable and the surrogate is entitled to control and make decisions about her pregnancy, regardless of any statement to the contrary in a surrogacy contract (ss. 10(1), 11).

Western Australia The formal regulation of surrogacy in Western Australia was initiated by the *Surrogacy Bill 2007*, which was replaced by the *Surrogacy Bill 2008*.[36] The Bill was passed as the *Surrogacy Act 2008* by the Western Australia Parliament in late 2008, and entered into force in March 2009.[37] Like other Australian regulatory schemes, this statute criminalizes parties who enter commercial surrogacy agreements, as well as those who advertise or facilitate this practice (ss. 8-11). Gratuitous surrogacy is, however, permitted and a surrogate is entitled to recovery of reasonable expenses or losses associated with her surrogate pregnancy. This latter entitlement is the only part of a surrogacy contract that is enforceable in Western Australia (s. 7).

Western Australian law further includes a mechanism for parentage orders (Division 3). Such orders, which transfer parental status from the surrogate to the intending parents (s. 26), may issue only where the state's "Reproductive

36 Austl, Western Australia, Reproductive Technology Council, *Surrogacy in Western Australia*. Available at: http://www.rtc.org.au/consumer/surrogacy_wa.html [accessed: 9 October 2012].

37 Austl, Western Australia, Reproductive Technology Council, *Surrogacy in Western Australia*. Available at: http://www.rtc.org.au/consumer/surrogacy_wa.html [accessed: 9 October 2012].

Technology Council" has approved a surrogacy arrangement (s. 16). The court petitioned to grant the parentage order must also be satisfied of a number of other statutory criteria, which include: residency and minimum age requirements for the intending parent(s) (s. 19(1)), the issuance of consents and provision of counseling and independent legal advice to relevant parties (s. 17), the presence of medical justifications for turning to surrogacy (s. 19(2)(3)), and heterosexual intending parents in a married or *de facto* union relationship (s. 19(2)).

Australian Capital Territory Surrogacy in the Australian Capital Territory has been regulated by the *Substitute Parents Act 1994* (SPA), and subsequently by the *Parentage Act 2004*. The SPA provided a basic framework for regulating surrogacy and emerged pursuant to vigorous legislative discourse, which sought to instantiate a clear stance against commercial surrogacy.[38] The introduction of the *Parentage Bill 2003* was aimed at creating a unified approach to parentage in the Australian Capital Territory, rather than having the issue addressed through multiple legislative texts.[39] It further sought to create a statutory regime that allowed formal recognition of same-sex parents.[40] Surrogacy was not addressed during debates over this Bill. However, when it came into force as the *Parentage Act 2004*, the statute included provisions that addressed surrogacy arrangements or "substitute parent agreements" (Part 4). The statute criminalizes intentional entry into commercial agreements (s. 41), but allows reimbursement of expenses linked to the surrogate pregnancy and the birth and care of the child (s. 40). Procuring another's entry into a surrogacy agreement with a third party, publishing surrogacy advertisements, and providing services to someone known to be party to a commercial agreement are also prohibited (ss. 42-44). As in New South Wales and Queensland, in the Australian Capital Territory it is an offence for someone ordinarily resident in the state to commit surrogacy-related offences in another jurisdiction (s. 45).

The *Parentage Act 2004* otherwise allows surrogacy arrangements and provides that a surrogate and, if applicable, her spouse or civil partner will be presumed as the parent(s) of a child born to a surrogate (ss. 7, 11(1)). This presumption can be set aside through a parentage order in favour of the intending parents. Such an order can issue on the satisfaction of set criteria comparable to those in other jurisdictions with parentage order schemes (ss. 23ff.). Distinct within the Australian Capital Territory legislation, however, are the requirements of a genetic connection with at least one intending parent and that no such connection exist

38 Austl, Australian Capital Territory, Legislative Assembly, *Parliamentary Debates* (11 October 1994) at 3467 (Mr Connolly).

39 Austl, Australian Capital Territory, Legislative Assembly, *Parliamentary Debates* (20 November 2003) at 4376 (Mr Stanhope); Austl, Australian Capital Territory, Legislative Assembly, *Parliamentary Debates* (10 February 2004) at 127 (Mrs Cross).

40 Austl, Australian Capital Territory, Legislative Assembly, *Parliamentary Debates* (20 November 2003) at 4377 (Mr Stanhope).

between the child and surrogate (s. 24). These requirements have been critiqued for excluding traditional surrogacy agreements from regulation and for rendering it impossible to engage in legal surrogacy in the Australian Capital Territory if both ova and sperm donations are required for conception (Johnson 2010: 620).

Northern Territory Australia's Northern Territory has not, to date, enacted legislation governing surrogacy nor has it conducted public inquiries into the practice. Assisted reproduction services must, according to the Northern Territory Department of Health, conform to regulations in South Australia. Furthermore, because no parentage order or other regime is in place to recognize the parental status of intending parents, the latter must proceed by adoption to be substituted for the surrogate as the legal parents of a child conceived by surrogacy (Johnson 2010: 625).

This contemplation of Australian law reveals the comparable paths of states and territories that have enacted statutory provisions pertaining to surrogacy. These jurisdictions criminalize commercial surrogacy, with proscriptions extending to the surrogate mother herself. In some states, gratuitous arrangements have also been criminalized until recently (Queensland in 2010, Tasmania in 2012). Unpaid surrogacy might lead to successful judicial orders recognizing the parentage of intending parents. However, private arrangements to this end are deemed unenforceable except, in some cases, insofar as reimbursement of the surrogate for her expenses are concerned. While it may be contended that Australia would be better served by implementing national legislation, it is noteworthy that other federalist states that govern surrogacy at the national level, such as Canada, still leave open a range of issues that fall to local legislatures to address (Burpee 2009: 337-338).

Legislative Overview

Legal approaches developed within Canada, the United Kingdom, and Australia are oriented toward the prohibition of commercial surrogacy. However, each of these jurisdictions appreciates the notion of "commercialization" somewhat differently. In Canada and Australia, this is understood as payment for surrogacy whereas in the United Kingdom, lucrative, for-profit initiatives designed to promote, facilitate and oversee surrogacy services are the target of legislative efforts. Each jurisdiction also criminalizes different actors involved in surrogacy: clients and brokers in Canada, brokers alone in the United Kingdom, and in Australia, potentially all parties to the paid surrogacy agreement, including the surrogate herself. The discussion that follows undertakes a critical evaluation of the regulatory frameworks explained here. It reflects on the ideals driving state law chronicled in this Part, the way in which state law interacts and competes with non-state norms shaping surrogates' choices, and the overarching effect of state law, and legislative prohibitions in particular, on such choices. Ultimately, Part 3 demonstrates how state law fails to realize its intended effects and goals primarily because of its coexistence with plural normative factors that bear influence on women's choices in relation to surrogate motherhood.

Part 3: Evaluating State Law

This part relies on data set out in the two forgoing sections to develop a critical evaluation of legal rules governing surrogacy in Canada, the United Kingdom and Australia. It draws on social science empirical work illuminating how surrogates ascribe meaning and value to surrogacy so as to assess whether legal rules crafted by the state reflect surrogates' realities, and to gauge the influence of such legal rules on surrogates' choices.

State Law's Presumptions and Objectives in Relation to Surrogacy, Women and Choice

Surrogacy legislation and policy in the three jurisdictions contemplated in this book are driven primarily by concerns about women and children, and their perceived vulnerabilities. Juridical stances in these places are probably best described as cautious, skeptical and protectionist in relation to surrogacy. This convergence in themes emergent in legal and political discourse in Canada, the United Kingdom and Australia is largely attributable to their comparable legal cultures and to shared political and social features relevant to surrogate maternity. Namely, these are three Western secular states where multiculturalism and immigration are prominent social and demographic features. An analysis of surrogacy's formal governance in other jurisdictional contexts might reveal different influences on its governance. Elly Teman's work on surrogacy in Israel offers a rich example, as it shows how a strong pronatalist state policy intimately tied to a religious juridical tradition that promotes procreation can yield more openness to and tolerance for surrogacy in legal regimes and in the public discourse that circulates around it (Teman 2010: 12-13).

The discussion that follows draws on legislative committee reports and political debates to illuminate the goals and presumptions that underpin legal approaches to surrogacy in Canada, the United Kingdom and Australia. It looks also to relevant judicial analyses, but to a lesser extent, as courts have not been frequently faced with surrogacy litigation. These authorities indicate that state law governing surrogacy in these jurisdictions is shaped by perceptions about surrogates as susceptible to exploitation and manipulation by intending parents. This perceived vulnerability is connected to a second presumption, namely that surrogates are motivated primarily, if not only, by money. A third preoccupation relates to the first two. It pertains to an interest in avoiding the objectification and commodification of reproduction through surrogacy practices. These points are the focus of elaboration in the ensuing discussion.

Surrogates' vulnerability Exposure to exploitation and harm are key tropes within political discourses on surrogacy and its governance. Discussions zero in on the particular risks for the women who become surrogates. As discussed in Part 1 and as noted by other scholars, at least some surrogates are "far from being vulnerable" and "empowered by their ability to exercise control over their bodies and the altruism that underpins surrogacy arrangements" (Horsey 2010: 451). Nevertheless, discussions surrounding the formation of legal regimes regulating this practice evidence deeply held presumptions that surrogates are "easily exploited" (Horsey 2010: 451). Moreover, in the surrogacy narrative, they are viewed as making an immeasurable sacrifice at the expense of their own health and wellbeing; one judge has likened the surrogate to "Cinderella trapped in act 1, and does not go to the ball" (*Re A. and B.*: 324). These discussions further insinuate that surrogates are not actively or rationally choosing their path, but are instead driven to it by desperation or coercion. This perception of the surrogate has generated state responses that may be characterized as "overly paternalistic" (Horsey 2010: 452).

Canadian legislative debates and reports on surrogacy have centred explicitly on preoccupations with women's supposed vulnerabilities. Surrogates' interests are viewed as threatened by virtue of "disparities in power between themselves and those paying for their services."[41] This concern is likely at the root of the Canadian law that criminalizes those who pay for or broker surrogacy services, but not the surrogate herself (Harvison Young and Wasunna 1998: 268).

Similar concerns and approaches were touted in British and Australian debates. Conversations surrounding the HFEA 1990 claimed that commercial surrogacy leads "very often [to] the rich exploiting the poor,"[42] prompting deep concerns about surrogates' propensity to become victims of manipulation by intending parents (Gibson 1994: 404). Such perceived power imbalances are characterized as deeply gendered, with politicians stressing "the exploitation of vulnerable women" that results from commercial surrogacy.[43] Similarly, in New South Wales, political discussions supporting the prohibition of commercial surrogacy, even when carried out extraterritorially, spoke of the need to protect "women who hire out their bodies because they are poor," particularly given the supposed allure of the surrogacy industry to women in "extremely poor countries."[44] By one British parliamentarian's account, the intending father has the greatest clout in surrogacy

41 Canada, *House of Commons Debates*, 35th Parl, 2nd Sess, No 89 (23 October 1996) at 5617 (Joseph Volpe).

42 UK, HL, *Parliamentary Debates*, vol 491, col 1471 (15 January 1988) (Duke of Norfolk).

43 Austl, Australian Capital Territory, Legislative Assembly, *Parliamentary Debates* (11 October 1994) at 3467 (Mr Connolly).

44 Austl, New South Wales, Legislative Council, *Parliamentary Debates* (11 November 2010) at 27678 (Linda Burney); Austl, New South Wales, Legislative Assembly, *Parliamentary Debates* (10 November 2010) at 27599 (Pru Goward).

relationships. He noted the "grossly unequal bond" between the "donor father," the surrogate and his own spouse. The intending father is characterized as the party who pays for the services and thus obtains extensive, personal information about the surrogate before "choosing" her, whereas the surrogate has no such information. The parliamentary member thus stated: "such voyeuristic relations are not uncommon in Soho, but are usually condemned as deeply exploitative and insulting to women."[45]

British debates have further focused on the need to protect rather than criminalize the surrogate mother. In describing the purpose of the *Surrogacy Arrangements Act 1985*, the Secretary of State for Social Services affirmed that the statute was not aimed at "penalis[ing] the surrogate mother" but at guarding her against the risk of exploitation by "commercial agencies."[46] British debates thus clearly situated surrogacy's potential malice with such agencies, identifying a "misery" that both surrogates and intending parents might share that could facilitate their exploitation.[47]

While most policy and political discussions focus on the harms to women that commercial surrogacy engenders, there is some recognition that exploitation can occur when surrogacy occurs without payment. In Queensland, one taskforce noted that coercion and exploitation can occur within unremunerated surrogacy arrangements formed between friends and family members.[48] Similar remarks were made in Tasmanian and Australian Capital Territory legislative debates regarding commercialization's relationship with exploitation risks.[49]

Legislative and policy discussions also depict surrogates as exposed to harm by virtue of being forced to relinquish a child promptly after giving birth. Women are presumed ill-placed to predict how they will feel about handing a child over immediately following delivery.[50] A "fragility of intentions" may be presumed to trigger "deep emotional disturbance" postpartum (*Re A. and B.*: 324). One legislator in Western Australia posited that a surrogate who "changes her mind" would suffer "the greatest possible guilt," particularly where the surrogate is

---

45 UK, HC, *Parliamentary Debates*, vol 77, col 40 (15 April 1985) (Harry Cohen).

46 UK, HC, *Parliamentary Debates*, vol 77, col 24 (15 April 1985) (Norman Fowler); UK, HL, *Parliamentary Debates*, vol 464, col 1520 (14 June 1985) (Earl of Caithness).

47 UK, HL, *Parliamentary Debates*, vol 465, col 934 (28 June 1985) (Baroness Warnock).

48 Austl, Queensland, Taskforce on Women and the Criminal Code, *Women and the Criminal Code* (Brisbane: Office of Women's Policy, 2000) at 296.

49 Austl, Tasmania, House of Assembly, *Parliamentary Debates* (12 April 2011) (Ms Petrusma); Austl, Australian Capital Territory, Legislative Assembly, *Parliamentary Debates* (11 October 1994) at 3463 (Mr Humphries).

50 Canada, Royal Commission on New Reproductive Technologies, *Proceed with Care: Final Report of the Royal Commission on New Reproductive Technologies* (Ottawa: Minister of Government Services, 1993) at 685.

the child's genetic mother.[51] Debates in the Australian Capital Territory referred to paid surrogacy in the United States as giving rise to "a lot of distress and a lot of trauma to innocent people," which Australian law should seek to avoid.[52] Thus, Queensland's Investigation into Altruistic Surrogacy Committee noted the relevance of a regulatory framework that protected against the "forced relinquishment" of children conceived via surrogacy (Johnson 2010: 629).

Legislative debates and analyses also commonly depict intending parents as exercising control over surrogates' lives and person. Policy commentators have expressed concern about intending parents' ability to dictate terms of surrogacy arrangements that affect a range of factors, such as the choice of physicians who will oversee pregnancy and delivery, and circumstances that may lead to a surrogate pregnancy's termination.[53] Voices within debates thus characterize surrogacy, particularly when taken up for money, as "cast[ing] aside and trampl[ing] on" women's rights to control their own bodies.[54] Viewed in their totality, these concerns fuel state law's overarching presumption of paid surrogacy as "positively exploitative" and deleterious to women's interests.[55]

Surrogacy as a financially motivated endeavour Concerns about surrogates' susceptibility to exploitation are intimately connected to a perception that they are chiefly motivated by money. While, as noted, some legislative discussions indicate that coercive pressures may be present and acute even in gratuitous surrogacy arrangements, the bulk of the political discourse on this topic links exploitation to commercialization. Thus, legislation that outlaws commercial surrogacy is premised on the rationale that it will reduce opportunities for preying upon women who turn to surrogacy because of financial need.

The idea that remuneration serves as a central incentive to become a surrogate emerges in legislative debates and policy analyses in all three jurisdictions studied here, but particularly in the United Kingdom. In that jurisdiction, the earliest political discussions focused on legislative action that would serve to prevent

---

51 Austl, Western Australia, Legislative Council, *Parliamentary Debates* (25 November 2008) (Hon Helen Morton).

52 Austl, Australian Capital Territory, Legislative Assembly, *Parliamentary Debates* (11 October 1994) at 3465 (Mr Connolly).

53 Canada, Royal Commission on New Reproductive Technologies, *Proceed with Care: Final Report of the Royal Commission on New Reproductive Technologies* (Ottawa: Minister of Government Services, 1993) at 684.

54 UK, HC, *Parliamentary Debates*, vol 77, col 39 (15 April 1985) (Harry Cohen). See also in Australia—Austl, New South Wales, Legislative Assembly, *Parliamentary Debates* (10 November 2010) at 27599 (Pru Goward).

55 UK, HC, "Report of the Committee of Inquiry into Human Fertilisation and Embryology," Cm 9314 in *Sessional Papers* (1984) 1 at 46. See also UK, HC, "Review for Health Ministers of Current Arrangements for Payments and Regulation," Cm 4068 (1998) 1 at 11.

women, "attracted by the lure of money,"[56] to relegate themselves to serving as "breeding machines" for other couples. Criminalizing commercial surrogacy was viewed as essential to prevent "poor women from being induced into pregnancy ... for the money."[57] Some British legislators have further questioned the authenticity of surrogates' claims about their altruistic motivations, indicating a conviction that "the attraction of the financial element is paramount."[58] Others suggest an openness to unremunerated surrogacy as a practice "impractical to prohibit," while stressing a need to criminalize commercial forms of the practice. To this end, legislators aim to preempt those "wishing to make a profit out of the plight of the childless," who may include the surrogate herself.[59]

Britain's Brazier Report, discussed above, conveyed preoccupations about payment for surrogacy. It concluded that payment contravenes moral and social norms about the commodification of human life. More relevant to the present discussion, the Brazier Report indicated that remuneration represented a potential inducement or prompt for women to become implicated in surrogacy at considerable risk to their own physical and psychological wellbeing. It further stated that when a surrogate is motivated by the prospect of financial gain, she is less likely to be capable of making an informed choice about becoming a surrogate and more susceptible to exploitation in this process.[60]

Comments about surrogates' supposed financial motivations are evident also in Canada and Australia. In Canada, legislative debates characterized surrogacy as treating "reproduction as an economic activity"[61] and as a "profit making transaction."[62] As a result, legislative efforts were targeted at ensuring that surrogacy would not develop into "another industry with great dollars and people choosing it as a career using their bodies to produce children for other people."[63]

In Australia, the Australian Capital Territory's legislative debates reflect an understanding of surrogacy as a "means of making money"[64] and as a method

---

56 UK, HC, *Parliamentary Debates*, vol 77, cols 46-47 (15 April 1985) (David Amess).

57 UK, HC, *Parliamentary Debates*, vol 77, col 28 (15 April 1985) (Norman Fowler).

58 UK, HC, *Parliamentary Debates*, vol 77, col 37 (15 April 1985) (Anna McCurley).

59 UK, HL, *Parliamentary Debates*, vol 515, col 1283 (13 February 1990) (Baroness Hooper).

60 UK, HC, "Review for Health Ministers of Current Arrangements for Payments and Regulation," Cm 4068 (1998) 1 at 35-36.

61 Canada, *House of Commons Debates*, 37th Parl, 2nd Sess, No 134 (6 October 2003) at 8191 (Marlene Jennings).

62 Canada, *House of Commons Debates*, 37th Parl, 1st Sess, No 188 (21 May 2002) at 11523 (Anne McLellan).

63 Canada, *House of Commons Debates*, 37th Parl, 2nd Sess, No 47 (28 January 2003) at 2774 (James Lunney).

64 Austl, Australian Capital Territory, Legislative Assembly, *Parliamentary Debates* (11 October 1994) at 3459 (Mrs Carnell); Austl, Australian Capital Territory, Legislative Assembly, *Parliamentary Debates* (11 October 1994) at 3461 (Ms Szuty).

for establishing a "commercial business" that ought to be discouraged for its propensity to exploit vulnerable persons.[65] Moreover, all state governments in Australia, when contemplating the regulation of surrogacy, focused exclusively on gratuitous arrangements, truncating contemplations of commercial surrogacy from public discussions. Keeping the issue of remuneration off the table signaled intense legislative wariness about commercial surrogacy. This point has been subject to critique, however, given the missed opportunity for exploring how payment might shift issues of gender equality, consent, choice and power in surrogacy arrangements (Millbank 2011: 12-13).

Surrogacy as commodifying personhood and reproduction A final theme that surfaces within political discussions and debates concerning surrogacy points to the practice's presumed ethical shortcomings. Moral objections to surrogacy commonly suggest that it permits individuals to "treat others as a means to their own ends,"[66] it "denigrates the position of women in society"[67] and, when practiced for profit, it resembles "a trade in humans."[68] These preoccupations are interwoven with a goal of preempting women's exploitation and surrogates' financial motivations; commodification, then, might be viewed as a "species of exploitation" (Gibson 1994: 410). Discussions surrounding surrogacy's governance thus indicate that when paid, surrogates are vulnerable to coercion and the exploitation of their reproductive capacities.[69] This concern firmly undergirds the design of Canada's AHRA (*Dans L'affaire du Renvoi fait par le gouvernement du Québec en vertu de la loi sur les renvois à la Cour d'appel, L.R.Q. ch. R-23, relativement à la constitutionnalité des articles 8 à 19, 40 à 53, 60, 61 et 68 de la Loi sur la procreation assistée, L.C. 2004, ch. 2, Procureur Général du Quebec c. Procureur Général du Canada*: 7, Baker 1996: 34).[70] It also drives the regulation of surrogacy in the United Kingdom and Australia. Thus, in

65 Austl, Australian Capital Territory, Legislative Assembly, *Parliamentary Debates* (11 October 1994) at 3464 (Mr Moore).

66 UK, HC, "Report of the Committee of Inquiry into Human Fertilisation and Embryology," Cm 9314 in *Sessional Papers* (1984) 1 at 46.

67 Austl, New South Wales, New South Wales Law Reform Commission, *Artificial Conception Report 3: Surrogate Motherhood* (Report No 60) (Sydney: New South Wales Law Reform Commission, 1988) at 39.

68 Austl, Western Australia, Legislative Council, *Parliamentary Debates* (13 November 2008) (Hon Barbara Scott). See also Austl, Victoria, Victorian Law Reform Commission, *A.R.T., Surrogacy and Legal Parentage: A Comparative Legislative Review* (Melbourne: Victorian Law Reform Commission, 2004) at 5.9.

69 Canada, *House of Commons Debates*, 35th Parl, 2nd Sess, No 89 (23 October 1996) at 5627 (John Murphy); Canada, *House of Commons Debates*, 37th Parl, 2nd Sess, No 134 (6 October 2003) at 8191 (Marlene Jennings).

70 Canada, *House of Commons Debates*, 37th Parl, 2nd Sess, No 85 (7 April 2003) at 5160-5161; Canada, *House of Commons Debates*, 37th Parl, 2nd Sess, No 72 (18 March 2003) at 4339.

an effort to preclude "baby farming" (*A. v. C.*: 459), "instrumentaliz[ing] human beings"[71] and a "dehumanizing" practice involving payment for reproduction,[72] legislators generally adhere to the view that paid surrogacy should be prohibited. In consequence, regulatory frameworks have advanced a "morality policy" (Snow 2009: 23) based on moralistic or "non-harm" (Gaffney 2009) rationales for criminalization. Such rules reflect majoritarian wariness of commercial surrogacy's ostensible social and moral implications, particularly in relation to commodifying women's sexuality and children (Snow 2009: 34).

The narrative that connects payment for surrogacy to human commodification commonly draws on conceptions of human dignity and human life and personhood as inalienable.[73] These notions are entrenched in Quebec's particular juridical approach, pursuant to which surrogacy contracts are unenforceable and viewed as contravening public order (Giroux 1997: 536-537).[74] They are also embedded in policy findings in both the United Kingdom[75] and Australia,[76] yielding regulatory frameworks that preclude payment for surrogacy.

Legislative disquiet over surrogacy's commodification potential is often expressed with reference to concepts of maternity, depicted in policy discussions as having immeasurable, sometimes nearly spiritual or sacred, value. One Canadian federal legislator described commercial surrogacy as "cheapen[ing] the invaluable act of motherhood upon which a price cannot be placed."[77] Comparably, Women's Forum Australia posited that surrogacy devalued "the intrinsic meaning of motherhood by re-constructing [it] as something that can be given away."[78] The idea was similarly expressed by a parliamentary member in the Australian

---

71 Canada, Royal Commission on New Reproductive Technologies, *Proceed with Care: Final Report of the Royal Commission on New Reproductive Technologies* (Ottawa: Minister of Government Services, 1993) at 683.

72 Austl, Queensland, *Investigation into Altruistic Surrogacy Committee: Report* (2008) at 4.

73 Canada, Royal Commission on New Reproductive Technologies, *Proceed with Care: Final Report of the Royal Commission on New Reproductive Technologies* (Ottawa: Minister of Government Services, 1993) at 683.

74 Canada, Quebec, Commission de l'éthique de la science et de la technologie, *Ethique et procréation assistée: des orientations pour le don de gametes et d'embryons, la gestation pour autrui et le diagnostic préimplantatoire* (Quebec: Commission de l'éthique de la science et de la technologie, 2009) at 80.

75 See e.g., the Brazier Report: UK, HC, "Review for Health Ministers of Current Arrangements for Payments and Regulation," Cm 4068 (1998) 1 at i.

76 Austl, Queensland, *Investigation into Altruistic Surrogacy Committee: Report* (2008) at 41.

77 Canada, *House of Commons Debates*, 37th Parl, 2nd Sess, No 78 (26 March 2003) at 4726 (Jason Kenney).

78 Austl, New South Wales, Standing Committee on Law and Justice, *Legislation on Altruistic Surrogacy in NSW* (Report No 38) (Sydney: Standing Committee on Law and Justice, 2009) at 25.

Capital Territory, who referred to surrogacy's "corruption of the simple traditional relationship between mother and a child" even when performed altruistically or "for love" over money.[79] The subsection below ("Interface between State and Non-State Law") illuminates the way in which state law's engagement with informal norms governing surrogacy both reinforces and challenges these idealized representations of maternity.

Overarching role of choice in state law's presumptions and objectives The foregoing discussion illuminates central presumptions and goals underlying formal legal approaches to surrogacy in Canada, the United Kingdom and Australia. In these jurisdictions, surrogacy is viewed as a practice fueled by a profit motive, as exploitative of women's reproductive capacities, and as commodifying intimate and physical aspects of their personhood and the children they bear. While these are dominant themes within discussions that circulate at the level of state law and policy, allusions to a counter-narrative emerge within pockets of these debates. On a few occasions, legislative members have suggested that women should have the ability to make independent determinations as to the propriety of their own involvement in surrogacy. In this connection, comments are anchored to the idea of "choice" or a "right to choose" in regard to reproductive practices.[80] Some politicians have thus advocated for recognizing surrogates' choices, viewing the latter as having "knowingly entered" their arrangements and as able to "understand the repercussions of what they are doing."[81] In support of this position, some have argued for "structures to inform [surrogates'] decision making," so as to promote and broaden opportunities for informed choice.[82]

References to choice in legislative debates lack universal normative weight, as they might be invoked to support surrogacy only in certain forms. In Queensland, for example, supporters of surrogacy's decriminalization argued that a ban on surrogacy infringed on reproductive freedom and involved the state's interference in individuals' private lives.[83] Such remarks, however, were confined

79 Austl, Australian Capital Territory, Legislative Assembly, *Parliamentary Debates* (11 October 1994) at 3463 (Mr Humphries). Millbank (2011) contemplates these themes more widely within Australian policy.

80 UK, HC, *Parliamentary Debates*, vol 170, col 968 (2 April 1990) (D.N. Campbell-Savours).

81 Austl, Victoria, Legislative Assembly, *Parliamentary Debates* (7 October 2008) at 3797 (Ms Thomson).

82 Canada, Ontario, *Raising Expectations: Recommendations of the Expert Panel on Infertility and Adoption* (Toronto: Ministry of Children and Youth Services, 2009) at 20, 129; Austl, New South Wales, Standing Committee on Law and Justice, *Legislation on Altruistic Surrogacy in NSW* (Report No 38) (Sydney: Standing Committee on Law and Justice, 2009) at 24.

83 Austl, Queensland, Legislative Assembly, *Parliamentary Debates* (26 November 2009) at 3668 (Hon C.R. Dick); Austl, Queensland, *Investigation into Altruistic Surrogacy Committee: Report* (2008) at 18.

to unremunerated surrogacy, further illuminating the presumed alignment between payment and risk. Moreover, stark references to choice seem rooted in liberalism and idealism (Snow 2009: 41), and pay minimal heed to the varied normative forces that might constrain or foster surrogates' agency. The risk, therefore, of sliding into a passive and uncritical acceptance of choice is the attribution of adverse outcomes to the presumed chooser. This hazard reflects the shortcomings of a lax ascription to choice of circumstances that are actually shaped by a blend of constraining forces and active resistance to them. The discussion that follows considers the informal and non-state normative factors that shape surrogacy-related choices and their interface with state law's schemes for governing surrogacy.

Interface between State and Non-State Law

State law's interactions with non-state norms that drive women's choices about surrogacy illuminate the lacunae within the formal regulatory frameworks governing this practice. Three particular junctions between state and non-state law are illustrative, and can be described as norms related to: conceptions of vulnerability, possible sources of coercion, and paradigms of maternity.

Conceptions of vulnerability As shown above, state law governing surrogacy is often premised on the view that women will not choose freely to engage in this practice but instead are susceptible to coercion at the hands of intending parents and commercial brokers. This perception of vulnerability underpins legal approaches to paid surrogacy, which strive to protect women from pressure or coercion. State law's efforts in this respect are most evident in criminal legislation that prohibits the activities of surrogacy brokers or intending parents, but not the surrogate herself. State law has also shown itself concerned with surrogacy contracts that might impair the surrogate's autonomy (Ince 1994), and further resists holding a woman to her promise to give up a child she carried during pregnancy.

Empirical data on surrogates' experiences suggest that most surrogates do not come to the bargaining table in the disempowered state that legislators seem to envisage. Aware of formal law's limits, they may understand that their surrogacy contracts "are not worth the paper they are written on" (Kashmeri 2008: 59) and thus cannot compel involuntary behaviour. A surrogate may also see herself as empowered by her role in the lives of people eager to become parents, her fertility serving as "a levelling device" for the disadvantage with which she might otherwise enter negotiations (Ragoné 1996: 358). Parties' bargaining stances thus may not be unbalanced even if the surrogate is unpaid or bears the risk of intending parents' default on payment.

Furthermore, state law's exclusive preoccupation with money as a potential source of coercion for surrogates seems misguided, given the multiple factors that influence surrogates' choices. Even in jurisdictions where remunerated surrogacy is permissible and surrogates overtly ascribe value to surrogacy's financial benefits, surrogates will emphasize the psychosocial benefits they draw from their experiences (Teman 2010: 23). In this way, state law overlooks and conflicts with the normative pluralism underlying the meaning and value of surrogates' decisions.

Juridical misgivings about holding women to the terms of surrogacy contracts also call for scrutiny. There are plain gender stereotypes embedded in the suggestion that women lack the emotional capacity for rational, self-protective decisions when all options on offer carry a considerable tradeoff, particularly when such decisions affect reproduction and maternity. Although this claim may seem more benign when cloaked in the discourse of protecting women from the emotional injury of their own choices, it nonetheless should trigger feminist critique and objection (Suk 2010).

A connected analysis would redirect the inquiry to examine the baseline against which vulnerability is measured. The reference point for the human condition in legal thought is a reasoned, self-sufficient and empowered individual. State law sees the surrogate as departing from this norm, largely on account of presumptions premised on gender, class, her physical and emotional state while pregnant and postpartum, and possibly also her age. Such identity-shaping factors would, as in any decision-making context, operate to exert some influence on the surrogate's choices. Yet interpreting these traits as proxies for decisional frailty or incapacity misses the universality of vulnerability, and its presence in the lives of all individuals at different moments. Overlooking this point results in a weakened understanding of the state's responsibility to relieve social and economic hardships caused by vulnerability (Fineman 2010). Furthermore, and more centrally to the present project, this oversight of vulnerability's universality reinforces the victim–agent dyad that renders deeply problematic formal legal responses to women's morally-fraught choices.

Potential sources of coercion A second junction between state and non-state law relates to the first. State law's focus on remuneration for surrogacy is predicated on a simplistic correlation between payment and the risk of exploitation. It proceeds on the understanding that eliminating the prospect of financial gain will purify the practice of surrogacy and mitigate surrogates' vulnerabilities. Such conclusions overlook the point, evident to scholars who have surveyed empirical literature on surrogacy, that although money might be relevant to surrogacy agreements, "there is no empirical research supporting the assertion that women are becoming surrogate mothers because they are facing financial distress" (Busby and Vun 2010: 55). The extent, then, to which money constrains or compels choices about surrogacy is not as clear as state law suggests, given the multiple expectations and norms operative in this context. That said, state approaches account minimally for the plurality of pressures pertaining to reproduction, marriage and family life that may direct surrogates' decision-making more than any economic force. Most notably, state law's failure to provide checks on coercion arising from family and community norms illuminates a shortcoming with understanding money as the sole inducement that can erode meaningful choice.

Furthermore, while resistance to payment is heralded in legal debates, on closer inspection, it is revealed as potentially aggravating the problems it seeks to avoid. For some women, payment facilitates and rationalizes emotional detachment from a surrogate pregnancy and the children they conceive, reducing the risk of second-guessing or retracting from the terms of their surrogacy agreements. Moreover, barring payment for surrogacy strikes as emblematic of inclinations, conventional within Western legal traditions, to undervalue caregiving and reproductive labour. Empathy, human connection, altruism are the "rewards" that women can legally obtain for serving as a surrogate. State law presumes such traits, perceived to lie at the core of women's moral presence, as sufficient on their own to infuse their surrogacy experiences with meaning and importance (Maguire Shultz 1990: 380, Shaw 2008: 15-16). Women's interests in altruistic surrogacy contexts thus might be subject to even greater exploitation than in "a free for all kind of situation" where surrogacy is unregulated.[84] Moreover, if allowing surrogates to receive payment might augment the value of women's social roles (Daunt 1991), the state's approach to surrogacy may be complicit in quashing unconventional routes to their social and economic empowerment.

Finally, one might probe at the persuasiveness of the distinction between altruism and commercialism and their respective connections to coercion. Legislative discussions related to surrogacy have shown strong tendencies to equate unpaid surrogacy with generosity and benevolence, while associating paid surrogacy with corruption and bad morals. The exploitation risks that are so central to legal analyses seem pertinent only when surrogacy occurs in exchange for money. Yet drawing blunt conceptual divisions between altruistic and paid surrogacy is unhelpful and potentially misguiding.[85] Engaging with the narratives of surrogates exposes the potential for altruistic surrogacy—especially when intra-familial—to be coercive, and for commercial surrogacy to result from reasoned and deliberated choice. This experiential knowledge problematizes simple associations between payment and coercion in surrogacy arrangements. It suggests a need for more nuanced legislative and policy approaches recognizing the equally problematic nature of conceptualizing surrogacy—like organ or tissue donation—as either an altruistic "gift" or as a "commodity" driven by self-interest (Healy 2006).

Paradigms of maternity Last, legal rules governing surrogacy crafted by the state often suggest that the practice appropriates and contorts the naturalness and innate worth of pregnancy, childbirth and maternity. This suggestion is particularly evident when legal and political conversations position surrogacy

84 Austl, New South Wales, Standing Committee on Law and Justice, *Legislation on Altruistic Surrogacy in NSW* (Report No 38) (Sydney: Standing Committee on Law and Justice, 2009) at 103.

85 Austl, New South Wales, Standing Committee on Law and Justice, *Legislation on Altruistic Surrogacy in NSW* (Report No 38) (Sydney: Standing Committee on Law and Justice, 2009) at 102.

within the rubric of "new" and "assisted" reproductive technologies and when the practice is characterized as commercializing women's procreative ability, their maternity and their children. These accounts cast surrogacy as corroding traditional maternity ideals. The following comment of one Canadian Member of Parliament is illustrative:

> [T]here is something fundamentally offensive with the notion that the act of human reproduction can and should be commodified, that it can and should become a market service, that to compel somebody, through financial incentive, to bear someone else's child in a sense cheapens the invaluable act of motherhood upon which a price cannot be placed.[86]

Surrogates' own narratives do not reflect instrumentalist or pejorative perceptions of maternity and parenthood. Rather, many surrogates expound upon the roles of mother and parent in orthodox and idealistic ways. Their contribution to the transformation of people into parents is cast, in their own terms, as the "ultimate gift" (Ragoné 1996: 355) or as "the gift of life" (Berend 2010: 243). Surrogates also typically enjoy pregnancy as a feminine life experience that yields favourable attention (Parker 1983: 118, York 1990). Women who expressed their willingness to become surrogates in one study indicated positive perceptions of becoming a parent and privileged traditional reasons for parenthood (Poote and van den Akker 2009: 143); this may explain some surrogates' ascription of value to a practice that facilitates genetic parentage. Thus, rather than being engaged in an experimental, *avant-garde* process that overhauls social and legal understandings of filiation, surrogates might be better understood as motivated by helping others achieve biological parenthood. And instead of perceiving surrogacy as derogating from the sanctity and wholesomeness of reproduction and maternity, surrogates instead draw upon cross-cultural social norms that privilege fertility and parentage. Surrogates have even shown themselves capable of appropriating descriptions of their bodies as vessels or instruments for reproduction, which often trouble feminists. This imagery is seized to develop a sense of control over a surrogate pregnancy, and can rationalize the application of their own physical forces to a surrogacy project, which bestows benefits on intending parents and on the surrogate herself.

All this being said, surrogates' renditions of their experiences are nuanced by the fact that their roles are premised on an intention to relinquish the children they gestate moments after delivering them into the world. This seeming paradox within the surrogate's narrative—prioritizing maternity while promising, prior to conception, to give up a child—complicates juridical approaches to surrogacy. State law grapples with this complexity through rules, existent in the jurisdictions considered here, which protect the surrogate from being compelled to deliver a child to the intending parents. However, knowledge of how surrogates appreciate

86 Canada, *House of Commons Debates*, 37th Parl, 2nd Sess, No 78 (26 March 2003) at 4728 (Jason Kenney).

their pregnancies suggests that this risk may be less acute than assumed. Moreover, while state law addresses the risk of a surrogate retreating from a surrogacy agreement's terms, it remains silent on the eventuality of intending parents doing so. In the result, surrogates bear the risk of being left to care for a child whom they did not plan to raise. State law accordingly communicates two messages. A first is that a surrogate is vulnerable to reneging on her commitments because of the natural bond she should have with the child she carries. Second, a lack of legal attention to, or remedy for, a breach of contract by intending parents suggests that such circumstances should not be viewed as a loss. Rather, a woman who gives birth occupies the natural and expected role of "mother" unless and until she decides to place the child for adoption.

These implications reflect state law's failure to account for the relevance of multiple norms pertinent to reproduction and maternity at play in surrogates' choices. These norms privilege parenthood while challenging traditional maternal images, shaping the experience of surrogate motherhood as a vocation that furthers a parental mission, but one that, for the surrogate, ends upon the completion of her reproductive labour.

Each of these three identified points of intersection between state and non-state law sheds light on state law's shortcomings. While state law presumes surrogates as economically dependent and susceptible to exploitation, empirical study reveals the power they may hold within surrogacy negotiations and the range of social and psychological factors underpinning their decisions. Given that their motivations stem from more than anticipated financial gain, surrogates are likely less vulnerable to economic pressure than legal and political actors seem to assume. Surrogacy legislation's heavy focus on payment conflicts with non-state norms in a second way, by overlooking sites of gender oppression rooted in cultural norms. Removing the element of remuneration will not fully alleviate risks for women who serve as surrogates to meet social expectations and to retain inclusion within families and communities. Precluding payment also forces surrogacy to be recognized according to norms of service and volunteerism, devaluing the social and economic worth of a surrogate's contribution. Finally, state law's casting of surrogacy as destabilizing and threatening to conventional ideas of motherhood overlooks the conservative, traditionalist outlook on family and parenthood that may prompt surrogates' choices.

Experiential knowledge gleaned from surrogates' own narratives recounted through empirical research thus foregrounds gaps in state law's understanding of how women make decisions about conceiving and bearing a child for another. This knowledge also reveals the over- and under-inclusiveness of juridical efforts to mitigate or eliminate harm to surrogates; they reach too far by presuming surrogates' general economic vulnerability and fall short by neglecting the range of factors that might constrain meaningful choice. These pitfalls suggest that state law bears a weak grip on surrogates' decision-making, particularly in contrast to the normative force of social, economic and psychological influences. As explained below, however, state-crafted legal rules do affect surrogates' choices, only not in the manner predicted by legislators and political actors.

Criminal Law's Persuasion over Surrogacy Choices

Juridical efforts in the three jurisdictions considered here have been oriented toward stamping out surrogacy in its commercial form, with a view to protecting the interests of women and children. An investigation into the experiences of women who have taken up the role of surrogate mother permits an assessment of criminal law's success in this mission. Plainly put, and unsurprisingly, the prohibition of paid surrogacy does not halt this practice (Burrows 2011: 60-61). Empirical research illuminates how the threat of criminal sanction, particularly when appreciated as unreasonable or unsubstantiated, can produce effects that counter state law's objectives. That is, individuals will be more likely to engage in "non-compliance, creative compliance, criminal behaviour or overt opposition" (Murphy et al. 2009: 2), to circumvent prohibitions or prosecution. Criminalization thus propels the practice to sites obscured from legal surveillance and devoid of regulation or protection for the parties involved. With respect to commercial surrogacy, prohibition often prompts its relocation to foreign jurisdictions where the practice does not carry a threat of prosecution. In Canada, following the AHRA's introduction, many couples travelled to countries where paid surrogacy can be practiced without risk of legal sanction (Kashmeri 2008: 31, 39).[87] Paid surrogacy's ban has thus been critiqued as having simply "exported" surrogacy's challenges rather than seeking to regulate it effectively (Kashmeri 2008: 40). Such instances of "surrogacy shopping" are observed also within Australia (Burpee 2009: 333).

When not pushed to alternate jurisdictions, commercial surrogacy continues domestically, only it usually moves "underground" (Menon 2009: 20-21, Gazze 2007, Anonymous 2007).[88] In Canada, an Expert Panel on Infertility and Adoption in Ontario remarked that legislative prohibitions compel actors to turn to prohibitively expensive, unethical or dangerous alternatives.[89] Part of criminalization's black market effect is manifest in participants' efforts to eliminate paper trails associated with a surrogacy arrangement. In some instances, this involves "reimbursing" the surrogate only in cash or in gifts (Anonymous 2007), sometimes in a manner that well exceeds the surrogate's out-of-pocket expenses, resulting in an illegal for-profit arrangement (Menon 2009: 20). In others, parties avoid the formation of

87 Canada, Ontario, *Raising Expectations: Recommendations of the Expert Panel on Infertility and Adoption* (Toronto: Ministry of Children and Youth Services, 2009) at 128.

88 Canada, House of Commons, Standing Committee on Health, *Assisted Human Reproduction: Building Families* (December 2001) (Chair: Bonnie Brown).

89 Canada, Ontario, *Raising Expectations: Recommendations of the Expert Panel on Infertility and Adoption* (Toronto: Ministry of Children and Youth Services, 2009) at 129.

written contracts (Burpee 2009: 328).[90] At the time of giving birth, surrogates might even admit themselves to a hospital or birthing centre under the intending mother's name so as to avoid postpartum parentage challenges (Burpee 2009: 334-335). Efforts to conceal facts surrounding surrogacy arrangements may be impugned as fraudulent and morally flawed. More significantly, they impose risk to the parties concerned, particularly the surrogate whose health and safety may be adversely affected by the absence of or inaccurate documentation. This phenomenon of exiling criminalized practices, with hazardous implications for the women concerned, is witnessed also in connection with the proscription of polygamy and sex work.

In some cases, however, surrogacy happens in plain view of juridical actors even though the terms of the arrangement should raise questions about its formal legality. In Quebec, surrogacy arrangements have been judicially sanctioned through the modality of special consent adoption, even though they are—according to formal law at least—null in the province (*Adoption – 09184*, *Adoption – 09367*, *Adoption – 10329*). This remains the case even when there is uncertain evidence about the exchange of money between the parties to the agreement (*Adoption – 09367*). In the United Kingdom, state law's exclusion of surrogates and intending parents from its prohibitions has been suggested as a defective mode of banning commercial surrogacy (Theis et al. 2009: 342). The legislative scheme has thus been described as "half-hearted and piecemeal" (Welstead 2010: 216), creating leeway for judicial recognition of surrogacy agreements, even in commercial form, in the name of children's interests (Horsey and Sheldon 2012: 78). Australian courts also have been willing to render decisions giving effect to surrogacy agreements that explicitly or potentially contravene legislative enactments by drawing on pragmatic concerns related to children's interests (*Re Evelyn*, *Re A. and B.*, *Re Mark: an application relating to parental responsibilities*). While perhaps reaching their conclusions with reluctance (Stuhmcke 2004: 24), Australian judges have held that children's interests must "override any public policy considerations" regarding surrogacy's questionable legality (*Re A. and B.*: 318, 324-325, but see contra *Re Appln pursuant to the BIRTHS DEATHS AND MARRIAGES REGISTRATION ACT 1997 – BC200002350*). Case law thus reveals social and judicial tolerance for surrogacy despite legal rules' skepticism. The point casts doubt about the efficacy of state-made rules, both in terms of their ability to control or circumscribe the practice and in offering the protection to women on which these rules claim to be premised.

In the final analysis, although criminalizing payment for surrogacy does not eliminate this practice, it affects surrogates' choices about their engagement with it. They may undertake their arrangements clandestinely. If the arrangement is brought into public view, its purpose and effect are generally cast in palatable terms, underscoring its service to children's interests. Juridical responses to

---

90 Canada, Ontario, *Raising Expectations: Recommendations of the Expert Panel on Infertility and Adoption* (Toronto: Ministry of Children and Youth Services, 2009) at 130.

surrogacy further affect the way surrogates discuss and explain their choices about this practice. Aware of state law's rejection of remunerated surrogacy, surrogates commonly deploy a discourse centred on altruism, which downplays the relevance of surrogacy's commercial benefits, to explain their choices. Pitching their accounts this way purifies their role, allowing them to distinguish themselves from surrogates—more "wicked"—who accept payment for their services (Ragoné 1996: 356). Their endeavours thus become more socially acceptable (Ruparelia 2007: 35). As discussed, however, surrogacy is rarely, if ever, altruistic; even when it is unpaid, surrogates' narratives reveal their sense that surrogacy yields a personal return. Yet it would be a mistake to presume as disingenuous claims about altruism within surrogacy narratives. As discussed in Part 1, a genuine desire to make a social difference or contribution drives many surrogates' decisions and explains the importance they attach to their experiences. It is important to note, too, that the actual role money plays in surrogates' choices remains enigmatic. Because state law stigmatizes this aspect of the practice so intensely, clear reporting in its regard will be difficult to obtain.

Surrogacy's juridical precariousness also has ramifications on the planning and strategizing that happens around issues of filiation. Commercial surrogacy's proscription, coupled with the general unenforceability of surrogacy contracts and paucity of state law governing the practice, operates to premise the relationship between surrogates and intending parents on mutual trust over juridical obligations (Hohman and Hagan 2001: 83, Menon 2009: 66, Kashmeri 2008: 68). Parties to surrogacy agreements are generally aware that their counterparts might refuse to uphold their respective promises without direct legal consequence. Surrogates might thus insist on gestational rather than genetic surrogacy, given the perception that intending parents will be less likely to renege on a surrogacy agreement if they are genetically related to the child the surrogate carries. Genetic surrogacy is also understood to temper surrogates' bonding with the fetus, reducing the risk that she will not follow through with her preconception intentions (Kashmeri 2008: 91).

Finally, legal prohibitions subject surrogates to considerable emotional risk. Emotional stressors that may be associated with becoming a surrogate are considerably mitigated by the presence of competent therapeutic interventions that guide women in relation to their expectations and emotions before, during and after their surrogate pregnancies. Access to professional psychological care and guidance appears to increase surrogates' satisfaction with their experiences. That being said, outlawing surrogacy intermediaries creates a critical impediment to the provision of such support (Ciccarelli and Beckman 2005: 33-34).

Even though non-state norms play a key role in driving surrogates' choices and these often conflict with state law governing surrogacy, the latter continue to shape the practice, only not in the manner legislators generally intend. Surrogacy regulation, ostensibly preoccupied with women's safety and exposure to manipulation and harm, seeks to reduce or eliminate instances of this practice, particularly when undertaken for payment. Criminalization and non-recognition have, however, had the effect of exporting the practice primarily to jurisdictions where surrogacy does not trigger potential penal consequences and where it is largely unregulated. Alternatively, practitioners are driven to engage in surrogacy covertly. Thus, even when legislative prohibitions do not target the surrogate and leave her free of any risk of prosecution, her engagement with surrogacy will resemble and carry many of the risks of criminal behaviour. This is particularly evident when one considers the stigma, deceit and harm surreptitious surrogacy can engender, and the costs and losses that parties to a surrogacy arrangement will be forced to assume in the event of conflict or unfulfilled undertakings.

Conclusion

Women's choices about becoming surrogate mothers are generated by a diversity of factors that include, but are plainly not limited to, formal laws designed by the state to govern this practice. Moreover, criminal law wields effects on surrogates' choices that do not match its underlying assumptions and ambitions. As this chapter reveals, surrogacy in practice eludes state law's reach, a reality brought to light through interdisciplinary empirical research focused on obtaining and communicating surrogates' experiential knowledge.

Part of state law's inability to regulate surrogacy according to its own intentions and foundational premises can be traced to its acceptance of a binary model of choice affecting genderized social practices fraught with controversy. Legislative and policy discussions on surrogacy are built on an understanding of women as either victimized or empowered (Goslinga-Roy 2000: 122). These conversations overlook the possibility that surrogates are enriched by their experiences, even if being a surrogate mother might involve considerable tradeoffs. At the same time, such conversations reflect negligibly on state law's own contribution to heightening women's vulnerability and to limiting their options with a view to ensuring their own security, dignity and protection. This is most evident in state law's refusal to consider how its rejection of legal payment for surrogacy might hurt, rather than help, women.

Parallels between surrogacy and sex work are easily discerned; indeed, some feminists have referred to surrogacy as a form of "reproductive prostitution" (Dworkin 1983: 181-182, Ince 1994). Both practices are contentious primarily because they present as instances of control, exploitation and commercialization of women's bodies: in one case for reproduction, in the other for sex. The architecture of state law's response to sex work thus closely resembles that which responds to surrogacy. It is prompted by presumptions that the women concerned invariably make choices constrained by gender-based power dynamics. Nevertheless, empirical research provides a counter-narrative to this dominant perception. As is true with respect to surrogacy, a proclaimed goal of protecting seemingly vulnerable women animates legislation and policy governing sex work. Yet as the upcoming chapter shows, state law pushes the ostensible subject of that protection, much like the polygamous wife and the paid surrogate, underground and out of view to sites where meaningful, self-actualizing choices truly can become unrealizable.

Chapter 4
Law's Engagement with the Sale of Sex

State law and policy makers in the West have given sex work far more attention than they have polygamy or surrogacy. This is true of both historical and current legal discussions within the three jurisdictions under consideration in this book. One might presume that the intensity and scope of state law's focus on sex work stems from its historical prevalence. Yet polygamy and surrogacy, while not having been the subject of such extensive juridical focus, are biblically recorded practices.[1] Polygamy and surrogacy are not new, only they have not received the public scrutiny given to sex work. The state's concern with sex work stems from its visibility and ubiquity. Unlike polygamy and surrogacy, which typically occurs discretely, sex work is often starkly viewable and public. It vexes many of those who neighbour and witness the practice and, as discussed in this chapter, their concerns are often at the root of legislative responses to sex work.

While the sex worker might have greater social prominence than the polygamous wife or the paid surrogate, state law impugns her choices and lifestyles for reasons that resonate with its indictment of these two other practices. Like the plural wife, the sex worker is viewed as the prey of lewd men who use her for their own sexual gratification. And, similar to the commercial surrogate, the sex worker is seen as deploying her body and her physical, intimate self to extract financial gain. Thus, as in other contexts considered in this book, state law's uneasiness with sex work is grounded in its perceived potential to distort orthodox sexual and family relationships.

This chapter is structured pursuant to the framework explained in Chapter 1 for the juridical study of women's morally controversial choices. Part 1 contemplates the narratives relayed by sex workers as recorded through empirical research. It seeks to discern the meaning or explanation women give for engaging with erotic labour. It further aims to identify how women value, or normatively assess, their engagement with this activity. Part 2 explores sex work's governance through formal laws crafted by the state in Canada, the United Kingdom and Australia. This discussion illuminates state law's historical and contemporary prohibition of activities associated with the trade of money for sex, rather than that exchange itself. Part 3 proceeds to identify presumptions and objectives driving state law,

---

1 On polygamy see e.g., Genesis 4:19, which refers to Lamech's two wives: Adah and Zillah, and Genesis 16:3, referring to Abraham being married to Sarah while also taking Hagar "as a wife." The Book of Genesis (16:1-16) also recounts Abraham's wives acting as surrogates for one another (Hagar as Sarah's surrogate), and (30:1-43) of Bilhah, the handmaid of Rachel, who conceived and bore a child for her.

and juxtaposes these against non-state norms and considerations—such as social, cultural and economic forces—prompting women's choices in relation to sex work as discerned from the empirical research discussed in Part 1. Part 3 further analyses state law's effects on the practice of sex work, which are comparable to the ramifications observed in relation to formal rules governing polygamy and surrogacy. More to the point, criminalizing these women ostracizes and marginalizes them, paradoxically heightening the vulnerability that state law commonly invokes as its rationale when outlawing particular choices.

Prior to embarking on this analysis, the discussion here would be remiss in failing to signal the capitalist and postcolonial forces shaping sex work in the jurisdictions under study. Sex work is predominantly undertaken to earn an income. As discussed here, this does not mean that all sex workers are economically desperate or destitute, but sex work—as any work—is largely driven by a remuneration incentive. Where associated with criminalization, however, the sex industry is largely unregulated and transactions occur in a hidden market. Few incentives exist for ensuring workers' fair wages and safe labour conditions. In the result, sex workers bear the onus of crafting informal strategies for resisting and overcoming the fallout of this predicament. This chapter reveals the resilience, resourcefulness and intellectual dexterity women exhibit in devising methods to identify and confront the risks of sex work, which are exacerbated by criminalization.

The distinct postcolonial realities existent in Canada, the United Kingdom and Australia are also critical to acknowledge, as these contribute to sex work's demographics in these jurisdictions. Available evidence indicates that Aboriginal women in Canada are disproportionately represented in the sex trade, particularly at street level (Day 2008, Rabinovitch 2003: 249).[2] Australian data is less explicit and detailed on this point, although historical scholarship emphasizes the prevalence of Aboriginal sex workers during the country's colonial period (Frances 1994). Contemporary research also speaks to indigenous women's involvement in transactional sex particularly as a result of stark economic marginalization and homelessness (Holmes and McRae-Williams 2011). Moreover, migrant and trafficked women, particularly from Asia, Eastern Europe and Latin America, appear to make up a significant and growing number of sex workers in the jurisdictions considered in this book (Timoshkina and McDonald 2009, Remple et al. 2007: 162, TAMPEP 2009: 16-24, Frances 1994, Queensland Crime and Misconduct Commission 2011: 11). These women may contest a plurality of subordinating forces at once: racism, undocumented status, language barriers, compromised economic circumstances, social stigma and criminalization. Such factors are core to the way in which women experience sex work and its governance.

2 Canada, British Columbia, Sisterwatch Project of the Vancouver Police Department and Women's Memorial March Committee, *The Tragedy of Missing and Murdered Aboriginal Women in Canada: We Can Do Better* (2011) at 10, [Online]. Available at: http://vancouver.ca/police/assets/pdf/reports-policies/missing-murdered-aboriginal-women-canada-report.pdf [accessed: 8 June 2013].

A last introductory remark about scope and terminology is required. This chapter generally relies on the term "sex work" rather than "prostitution," although the latter term is used in the explanation and assessment of legislative provisions that directly invoke the language of "prostitution." By drawing primarily on the terminology of "sex work," this project adopts the views of feminists who have argued that this is more than a rhetorical label, but bears critical political connotations. It resists the victimizing and stigmatic insinuations that the term "prostitution" has historically conveyed. "Sex work" lexicon is further attuned to the control and power some women derive from sexual labour (Sanders et al. 2009: 9, Bindman and Doezema 1997). These connotations resonate strongly with this book's central argument regarding the way in which women, even in intensely compromising life circumstances, can appropriate agency and choice.

The meaning of "sex work" within this chapter merits definition. The term can encompass a range of services that may extend beyond the sale of direct sexual contact, such as pornography and erotic dance (e.g., Harcourt and Donovan 2005: 201 identify "at least 25 types of sex work"). While hazy lines separate these practices, they raise distinct concerns (Weitzer 2010). This project's scope does not permit a full inquiry into the varied practices to which "sex work" might refer. Its focus is on transactional sex, whether commissioned directly by a sex worker, or arranged by a third party. Moreover, while not all sex workers are women, they remain the concentration here in view of sex work's highly genderized nature as well as this project's focus on women's proscribed lifestyles and choices.

Part 1: Plural Narratives about Choice

The breadth of social science research relevant to sex work is vast, particularly when compared with that which has examined the practices of polygamy and surrogacy. The body of literature on which this chapter draws is delineated by three main characteristics. First, it focuses on sex work as practiced in the jurisdictions considered in this book: Canada, the United Kingdom and Australia. Second, it is premised on data derived primarily through qualitative research methods and field studies, in view of this book's commitment to learning from empiricism and experiential knowledge. Authorities relied on thus emanate primarily from sociology, anthropology, psychology, criminology, health and medicine, and socio-legal studies. Third, the analysis that follows builds on women in sex work, and on adult sex work. A few authorities, however, include male and transgender research participants or describe the experiences of sex workers who engaged in this practice before reaching the age of majority (e.g., Jeffrey and Macdonald 2006a, Lewis et al. 2005, Boyle et al. 1997, Benoit and Millar 2001), and these are relied on for what they impart about women's experiences in the sex trade.

This body of empirical research is affected by limitations similar to that which relates to polygamy and surrogacy. In the jurisdictions under contemplation here, sex workers live under heavy social stigma and an ongoing risk of criminal prosecution. In consequence, they are a "relatively hard-to-reach" population for field research (*Bedford v. Canada*: para. 97). Sex work is also characterized by marked fluidity; women will be engaged sometimes regularly or sometimes sporadically or on single occasions in the sex trade (Sanders 2007: 76). Many will simultaneously pursue educational programs or work for pay in jobs outside of sex work (Bilardi et al. 2011: 119, Groves et al. 2008: 394, Sanders 2004a: 561, Benoit and Millar 2001: 22). Whether one self-identifies as a sex worker will depend largely on experiences and desires. For instance, some women might exchange sex for goods or services in kind rather than money, and in such circumstances might not consider themselves as sex workers (Boyle et al. 1997: 38-39). Their narratives may be omitted from empirical study on sex work, and this suggests the possibility of an under-inclusive body of research. Conversely, research on "sex work" might be over-inclusive, capturing those who engage in forms of erotic labour, such as pornography or non-contact erotic dance, which fall outside of what is conventionally understood as "prostitution" or "sex work."

The present work is mindful of these drawbacks to the scope of published research on sex work. Nevertheless, this body of research is characterized by ample studies that generate overlapping themes and conclusions, infusing it with credibility and relevance. Moreover, empirical evidence, though not without limits, is crucial to nourishing juridical understandings of and approaches to sex work (*Bedford v. Canada*: para. 83). Thus, as in preceding chapters, the investigation that follows affirms this book's commitment to drawing on women's narratives, as communicated primarily through field studies, to discern their experiences and choices in connection with practices that prompt social, moral and legal objection.

Following the structure established for each case study in this book, this Part investigates two questions. The first is how women give meaning to their involvement in sex work. This inquiry assesses the motivations or explanations women ascribe to their decisions to take up sex work. A second question relates to how women attribute value to sex work. This strand of analysis is more normative in nature than the first. It contemplates how women assess their experiences as sex workers, that is, whether they attribute positive or negative value to such experiences and on what bases.

The Meaning Women Ascribe to Engaging in Sex Work

Sex workers explain, or give meaning to, their involvement with this work by referring to factors that suggest a history or status of social and economic marginalization. Women who are financially privileged, highly educated and have enjoyed social, emotional and economic stability throughout their lives do not typically resort to work in the sex trade. Moreover, unlike many women who engage in polygamy or surrogacy, few sex workers explain their choices by drawing on notions of spiritual, moral or social fulfillment and contribution. Most see sex work as a means of earning an income. In some cases, this work is tied to substance dependence. Finally, some women might consider sex work as an extension of, or as a way to explore, their sexual identity. These factors, which illuminate the meaning or rationale women ascribe to sex work, are explored in turn.

Economic pressures and incentives Engagement with sex work is largely driven by economic need or desire. This is true with respect to both entry into and remaining within the sex trade (Groves et al. 2008). Regardless of where sex work occurs and the legal regime that applies to its governance, women make sense of their involvement in this practice through reference to it as a source of income. This may be viewed as intuitive or logical, as money "reflects why most persons work," including those who work in the sex trade.[3] Yet not all correlations between a person's economic circumstances and sex work are of the same quality. Depending on women's socioeconomic state, movement into sex work might be qualified either as resulting from economic desperation or from an attraction to a relatively lucrative opportunity this way of life presents.

Women who describe their motivations in terms of pure economic "necessity" (Pivot Legal Society 2004: 13) are typically those most disadvantaged socially and economically. They are more likely to be involved with street work and to live with substance dependencies. Many also will report having been homeless, at least at one point in their lives, and will feel the need to relocate often to avoid having their identity as a sex worker uncovered.[4] One study of sex work in Vancouver's Downtown Eastside concluded that of the 91 affiants whose views were culled, poverty was "overwhelming" and many affirmed that their entry into sex work was prompted by "inadequate social assistance" (Pivot Legal Society 2004: 13). This study, having been conducted in one of Canada's most impoverished communities, perhaps cannot be "generalized to the sex worker population overall" (Pivot Legal Society 2004: 8). Yet other research suggests that joblessness, the need to care for dependents, an absence of private or family support, housing challenges and inadequate social assistance often combine to prompt entry into sex work (Hallgrimsdottir et al. 2006: 276). The point emerges in the remarks of a Queensland sex worker, describing her entry into the sex trade as a 12 year-old runaway:

> Nowhere to live, no money and an offer came along and it just seemed alright at the time too, and drugs … I was into drugs too so I had to get money for drugs. (Boyle et al. 1997: 39)

Not all sex workers enter this trade as a result of acute economic need. Some women indicate that the income potential of sex work presents an "incentive"

3 Austl, Queensland, Prostitution Licensing Authority, *Submission to the Crime and Misconduct Commission Review of the Prostitution Act 1999* (Brisbane: Crime and Misconduct Commission, 2010) at 6.

4 Edmonton Social Planning Council, *Street Prostitution in Edmonton* (Edmonton: Edmonton Social Planning Council, 1993) at 1.

or "opportunity" rather than a way to meet basic necessities. Sex work might be viewed as both profitable and flexible, facilitating the maintenance of children or the fulfillment of other financial obligations or objectives (Sanders and Campbell 2007: 7). Women may view sex work as the most viable among a range of income-earning options, particularly where such options offer low wages or impose onerous and stressful work conditions (Jeffrey and MacDonald 2006a: 319-320, Bilardi et al. 2011, Willman 2010: 143-146, Jackson et al. 2007: 262-263). A participant in a Canadian study thus explained her reasons for taking up sex work:

> The money's really good and I am a single mom … to support my kids and the things they need. The [non sex-work] jobs that I applied for before; they're all minimum wage. I don't really have a lot of education to go work for a big company. (Bungay et al. 2011)

Another woman in Queensland offered a comparable narrative, which alludes also to the flexibility for which sex work might be valued, as is described later in this chapter:

> I was used to the income of two wages and then when I split up [with my husband] I didn't realise it would be so hard … the children were used to a certain living standard, and I was living in a hovel and I just couldn't do it, my children weren't used to it … I go out to work, a normal job, by the time I pay out child care, I don't see the children from seven in the morning until seven at night … having the children with no father, why should they have no mother as well? (Boyle et al. 1997: 71)

Clearly, then, not all sex workers are "simply pushed into the trade by economic forces" (Jeffrey and MacDonald 2006a: 314, see also Koken 2010: 41). Sex work can present an opportunity to make, in the words of one escort, "a good living" (Hallgrimsdottir et al. 2006: 276). It might also be a way to earn both "big" money (that is, large sums) and "easy" money (that is, obtained rapidly or relatively simply) (Jeffrey and MacDonald 2006a: 317-318). This money might be used for meeting basic survival needs or for narcotics. It might also be relied on to pursue mainstream or mundane financial goals, such as offsetting debt, preparing for the costs of a new baby, planning for the expenses of Christmas, financing tuition fees and supporting dependents (McKeganey and Barnard 1996: 26-27, Groves et al. 2008: 393, Bruckert et al. 2003: 22-23).

Apart from shaping decisions about whether women partake in sex work or remain in this practice, economic factors might also influence the scope of a sex worker's services. Women may accept to do "full service" sex work for clients if they perceive this as a way to earn a greater income (Bungay et al. 2011). This might also involve engaging in unprotected sex should a client offer more money for this (Boyle et al. 1997: 84). The risks of such services are clear, and they are explored more fully in a later subsection ("The Value Women Ascribe to Engaging in Sex Work").

Substance dependence Although it is often presumed that drug use and sex work coincide, the prevalence of addiction as a motivator for sex work is impossible to determine. Some women are explicit about substance dependence as the reason for their engagement in sex work (McKeganey and Barnard 1996: 26, Cusick and Hickman 2005: 370, Hallgrimsdottir et al. 2006: 276, Benoit and Millar 2001: 36-37). In some cases, workers might be financing a partner's dependence (McKeganey and Barnard 1996: 47). Sex work might be used as a way to earn money to buy illegal drugs, or it may be directly exchanged for narcotics (Kwiatkowski and Booth 2000, Gossop et al. 1994). Where dependence is at the root of sex work, a pattern emerges that might be described as a "'work-score-use' cycle" (Jeal et al. 2008, see also Porter and Bonilla 2010: 164). Other researchers have characterized circumstances of simultaneous engagement with sex work and drug use as "trapping" for participants, leaving them with few viable options for subsistence (Cusick and Hickman 2005, see also Gossop et al. 1994: 967). Addiction-related needs might be exacerbated in circumstances or settings where drugs are scarce. This can leave substance-dependent sex workers "at the mercy of customers, pimps and drug dealers," potentially compelling them to partake in practices that expose them to sexually-transmitted infection and violence (Pivot Legal Society 2004: 22).

Substance dependence explains women's involvement in sex work largely in connection with urban street work. This point is suggested both by studies that focus only on outdoor sex work (e.g., Jeal et al. 2008, McKeganey and Barnard 1996: 36ff.) and by those that include both street and indoor workers within their research population sample (e.g., Pyett and Warr 1999: 185-196).[5] Indoor establishments might also set norms that bar and sanction the use of illegal drugs (Boyle et al. 1997: 102). In the State of Victoria, for example, where brothels are licensed, illegal drugs are prohibited and managers are typically unlikely to hire women known to use or be addicted to drugs (Pyett and Warr 1999: 189). Women in such settings may be less likely to use stupefying substances or be dependent on them.

Accordingly, sex workers' relatively high rate of substance use or dependence (e.g., Cler-Cunningham and Christensen 2001)[6] does not unequivocally point to substance dependence as a cause or necessary precursor to sex work. Dependence might predate sex work, but might also be caused or deepened by it; drugs might serve as a "coping mechanism" for sex work's stresses (Boyle et al. 1997: 100). Regardless of chronology, the coincidence of dependence and sex work can

5 See also, C. Woodward et al., *Selling Sex in Queensland 2003: A Study of Prostitution in Queensland* (Brisbane: Prostitution Licensing Authority, 2004).

6 See also, Edmonton Social Planning Council, *Street Prostitution in Edmonton* (Edmonton: Edmonton Social Planning Council, 1993).

complicate an exit from sex work for a woman who seeks that option (Gossop et al. 1994). Leaving sex work may be frustrated by the economic costs of substance dependence, and by the limited social and medical resources, as well as work opportunities, that are realistically available to women seeking to overcome addiction while emerging from a socially and legally impugned lifestyle.

Just as the extent to which economic need varies as a motivator for sex work, there is no clear or consistent correlation between substance dependence and this labour. Drug use is more prevalent among sex workers than the general population, although it cannot be inferred that one practice is the direct cause of the other (Jeffrey and MacDonald 2006b: 39-44, 191). The relationship between childhood trauma and sex work is comparable; while understood as "risk factors" (Nixon et al. 2002: 1023-1024, Hallgrimsdottir et al. 2006: 275), encounters with abuse, trauma or instability will not inevitably lead to sex work and this history is not universal among sex workers (Nadon et al. 1998, Vanwesenbeek 2001: 259-262, Koken 2010: 45).

As a final point, it is worth noting that the implications of drug use in sex work contexts are more nuanced than might be initially presumed. Addiction can compound sex workers' health and safety risks (Nixon et al. 2002: 1034). For instance, the urgency of drug withdrawal and the desire to "score" might prompt sex workers to tolerate violent clients or those who seek unprotected sex (Jackson et al. 2005: 99). One British street worker described this situation in the following stark terms:

> Sometimes they [clients] didn't use condoms I'll be honest with you but that's the way it is init you know. If you've got a habit you've got to do it, no choice you know what I mean. (Jeal et al. 2008: 382)

At the same time, drugs might be a method for negotiating health challenges. Notably, it might facilitate "the management of stress and positive domain separation," that is, the ability to demarcate one's self from one's sex work (Harris et al. 2011: 395). Drug use therefore might offer a necessary strategy for negotiating sex work's mental health challenges. The observation is not intended to palliate or offset the plain and well-documented risks of substance misuse, especially for sex workers (e.g., Pivot Legal Society 2004: 21-23). It is instead meant to underline methods sex workers may adopt to navigate the intense burdens of sex work and associated state-based legal regimes, particularly those premised upon criminalization, which obstruct the provision of health and social services to the sex worker community. This argument is developed more robustly in Part 3 ("Interface between State and Non-State Law").

Sexual curiosity and enjoyment The two foregoing factors—financial pressures and incentives, and substance dependence —suggest that sex workers are typically disenfranchised women. A third dynamic lacks such connotations and suggests that sex work might draw women from any walk of life. Sexual interest, or a desire to explore one's own sexual identity or service others' sexual needs, might motivate sex work (Petro 2010: 157). As one Canadian woman explained, "My life before I started working in the sex trade? I was just going to school and I was extremely curious about prostitution" (Benoit and Millar 2001: 36-37).

Some women cite their enjoyment of sex or the satisfaction derived from providing sexual services, as a basis for their work (Groves et al. 2008: 393). The take up of sex work might therefore evolve from long-standing attractions to "eroticism and sex work" and may represent "a natural extension of [one's] lifestyle" (Bruckert et al. 2003: 22-23). At least in the context of licensed sex work, "the glamour of the [sex] industry" could be a draw (Groves et al. 2008: 393-394). Comparably, other women may see this as a way to "escape isolation" and forge human connections (Bruckert et al. 2003: 22, see *contra*, Pivot Legal Society 2004: 22, asserting that women do not work in the sex trade "for the fun of it"). Although this is not a prevailing view within the empirical literature, the possibility of sex work as personally gratifying surfaces in some corners of empirical study and merits acknowledgement, given that it suggests that sex work could draw women from diverse social and economic brackets, not only those who are most marginalized. Moreover, this dimension of sex work stresses the relevance of social connections that some women find in sex work, which can infuse the practice with value in addition to meaning. The ensuing analysis explores this feature and others that sex workers deem pertinent within their evaluations of their experiences in the sex trade.

The Value Women Ascribe to Engaging in Sex Work

Women's evaluations of their encounters with sex work are premised on the extent to which they view their work as compromising their health and security, affording independence, and facilitating social relationships.

Health and security The risks associated with sex work are easily imagined and thoroughly recorded. Sex workers face elevated exposure to sexually-transmitted infections. The risk is aggravated for women who provide services without condom use, either because they work while using drugs and thus have diminished control over their encounters or because they accept a client's request for unprotected sex in return for higher payment (Pyett and Warr 1997, Benoit and Millar 2001: 75).

Sex workers' physical health is also undermined by violence, which workers often see as endemic to their trade (Porter and Bonilla 2010: 164). Many women have been assaulted in the course of their work (Pyett and Warr 1999), and risks of such violence are especially acute for street workers (Jeal et al. 2008, Sanders and Campbell 2007: 1-2, O'Doherty 2011a, Church et al. 2001, McKeganey and Barnard 1996: 70). Even those who have not been directly subject to violence are deeply aware of and anxious about its risk. Workers therefore take active steps to prevent or reduce their susceptibility to assault or other criminal activity (Sanders

2004a: 563-564, Benoit and Millar 2001: 50-59). Such risk-mitigating strategies are explored more fully in Part 3 ("Interface between State and Non-State Law").

Empirical studies evidence sex workers' ability to respond to physical hazards. Within the indoor market, safe sex is generally a routine and enforced practice (Sanders 2004a: 562, Bungay et al. 2011: 24), although condom use may sometimes be restricted to the riskiest practices (Benoit and Millar 2001: 73). Street workers who do not have the support of an agency or brothel can develop skills to negotiate condom use with resistant clients (Pyett and Warr 1999: 191). Most also will refuse unprotected sexual encounters as a means of competing with other sex workers or of elevating their compensation (Pyett and Warr 1997: 542, see *contra*, Jeal et al. 2008: 382).

While the physical hazards of sex work are formidable, some workers will see these as less menacing than the emotional risks of their work. The latter are seen to be less readily controlled and remedied than dangers to physical security. Sex work's emotional risks also are viewed as pervasive, with its effects persisting even outside of work-related encounters, and as threatening irreparable harm. In consequence, while many sex workers believe they could recover from a work-related physical injury, the emotional distress, criminal liability, stigma and family dissolution that might accompany public identification as a sex worker could be "insurmountable" (Sanders 2004a: 568). These emotional stressors may be accentuated for women with pre-existent mental health conditions; a relatively high proportion of sex workers have psychiatric illnesses. Some women might attribute poor mental health status to adverse experiences or to the social shame and stigma associated with sex work (Jeal et al. 2008: 382, Jackson et al. 2007: 266, Benoit and Millar 2001: 69-71). As with drug dependence, however, a direct and unequivocal correlation between mental health challenges and sex work is not established (Bilardi et al. 2011: 121).

These health and safety risk factors influence women's choices about how they engage with the sex industry. It leads many to opt for indoor over outdoor sex work even though indoor independent work (Lewis et al. 2005: 150, 153-154, Boyle et al. 1997: 34-35, Queensland Crime and Misconduct Commission 2011: 42-43) and out-call work (Shaver et al. 2011: 51) can also impose considerable risks. Indoor sex workers' physical integrity and security is thus not unequivocally protected (Sanders and Campbell 2007). Moreover, organized sex establishments might impose worksite policies that increase risk, for example, by failing to screen out dangerous clients or by requiring or incentivizing risky sex services (Pyett and Warr 1999: 190).

Sex workers who prefer brothel work underscore the presence of support staff onsite and measures typically in place for screening clients (Sanders and Campbell 2007: 11, Jeffrey and Sullivan 2009: 65). An Australian worker conveyed this sentiment:

> I've done a little bit of escort work, but didn't like it. You can't relax, you're in someone else's private home, you don't know who is there other than yourself

> and the client. I much prefer the parlour because you've got more protection and other girls around you. It's a much safer environment. (Boyle et al. 1997: 35)

Sex work's health and safety risks therefore affect choices women make about how they take up this work. Recognizing that they must negotiate the interests of their sanity, their physical safety and their economic survival (Sanders 2004a: 559), workers determine the tradeoffs they are willing to make within the pursuit of their work. Balancing the emotional, physical and economic dimensions and risks of sex work is a formidable feat. Yet as discussed in Part 3, recognizing how sex workers navigate risk is essential to an appreciation of how their narratives defy state law's presumptions about the sex worker as invariably victimized by her circumstances.

Work and financial independence While sex work's adverse health experiences may compel women to assess experiences negatively or to craft strategies for negotiating related risks, women may value sex work over other types of employment due to the independence and flexibility it may afford (Bilardi et al. 2011: 119, Groves et al. 2008). It can free them of authoritative hierarchies in the workplace, allowing them to "be [their] own boss" (Sanders 2005: 324, Jeffrey and MacDonald 2006a: 322). Workers thus may be positioned to decide for themselves how, when and where they service clients, giving them "control over the pace and price of their work" and their potential income yield (Jeffrey and MacDonald 2006a: 319). In relation to income, sex work may be valued not only for the size of potential earnings, but also for its liquidity; the work yields "clear" income that produces "cash-in-hand" (Hallgrimsdottir et al. 2006: 277, Boyle et al. 1997: 71, Weldon 2010: 150). Thus, although women recognize sex work's risks, they might choose it in preference to other options that impose greater rigidity and discipline (Jackson et al. 2007: 262, Jeffrey and Macdonald 2006a: 321).

Valuing positively sex workers' vocational and financial autonomy is somewhat paradoxical. Street-based and indoor sole operators appear to enjoy the largest breadth of flexibility and control. In contrast, brothel workers and escorts often lose the ability to negotiate directly with clients and may be subject to terms that limit their independence and sanction them economically. Managers and agents typically collect fees from workers' earnings. They are also prone to dictating worker's schedules, attire, the services they will provide (which sometimes go unpaid and sometimes include mundane tasks having nothing to do with sex, such as laundry), acceptable bases for refusing clients and the health screenings that workers must undergo (Sullivan 2008: 81, Bungay et al. 2011: 21, McKeganey and Barnard 1996: 20, Pyett and Warr 1999: 191, Benoit and Millar 2001: 45-47, and Bruckert et al. 2003: 25-26 but see *contra*, on the issue of extracting fees, Cler-Cunningham and Christensen 2001: 33). Managers or agents might sanction women who resist these requirements by moving them to "quiet" shifts, removing them from the work schedule, dismissing them or fining them (Jeffrey and Sullivan 2009: 66). Some thus suggest that it is "class prejudice" to view street workers as exposed to heightened risks or less humane social conditions as compared with indoor sex workers (Farley 2004: 1101, Benoit and Millar 2001: 44-45).

For those working on the streets or independently indoors, what is lost in terms of the "relative comfort and safety" of structured indoor work (McKeganey and Barnard 1996: 20) may be made up in terms of outdoor sex work's offer of "better money," control and independence (Jeffrey and MacDonald 2006a: 324, Weitzer 2010: 9-11, Harcourt and Donovan 2005: 202, Lewis et al. 2005: 154). Other women, however, will privilege safety over the flexibility and earnings that street or independent work can offer (Jeffrey and Macdonald 2006b: 31). The point critical to the present analysis pertains to women's awareness of tradeoffs and risks that accompany different forms of sex work, and their consequential choices about worksites and services.

Companionship and support A final factor emergent from empirical research on sex workers' experiences has received minimal attention. Women's relationships in sex work contexts affect the way they evaluate their experiences. Support and friendship can reduce the stress and anxiety often associated with this work, and may found professional and social alliances. Women's narratives stress the relevance of such relationships most prominently when discussing safety strategies. Many will refuse independent work and will collaborate with at least one other worker or with a "chaperon" stationed nearby (Sanders 2004a: 564).[7] They may also share information to help each other avoid dangerous clients or settings (McVerry and Lindop 2005: 112), or coordinate efforts to provide backup in the event a client presents "trouble" for one woman (McKeganey and Barnard 1996: 27).

Aside from these professional alliances, sex workers will often refer to women they have met through their work as "friends" (Harris et al. 2011: 392, Sanders 2004a: 564, Jackson et al. 2007: 263). That being said, some women prefer to demarcate and separate their personal from professional bonds (Bruckert et al. 2003: 36).

Relationships among sex workers are not universally positive, and conflict can emerge among particular women or groups of women, which adversely affects their experiences. Such disputes frequently arise from competition for clients. Practices viewed as problematic include undercutting one another's prices or venturing into territory already staked out by other workers. Those engaging in such competitive practices may fear retaliation, even in the form of violence, by other sex workers (Jackson et al. 2007: 263). Some research indicates that street workers may be more likely to engage in competitive and hostile behaviour with one another, whereas allegiances are more likely to be formed among indoor sex workers (Pyett and Warr 1997: 541).

---

7 See also, A. Edwards, *Selling Sex; Regulating Prostitution in Queensland: A Report to the Prostitution Licensing Authority* (Brisbane: Prostitution Licensing Authority, 2009) at 20.

Disputes might also arise between sex workers who use drugs and those who do not. Divisions are often triggered by the view that a drug user will be more willing to have unprotected sex, and will attract clients seeking sex without condoms (Harris et al. 2011: 392, McKeganey and Barnard 1996: 28-29).

Women's relationships within sex work contexts are tied to the issue of health and safety and its effect on the way they evaluate their experiences. Specifically, communal support can enhance safety whereas strife may trigger stress and dissatisfaction. Yet these relationships are treated under their own heading here in view of their nuanced nature. The impact of sex workers' interactions and relationships is not unequivocally healthy or harmful. Some find friendship formed through an "implicit code of solidarity" that binds women in the sex trade together (Harris et al. 2011: 392). At the same time, a breach of this code could trigger more stress and disturbance than any potential harm threatened or inflicted by a client. These relationships are thus delicate, "undoubtedly strained" but not precluded by competition (McKeganey and Barnard 1996: 29), and potentially a source of safety and survival while also the possible root of deep anxiety.

The multidimensional nature of relationships among sex workers calls to mind those among the polygamous wives discussed in Chapter 2. While these contexts are markedly distinct, the reader will recall the way in which plural wives who shared a husband attributed considerable importance to their relationships with each other in connection with the overall satisfaction they drew from polygamous life. While these women dealt with issues of jealousy and competition, they also benefited from mutual support and solidarity. The point underlines the significance of social connections among women to their valuing of morally contentious life choices.

The point emerges also in connection with women in surrogacy circumstances, albeit with somewhat of a twist. Empirical research does not suggest the existence of a community of surrogates who either rival or support each other directly as apparent among plural wives or sex workers. Yet, as highlighted in Chapter 3, social connections are critical to surrogates' assessments of their experiences. Surrogates' relationships with intending parents are central to normative analyses of their roles in surrogacy. They are more likely to value their experiences when they feel that intending parents respect them and meet their expectations with respect to the surrogacy arrangement.

While accounting for the sharp differences in the social and legal issues generated by polygamy, surrogacy and sex work, the discussion here reveals how relational factors nourish normative reflections on one's own difficult choices. This is not surprising, and harmonizes with feminist analyses that understand a woman's choices and outcomes as shaped by her relationships and by perceptions of the self as constituted by connections with others (Nedelsky 2011, Minow and Shanley 1996, Gilligan 1982, Keller 1997). The discussion that follows turns to an analysis of formal laws crafted by the state for the governance of sex work. As shown here, these laws suggest legislators' minimal awareness of the factors that matter to women in both choosing and managing sex work.

Part 2: State Law's Approach to Sex Work in Canada, the United Kingdom and Australia

The discussion in this Part explains the formal governance of sex work under Canadian, British and Australian law. The reader will observe that regulatory frameworks in each of these jurisdictions concentrate on outlawing or restricting activities associated with sex work, rather than on the actual act of giving or taking remuneration for sex. The focus of the present discussion will thus be on legal rules rooted in criminal law. Excluded from the ambit of analysis are the implications for sex work of municipal law, landlord-tenant law, employment law and immigration law, which may be as significant as criminal prohibitions in affecting women's decisions about engaging in sex work. While the relevance to sex work of these regulatory approaches merits recognition, their full exploration is not possible within the parameters of this project, which concentrates on the state's proscriptive responses to women's controversial choices. Moreover, it must be underscored that even a focus on criminal law does not allow for thorough coverage of all relevant legal developments, given their breadth. This Part therefore canvasses criminal law's engagement with sex work in Canada, the United Kingdom and Australia, but refrains from delving into the full details of these legislative schemes and their history in each jurisdiction.

Canada

Canada's prohibitions of sex work-related activities have been subject to extensive judicial interpretation and scrutiny over time, particularly during the period of this book's development. As of the time of writing, the Supreme Court of Canada has reserved judgment following its hearing of arguments in an appeal from a decision of the Ontario Court of Appeal striking down as unconstitutional various prohibitions pertaining to sex work (*Canada (Attorney General) v. Bedford*). Although adult payment, or taking payment for, sex is not a crime in Canada (*Bedford v. Canada*: para. 227), directly associated activities are outlawed. Canada's offences relate to: the keeping of bawdy houses, procuring and living on the avails of prostitution, and communicating for the purposes of prostitution. Each of these categories of prohibitions is described in turn here.

Bawdy houses (Criminal Code s. 210) Canada's *Criminal Code* prohibits keeping a "common bawdy-house" (s. 210(1)). Being an inmate of, being present without lawful excuse in, or owning, occupying or otherwise controlling a place while knowingly allowing it to be used as a bawdy house is also a criminal act (s. 210(2)), as is knowingly transporting or directing another individual to a bawdy house, or offering to do so (s. 211).

The broad framing of the *Criminal Code*'s bawdy house provisions ensures that sex workers, their clients and those with or for whom they work are all subject to the offence. The prohibitions have been further expanded by courts' interpretation of the term "bawdy house." The *Criminal Code* defines such a site as "a place that is (a) kept or occupied, or (b) resorted to by one or more persons for the purpose of prostitution or the practice of acts of indecency" (s. 197(1)). Canadian courts have affirmed that a bawdy house need not be understood solely as a brothel; any space "frequently or habitually" (*R. v. Patterson*) used for sex work or indecency may fall subject to these prohibitions. Thus, hotels, houses and parking lots have qualified as "bawdy houses."[8]

Provisions pertaining to the keeping or use of brothels predate Canadian confederation. Early articulations of such offences within provincial legislation derived from Britain's *Disorderly Houses Act 1751* (*An Act for the more speedy and effectual punishment of Persons keeping Disorderly Houses*), setting the groundwork for *An Act respecting Vagrants* (1869), federal legislation that included within the definition of a vagrant "all keepers of bawdy-houses and houses of ill-fame, or houses for the resort of prostitutes, and persons in the habit of frequenting such houses, not giving a satisfactory account of themselves." Subsequent legislation broadened this definition to include, within the meaning of a vagrant, "inmates" of bawdy houses (*An Act respecting Offences against Public Morals and Public Convenience*).

Canada's first *Criminal Code*, formed in 1892, included prohibitions against sex work-related activities under the heading, "Offences against Religion, Morals and Public Convenience." These prohibitions banned keeping, frequenting or being an inmate of a bawdy house and, similar to offences set out in antecedent legislation, drew explicit connections between sex work and vagrancy (*Criminal Code, 1892*: ss. 195ff.). Over time, the *Criminal Code*'s bawdy house provisions were subject to various amendments, such as one 1907 revision clarifying that a bawdy house included premises used by only one person (*Criminal Code Amendment Act, 1907*). Other amendments (*Criminal Code Amendment Act, 1913*: ss. 228-229) were aimed at capturing a larger range of actors involved in sex work and at facilitating their prosecution.[9]

By 1915, these offences were removed from the vagrancy section of the *Criminal Code* and a separate provision was enunciated to address the act of being an inmate in a bawdy house (*Criminal Code Amendment Act, 1915*). This statutory reform reflected a transition in the political narrative associated with sex work at that time. While originally oriented toward the correction of wayward vagrants, politicians and legislators had, during the Victorian period, begun to see sex work as amenable to elimination through social engineering and rehabilitation.

---

8 Canada, Parliamentary Information and Research Service, L. Barnett and J. Nicol, *Prostitution in Canada: International Obligations, Federal Law, and Provincial and Municipal Jurisdiction* (Ottawa: Library of Parliament, 2012). See also *R. v. Sorko*, *R. v. Evans*, *Rockert v. R.*, *R. v. Ikeda*, *R. v. Lahaie*, *R. v. Labaye*, *R. v. Kouri*, *R. v. Pierce*, *R. v. McLellan*.

9 Canada, *House of Commons Debates*, 12th Parl, 2nd Sess, Vol 111 (16 May 1913) at 10072 (C.J. Doherty).

Some additional revisions were made to the Canadian bawdy house prohibitions from the 1920s onward. Most notably, such provisions were relocated as part of the *Criminal Code*'s revision in 1954 to its Part V, pertaining to "Disorderly Houses, Gaming and Betting" (*An Act respecting the Criminal Law*). By that point in time, Canada's bawdy house provisions contained the essential elements of the offence that persist within the contemporary *Criminal Code* (*Bedford v. Canada*: para. 237).

The legality of these offences is currently uncertain. Canada's ban on keeping bawdy houses was subject to an initial unsuccessful constitutional challenge before the Supreme Court in 1990 (*Reference re ss. 193 and 195.1(1)(c) of the Criminal Code*). In 2012, however, the Court of Appeal for Ontario upheld the trial-level decision in *Bedford v. Canada* concluding that the *Criminal Code*'s bawdy house provisions violated the right not to be deprived of "life, liberty and security of the person except in accordance with the principles of fundamental justice" as guaranteed by the *Charter of Rights and Freedoms* (s. 7). In this connection, the Ontario Court of Appeal underscored how efforts to eradicate bawdy houses bar access to legal and safe sites for sex work. As such, the Court concluded that the bawdy house offences effectively deprive persons in the sex trade of their right to security and autonomy. Moreover, the prohibitions were viewed as overbroad and grossly disproportionate to their legislative objective (*Canada (Attorney General) v. Bedford*: para. 172). While the provisions were declared constitutionally invalid, the Court of Appeal's order has been stayed pending the outcome of the appeal from this decision, which was heard by the Supreme Court of Canada in June 2013.

Procuring and living on the avails (Criminal Code s. 212) Canada's *Criminal Code* prohibits attempts to procure, entice, solicit or induce another person into "illicit sexual intercourse" or prostitution (s. 212(1)(a), (d)), as well as inducements and activities related to frequenting bawdy houses (s. 212(1)(b), (c), (e)). They further address prostitution trafficking (s. 212(1)(f), (g)), control over prostitution for gain (s. 212(1)(h)) and using intoxicating substances to enable prostitution (s. 212(1)(i)). Also included within the *Code*'s procuring provisions is the offence of living "wholly or in part on the avails of prostitution of another person" (s. 212(1)(j)).

This group of provisions targets two separate but related activities taken up by those who control or direct the activities of sex workers. The first relates to practices that lure or compel individuals into sex work, and the second to the extraction of a profit from sex work. The first, "procuring," dimension requires evidence of persuasion over another person to enter the sex trade.[10] The second, "living on the avails," dimension targets pimps living in a "parasitic" relationship

10 Canada, Parliamentary Information and Research Service, L. Barnett and J. Nicol, *Prostitution in Canada: International Obligations, Federal Law, and Provincial and Municipal Jurisdiction* (Ottawa: Library of Parliament, 2012) at 8.

from a sex worker's earnings (*R. v. Grilo*: 522, *Canada (Attorney General) v. Bedford*: paras. 225-236). It applies also to those who receive payment for goods or services provided to a sex worker "for the purpose of her prostitution" (*Canada (Attorney General) v. Bedford*: para. 236, *R. v. Barrow*: para. 29).

The history of these provisions largely tracks the contemporary division between procuring and living on the avails. Two separate statutes addressed the matter shortly following Canada's confederation. A first prohibited procuring by fraud women under age 21 into sexual activity with men other than the procurer (*An Act respecting Offences against the Person*: s. 50), and a second included those living on the avails of sex work within the offence of vagrancy (*An Act respecting Vagrants*). The procurement offence was amended in 1890 so as to prohibit the persuasion, by false pretenses, of a woman of any age into sex work provided that she was not already "a common prostitute or of known immoral character" (*An Act further to amend the Criminal Law*: s. 9).

Canada's first *Criminal Code* codified the procuring offence in language that largely reflects the contemporary articulation of this offence (*Criminal Code, 1892*: s. 185). Living on the avails was at that time encompassed by the vagrancy prohibition, and was treated as distinct from procuring (*R. v. Grilo*: paras. 7, 11, *Bedford v. Canada*: para. 256). By 1913, however, the *Criminal Code*'s procuring provisions were amended to include the act of living on earnings from prostitution (*Bedford v. Canada*: para. 256). In consequence, the procuring and vagrancy offences operated in parallel to capture activities related to living on prostitution's avails. This state of affairs was modified by the *Criminal Code* revision in 1953-1954 consolidating these offences within the single procuring provision (*An Act respecting the Criminal Law*: s. 184). Subsequently, the provision's language was amended to extend its reach to female as well as male pimps (*Criminal Law Amendment Act, 1972*), and to render the prohibition gender-neutral so as to afford its protection to female and male sex workers alike (*An Act to amend the Criminal Code in relation to sexual offences and other offences against the person and to amend certain other Acts in relation thereto or in consequence thereof*).

While Canada's procuring provisions have not been subject to challenge in recent constitutional litigation, the offence of living on the avails (*Criminal Code*: s. 212(j)) has. The trial level and appeal courts in *Bedford* concluded that this provision violates the right to life, liberty and security of the person in accordance with the principles of fundamental justice, as guaranteed by the *Charter*. More precisely, the Ontario Court of Appeal held the provision to be overbroad, capturing more than necessary to pursue its objective of protecting sex workers. The court indicated that a narrower provision, requiring evidence of exploitation by the accused charged with living on the avails, would prevent incriminating those who supported or protected sex workers (*Canada (Attorney General) v. Bedford*: paras. 249-252). It thus held that the living on the avails provision could be remedied by reading in the words "in circumstances of exploitation" so as to tailor the offence to the particular harm it sought to target. This amendment to the provision is, however, subject to the Supreme Court of Canada's ruling in the appeal from this decision.

Communication for the purpose of prostitution (Criminal Code s. 213) A third category of provisions targets communications associated with arranging sex work, envisaging street workers primarily. The *Criminal Code* (s. 213(1)) prohibits the following activities from being carried out "in a public place" or a "place open to public view": stopping or attempting to stop a motor vehicle, impeding pedestrian or vehicular traffic or blocking entrances or exits from public places, or stopping, attempting to stop, or "in any manner communicat[ing] or attempt[ing] to communicate with any person" for the purposes of engaging in prostitution or obtaining sexual services from a prostitute. The term "public place" is broadly construed, and includes any site to which the public has access by invitation or as of right, as well as vehicles located in a public place or a place open to public view (s. 213(2), *R. v. Smith*).

Historically, street sex work was treated as a form of vagrancy. Canada's first *Criminal Code* criminalized a "nightwalker" or "common prostitute" in a public place if she did not, when required, provide a satisfactory account of herself (*Criminal Code* 1970: s. 175(1)(c)). The offence eventually fell subject to criticism, as it was based on one's status (as a nightwalker or common prostitute) rather than a particular act. Requiring a suspected sex worker to account for herself also raised questions as to the provision's consistency with the common law privilege against self-incrimination and, as of 1960, with the Canadian *Bill of Rights*.[11]

This early provision was repealed in 1972 and replaced by the offence of solicitation for prostitution (*Criminal Law Amendment Act, 1972*: s. 12). The new provision stated simply that any person soliciting in a public place for the purposes of prostitution was guilty of a criminal offence.[12] As such, it removed the requirement of self-accounting and linked liability to a positive act (solicitation) rather than to status or to an omission. Moreover, unlike its predecessor, this new offence was worded neutrally with respect to gender, rendering it equally applicable to men and women.[13]

The 1972 solicitation offence was not, however, considered effective. Its construal as requiring "pressing and persistent" communication by sex workers (*Hutt v. The Queen*) was viewed as imposing too high a burden on police officers and prosecutors. Moreover, its silence as to its applicability to users of sex workers' services left open the argument that clients' communications constituted non-criminal behaviour (compare *R. v. Dudak* and *R. v. DiPaola*). Finally, despite

11 Canada, Parliamentary Information and Research Service, J.R. Robertson, *Prostitution*, CIR 82-2E (Ottawa: Library of Parliament, 2003).

12 Canada, Parliamentary Information and Research Service, J.R. Robertson, *Prostitution*, CIR 82-2E (Ottawa: Library of Parliament, 2003).

13 Canada, *House of Commons Debates*, 28th Parl, 4th Sess, Vol 2 (27 April 1972) at 1708 (Grace MacInnis).

the provision's gender-neutral language, courts interpreted it as applying only to the practices of female workers.[14]

In 1983, the federal Justice Minister convened a Special Committee on Prostitution and Pornography (the Fraser Committee), which recommended a legislative approach to sex work focusing on the social and economic factors conducive to the practice. It advocated heavier penalties for solicitation offences, while calling for restricting the scope of other sex work-related offences and, more contentiously, for the licensing and regulation of commercial sex establishments.[15]

Shortly following the Fraser Report's release in 1985, the Minister of Justice introduced Bill C-49, which came into force months later. This Bill amended the *Criminal Code* to replace the solicitation offence with the current prohibition (now at s. 213). This offence has been subject to constitutional review by appellate courts on several occasions. In the 1980s, courts of appeal gave inconsistent opinions on whether the communication restrictions included within the offence violated the freedom of expression guarantee (s. 2(b)) in the *Charter of Rights and Freedoms* (*R. v. Skinner*, *R. v. Jahelka*). The Supreme Court ruled on the matter in 1990, upholding the validity of the impugned provisions (*Reference re ss 193 and 195.1(1)(c) of the Criminal Code*). A majority held that any limitation on constitutional liberty was consistent with the principles of fundamental justice and while the ban curtailed free expression, this restriction was justified as a reasonable infringement on a constitutional right.[16]

This conclusion was upheld at the appellate court level in *Bedford*. Although at first instance the applications judge held that the offence violated sex workers' right to personal security, a majority of the Ontario Court of Appeal disagreed.[17] The solicitation offence thus remains in place as a constitutionally sound prohibition, subject to the Supreme Court of Canada's ruling on this matter, which at the time of writing remains pending.

Overview—Canada Canada's legal approach to sex work has refrained from criminalizing the actual exchange of sexual services for money. Instead, criminal law targets activities surrounding this practice. It is an offence to: operate, be an "inmate" of or generally to be found in a bawdy house; procure or live on the avails of prostitution; and communicate in public for the purposes of prostitution. Several

14 Canada, Parliamentary Information and Research Service, J.R. Robertson, *Prostitution*, CIR 82-2E (Ottawa: Library of Parliament, 2003).

15 Canada, Parliamentary Information and Research Service, J.R. Robertson, *Prostitution*, CIR 82-2E (Ottawa: Library of Parliament, 2003).

16 Section 1 of the Canadian *Charter* provides that interference with constitutional guarantees can be upheld where these are established as "reasonable limits" that can be "demonstrably justified in a free and democratic society."

17 MacPherson J.A. dissented alone on the analysis of s. 213(1)(c) *Criminal Code*, holding that the applications judge was right to determine that the provision violates s. 7 of the *Charter* and is thus unconstitutional.

of these prohibitions bear fault lines made visible within litigation challenging their constitutional validity. For the moment they continue to represent the state of Canadian law, pending the Supreme Court's analysis in the *Bedford* litigation. Beyond *Bedford,* further litigation will be proceeding before the Canadian judiciary in coming years. The Canadian Supreme Court recently granted standing to a sex worker advocacy group and former sex worker to advance a broad constitutional challenge of the country's sex work-related offences, including *Criminal Code* provisions that are not encompassed by the *Bedford* challenge (*Canada (Attorney General) v. Downtown Eastside Sex Workers United Against Violence Society*). If successful, this more recent constitutional challenge could lead to the comprehensive abrogation of Canada's current sex work governance scheme anchored to criminalization.

The United Kingdom

As in Canada, British law prohibits practices aimed at facilitating, promoting or extracting a financial advantage from sex work. Most sex work-related offences are set out in the *Sexual Offences Act 2003*, although some remain in effect from earlier statutes (e.g., *Street Offences Act 1959*, *Sexual Offences Act 1956*). The discussion here concentrates on three primary categories of sex work offences in the United Kingdom, which generally track those in place in Canada: keeping a brothel, inciting or controlling prostitution for gain, and solicitation or loitering for sex work purposes.

Keeping a brothel The *Sexual Offences Act 1956* makes it an offence to keep, manage or support the management of a brothel (s. 33). While a "brothel" is not statutorily defined, it is understood as premises women resort to "for the purpose of illicit sexual intercourse or sexual lewdness with more than one man" (*Abbott v. Smith*: 663). As in Canada, a property need not be used exclusively or entirely for sex work to qualify as a brothel (*Sexual Offences Act 1956*: s. 33A). Leasing particular rooms for prostitution within a building may yield a finding that the premises as a whole are used as a brothel (*Abbott v. Smith*: 664-665). A sex worker or a person who resides onsite may be charged with keeping a brothel only if she or he takes an active part in running or controlling its business activities, or in facilitating the brothel's management (*Gorman v. Standen*, *Abbott v. Smith*: 665-666, *Jones and Wood v. Director of Public Prosecutions*: 132).

The brothel-keeping offence was adopted from the *Criminal Law Amendment Act 1885*, which was directed at eradicating public prostitution, especially that involving girls and young women (Mead and Bodkin 1885). Its provision targeting the "suppression of brothels" (s. 13) generally mirrors current provisions pertaining to brothel-keeping in the *Sexual Offences Act 1956* (ss. 33-36). As such, early judicial analyses predating the 1956 statute reflect contemporary approaches to and appreciations of the elements of Britain's brothel-keeping offence (e.g., *Caldwell v. Leech*, *Woolfe v. Woolfe*).

Causing or inciting prostitution; controlling prostitution for gain When compared with section 212 of Canada's *Criminal Code*, which sets out the offences of procuring and living on the avails of prostitution, the United Kingdom's framing of comparable prohibitions is relatively confined. The *Sexual Offences Act 2003* prohibits causing or inciting prostitution for gain (s. 52), whether by force or by coaxing or arranging another's involvement in prostitution-related activities (*Sexual Offences Act 2003*: Explanatory Notes para. 99). The statute further makes it an offence to control intentionally another person's activities in relation to prostitution anywhere in the world with the expectation of personal gain or gain to a third party (s. 53(1)). The notion of "gain" is understood as a financial advantage or the goodwill of a person likely to yield such advantage (*Sexual Offences Act 2003*: s. 54(1)).

These two offences—intentionally inciting prostitution and controlling prostitution-related activities—are distinct from the conventional concepts of procuring and living on the avails of prostitution, which continue to exist in Canadian law. The British provisions' language restricts their application to situations in which the inciting or control is intentional and aimed at extracting personal or third party gain. Thus, in contrast to the situation in Canada, persuading someone to engage in, or living on the avails of, prostitution is not by itself a criminal act. Instead, the activities must be correlated to the actor's expectation of benefit.

The controlling for gain offence requires more than a demonstration that the accused benefitted from the avails of sex work; she or he must have exercised intentional authority or command over another's prostitution-related activities. While the element of "control" narrows the application of the offence, it does not necessarily connote coercion, compulsion or force. Control has been judicially understood as "directing a relevant activity" pertaining to sex work, such as workers' fees or sites of service-provision (*R. v. Massey*, see also *Sexual Offences Act 2003*: Explanatory Notes paras. 96, 100).

The predecessors to the inciting and controlling for gain provisions within the *Sexual Offences Act 2003* were found within the *Sexual Offences Act 1956*, which criminalized "encouraging" and "living on earnings of" prostitution. The former offence required proof that the accused caused or encouraged prostitution of "a woman who is a defective" (s. 29). The "living on earnings" offence required a demonstration that a man lived "wholly or in part" on the earnings of prostitution (s. 30(1)). It further presumed that a man habitually in a prostitute's company knowingly lived on her earnings from prostitution (s.30(2)). The statute further prohibited the exercise of control or influence over a prostitute's activities in a manner indicative of facilitating or compelling prostitution (ss. 30(2), 31).

A 2000 Home Office report issued pursuant to an inquiry on law reform regarding sexual offences[18] recommended the revision of the living on the

18 UK, Home Office, *Setting the Boundaries: Reforming the Law on Sex Offences*, vol 1 (London: Home Office, 2000).

avails prohibitions, so as to distinguish between persons living with prostitutes in "genuine" supportive relationships and those who cohabited with prostitutes to exploit them.[19] The report emphasized that the criminal law should target specifically those who recruit or manage the activities of sex workers for gain, and those who partake in exploitation to extract financial benefits from them.[20] These recommendations yielded the current articulation of provisions within the *Sexual Offences Act 2003*, which are tailored to focus on the intentional causing of or control over sex work motivated by gain.

Soliciting or loitering for the purposes of prostitution As in Canada, solicitation offences in the United Kingdom are rooted in their perception as a public nuisance. British law addresses separately solicitation by sex workers and that by clients. The *Street Offences Act 1959* prohibits "persistently" loitering or soliciting on the street or a public place for prostitution (s. 1(1)). "Loitering or soliciting" for prostitution in this statute pertains to "offering services," thereby capturing sex workers, but not their clients (s. 1(4)(b)). While originally the provision applied to women only, its language was amended in 2003 so as to apply both to female and male sex workers (*Sexual Offences Act 2003*: Schedule I, para. 2). The requirement that the solicitation be "persistent" was included in 2009 and defined broadly to mean "two or more occasions in any period of three months" (s. 1(4)(a)). The term "street" is also given a wide meaning (s. 1(4)(c)).

The *Street Offences Act 1959* replaced offences that existed under earlier statutes such as the *Metropolitan Police Act 1839*, the *Town Police Clauses Act 1847* and the *City of London Police Act 1839*. It was prompted by the Wolfenden Report[21] and, as discussed more fully in Part 3 (within the subsection "State Law's Presumptions and Objectives in Relation to Sex Work, Women and Choice"), was oriented toward reducing street sex work as a nuisance and as evidence of public immorality. At the same time, the solicitation offence did not include an element of nuisance, thus making a conviction for this offence possible even where a sex worker's public presence was not established as annoying or menacing to a community. The statute's subjection of "common prostitutes" to potential arrest and prosecution for merely "walking, standing still, or looking into a shop window" attracted criticism, particularly given its genesis in targeting public nuisance.[22] Currently, a nuisance element is not explicitly referenced in the statute, although the requirement that the solicitation be "persistent" would seem to limit the ambit of the offence.

19 UK, HL, *Parliamentary Debates*, vol 654, col 1638 (13 November 2003) (Baroness Scotland of Ashthal).

20 UK, Home Office, *Setting the Boundaries: Reforming the Law on Sex Offences*, vol 1 (London: Home Office, 2000) at para. 7.7.1.

21 UK, *Report of the Committee on Homosexual Offences and Prostitution* (London: Her Majesty's Stationery Office, 1957).

22 UK, HL, *Parliamentary Debates*, vol 216, col 784 (9 June 1959) (Lord Stonham).

Beyond targeting sex workers, British legislation includes provisions proscribing client solicitation. The *Policing and Crime Act 2009* (s. 19) amended the *Sexual Offences Act 2003* to include a solicitation offence (s. 51A) prohibiting a person in a street or public place from soliciting another to obtain the latter's sexual services. This provision explicitly applies to persons in motor vehicles in streets or public places (s. 51A(2)) and incorporates by reference the broad meaning of "street" within the *Street Offences Act 1959* (s. 51A(4)), noted above. This 2009 amendment subjected, for the first time in the United Kingdom, soliciting clients to charges for a first offence. Prior to this amendment, solicitation by users was prohibited only where it occurred "persistently" (*Sexual Offences Act 1956*: s. 32, *Sexual Offences Act 1985*: ss. 1-2).

Overview—United Kingdom As in Canada, British law criminalizes activities associated with sex work but not the trade in sexual services itself. It is an offence to keep or manage a brothel or to assist in its management, but working or residing in a brothel is not prohibited in its own right. Inciting another person to enter sex work is a crime where this is done with the expectation of personal gain, or gain to a third party. Likewise, control over sex work with the expectation of such gain is prohibited. Finally, loitering and solicitation for the purposes of prostitution are criminalized, with separate strands of the criminal law applying to sex workers and those who seek out and use their services.

Australia

This discussion of Australian legal responses to sex work follows an approach that differs from that deployed to consider Canadian and British law. Sex work-related activities in Australia are governed at the state and territorial levels. Although Chapter 3 outlined the formal governance regimes in place pertaining to surrogacy in all Australian states and mainland territories, the scope of this chapter does not permit such an exploration. Sex work has been far more amply legislated in Australia than polygamy or surrogacy. Moreover, Australian states and territories take distinct approaches to activities associated with the trade in sexual services. As such, this section focuses on three particular states, namely, Tasmania, New South Wales and Queensland, which exemplify different governance strategies adopted by the country's states and territories.

Tasmania (criminalization model) While trading sex is itself not subject to criminalization in Tasmania, the *Sex Industry Offences Act 2005* prohibits a number of related activities. The statute makes it an offence to be a "commercial operator" of a "sexual services business" (s. 4), that is, a business that provides "sexual services for fee or reward" (s. 3(1)). Commercial operators of such enterprises include corporations or persons who own, operate or control a sexual services business and who do not qualify as "self-employed sex workers." The latter term includes a person who, alone or with a maximum of one other worker who is not her employee or employer, owns and operates a business providing sex services (ss. 3(1), 3(2)). An individual falls outside the ambit of this ban if she works alone or with just one other independent worker.

The *Sex Industry Offences Act 2005* also makes it an offence, generally, to receive knowingly commercial sex services (ss. 4-5). It prohibits inducing—through various enumerated threats, incentives or pressures—another to provide "sexual services in a sexual services business" (s. 7(2)). Finally, this statute criminalizes the acts of accosting another person, or soliciting or loitering in a public place for the purpose of "offering or procuring sexual services in a sexual services business" (s. 8(1)).[23] This ban extends to individual sex workers, even those who do not qualify as "commercial operators."

Some provisions within the *Sex Industry Offences Act 2005* seek to protect sex workers. The statute lists separate offences related to threatening or assaulting sex workers or supplying them with narcotics in different contexts (s. 7(1)). It further includes requirements pertaining to the use of condoms and prophylactic devices to control the spread of sexually-transmitted infections (s. 12).

Tasmania's current legislative framework emerged pursuant to legislative inquiry and debate initiated in the late 1990s. At that time, many practices associated with sex work were criminalized under the *Criminal Code Act 1924* and the *Police Offences Act 1935*. A 1999 Report ("CDC Committee Report") recognized the need for statutory reform to ensure greater protection for: public health, workers' welfare and occupational health and safety, communities' social and physical environment (specifically, by controlling the location of brothels), and minor children.[24] The CDC Committee Report further recommended legislative provisions implementing a sex work licensing system, measures to deter the spread of sexually-transmitted infections, and sanctions against those who used violence, threats or stupefying substances to induce prostitution.[25] In consequence, the *Sex Industry Regulation Bill 2003*, which proposed a registration system for sexual services businesses, was drafted and released for consultation in 2004. This Bill was received and read in the legislature, but did not pass.

In October 2005, the *Sex Industry Offences Bill 2005* was presented and read in the Legislative Council. It moved through the legislative process in a matter of weeks, receiving royal assent in November 2005 and coming into force on 1 January 2006. This statute, which continues to govern sex work-related activities in Tasmania, did not integrate the licensing system that the 2003 Bill had proposed.

---

23 Note that a separate subsection of this provision (s. 8(2)) addresses the solicitation of children and carries a far more onerous penalty.

24 Austl, Tasmania, *Community Development Committee Report on the Need for Legislative Regulation and Reform of the Sex Industry in Tasmania*, Report No 8 (1999) at 3.

25 Austl, Tasmania, *Community Development Committee Report on the Need for Legislative Regulation and Reform of the Sex Industry in Tasmania*, Report No 8 (1999) at 4.

It did, however, include other provisions from this proposed legislation, such as those outlining specific offences perpetrated upon sex workers and those aimed at controlling sexually-transmitted infections. Thus, an initial policy push in the direction of regulating and licensing sexual services brothels was short-lived and replaced by legislation that perpetuated Tasmania's approach founded on the criminal law. The Deputy Premier of Tasmania in 2010 articulated an intention to develop a discussion paper oriented toward sex work legislative reform.[26] This discussion paper was released in 2012, investigating legislative models for the governance of sex work worldwide and inviting consultation and submissions for reform, with a particular view to ensuring greater protection of sex workers' human rights, health and safety.[27]

Prior to considering two other distinct legal approaches taken up in Australia, it is worth noting other states that share policy approaches similar to Tasmania's. South Australia (*Summary Offences Act 1953*), Western Australia (*Police Act 1892*, *Criminal Code 1902*, *Prostitution Act 2000*) and the Northern Territory (*Prostitution Regulation Act 2004*) prohibit activities associated with sex work. Although private sex work is not outlawed, brothels and street-based work are considered criminal offences. Some exceptions to this general stance exist. For example, in the Northern Territory, escort agencies may be licensed, but brothels may not. In Western Australia, solicitation, procurement and brothel-keeping are prohibited, however, police have applied an informal containment policy allowing some sex work-related businesses to operate subject to specific conditions.[28] At the time of writing, proposed legislation had been introduced in Western Australia that would ban brothels from residential neighbourhoods, allowing them elsewhere, subject to licensing and monitoring (*Prostitution Bill 2011*).

New South Wales (general decriminalization model) New South Wales is understood as having the most liberal approach to sex work in Australia, as some related activities have been decriminalized in this state without an accompanying licensing system. New South Wales' decriminalization process occurred through legislative reform targeting the removal of individual practices from the sphere of criminal law. Yet it would be inaccurate to characterize this state's approach to sex work as based on a policy of absolute decriminalization. Certain associated

---

26 Austl, Tasmania, House of Assembly, *Parliamentary Debates* (22 June 2010) at 48 (Lara Giddings).

27 Austl, Tasmania, Hon. Brian Wightman, MP, Attorney General and Minister for Justice, *Regulation of the Sex Industry in Tasmania (Discussion Paper)* (Hobart: Minister for Justice, 2012). Available at: http://www.justice.tas.gov.au/__data/assets/pdf_file/0008/188738/Regulation_of_the_Sex_Industry_Discussion_Paper.pdf [accessed: 16 June 2013].

28 Austl, Western Australia, *Prostitution Law Reform for Western Australia: Report of the Prostitution Law Reform Working Group* (Perth: Office of the Attorney General, 2007) at 14-15.

practices remain illegal in the state and those that are permitted are subject to legal delineation and restriction, albeit through land use and planning, rather than criminal, law.

Brothel-keeping

Owners and occupiers of brothels are not subject to criminal prosecution in New South Wales on the sole basis of owning or residing in brothels (*Restricted Premises Act 1943*: s. 16). Nevertheless, the *Restricted Premises Act 1943* extends considerable power to local councils to approve legal commercial businesses, which includes brothels now that they are decriminalized.[29] Local councils may thus apply to the Land and Environment Court to close a brothel if residents, workers or parents of children using facilities in a given area advance sufficient complaints (*Restricted Premises Act 1943*: s. 17, *Brothels Legislation Amendment Act 2007*, see also Sullivan 2010: 97).

Although currently subject to permissive regulation, brothel-keeping was a criminal offence in New South Wales until 1995. The activity was subject to prosecution under the *Disorderly Houses Act 1943*. Prosecutions under such legislation were rare until the 1980s when police sought declarations deeming particular properties "disorderly houses," rendering their owners or occupiers criminally liable (Brown et al. 2006: 888). In 1988, the Criminal Court of Appeal ruled that premises could be subject to such declarations when they are habitual sites of sex work, even if they are not "disorderly" in the ordinary sense of this term (*Sibuse Pty Ltd v. Shaw*). The ruling prompted police applications for the closure of many brothels and generated concern about widespread movement of sex work from these sites to the streets.[30] It further sparked the revival of the common law offence of brothel-keeping (Brown et al. 2006: 888, *R. v. Rahme*).

In an effort to address these circumstances, the Attorney General introduced the *Disorderly Houses Amendment Bill 1992*, which did not pass beyond second reading. Subsequent revelations of police corruption in connection with sex work generated the *Disorderly Houses Amendment Bill 1995*, incorporating the provisions of the 1992 Bill.[31] Receiving assent in November 1995, this new legislation instituted a regime premised on the general, although not outright, decriminalization of brothels.

---

29 Austl, New South Wales, Parliamentary Library Research Service, Stewart Smith, *The Regulation of Prostitution: A Review of Recent Developments* (Briefing Paper No 21/99) (Sydney: New South Wales Parliamentary Research Service, 1999) at 5. See also *Walsh v. Bankstown City Council*.

30 Austl, New South Wales, Parliamentary Library Research Service, Stewart Smith, *The Regulation of Prostitution: A Review of Recent Developments* (Briefing Paper No 21/99) (Sydney: New South Wales Parliamentary Research Service, 1999) at 6.

31 Austl, New South Wales, Parliamentary Library Research Service, Stewart Smith, *The Regulation of Prostitution: A Review of Recent Developments* (Briefing Paper No 21/99) (Sydney: New South Wales Parliamentary Research Service, 1999) at 4-5.

Soliciting

Soliciting for the purpose of sex work, by workers or clients, is generally permitted in New South Wales, although it may not occur near or within view from a dwelling, school, church or hospital (*Summary Offences Act*: s. 19). Soliciting in these areas need not be persistent to constitute an offence. Thus, unlike earlier Canadian judicial analyses and current British legislation, which penalize solicitation by sex workers that is persistent or badgering, in New South Wales the offence may apply to "[t]he mere approach by a prostitute to a person who is a potential customer, when she is dressed in a suggestive manner, perhaps with appropriate gestures or words ..." (*Coleman v. D.P.P.*: para. 42).

As in Canada, solicitation in New South Wales was treated originally as a form of vagrancy. The *Vagrancy Act 1902* prohibited solicitation by a "known prostitute" in a public place (s. 4(1)(c)). The offence was expanded in 1968 to include solicitation or loitering for prostitution in or near a public place, even if one was not "known" to be a prostitute (*Summary Offences Act 1970*: s. 28, Brown et al. 2006: 887). By 1979, the *Cognate Summary Offences Bills*, which included a *Prostitution Bill*, established "provisions which the Government considered necessary to control the more repugnant aspects of prostitution not otherwise the subject of criminal law."[32] When the *Prostitution Act 1979* took effect, however, it eliminated the offence of soliciting in public for the purposes of prostitution (Brown et al. 2006: 887).

The resultant full decriminalization of solicitation lasted only briefly. Legislation passed in 1983 amended the *Prostitution Act 1979* by prohibiting solicitation near residences, schools, churches or hospitals (*Prostitution Amendment Bill 1983*: Schedule I, s. 3). The statute was repealed in 1988, and its provisions were absorbed within the *Summary Offences Act 1988*, which currently remains in force (Brown et al. 2006: 888). The *Summary Offences Act 1988* continues to allow solicitation except in the vicinity of residences, schools, churches or hospitals.

Other sex work-related offences

Although brothel-keeping and solicitation have been subject to decriminalization processes, other sex work-related activities remain prohibited. Most notably, as in Canada and the United Kingdom, anyone who "procures, entices or leads away any person (not being a prostitute)" into prostitution is subject to criminal sanction (*Crimes Act 1900*: s. 91A). Procuring prostitution through the use of violence, fraud or by intoxicating substances is also criminalized (*Crimes Act 1900*: s. 91B). Moreover, living on the earnings of another person's sex work remains an offence in New South Wales, although this provision does not apply to owners, managers or employees of brothels (*Summary Offences Act 1988*: s. 15). The offence applies where a person habitually receives financial gain from the proceeds of prostitution, such that isolated instances of benefiting do not fall within the prohibition's scope

32 Austl, New South Wales, Legislative Assembly, *Parliamentary Debates* (23 April 1979) at 4923 (Mr. Walker).

(Brown et al. 2006: 892). The provision that sets out the offence of living on the avails of prostitution is generally framed, and includes no element of coercion or control. Thus, while New South Wales is held out as having adopted one of the most liberal and progressive regulatory approaches to sex work, the state's living on the avails offence is framed in a manner that the Court of Appeal for Ontario in *Bedford* deemed unconstitutional for capturing relationships that may in fact support and protect sex workers' interests.

Queensland (licensing/registration model) Queensland's regulatory approach represents a model that rests between the poles of prohibition and decriminalization, but only insofar as brothels are concerned. Other activities, such as solicitation and procuring for prostitution, remain criminalized. Evidence of widespread police corruption in connection with brothels (Schloenhardt and Human Trafficking Working Group 2009: 7, *Bedford v. Canada*: paras. 202-204) was a key factor that prompted Queensland's enactment of the *Prostitution Act 1999*, which recognizes brothels as legal businesses, provided that they follow legislated protocols for acquiring and maintaining appropriate licenses (*Prostitution Act 1999*). This approach is adopted also in Victoria (*Prostitution Control Act 1994*). The Australian Capital Territory's regulatory model is similar but based on a registration rather than licensing framework (*Prostitution Act 1992*).

Being a "sole operator" is not illegal in Queensland as long as one does not offer services from the same premises as one or more other sex workers, even at different times, unless the site is a licensed brothel or the person concerned has a "reasonable excuse" (*Criminal Code Act 1899*: s. 299I, *R. v. Newcombe and Barns*). Sole operators are not immune from liability under other related provisions, such as those regarding solicitation (Schloenhardt and Human Trafficking Working Group 2009: ss. 5.1, 6.2). Additionally, Queensland's *Prostitution Act 1999* creates an elaborate framework for regulating the licensing of brothels. This statute stipulates the process for obtaining brothel licenses and the penalties associated with keeping a brothel while failing to adhere to these provisions (Part 3). Apart from license requirements, the legislation sets out detailed parameters for operating brothels (Part 6, Div 2).

Sex work-related activities outside of brothels remain criminalized in Queensland. Notably, the *Prostitution Act 1999*'s framing of the solicitation offence is broad, and makes it an offence to "publicly solicit for prostitution." This offence applies both to sex workers and clients where the solicitation occurs in a public place, within view or hearing of a person in a public place, or while loitering either in a public place or within view from a public place (ss. 73-75). The statute also creates a nuisance offence targeting unreasonable annoyances or disruptions to privacy in areas "reasonably suspected" of use for prostitution, which are caused "to a significant extent" by the presence or suspected presence of prostitution (s. 76).

Additionally, the statute includes offences against procuring for prostitution. Articulated as an offence against exercising "duress" in connection with prostitution, these provisions prohibit the use of intimidation, harassment or fraud to compel a person to continue providing prostitution services (s. 77). This provision adds to the procuring offence delineated in Queensland's *Criminal Code Act 1899*, which makes it an offence to "knowingly entice or recruit for the purposes of sexual exploitation" another person to engage in prostitution within the state or abroad (s. 229G).

The scope of legally permissible prostitution in Queensland is thus limited. Apart from work by independent sole operators, which is largely unregulated, and that within licensed brothels, which is heavily regulated, sex work remains generally subject to criminal law. The presumptions framing the state's legislative response to sex work conveys a clear preference for indoor over street work, the former being viewed as safer and less debasing to women's integrity. But while indoor brothel work is legalized in Queensland, a parallel illegal economy in the sex trade exists within the state wherein women face the same risks and tradeoffs as they do in jurisdictions where all activities associated with sex work are outlawed. Moreover, even within legalized zones, sex workers face the risk of violence and exploitation at the hands of clients as well as managers and operators of indoor sex establishments.[33]

Overview—Australia Australia's governance of sex work is marked by a spectrum of approaches. Some states, such as Tasmania, adopt a model based on general proscription, whereas New South Wales exemplifies a legislative strategy premised largely on decriminalization, allowing some sex work-related activities. Situated between the approaches of prohibition and permission is a model grounded upon regulation and licensing, as witnessed by Queensland's legislative framework.

In contemplating Australia's juridical response to sex work, a couple of points should be borne in mind. A first is that the labels attached to governance models in varying states (criminalization, decriminalization, licensing) capture only partially state law's essence in each place. For example, although New South Wales is commonly understood to have decriminalized sex work-related activities, many practices remain outlawed and those that are permitted are subject to restrictive criteria. Likewise, licensing in Queensland is framed by strict regulations pertaining to brothels, while other activities remain criminalized.

A second point worth underlining pertains to the effects of decriminalization and regulation. While these are viewed as liberal modes of governance, as in New South Wales and Queensland, they may be accompanied by concomitant initiatives anchored to administrative rather than criminal law, which are severely restrictive. It is thus not clear whether greater permissibility arises as a result of a governance design premised on regulatory approaches outside of the criminal law.

---

33 A. Edwards, *Selling Sex; Regulating Prostitution in Queensland: A Report to the Prostitution Licensing Authority* (Brisbane: Prostitution Licensing Authority, 2009).

iscussion that follows critically evaluates juridical approaches to sex anada, the United Kingdom and Australia. It explores the objectives and ions underpinning state law in these jurisdictions. It further considers 's engagement with non-state law and norms that shape choices about sex work and the effect of state law—especially criminal law—on sex workers' lived experiences.

Part 3: Evaluating State Law

This Part appraises state law's responses to sex work. It contemplates the presumptions and objectives driving this law and proceeds to consider, by deploying the empirical data studied in Part 1, how such presumptions and objectives align with informal norms that shape women's choices about sex work. Last, this Part examines state law's impact on these choices to assess whether the objectives of state law are materially realized by sex workers' realities and experiences.

State Law's Presumptions and Objectives in Relation to Sex Work, Women and Choice

Two predominant themes may be said to characterize the vision and goals driving legislative approaches to sex work, as well as state law's perception of choice in relation to this practice. A first relates to the perceived identity of the sex worker, while the second is concerned with distinguishing public from private forms of sex work. Each of these conceptual strands is discussed here.

Sex worker as coerced victim and moral offender Legal and political discussions draw heavily on a distinct image of sex workers and their capacity for reasoned decision-making. Most strikingly, a survey of legislative debates and policy discussions on sex work reveals that the practice is understood as invariably gendered: sex workers are always women and girls, and clients and those who control the sex trade (respectively, "johns" and "pimps") are always men. This supposition sets the groundwork for the power dynamics and vulnerabilities that state actors perceive in relation to sex work. While the focus of this book is on women in sex work, a look at the empirics on this topic complicates presumptions about gender identity underpinning state governance. Moreover, while lying outside the scope of this book, an analysis of men and trans peoples in sex work would likely reveal diverse first-hand narratives and would further call for varied lenses through which to study effectively questions about choice in relation to sex work (see e.g., Minichiello et al. 2001, Harcourt et al. 2001, Allman and Myers 1999).

State law presents women in sex work as at once morally depraved and easily preyed upon by others. Early juridical conversations addressed their waywardness, and stressed an interest in bringing them "under control" through projects of moral and social "reformation."[34] At the same time, these discussions described sex workers as "unfortunate girls"[35] who had fallen victim to "the dastardly wiles of a clandestine and vile league of exploiters" (McLaren 1986: 130-131, 155). In what may be understood as a "schizophrenic" outlook, sex workers were cast as predisposed to "sexual irresponsibility" while coerced by "rogues and bounders" (McLaren 1986: 139), rationalizing interventions oriented toward their simultaneous rehabilitation and protection. Yet this public narrative also perceived some sex workers as "fallen women," too damaged and culpable for rescue or reform (Hallgrimsdottir et al. 2006: 272).

While the dualistic image of the sex worker as both moral offender and victim persists within modern discussions, contemporary discourse has become overrun by references to their susceptibility to harm and exploitation. Much like the polygamous wife and the surrogate, the sex worker is understood as limited in her ability to withstand pressures operating to her detriment. Related preoccupations about her vulnerabilities course prominently through legislative and policy debates, ignoring the dependencies that characterize the human condition more broadly, without restriction to marginalized circumstances (Fineman 2008). Within such debates, sex workers are referred to as "victims" of those who place them in conditions of "quasi and even outright slavery,"[36] expose them to "serial abuse"[37] and "exploit them to the max."[38] Sex work is thus presumed restricted to the "most vulnerable" women whose frailties are exacerbated by the practice's "exploitation and degradation … and violence."[39] Such uncritical connections between sex work and vulnerability, although drawn in the name of protecting women, serve to substantiate blunt and regressive legal interventions that bolster state authorities' power while undermining the liberties of those presumed to be at risk (Munro and Scoular 2012: 196-197). This in turn exacerbates any real preexistent vulnerabilities and reinforces a simplistic victim–offender dyad in which sex workers are envisaged either as needing protection and salvation, or as requiring discipline and correction (Carline 2012).

State law's binary understanding of sex work neglects the constant fluidity and coincidence between victim and offender status seen here and in the other case

---

34 Canada, *House of Commons Debates*, 12th Parl, 5th Sess, Vol 120 (18 March 1915) at 1227 (Mr. Doherty).

35 Canada, *House of Commons Debates*, 12th Parl, 5th Sess, Vol 120 (18 March 1915) at 1227 (Mr. Doherty).

36 Canada, *House of Commons Debates*, 33rd Parl, 1st Sess, Vol 5 (9 September 1985) at 6421 (Don Boudria).

37 Austl, Queensland, Legislative Assembly, *Parliamentary Debates* (1 December 1999) at 5711 (Mr. Borbidge).

38 Canada, House of Commons, Subcommittee on Solicitation Laws of the Standing Committee on Justice, Human Rights, Public Safety and Emergency Preparedness, Evidence, 38th Parl, 1st Sess, No 6 (9 February 2005) at 13 (Art Hanger).

39 Austl, Tasmania, Legislative Council, *Parliamentary Debates* (19 October 2005) at 20 (Ms. Forrest).

studies developed in this book. Furthermore, regardless of where state law situates sex workers on its imagined victim–offender spectrum, it casts them as lacking agency, compelled into sex work by social and economic forces beyond their control. Any connection drawn between sex work and the notions of choice and agency has traditionally been tainted by the view that only women of a particular "psychological make-up" would willingly engage in this practice. Such women are understood as lured to the sex trade by an "easier, freer and more profitable" life than they would face outside the practice.[40] Modern discussions continue to see sex work as fueled by the prospect of "easy money outside the taxman's grasp and payment for illegal drugs."[41] Where spoken of as making choices, then, sex workers' motivations are deemed devious and antisocial.

Resistance to identifying sex work as a choice is explained by its predominant legal and social appreciation as "degrading and dehumanizing" and as "amount[ing] to exploitation and sexual abuse."[42] A Canadian policy report thus described sex work as "most often an act of despair, a means of survival" (Boivin 1984: 3). The United Kingdom's Home Office adopted a similar view, describing this work as a means of getting by in circumstances of acute "deprivation."[43] This stance has surfaced also within Tasmanian debates, which generally decline to see women as freely or knowingly choosing sex work.[44] Rather, sex workers are understood as driven by "coercion, poverty, homelessness, hunger, disadvantage and powerlessness."[45] In New South Wales, sex workers have further been described as victims "trapped in the web of prostitution."[46] These characterizations converge on notions of women's victimization and vulnerability, and leave negligible room for imagining choice or agency. Core to such policy reasoning is a rejection of sex

---

40 UK, *Report of the Committee on Homosexual Offences and Prostitution* (London: Her Majesty's Stationery Office, 1957) at para. 223. See also Sullivan (1994: 193).

41 Austl, Queensland, Legislative Assembly, *Parliamentary Debates* (1 December 1999) at 5721 (Mr. Feldman).

42 Austl, New South Wales, Legislative Council, *Parliamentary Debates* (15 November 1995) at 3188-3189 (J.P. Hannaford).

43 UK, Home Office, *Paying the Price: A Consultation Paper on Prostitution* (London: Home Office, 2004) at para.7.1.

44 Austl, Tasmania, Legislative Council, *Parliamentary Debates* (22 June 2005) at 25 (Mr. Dean); Austl, Tasmania, Legislative Council, *Parliamentary Debates* (22 June 2005) at 29 (Mr. Dean).

45 Austl, Tasmania, Legislative Council, *Parliamentary Debates* (19 October 2005) at 20 (Ms. Forrest).

46 Austl, New South Wales, Legislative Council, *Parliamentary Debates* (15 November 1995) at 3152 (F.J. Nile); Austl, Queensland, Legislative Assembly, *Parliamentary Debates* (1 December 1999) at 5703 (Mr. Horan).

work as legitimate "work,"[47] and a belief that if any choice existed for sex workers, they would exit this way of life.[48]

State law's response to sex work reveals the implications for liability attribution of adopting a simplistic choice-based discourse in the contemplation of women's morally fraught decisions. More precisely, these responses equate choice with responsibility and cast coercion and victimization as bases for liability-exemption. But regardless of whether they are imagined within a framework of agency and blameworthiness or one of victimhood, sex workers are appreciated as bearing a weakened moral and emotional constitution "either because they 'chose' to be a prostitute, or as the inevitable result of being a victim of the sex trade" (Jackson et al. 2007: 268).

The point is exemplified by a 2006 report issued by the British Government, which envisaged sex work as a product of women's exploitation.[49] It thus advocated a "rehabilitative approach" offering strategies to prevent entry or to facilitate exit from sex work.[50] This approach contrasts with common policy reactions to "chosen" sex work. Where "women and men choose to prostitute themselves," they are held "responsible for the decisions they make,"[51] and legislators have questioned the propriety of extending state protection to "those who engage in prostitution

---

47 Canada, House of Commons, Subcommittee on Solicitation Laws of the Standing Committee on Justice and Human Rights, Evidence, 37th Parl, 2nd Sess, No 3 (21 October 2003) at 1700 (Cherry Kingsley); Canada, House of Commons, Subcommittee on Solicitation Laws of the Standing Committee on Justice, Human Rights, Public Safety and Emergency Preparedness, Evidence, 38th Parl, 1st Sess, No 5 (7 February 2005) at 20 (Yolande Geadah); Canada, House of Commons, Subcommittee on Solicitation Laws of the Standing Committee on Justice, Human Rights, Public Safety and Emergency Preparedness, Evidence, 38th Parl, 1st Sess, No 6 (9 February 2005) at 13 (Lyne Kurtzman); Austl, Tasmania, Legislative Council, *Parliamentary Debates* (19 October 2005) at 24 (Ms. Forrest); Austl, Queensland, Legislative Assembly, *Parliamentary Debates* (2 December 1999) at 5825 (Mrs. Pratt).

Yet this perspective is not universal; some voices in political debates advocate the recognition of sex work as "a legitimate choice of work." See Austl, New South Wales, Legislative Council, *Parliamentary Debates* (14 November 1995) at 3074 (Dr Meredith Burgmann); Austl, New South Wales, Legislative Council, *Parliamentary Debates* (15 November 1995) at 3149 (I. Cohen). See also Austl, Australian Capital Territory, Standing Committee on Justice and Community Safety, *Inquiry into the Prostitution Act 1992* (Report No 9) (2012) at ix and 41.

48 Austl, New South Wales, Legislative Council, *Parliamentary Debates* (14 November 1995) at 3075-3076 (Dr. Meredith Burgmann).

49 UK, Home Office, *A Coordinated Prostitution Strategy and Summary of Responses to Paying the Price* (London: Home Office, 2006) at 1.

50 UK, Home Office, *A Coordinated Prostitution Strategy and Summary of Responses to Paying the Price* (London: Home Office, 2006) at 8.

51 Austl, Tasmania, Legislative Council, *Parliamentary Debates* (19 October 2005) at 7 (Mrs. Jamieson).

entirely of their own volition."[52] Yet it is worth signaling the Ontario Court of Appeal's recent gesture at an alternate, textured appreciation of the intersection between choice, responsibility and protection. There, the court affirmed that engaging, even willfully, in sex work should not deprive an individual of the constitutional protection afforded to others who engage in "other dangerous, but legal enterprises" (*Canada (Attorney General) v. Bedford*: para. 123).

The circumstances in which women occupy concurrently the status of victim and offender are not unique to sex work and are visible in other contexts that this book addresses. The reader will recall Chapter 1's discussion of women living in abusive intimate partnerships who use violence as a mode of self-protection. Such women are more prone to be viewed as acting in self-defense, and thus justified in their use of force, when they are pathologized. To be precise, where they have developed "battered woman's syndrome" and see themselves as trapped within a dangerous situation from which exit requires violence, their actions may not trigger criminal liability. By contrast, women who self-perceive as having an alternative to violence will be understood to have chosen their path, and will thus be held legally accountable for it.

Juridical conversations related to polygamy also reflect this binary image of women. Casting them as victims substantiates blunt paternalistic criminal laws, which are rationalized as instruments designed for their protection. At the same time, when a polygamous wife is viewed as "the capable consenting spouse," she is likely to be viewed as a perpetrator of harm who should shoulder legal responsibility for her actions (*Reference re: Section 293 of the Criminal Code*: para. 1197).

Like the polygamous wife and the woman living in circumstances of intimate partner violence, sex workers have been subject to polarized juridical analyses, in which they are viewed either as passive victims or as offenders fully capable of choice. These analyses imagine sex workers as preyed upon by those who coerce and exploit them, or as calculating and maladjusted social threats that merit sanction and call for rehabilitation. Such discussions reflect little recognition of the potential for agency to be exercised even in oppressive environments, or conversely, of the existence of constraints and possible need for support even where some degree of choice is discerned (Jackson et al. 2007: 268). The absolutism in the victim–offender dyad is thus unhelpful to contemplating ways in which women's experiences may be multifaceted and dynamic, and this in turn yields legal reactions to their lifestyles and choices that fail to respond to and reflect accurately their lived realities and interests.

In a related vein, legal and political conversations about sex work tend to essentialize women. While some voices in these discussions note the impropriety

52 UK, HL, *Parliamentary Debates*, vol 648, col 183 (13 May 2003) (Baroness Blatch).

of casting sex workers "as being under any one single umbrella,"[53] and recognize the naivety in presuming that they form a monolithic, "emotionally scarred" collectivity,[54] this is a minority perspective. Sex workers' perceived inability to make free choices is anchored to their being broadly envisaged as poor and drug-dependent, often racialized and homeless.[55] Juridical actors have thus been inclined to position sex workers as a counterpoint to "wives and mothers, sisters and daughters and sweethearts."[56] The latter are imagined as women far removed from the world of the sex trade, warranting shelter from its corrosive influence. In contrast to this purified feminine image, sex workers are typically lumped together under broad epithets such as "vulnerable young women with disturbed backgrounds" (*R. v. Massey*: para. 21), or "poor women, disadvantaged women and native women" often with "a history of childhood abuse" and "few employment skills."[57] Generalizing about sex work from such presumptions ultimately suppresses inquiries into the manner in which sex workers may identify and weigh options, resist multiple pressures, rationalize their decisions, and experience their work heterogeneously and dynamically.

Preferring private sex work Apart from suppositions related to sex workers' identity, state law and policy in this domain are driven by a perception that "private" or "indoor" sex work can be distinguished from, and should be preferred to, "public" sex work, known also as "outdoor" or "street" work. Legislative initiatives throughout the West have thus concentrated on exporting sex work and containing it within sites shielded from public observation. This largely explains

---

53 Austl, Tasmania, Legislative Council, *Parliamentary Debates* (19 October 2005) at 26-27 (Ms. Ritchie).

54 Austl, New South Wales, Legislative Assembly, *Parliamentary Debates* (18 October 1995) at 1941 (Mr. Rogan); Austl, New South Wales, Legislative Council, *Parliamentary Debates* (14 November 1995) at 3072 (Hon Symonds).

55 UK, Home Office, *A Coordinated Prostitution Strategy and Summary of Responses to Paying the Price* (London: Home Office, 2006) at 37; UK, Home Office, *Paying the Price: A Consultation Paper on Prostitution* (London: Home Office, 2004) at s. 5.2; Canada, Department of Justice, *Pornography and Prostitution in Canada: Report of the Special Committee on Pornography and Prostitution*, vol 2 (Ottawa: Minister of Supply and Services Canada, 1985) at 351; Austl, New South Wales, Legislative Assembly, *Parliamentary Debates* (18 October 1995) at 1938 (Mr. Harrison); Austl, New South Wales, Legislative Council, *Parliamentary Debates* (14 November 1995) at 3076 (Dr. Meredith Burgmann); Austl, New South Wales, Legislative Council, *Parliamentary Debates* (15 November 1995) at 3150 (I. Cohen); Austl, Queensland, Legislative Assembly, *Parliamentary Debates* (2 December 1999) at 5820 (Mrs. Cunningham).

56 Austl, New South Wales, Legislative Assembly, *Parliamentary Debates* (18 October 1995) at 1939 (Mr. Harrison).

57 Canada, *House of Commons Debates*, 33rd Parl, 1st Sess, Vol 5 (9 September 1985) at 6410 (Margaret Mitchell); Austl, Tasmania, Legislative Council, *Parliamentary Debates* (22 June 2005) at 25 (Mr. Dean).

the prohibition or strict control of solicitation even within jurisdictions that adopt decriminalization or regulatory approaches.

Legal actors explicitly justify efforts to export sex work to private and invisible sites by invoking public or community interests. Writing for the majority in the Supreme Court of Canada's 1993 constitutional assessment of the solicitation ban, Chief Justice Dickson affirmed that this prohibition "does not attempt, at least in any direct manner, to address the exploitation, degradation and subordination of women that are part of the contemporary reality of prostitution" (*Reference re ss 193 and 195.1(1)(c) of the Criminal Code*: para. 2). Rather, as noted by the trial court in *Bedford*, Canada's solicitation provisions are aimed at "combatting neighbourhood disruption or disorder and safeguarding public health and safety" (*Bedford v. Canada*: para. 242).

These judicial observations are consistent with legislative commentary surrounding the introduction of Bill C-49, which establishes Canada's current solicitation offence. The Bill was described as a tool designed "to help the citizens of this country who live in certain of our major urban areas and the police forces of the country to regain the streets."[58] It was further presented as aiming to "protect ordinary law-abiding citizens"[59] by eliminating sex work's "nuisance effects," specifically by driving it away from public view.[60] Public discourse has thus concentrated on the goal of "clear[ing] the streets of prostitution," for example, to avoid the "embarrassment" that "whores" provoke when "families go downtown for dinner" (Hallgrimsdottir et al. 2006: 272). Such objectives have been fueled by a belief that the threat of arrest can "deter and incapacitate"[61] those who engage in street work, or at least "remove the opportunity for them to carry out their business in public."[62]

Comparable goals have been expressed in connection with the United Kingdom's loitering and solicitation offences. The House of Lords' debates surrounding the *Sexual Offences Act 2003* stressed an interest in restricting sex work to the private sphere. Lord Lucas emphasized the desire to prevent sex work from being "thrust in our faces as we walk around most parts of most cities." He perceived, however, that where sex work is "carried on decently in private"

---

58 Canada, *House of Commons Debates*, 33rd Parl, 1st Sess, Vol 5 (9 September 1985) at 6373 (John Crosbie).

59 Canada, *House of Commons Debates*, 33rd Parl, 1st Sess, Vol 5 (9 September 1985) at 6378 (John Crosbie).

60 Canada, Department of Justice, *Street Prostitution: Assessing the Impact of the Law: Synthesis Report* (Ottawa: Department of Justice, 1989) at 7; Canada, *House of Commons Debates*, 33rd Parl, 1st Sess, Vol 5 (9 September 1985) at 6375 (John Crosbie); Canada, *House of Commons Debates*, 33rd Parl, 1st Sess, Vol 5 (9 September 1985) at 6409 (Margaret Mitchell).

61 Canada, Department of Justice, *Street Prostitution: Assessing the Impact of the Law: Synthesis Report* (Ottawa: Department of Justice, 1989) at 7.

62 Canada, *House of Commons Debates*, 33rd Parl, 1st Sess, Vol 5 (9 September 1985) at 6375 (John Crosbie).

with consent, state lawmakers would be "prepared for it to exist."[63] His Lordship suggested that moving sex work to "inside premises" would be "more pleasant for residents and those travelling through the areas where prostitutes ply their trade" while also "safest for the women concerned."[64] These remarks reflect Britain's historical vision of sex work as "a self-evident public nuisance"[65] that threatened "public morality."[66] Such perceptions persist in contemporary discussions, which are anchored to a liberal separation between private and public social realms. This distinction posits that while public matters are subject to state monitoring and governance, unseen and private activities, regardless of their esteemed immorality, are "not the law's business" (Kantola and Squires 2004: 78-79).

Australian legal discussions reveal a less prominent focus on separating public from private sex work-related activity, although legislative approaches in various states suggest that such a distinction serves to rationalize governance design. For example, relatively permissive legislation in New South Wales communicates a distinct preoccupation with the physical sites in which sex work occurs. Although brothels and soliciting generally are not subject to criminalization, they may be outlawed if they constitute a public nuisance or threat. This legal framework is rationalized by a social interest in preserving public spaces as community sites free from harassment.[67] Governance structures in New South Wales are further justified as promoting public health and safety for sex workers and for the wider community.[68]

The bipartite regulatory approach to sex work's governance, which treats street and indoor practices differently, is incongruous with the realities of this work. Juridical preoccupations with protecting women seem misplaced or too confined in their concentration on bawdy houses and procuring activities given the gravity of the risks that street workers collectively face. The acute dangers associated with outdoor sex work are explored more fully in the ensuing discussion, which contemplates the ways in which the presumptions and goals driving state law engage and conflict with non-state law shaping sex workers' decisions.

---

63 UK, HL, *Parliamentary Debates*, vol 648, col 184 (13 May 2003) (Lord Lucas).

64 UK, HL, *Parliamentary Debates*, vol 648, col 189 (13 May 2003) (Lord Lucas).

65 UK, HL, *Parliamentary Debates*, vol 216, col 779 (9 June 1959) (Lord Stonham); UK, HL, *Parliamentary Debates*, vol 216, col 804 (9 June 1959) (Lord Chancellor); UK, HL, *Parliamentary Debates*, vol 216, col 830 (9 June 1959) (Lord Denning).

66 UK, HL, *Parliamentary Debates*, vol 216, col 787 (9 June 1959) (Lord Archbishop of Canterbury).

67 Austl, New South Wales, Legislative Assembly, *Parliamentary Debates* (31 May 1988) at 804 (Mr. Dowd).

68 Austl, New South Wales, Legislative Assembly, *Parliamentary Debates* (31 May 1988) at 806 (Mr. Dowd); Austl, New South Wales, Legislative Assembly, *Parliamentary Debates* (31 May 1988) at 805 (Mr. Dowd); Austl, New South Wales, Legislative Assembly, *Parliamentary Debates* (20 September 1995) at 1187 (Mr. Whelan).

Interface between State and Non-State Law

State law converges with non-state norms relevant to women's choices about sex work at three points: the conceptualization of the relationship between money, addiction and sex work; the stratification of different sex work practices; and appreciations of women's vulnerability and potential to negotiate and appropriate the circumstances and outcomes of their work. The discussion that follows contrasts the way in which state law regards these points with the way they play out in the lived experiences of sex workers, as recounted through the empirical scholarship explored in Part 1.

Relationship between money, addiction and sex work As just explained, state governance of sex work is largely premised on the assumption that women adopt this practice as a result of coercion or entrapment, and that such circumstances are induced by poverty, racialization, substance dependence, homelessness or other forms of disenfranchisement.[69] This narrative is inclined to trace sex work to economic desperation and in turn, to presume that this desperation often arises from addiction. Workers' own narratives offer alternate representations of their circumstances and identity. Erotic labour is indeed typically taken up as a source of income. But the pursuit of such work often is not impetuous. Instead, women may select sex work from a range of income-earning possibilities that, pursuant to a reasoned deliberation, seem untenable, or at least less tenable than sex work.

Similar observations might be made in connection with substance dependence. Some women attribute the meaning of, or explanation for, their involvement in sex work to an addiction. Others might initiate or intensify drug use after their entry into the sex trade. Moreover, many sex workers are not drug-dependent. Thus, a pervasive juridical supposition about substance dependence as a root cause of sex work, which cuts transversally across jurisdictional boundaries, is too simplistic. Juxtaposing these suppositions against narratives drawn from empiricism illuminates the gaps in state laws' presumed causal correlations between drug use, economic need and sex work. These laws miss the point that sex work is not universally fuelled by a need to feed addiction, and overlook the possibility that sex work—largely because of its subjection to criminal law's governance—fosters circumstances that facilitate or prompt substance misuse. Orienting state law and policy to respond to this reality would be a worthwhile effort. Juridical initiatives rooted in presumptions about addiction engendering sex work might be revisited to discern and reduce the impact of the features of this work that might contribute to substance dependence. To this end, it would be worth considering juridical responses that depart from criminalization and instead seek to identify and palliate the social and economic disadvantages often associated with entry into and life in the sex trade (Carline 2012).

---

69 See e.g., Austl, Tasmania, Legislative Council, *Parliamentary Debates* (19 October 2005) at 20 (Ms. Forrest); Hallgrimsdottir et al. 2006: 276.

While circumstances of marginalization characterize the experiences of many sex workers, state-based discourse suggests that involvement in sex work is invariably triggered by social and economic tragedy. Juridical analyses fail to heed the range of factors that might underlie choices about this work. Women's narratives illuminate the pertinence to such choices of financial considerations, work flexibility and independence, and sexual interest and curiosity.

Ultimately, a monolithic understanding of sex work and those who engage with it flattens legal conversations and inquiry. The reasons underlying women's entry into sex work are varied, as are their experiences. Their evaluations of their work range from "complacency and indifference to strong positions in favour of and against it" (Hallgrimsdottir et al. 2006: 276). These empirically drawn conclusions accentuate the simplicity within state law's imagination of sex workers, envisaging them as depraved by their own moral shortcomings or by the exploitation of others. Either characterization overlooks the spectrum of objectives that may explain and give value to choices about sex work.

Hierarchizing sex work State and non-state law shaping sex work practices meet at a second juncture, this one pertinent to the distinctions between categories of the practice. As considered earlier, the governance of sex work is based on a view of indoor, private forms of this practice as safer, more discrete and thus more palatable. State law may permit or informally tolerate practices such as brothel-keeping or independent indoor work. Alternatively, the criminalization of indoor work may attract judicial scrutiny and criticism (*Canada (Attorney General) v. Bedford*). Street work, in contrast, is presented as a distinct public threat and irritant, and is the form of sex work that state law rejects most bluntly.

The distinction state law draws between indoor and outdoor work is premised on an objective of eliminating or driving out of sight public forms of sex work, generally perceived as an urban blight. Rather paradoxically, then, legal actors invoke the relevance of community aesthetic and safety to rationalize legislation and policies that drive street work to covert, unsightly and dangerous spaces. These are zones in which women are susceptible to violence, disappearance and homicide. Such risks are entirely theirs to absorb and manage, as legal rules and their enforcement offer minimal protection (Lowman 2000). This point is taken up in greater detail in the subsection "Criminal Law's Persuasion over Sex Work Choices," below.

A governance framework premised on hierarchizing private over public sex work creates and nourishes three separate myths, each of which is nuanced or challenged by empiricism. First, it implies that public and private spaces can be definitively separated from one another, with state law's ken relegated to matters public. This notion, broadly criticized by feminists, overlooks the violence that state actors perpetrate when they remain inactive in the face of known risks to marginalized individuals on the grounds of respecting personal or private space (Higgins 2000, Schneider 1991, Minow 1990: 269-283, Boyd 1997, Koshan 1997, Goldfarb 2000, Hanna 2009).

Second, state law governing sex work is often developed and propagated for the ostensible benefit of a neighbourhood, as distinct from and to the exclusion of sex workers' interests. Within this conceptual structure, "outsider" women are viewed as importing sex work into otherwise safe and law-abiding spaces. This understanding forecloses consideration of sex workers' residential and social presence in their work communities. They may see themselves as "resident[s] too" of the streets that legislators aim to launder through legislation aimed at eliminating street sex work (Jakobsen and Perkins 1994: 61). Apart from "home operators" who reside and work in the same premises, outdoor workers may understand their work communities as living spaces. Many will face inadequate or transient housing arrangements (Pivot Legal Society 2004: 15, Jeal et al. 2008: 383, Bilardi 2011, Queensland Crime and Misconduct Commission 2011: 120),[70] and the streets they occupy for work might constitute a temporary home. Sex workers with permanent housing may also work within their own neighbourhoods. For instance, a participant in one study chose to work in a particular establishment because she lived "down the street" and could walk or bike to work, avoiding the cost of bus fare (Bungay et al. 2011: 23). Finally, there is a point to be made about community not necessarily occupying geographic space. Whether they work miles away from, next door to, or in the room in which they reside, sex workers are symbolically, but powerfully, revoked of social citizenship and belonging through juridical efforts that neglect their perspectives and aim to dispose communities of their presence. These efforts push sex workers to zones that promote their social and political isolation, where violence against them can occur with impunity. The message state law's initiatives thus convey is that sex workers are not seen, do not matter and do not belong. The dangers of street work, which state law's discourse frequently laments as an inevitable and inherent attribute of this practice, are likely better appreciated as the direct and foreseeable upshot of legislation and policy deliberately designed to marginalize sex work and render it invisible.

Third, state law and policy gesture at a hierarchy among sex workers, with those working indoors as having greater options and some sense of privilege over their colleagues working on the streets. More precisely, legal actors tend to view outdoor workers as being driven by exploitation[71] and as facing "enormous risk" (*Canada (Attorney General) v. Bedford*: para. 359) in their work. Street workers are thus understood as having the fewest opportunities and weakest sense of control over their circumstances. Sex workers' experiences suggest an alternate possible understanding of outdoor practices. As explained in Part 1, control and flexibility in relation to one's work pattern and income are central to the value that some women ascribe to their encounters with sex work. This autonomy is usually enhanced for women who work independently, beyond the reach of those who own

---

70 See also Edmonton Social Planning Council, *Street Prostitution in Edmonton* (Edmonton: Edmonton Social Planning Council, 1993) at 1-2.

71 UK, Home Office, *A Coordinated Prostitution Strategy and Summary of Responses to Paying the Price* (London: Home Office, 2006) at 1.

or operate indoor sex establishments. For some women, then, outdoor work might not mean eking out the bleak and desperate existence that state law imagines. Rather, it might be chosen following a process of identifying and selecting among varied income-earning strategies and, more narrowly, among types of work within the sex industry.

Legal and political discussions about sex work have drawn on a historical, but untenable, distinction between public and private zones of regulation in the name of protecting supposed community interests. These discussions craft an image of "the street" or "the public" as removed from private and presumably securer zones of sex work without acknowledging the dangers for women within these indoor spaces (Harcourt and Donovan 2005: 203, Sanders and Campbell 2007: 7-10, Jackson et al. 2007: 264, Benoit and Millar 2001: 53).[72] This distinction has the further result of prompting aggressive policing of outdoor sex work. Solicitation-related offences account for law enforcement's principal preoccupation with sex work. Street-level workers are thus arrested and charged far more frequently than those who work within indoor sex services establishments (Pivot Legal Society 2004: 23, O'Doherty 2011b: 219, Sanders 2004c: 1712-1713).[73] In the result, outdoor sex workers are subject to multiple oppressions exerted by social and economic marginalization, by heightened risks of violence and emotional strain, and by the operation and enforcement of formal legal rules.

State law's neglect of sex worker narratives generates a fallacy about geography and identity in the sex trade. State law's indoor/outdoor, private/public sex work dichotomies underpin a social reassurance that pitches sex work—especially its seediest version transacted in dark corners and city outskirts—as unwanted, unwelcome and therefore banished from "law-abiding" neighbourhoods. Empirics contrast this imagery, revealing the varied norms and pressures that lead to sex workers' presence in the very communities that governments aim to protect through sex workers' exile. Sex workers' accounts further counter presumptions regarding outdoor work's inherent danger and indoor work's security. Sex worker narratives show the presence of risk in either setting, as well as state law's role in compounding the hazards to which workers are exposed. For example, some workers might absorb the risks of street work violence if they feel that the rigidity and disciplinary protocols of indoor labour, discussed in Part 1 ("The Value Women Ascribe to Engaging in Sex Work"), are unmanageable. Accordingly, legalizing indoor sex establishments will not by itself eliminate street work nor will it achieve sex worker security. Street work will persist, with some workers transitioning

72 See also, A. Edwards, *Selling Sex; Regulating Prostitution in Queensland: A Report to the Prostitution Licensing Authority* (Brisbane: Prostitution Licensing Authority, 2009) at 8.

73 See also, C. Woodward et al., *Selling Sex in Queensland 2003: A Study of Prostitution in Queensland* (Brisbane: Prostitution Licensing Authority, 2004) at 38.

between indoor and outdoor sites depending on their needs and circumstances.[74] As considered below ("Criminal Law's Persuasion over Sex Work Choices"), risks encountered in either site will persist so long as sex work carries the threat of criminal penalty and stigma, and so long as sex workers remain unable to access support in the form of labour standards, social security and antidiscrimination legislation. Finally, empirical evidence brings to light the possibility of street work as desirable, or at least as more desirable than indoor work, for some women. The possibility of a preference for street work is easier to appreciate in view of the risk-reduction strategies sex workers deploy to mitigate potential dangers in their work, as described in the discussion that follows.

Scope for developing resistance and negotiating risk Sex work narratives derived from empirical study reinforce state law's underlying premise regarding the practice's potential physical and emotional hazards. Sex workers' own accounts make plain the physical, psychological and economic risks posed by encounters with clients, agents, managers and "pimps" or "protectors." While these narratives bring home the stark dangers of sex work, they do not yield the same conclusion that state law reaches. State law identifies risk as a basis for generally labeling sex work as coercive and as revoking women's agency and power. In contrast, empirical studies demonstrate the correlation between sex work's risks and the manner in which it is governed by the state. This point is taken up more fully in the following section of this chapter ("Criminal Law's Persuasion over Sex Work Choices"), but for the moment it remains critical to note that a threat of prosecution cultivates a risky environment for sex workers. Fear of criminal charges exports sex work to hidden sites where social and legal protections are absent. Sex work's emotional perils in the form of stigma and shame also stem from its prohibition.

Sex workers' narratives offer insight into their use of informal normative structures, or non-state law, to resist outside exertions of control and dominance, and to make choices that allow them to negotiate potential harms. Such appropriation of agency in relation to overcoming risk is apparent in three particular sex work contexts. First, sex workers use resources at their disposal to manage the psychological hazards of their work. Without minimizing or dismissing the impact of such stress, sex workers' experiential knowledge sheds light on strategies they craft to negotiate emotional risks. In an effort to avoid stigma arising from publicity of their identity as sex workers (Jackson et al. 2007), many women will conceal their work from family, friends and community members (Groves et al. 2008: 394). Other techniques for managing emotional risk, which are left unaddressed in juridical discussions, can include the use of humour (Sanders 2004b) or the imagination of the self as dissociated and distinct from one's natural, or private, persona (Sanders 2005: 325, Hallgrimsdottir et al. 2006: 277, McVerry and Lindop 2005: 113-114, Benoit and Millar 2001: 70, Bruckert et al. 2003: 34-36). Sex work

74 A. Edwards, *Selling Sex; Regulating Prostitution in Queensland: A Report to the Prostitution Licensing Authority* (Brisbane: Prostitution Licensing Authority, 2009).

is therefore described as "'acting out' a role" (McVerry and Lindop 2005: 113), as leading a "double life" (Bruckert et al. 2003: 86), or as sustaining a "mask, or series of masks" (Brewis and Linstead 2000: 84). In a related vein, many women go to lengths to distinguish sex work from personal sex. This may result in women foregoing altogether private sexual relationships (Sanders 2004a: 567, Pyett and Warr 1999: 190). Alternatively, it may mean drawing a conceptual distinction between work versus private sex, or declaring physically "off limits" certain body parts or practices to clients, reserving these for intimate partners (Sanders 2005: 326). As one woman explained:

> When you are working you are having sex, you are not making love you are having sex … so when you go back in your personal relationship you are doing the same but you are putting feelings to it, so it is not the same. I could not kiss a punter, I would not want anything to do with their mouth because I have to kiss my baby. And you would not want to kiss your man. Sex is with Durex so you are not really touching them. (Sanders 2004a: 567)

At least one author (Farley 2003: 264-265) has argued that this rupture of the body from the self is emblematic of surviving trauma, highlighting the potential adverse psychological impact of sex work. Moreover, other research indicates that sex workers' techniques for coping with emotional hardship are not always successful (Sanders 2004a: 567-569, Pyett and Warr 1999: 190, Cooper et al. 2004). This being said, such techniques can be crucial to getting a handle on and surmounting the physical and psychosocial challenges encountered in sex work.

Beyond emotional harms, sex workers manage physical risks by assuming control over the parameters of their labour. They set limits as to the services they will offer, the clients they will accept and the settings in which they will work. These are understood as measures that at once build confidence and stave off violence (Jackson et al. 2005: 99). Risk management may further call for developing the verbal skills required for talking down or "gentling" clients who become anxious or aggressive (Sanders and Campbell 2007: 11), or for becoming an "educator" to resistant or deviant clients, especially in regard to condom use (Bungay et al. 2011: 24, Jackson et al. 2005: 99).[75] Sex workers recount other self-protective techniques for averting violence including: memorizing clients' car license plate numbers; avoiding clients in rented cars or cars with interstate plates; leaving fingerprints or other traces of their presence in cars or other sites visited with clients; checking clients and their cars to ensure an absence of weapons; and carrying weapons themselves (Lewis et al. 2005: 161-163, Sanders 2004c: 1710-1711, Pyett and Warr 1999: 190-192, McKeganey and Barnard 1996: 75-78). Sex workers might also form alliances with others in the sex trade—such as

75 See also, A. Edwards, *Selling Sex; Regulating Prostitution in Queensland: A Report to the Prostitution Licensing Authority* (Brisbane: Prostitution Licensing Authority, 2009) at 20.

bodyguards, drivers or other workers—to mitigate risk. While such networks are generally informal, some, such as Britain's "Ugly Mugs" project, are structured. Ugly Mugs disseminates information about violent incidents against sex workers, including information about perpetrators. In so doing, the initiative advocates "the need for sex workers to be proactive in preventing violence" (Sanders 2004a: 564, see also McVerry and Lindop 2005: 113). Although this collectivity of efforts is indicative of the perpetual vigilance that sex workers exercise, it foregrounds workers' ingenuity and industriousness in mustering a degree of ownership over circumstances that otherwise severely compromise their interests. Sex workers thus cultivate agency "insofar as they attempt to adjust to the stressors and re-organize their lives to make their situation more manageable" (Jackson et al. 2007: 258).

A third dynamic demonstrative of women's power in sex work pertains to workers' formation of preferences for types of work both within and outside of the sex trade, and their consequential choices about income-earning options. While legal authorities represent sex work as either the fruit of compulsion or as a corrupt choice, women's accounts reveal their reasoning in identifying and weighing options in the face of risks and preferences. At times, decisions about sex work are premised upon risk negotiation, as just discussed. Sometimes, though, choices might be made pursuant to a contemplation of "competing preferences" (Sanders 2004a: 559). Beyond the avoidance or mitigation of risk, sex workers may seek "improved working conditions and environments that [interact] favourably with other aspects of life" (Bungay et al. 2011: 23). This may prompt transitioning between various types of sex work according to the income and conditions offered in different settings (Jeffrey and MacDonald 2006a: 323).

Dominant narratives about sex work concentrate on the severe constraints under which women operate, neglecting instances of resistance and agency women acquire even in compromising or menacing circumstances. State law's mistake is thus to premise its response to sex work almost fully on an assumption that sex workers' risks and tradeoffs, onerous though they may be, preclude the possibility of reasoned deliberation and decision-making. Women's own renditions of their experiences corroborate sex work's characterization as deeply hazardous. Yet they also bring to light sex workers' potential for developing meaningful control and choice in the face of a difficult and limited range of options. These notions of control and choice remain vital to those who emphasize that seeing one's self as resilient and in command of engagements with clients is crucial for self-empowerment and survival. Adverse or injurious experiences in the sex trade may therefore be described as stepping-stones to "becoming hardy," rather than moments of weakness or victimization (Harris et al. 2011: 395-396).

This analysis of women's resourcefulness in devising options and making choices to identify and negotiate risks is rendered possible through an analysis of empirics. It underscores the contribution of field studies to a fuller understanding of sex work. These studies do not, however, engage with juridical authorities. They therefore cannot contemplate a critical point that is the subject of the ensuing discussion, namely, the effect of criminal law on women's options and risks in sex work.

Criminal Law's Persuasion over Sex Work Choices

Criminalization does not halt polygamy, surrogacy or sex work. Rather, its main effect is the aggravation of risks to which those involved in these activities are exposed. A prohibition's failure to terminate a given practice does not render that prohibition unjustified or illogical. Neither does the fact that the prohibition heightens risk for participants of the outlawed activity. Various forms of socially offensive behaviour persist in the face of their criminalization, occurring in surreptitious circumstances because they are prohibited, increasing the risks of violence and harm for those involved. On their own, such circumstances are usually not a basis for impugning or repealing a criminal law. Yet the practices considered in this book are distinct in that the goals underlying their prohibition are paradoxically undermined by criminal law's operation. Juridical responses to polygamy, surrogacy and sex work are premised upon presumptions and justifications related to women's vulnerability and protection. Yet in each of these domains, state laws' impact is counterproductive and boosts women's exposure to harm.

The point is particularly stark in connection with sex work. Proscribing and refusing to recognize this as legitimate work amplifies the risks women encounter when they engage in this practice, while failing to address the circumstances of social and economic disadvantage that women encounter before or during their lives as sex workers (Munro and Scoular 2012: 194). Thus, in an effort to elude public and police attention, illegal sex work occurs "in the shadows,"[76] and such relegation to secluded areas elevates opportunities for violence (Pivot Legal Society 2004: 23). Moreover, provisions against procuring and living on the avails subject third parties to prosecution, dissuading them from behaviour and relationships that could otherwise enhance sex workers' safety (Pivot Legal Society 2004: 10, O'Doherty 2011a: 957). The same is true of provisions, such as those in Queensland, which allow sole operation sex work but bar two or more workers from providing services in the same place (Sullivan 2008: 84). Finally, soliciting bans force pre-service exchanges between sex workers and clients to happen hastily, which may put women at risk of accepting clients who they would, with more time and in a more open setting, have screened out as potentially dangerous (Pivot Legal Society 2004: 11-12, O'Doherty 2011a: 957, Sanders 2004c: 1713-1714). As MacPherson J.A. noted in *Bedford*, albeit in dissent, this prohibition "chokes off self-protection options for prostitutes who are already at enormous risk" (*Canada (Attorney General) v. Bedford*: para. 359). Communication prohibitions

76 Austl, Queensland, Prostitution Licensing Authority, *Submission to the Crime and Misconduct Commission Review of the Prostitution Act 1999* (Brisbane: Crime and Misconduct Commission, 2010) at 5.

also present a potential economic risk, forcing incomplete discussions about the terms of service, which may result in hostile sex worker–client exchanges and in the worker being unfairly paid (Bungay et al. 2011: 22).

In view of these factors, many sex workers take up their work independently and clandestinely, often with nefarious effects to their health, safety and economic well-being. Circumstances in Vancouver's Downtown Eastside are illustrative. As one set of researchers opines, "this system of quasi-criminalization [i.e., banning activities surrounding sex work but not the trade in sex itself] bears direct responsibility for the violent conditions suffered by women in Vancouver's street level sex trade" (Cler-Cunningham and Christensen 2001: iii, see also Pivot Legal Society 2004: 17-18). This position resonates with observations made elsewhere about the correlation between regulatory approaches and the harm to which sex workers are exposed and, more directly, criminalization's effect on intensifying violence within sex work (Sanders and Campbell 2007: 3-5). Evidence from Queensland, by contrast, suggests that licensed brothels offer secure workspaces for women (Sullivan 2008: 79). This being said, a regulatory scheme may allow for the imposition of onerous working conditions within brothels, leading some to advocate for decriminalization over licensing as a means of opportunity creation and harm reduction (Jeffrey and Sullivan 2009: 65-67, see *contra*, Farley 2004: 1094, who argues it is "a cruel lie" to propose that decriminalization or regulation reduces sex workers' exposure to risk). Moreover, in conceiving of regulatory and licensing models, it is critical to keep in mind the risk of "local" law, advanced at a municipal or administrative level, to be as blunt, homogenizing and undemocratic in its execution as the criminal law (Valverde 2012). Thus, any move by the state toward the creation of regulatory frameworks must internalize and reflect commitments to heeding and responding to sex workers' experiential knowledge with a view to ensuring equity and safety in their work.

Apart from undermining physical security, sex work-related prohibitions prompt circumstances and choices that compromise women's emotional health. As explained, sex work imposes significant stress triggered by the constant vigilance required to avert violence and the transmission of disease, and the burdens and constraints imposed by agents and managers. Sex work's stigma also causes emotional disquiet, shame and degradation, and leads many to refrain from disclosing their work, even within family circles (Harris et al. 2011: 391-392, Lewis et al. 2005: 156-157, Groves et al. 2008: 394, Benoit and Millar 2001: 70-71). State law has a hand in imposing these psychological burdens and presents a formidable barrier for those who might seek out resources for coping with them. Just as polygamy and surrogacy's prohibition deters some women who engage in these practices from seeking out support, shame and fear of prosecution may dissuade sex workers from obtaining "mainstream" counseling services to manage the stresses of, or to exit, the sex trade (Benoit and Millar 2001: 56). They may instead prefer to seek out the services of informal or community-based networks, which are sharply under-resourced (Jackson et al. 2007: 269). Such networks' own outreach efforts may also be frustrated by sex workers' need to operate anonymously and secretly.[77]

Engaging in a criminalized and stigmatized lifestyle further limits access to legal support and remedies against harm. Rather than viewing police or other legal actors as offering protection against crime and violence, many sex workers understandably eye those who enforce state law suspiciously and antagonistically. Criminal charges may lead to fines that women cannot pay without a return to sex work (Jeffrey and Sullivan 2009: 64). Even before any such charge is entered, the processes of police contact and arrest, particularly by male officers, can be traumatizing and deeply undignified (Nixon et al. 2002: 1030-1031, Bruckert et al. 2003: 31). Distrust of police is thus broad, amplified by the view—supported by some police officers themselves—that state actors will remain inert in the face of violence against sex workers (Shaver et al. 2011: 56, O'Doherty 2011b: 223-224). Such misgivings will be especially pronounced for Aboriginal women, given historical relationships with state institutions marred by abuse and racism.[78] Moreover, migrant and trafficked sex workers without documentation will recognize that filing a police report also means the possibility of triggering removal proceedings. It comes as no surprise, then, that women in the sex trade often refrain from reporting crimes carried out against them (O'Doherty 2011a: 957, Lewis et al. 2005: 160, Cler-Cunningham and Christensen 2001: iii, Harris et al. 2011: 395, Boyle et al. 1997: 137, Benoit and Millar 2001: 54-55). The disastrous effects of this social and legal framework are made plain within a recent Canadian Commission of Inquiry Report cataloguing the vast failures of police and other public actors in preventing, investigating and prosecuting the serial disappearance and murder of 67 women, many of whom were Aboriginal and most of whom had connections to the sex trade in Vancouver's Downtown Eastside. The Report illuminates social perceptions of these women as transient "nobodies" living high-risk lifestyles, explaining the sluggishness, indifference and negligence that characterized state responses to their disappearances and murders.[79]

A community's "tolerated residuum of abuse" should bear an inverse relationship to the presence of strict or excessive law enforcement targeting such abuse (Kennedy 1993: 144, 160). The scope of abuse sex workers—especially

77 Austl, Queensland, Prostitution Licensing Authority, *Submission to the Crime and Misconduct Commission Review of the Prostitution Act 1999* (Brisbane: Crime and Misconduct Commission, 2010) at 5.

78 Canada, British Columbia, Sisterwatch Project of the Vancouver Police Department and Women's Memorial March Committee, *The Tragedy of Missing and Murdered Aboriginal Women in Canada: We Can Do Better* (2011) at 10, [Online]. Available at: http://vancouver.ca/police/assets/pdf/reports-policies/missing-murdered-aboriginal-women-canada-report.pdf [accessed: 8 June 2013].

79 Canada, British Columbia, The Honourable Wally T. Oppal Q.C., Commissioner, *Forsaken: The Report of the Missing Women Commission of Inquiry* (Victoria: Ministry of the Attorney General, 2012). See also Lowman 2000.

those who work outdoors—absorb is enormous, largely on account of state actors' deliberate oblivion and passivity. Criminal law's social message, about who is law-abiding and who is an outlaw, and about who merits or is unworthy of its benefits and protection, is thus conveyed not only by its diction, but also by its deployment. In its formulation, as well as its purposive substantive application, criminal law marks and reinforces the boundaries that certify social citizenship, which in this context plainly proclaim sex workers' exclusion.

Beyond criminal law, sex workers, in a manner reminiscent of some women who have shared their personal narratives about life in polygamy, bear preoccupations in relation to child protection. Sex workers who are mothers will typically worry as much about losing custody of their children as about arrest (Jeffrey and Sullivan 2009: 64, O'Doherty 2011b: 224, Shaver et al. 2011: 57, see also Jackson et al. 2007: 265).

Finally, criminalization coupled with the absence of a framework for recognizing sex work as legitimate work offers fertile ground for abuse by managers and agents operating sex services establishments. As discussed earlier, working conditions in such spaces range from tolerable and safe to enslaving. Recourses open to women who find themselves on the disadvantaged end of this spectrum are entirely self-crafted. Where sex work is criminalized and unrecognized by the state, sex workers have no access to the body of employment and human rights legislation and jurisprudence developed to reduce exposure to physical, social and economic risk in the waged labour force. In view of the unavailability of outside protection from bodies such as unions or tribunals, sex workers devise for themselves methods to cope with or exit their workspace (Jackson et al. 2007: 268, Shaver et al. 2011: 53, Bruckert et al. 2003: 26). One woman in a Vancouver-based study thus remarked about her experiences as an indoor sex worker:

> The door girl keeps your money, that way if you get fined for anything throughout the day, not picking up a towel, not cleaning a sheet, not providing a service the gentleman wanted or so and so, then they fine you … they fine you $50 for being late … they will fine you $150 for calling in sick … I mean what are we going to do? Go to the labour board? (Bungay et al. 2011: 21)

State law's effects on sex work, as recounted through empirically gleaned knowledge, are significantly removed from the proclaimed goal of protecting women from the coercion and violence presumed inherent to sex work. Legislation and policies rooted in proscription do not rescue sex workers. Rather, they propel sex workers to operate off the state's radar, and they must absorb the consequential risks of doing so entirely through their own private networks, norms and resources. Where sex workers happen to befall public scrutiny, they risk punishment and stigma instead of support. Those who seek to exit the sex trade may well find legislative frameworks hindering rather than helpful, given the financial onus imposed by fines and the impediment that a criminal record can have on establishing housing and employment (Sanders 2007).

This discussion illuminates the parallel streams of norms crafted by sex workers themselves, as conveyed through empirical scholarship, and formal rules constructed by the state. An analysis of the impact of each suggests that informal norms bear formidable weight in sex work-related choices. State governance structures seem to have little effect on stopping, slowing or encouraging sex work. Where it is prohibited, the practice continues and conversely, decriminalization does not trigger a surge in its uptake. Instead, economic need, and preferences in relation to balancing personal life and work, and in relation to sexual expression seem more influential on decisions about engagement with sex work.[80]

Having said this, state law exerts its presence on choices made in relation to where and how sex work is practiced. This resonates closely with the observations drawn in Chapters 2 and 3 in relation to criminal law's persuasion over choices about polygamy and surrogacy. Considered here in the context of sex work, proscriptive rules wield effects that prejudice their own proclaimed aims pertaining to women's protection. They also advance a narrative of despondent and victimized women, particularly those working the streets, leaving aside accounts illuminating women's ability to appropriate control and choice, even within sex work's potentially constrictive parameters.

Conclusion

State law and policy conversations addressing sex work reveal three conventional pitfalls, identified in Chapter 1, of a simplistic understanding of choice in connection with women's controversial lifestyles. First, these conversations construct choice as an absolute, imagining minimal or no possibility for the presence of agency, resistance, control or desire where women confront and negotiate risks and constraints. Conversely, where choice is identified, limits on agency tend to be minimized or overlooked.

Second, legal discourse positions choice as a vector of responsibility. When cast as victims compelled by coercion or entrapment, sex workers are less susceptible to be held to account for their actions. They are described as needing the state's protection and deliverance from sex work's evils. In contrast, where choice is in play, responsibility is traced more readily to the actor, rationalizing juridical analyses that impugn and seek retribution for sex workers' choices and conduct.

Third, state law and policy rubrics develop an essentialized representation of sex workers. Sex workers are invariably women who are motivated by economic desperation, often as a result of substance dependence. State law's understandings further assume that street work is consistently more insidious than indoor sex work.

80 Austl, Queensland, Prostitution Licensing Authority, *Submission to the Crime and Misconduct Commission Review of the Prostitution Act 1999* (Brisbane: Crime and Misconduct Commission, 2010) at 6-7.

Integrating knowledge gleaned from empirical study with sex workers highlights the range of informal forces—economic, social and psychological—that coexist with formal, state-crafted rules to wield influence over deliberations and decisions about sex work. Empirical research allows an exploration of the diverse norms contouring women's choices about where, when and with whom to work, allowing them to identify and quell risk. It further reveals the way in which state law's effects counter its chief narrative of sex workers as victims needing protection, operating instead to create and exacerbate hazards. Finally, empirically drawn knowledge challenges juridical essentialism, revealing the plurality of factors that explain and give meaning to the practice of sex work for women, and that pertain in their evaluations of their experiences.

Ultimately, state law's underlying dichotomy between choice and agency on one hand, and coercion and victimization on the other, is not communicated by sex workers' experiential knowledge as relayed through empirical research. Rather, this knowledge nuances and problematizes these concepts, suggesting possibilities for their coexistence despite their apparent polarization. This observation is discernible also in relation to women's engagements with polygamy and surrogacy. It calls for scrupulous inquiry in relation to the dyadic relationship state law commonly envisages between agency and victimhood in relation to women's morally ambiguous choices. The conclusion to this book follows, taking up this point more robustly.

Conclusion

This book contends that women's choices are neither impervious to nor defined by law. All choices, even those that spark social and juridical objection and those that seem self-injurious, take place against the backdrop of state and non-state law. Moreover, such choices flow from an evaluation of diverse norms and the relative value, to the individual chooser, of internalizing and abiding by these norms.

Juridical analyses benefit minimally from casting women who make morally ambiguous choices as either helpless victims of oppression who require the state's protection, or as freedom warriors who break the law of the state as a political affirmation of individual rights. A more instructive appreciation of tough choices calls for greater nuance, and requires an investigation of the conditions that lie within the gap created by law's imagined bifurcation between complete coercion and pure choice (Jeffrey and MacDonald 2006b: 109-112, Koken 2010: 40-42). This more textured and robust appreciation of choice is furthered by juridical investigations characterized by openness to identifying instantiations of agency, power and resistance and by an awareness of the oppressions and constraints that operate to confine options and outcomes.

Recognizing choice respects the individual chooser provided that analyses refrain from presuming autonomy and remain alive to the risk of pressures that restrict possibilities and opportunities, particularly for disadvantaged populations. Moreover, identifying choice in any given context should not necessarily yield impositions of responsibility for poor outcomes to the ostensible chooser. Finally, compelling interpretations of choice cannot be premised upon suppositions or stereotypes in regard to the identity and characteristics of those who are competent to make choices, and those who are not.

An effective and equitable juridical framework for analyzing choice compels a turn to empirical evidence with a view to discerning why controversial choices are made and how they are valued. In this way, empirical data illuminate the multiple normative forces beyond state law that shape individuals' decision-making in regard to practices that trigger social debate and dissent. Moreover, empirically drawn knowledge highlights the role of state law in this process and can, as in the case studies that this book develops, reveal the important costs that state law might impose on the individuals it professes to protect.

The call for reliance on empiricism should prompt some probative questions. Notably, there is an issue in regard to disciplinary capacity, specifically as to whether jurists are trained to pursue, interpret or evaluate empirical data. Empirical inquiry and reasoning also spur questions about inclusivity and representativeness, particularly with respect to populations that live under the threats of state-imposed penalties and social stigma for taking part in practices central or essential to their ways of life. Research efforts to locate, study and engage with such populations will be fraught with practical and ethical challenges. These and other intricacies associated with empirically derived knowledge are examined in Chapter 1, and discussed in subsequent chapters with reference to choices about polygamy, surrogacy and sex work.

Regardless of the challenges that the pursuit of empirical research may present, it remains crucial to understanding socially contested choices. Such choices are commonly understood and labeled as aberrations from a presumed benchmark of normalcy, and this rationalizes state law's responses to them. Yet narratives offered by those who make these choices, which may be accessed through fieldwork and empirical investigation, throws into relief the relativity of juridical perceptions of difference and deviation. Beliefs and behaviours become abnormal or profane when these are assessed against imagined and constructed ideals of the ordinary or the tolerable. Given that these ideals tend to fuel the state's approaches to morally controverted matters, labels of "difference" have critical juridical implications (Minow 1990).

Integrating experiential knowledge within legal analyses facilitates appraisals of the state's law, which in turn blurs the presumably blunt divisions between the conventional and the unorthodox, and between what is legal and what offends. For example, narratives of women in polygamy discussed in Chapter 2 indicate the importance sister wives ascribe to marriage and spousal fidelity, as they simultaneously adapt the laws of the state to reform nuptial norms within their communities. Their stories contrast suppositions about polygamy that underpin state law's response to this practice in the West, and which characterize plural marriage as static, regressive and as serving primarily to satiate men's sexual avarice. State law thereby holds polygamy up as a marked departure from monogamous marriage; a position bolstered by legislative, judicial and policy discourses that overlook the tolerated prevalence of conjugal pluralism throughout Western legal cultures and societies. These same discourses tout monogamy as equality-producing, shunning contemplation of the inequalities that conventional marriage and its governance have long cultivated.

Comparably, experiences explored in Chapter 3 highlight the centrality of conventional family ideals to women's choices about surrogacy. Foundational to the meaning and value that women ascribe to surrogacy is a traditional vision of the family, typically one that is formed through genetic bonds. Surrogates view themselves as making critical social contributions by allowing others to realize the "dream" or "miracle" of biological parenthood. These narratives stand in contrast to assumptions underlying state law's approach to surrogacy. Legislation and policy discussions portray women as vulnerably lured to surrogate maternity by the prospect of economic gain, through a process that coerces, commodifies and converts the naturalness of reproduction. Surrogates' narratives further reflect their capacity to seize, rather than be victimized by, the separation that surrogacy imposes between reproduction and parenting so as to rationalize and develop a sense of control over a surrogate pregnancy.

Last, Chapter 4 illuminates the pragmatism and rationalism that undergirds choices about sex work. In contrast to the dominant narrative driving state law in this area, sex workers are not uniformly depraved, desperate or disposed to risk. Rather, their stories reflect an ability to identify and weigh realistic options and negotiate the potential hazards they encounter in their work. As Chapter 4 explains, these hazards are not purely inherent to sex work. The state's response to sex workers consigns them to spaces marked by obscurity and danger, prompting empirical narratives that circulate heavily around risk-navigation. Moreover, state law and institutions in the jurisdictions studied here cultivate reticence within the sex worker community in regard to resorting to public sources of support and security. Such reluctance to seek state assistance is logical. Rather than safety and security, sex workers' encounters with police, social workers, lawyers or judges often result either in passivity and inaction in the face of sex workers' concerns and interests, or in the infliction of physical, emotional or economic harms.

The synthesis of these cases studies in not indented to insinuate that polygamy, surrogacy and sex work raise parallel concerns and considerations. Choices made in regard to each of these practices carry distinct implications and tradeoffs. Yet each of these contexts calls attention to the indispensable quality of empirically derived experiential knowledge for developing enriched understandings of morally complex choices. This knowledge provides insight into the perspectives of those whose interests lie at the core of legal analyses. It further facilitates a critical evaluation of state law's success in meeting the goals it sets out to achieve by regulating or outlawing particular choices.

A study of women's experiences in polygamy, surrogacy and sex work further establishes the dilemma of absolutist approaches to choice. Outright exclusion of the possibility of choice neglects the dignity and capacities of women who muster agency and resolve in the face of adversity. Conversely, the identification of choice can problematically serve to rationalize the state's withdrawal from and abdication of responsibility within these contexts, typically to the peril of individuals and groups who already absorb considerable risk. This book therefore advances the position that juridical efforts to identify choice, even in the context of constricting and difficult life circumstances, are essential to social and political empowerment. Such efforts must, however, be coupled with initiatives at the state level aimed at reducing risk and broadening options and opportunities. These aspirations require legal actors such as legislators, policymakers and judges to hear and heed the narratives of those whose choices are in dispute, and on whose lives state law is directly brought to bear. Their experiential knowledge foregrounds their resilience and ingenuity in identifying multiple norms relevant to their choices, and in negotiating these norms to reason and choose according to their own values, needs and ambitions.

The framework developed here for assessing polemical choices begins by endeavouring to discern how those who make such choices ascribe meaning and value to them. This knowledge, which may be derived through empirical inquiry, is subsequently contrasted with the law of the state that seeks to govern the choices concerned. At this stage, an analysis of relevant state governance instruments (legislation, judicial decisions, polices) is required. Juxtaposing the assumptions and goals that drive state law with the narratives of those who are subject to that law commonly reveals the plurality of norms that influence morally obscure choices. This integration of narrative and state law can further highlight state law's conceptual and practical shortcomings. More precisely, at a conceptual level, it may reveal logical incongruences between the practices that state law accepts and those it rejects and prohibits. At a practical level, an analysis that integrates empirics with traditional legal authorities brings to light the deficiencies of state strategies that weaken the social, economic and political positions of those whose interests are ostensibly at the heart of these strategies. These deficiencies are most plain when criminal law subjects those whom the law professes to protect to deep social stigma and the risk of incarceration or other penalty.

This analytical framework for the juridical study of complex and controversial choices should bear transversal utility and relevance across a range of contexts and circumstances, which may or may not involve gender-related questions. Choices that stand to benefit from this framework may touch upon large-scale social and moral issues, such as assisted suicide or the refusal of essential medical care, or issues that seem narrower and more discrete, such as those pertaining to how an individual dresses, or where she lives. In some cases, the choices concerned will appear to have little direct or explicit connection to the laws of the state, as the personal story that opens this book demonstrates. A fuller juridical appreciation of such choices is nonetheless enabled by the analysis developed here.

Ultimately, this book's propositions aspire to forge a conceptual platform for the juridical study of choice that considers the experiences of relevant choosers, identifies the plurality of norms that shape their choices, and plumbs the effects of state law on widening or constricting their options and opportunities. Deploying this approach will not necessarily reform law. It will, however, have the more critical result of informing law. Analyses integrative of empirically recorded experiences promise to enrich juridical assessments of morally involved choices and the individuals who make them. Departing from oversimplified victim–agency and coercion–choice dyads, such analyses may expose the power and agency wielded by those traditionally presumed as disenfranchised. These investigations further spotlight state law's successes and failures in responding to social realities and public objectives that pertain to morally ambiguous choices. In this way, possibilities can be imagined for recognizing and respecting choices, even choices made in the face of formidable constraints. At the same time, this analysis reinforces the relevance of state laws that seek to promote personal security, integrity and nourishing social relationships, all with a view to widening options and opportunities. These objectives merit pursuit in all contexts where questions about choice and its authenticity are brought to the fore. Their significance is especially acute, however, where implications for the individual concerned lie in the domain of criminal law, resulting in her potential conversion from citizen to outlaw by choice.

Bibliography

Government Debates

Austl, Australian Capital Territory, Legislative Assembly, *Parliamentary Debates* (11 October 1994) at 3459 (Mrs Carnell).

Austl, Australian Capital Territory, Legislative Assembly, *Parliamentary Debates* (11 October 1994) at 3461 (Ms Szuty).

Austl, Australian Capital Territory, Legislative Assembly, *Parliamentary Debates* (11 October 1994) at 3463 (Mr Humphries).

Austl, Australian Capital Territory, Legislative Assembly, *Parliamentary Debates* (11 October 1994) at 3464 (Mr Moore).

Austl, Australian Capital Territory, Legislative Assembly, *Parliamentary Debates* (11 October 1994) at 3465 (Mr Connolly).

Austl, Australian Capital Territory, Legislative Assembly, *Parliamentary Debates* (11 October 1994) at 3467 (Mr Connolly).

Austl, Australian Capital Territory, Legislative Assembly, *Parliamentary Debates* (20 November 2003) at 4376 (Mr Stanhope).

Austl, Australian Capital Territory, Legislative Assembly, *Parliamentary Debates* (20 November 2003) at 4377 (Mr Stanhope).

Austl, Australian Capital Territory, Legislative Assembly, *Parliamentary Debates* (10 February 2004) at 127 (Mrs Cross).

Austl, Commonwealth, House of Representatives, *Parliamentary Debates* (19 September 1905) (King O'Malley).

Austl, Commonwealth, House of Representatives, *Parliamentary Debates* (26 October 1905) at 4188, *Estimates* (King O'Malley).

Austl, Commonwealth, House of Representatives, *Parliamentary Debates* (5 December 1912) at 6514 (J.H. Catts).

Austl, Commonwealth, House of Representatives, *Parliamentary Debates* (25 November 1948) at 3520 (Mr Caldwell).

Austl, Commonwealth, House of Representatives, *Parliamentary Debates* (25 November 1948) at 3532 (Mr Thompson).

Austl, Commonwealth, House of Representatives, *Parliamentary Debates* (12 November 1959) at 2697 (Mr Caldwell).

Austl, Commonwealth, House of Representatives, *Parliamentary Debates* (29 March 1960) at 671 (Mr Anderson).

Austl, Commonwealth, House of Representatives, *Parliamentary Debates* (19 May 1960) at 2006 (Sir Garfield Barwick).

Austl, Commonwealth, House of Representatives, *Parliamentary Debates* (20 May 1975) at 2484 (Mr Luchetti).

Austl, Commonwealth, Senate, *Parliamentary Debates* (11 April 1961) at 417 (Senator McKenna).
Austl, New South Wales, Legislative Assembly, *Parliamentary Debates* (23 April 1979) at 4923 (Mr Walker).
Austl, New South Wales, Legislative Assembly, *Parliamentary Debates* (31 May 1988) at 804 (Mr Dowd).
Austl, New South Wales, Legislative Assembly, *Parliamentary Debates* (31 May 1988) at 805 (Mr Dowd).
Austl, New South Wales, Legislative Assembly, *Parliamentary Debates* (31 May 1988) at 806 (Mr Dowd).
Austl, New South Wales, Legislative Assembly, *Parliamentary Debates* (20 September 1995) at 1187 (Mr Whelan).
Austl, New South Wales, Legislative Assembly, *Parliamentary Debates* (18 October 1995) at 1938 (Mr Harrison).
Austl, New South Wales, Legislative Assembly, *Parliamentary Debates* (18 October 1995) at 1939 (Mr Harrison).
Austl, New South Wales, Legislative Assembly, *Parliamentary Debates* (18 October 1995) at 1941 (Mr Rogan).
Austl, New South Wales, Legislative Assembly, *Parliamentary Debates* (18 October 1995) at 1958 (Mr Peacock).
Austl, New South Wales, Legislative Assembly, *Parliamentary Debates* (18 October 1995) at 1961 (Mr Windsor).
Austl, New South Wales, Legislative Assembly, *Parliamentary Debates* (10 November 2010) at 27599 (Pru Goward).
Austl, New South Wales, Legislative Council, *Parliamentary Debates* (14 November 1995) at 3072 (Hon Symonds).
Austl, New South Wales, Legislative Council, *Parliamentary Debates* (14 November 1995) at 3072-3073 (Hon Symonds).
Austl, New South Wales, Legislative Council, *Parliamentary Debates* (14 November 1995) at 3074 (Dr Meredith Burgmann).
Austl, New South Wales, Legislative Council, *Parliamentary Debates* (14 November 1995) at 3075-3076 (Dr Meredith Burgmann).
Austl, New South Wales, Legislative Council, *Parliamentary Debates* (14 November 1995) at 3076 (Dr Meredith Burgmann).
Austl, New South Wales, Legislative Council, *Parliamentary Debates* (15 November 1995) at 3149 (I. Cohen).
Austl, New South Wales, Legislative Council, *Parliamentary Debates* (15 November 1995) at 3150 (I. Cohen).
Austl, New South Wales, Legislative Council, *Parliamentary Debates* (15 November 1995) at 3152 (F.J. Nile).
Austl, New South Wales, Legislative Council, *Parliamentary Debates* (15 November 1995) at 3188-3189 (J.P. Hannaford).
Austl, New South Wales, Legislative Council, *Parliamentary Debates* (11 November 2010) at 27678 (Linda Burney).

Austl, Queensland, Legislative Assembly, *Parliamentary Debates* (1 December 1999) at 5703 (Mr Horan).

Austl, Queensland, Legislative Assembly, *Parliamentary Debates* (1 December 1999) at 5711 (Mr Borbidge).

Austl, Queensland, Legislative Assembly, *Parliamentary Debates* (1 December 1999) at 5721 (Mr Feldman).

Austl, Queensland, Legislative Assembly, *Parliamentary Debates* (2 December 1999) at 5820 (Mrs Cunningham).

Austl, Queensland, Legislative Assembly, *Parliamentary Debates* (2 December 1999) at 5825 (Mrs Pratt).

Austl, Queensland, Legislative Assembly, *Parliamentary Debates* (26 November 2009) at 3668 (Hon C.R. Dick).

Austl, South Australia, Legislative Council, *Parliamentary Debates* (21 June 2006) at 437 (J.S.L. Dawkins).

Austl, South Australia, Legislative Council, *Parliamentary Debates* (27 September 2006) at 764.

Austl, South Australia, Legislative Council, *Parliamentary Debates* (13 February 2008) at 1667 (J.S.L. Dawkins).

Austl, South Australia, Legislative Council, *Parliamentary Debates* (2 April 2008) at 2219.

Austl, Tasmania, House of Assembly, *Parliamentary Debates* (22 June 2010) at 48 (Lara Giddings).

Austl, Tasmania, House of Assembly, *Parliamentary Debates* (5 April 2011) (Mr Rockliff).

Austl, Tasmania, House of Assembly, *Parliamentary Debates* (12 April 2011) (Ms Petrusma).

Austl, Tasmania, Legislative Council, *Parliamentary Debates* (22 June 2005) at 25 (Mr Dean).

Austl, Tasmania, Legislative Council, *Parliamentary Debates* (22 June 2005) at 29 (Mr Dean).

Austl, Tasmania, Legislative Council, *Parliamentary Debates* (19 October 2005) at 7 (Mrs Jamieson).

Austl, Tasmania, Legislative Council, *Parliamentary Debates* (19 October 2005) at 20 (Ms Forrest).

Austl, Tasmania, Legislative Council, *Parliamentary Debates* (19 October 2005) at 24 (Ms Forrest).

Austl, Tasmania, Legislative Council, *Parliamentary Debates* (19 October 2005) at 26-27 (Ms Ritchie).

Austl, Victoria, Legislative Assembly, *Parliamentary Debates* (7 October 2008) at 3797 (Ms Thomson).

Austl, Western Australia, Legislative Council, *Parliamentary Debates* (12 November 2008) at 153b (Hon Norman Moore).

Austl, Western Australia, Legislative Council, *Parliamentary Debates* (13 November 2008) (Hon Barbara Scott).

Austl, Western Australia, Legislative Council, *Parliamentary Debates* (25 November 2008) (Hon Helen Morton).
Canada, *Debates of the Senate*, 6th Parl, 4th Sess, No 29 (25 February 1890) at 142 (Hon Mr Dickey).
Canada, *Debates of the Senate*, 6th Parl, 4th Sess, No 29 (25 April 1890) at 584 (Hon Mr Power).
Canada, *House of Commons Debates*, 5th Parl, 3rd Sess, No 19 (26 May 1885) at 2127 (Mr Paterson).
Canada, *House of Commons Debates*, 6th Parl, 3rd Sess, No 28 (3 April 1889) at 980 (Mr Doyon).
Canada, *House of Commons Debates*, 6th Parl, 4th Sess, No 30 (10 April 1890) at 3177 (Mr Blake).
Canada, *House of Commons Debates*, 6th Parl, 4th Sess, No 30 (10 April 1890) at 3177 (Mr Mulock).
Canada, *House of Commons Debates*, 6th Parl, 4th Sess, No 30 (10 April 1890) at 3178 (Mr McMullen).
Canada, *House of Commons Debates*, 6th Parl, 4th Sess, No 30 (10 April 1890) at 3178 (Sir John A. Macdonald).
Canada, *House of Commons Debates*, 12th Parl, 2nd Sess, Vol 111 (16 May 1913) at 10072 (C.J. Doherty).
Canada, *House of Commons Debates*, 12th Parl, 5th Sess, Vol 120 (18 March 1915) at 1227 (Mr Doherty).
Canada, *House of Commons Debates*, 28th Parl, 4th Sess, Vol 2 (27 April 1972) at 1708 (Grace MacInnis).
Canada, *House of Commons Debates*, 33rd Parl, 1st Sess, Vol 5 (9 September 1985) at 6373 (John Crosbie).
Canada, *House of Commons Debates*, 33rd Parl, 1st Sess, Vol 5 (9 September 1985) at 6375 (John Crosbie).
Canada, *House of Commons Debates*, 33rd Parl, 1st Sess, Vol 5 (9 September 1985) at 6378 (John Crosbie).
Canada, *House of Commons Debates*, 33rd Parl, 1st Sess, Vol 5 (9 September 1985) at 6409 (Margaret Mitchell).
Canada, *House of Commons Debates*, 33rd Parl, 1st Sess, Vol 5 (9 September 1985) at 6410 (Margaret Mitchell).
Canada, *House of Commons Debates*, 33rd Parl, 1st Sess, Vol 5 (9 September 1985) at 6421 (Don Boudria).
Canada, *House of Commons Debates*, 35th Parl, 2nd Sess, No 89 (23 October 1996) at 5617 (Joseph Volpe).
Canada, *House of Commons Debates*, 35th Parl, 2nd Sess, No 89 (23 October 1996) at 5627 (John Murphy).
Canada, *House of Commons Debates*, 37th Parl, 1st Sess, No 188 (21 May 2002) at 11523 (Anne McLellan).
Canada, *House of Commons Debates*, 37th Parl, 2nd Sess, No 47 (28 January 2003) at 2774 (James Lunney).

Canada, *House of Commons Debates*, 37th Parl, 2nd Sess, No 72 (18 March 2003) at 4339.
Canada, *House of Commons Debates*, 37th Parl, 2nd Sess, No 78 (26 March 2003) at 4726 (Jason Kenney).
Canada, *House of Commons Debates*, 37th Parl, 2nd Sess, No 78 (26 March 2003) at 4728 (Jason Kenney).
Canada, *House of Commons Debates*, 37th Parl, 2nd Sess, No 85 (7 April 2003) at 5160-5161.
Canada, *House of Commons Debates*, 37th Parl, 2nd Sess, No 134 (6 October 2003) at 8191 (Marlene Jennings).
Canada, *House of Commons Debates*, 41st Parl, 1st Sess, Vol 146, No 51 (22 November 2011) at 1410 (Mr Pierre Lemieux).
Canada, *House of Commons Debates*, 41st Parl, 1st Sess, Vol 146, No 52 (23 November 2011) at 1450 (Mr Kyle Seeback).
Canada, *House of Commons Debates*, 41st Parl, 1st Sess, Vol 146, No 52 (23 November 2011) at 1450 (Mr Rob Nicholson).
Canada, *House of Commons Debates*, 41st Parl, 1st Sess, Vol 146, No 54 (25 November 2011) at 1100 (Mr Maurice Vellacott).
Canada, British Columbia, Legislative Assembly, *Official Report of Debates (Hansard)*, 38th Parl, 4th Sess, Vol 30, No 5 (10 April 2008) at 11212 (Leonard Krog).
Canada, British Columbia, Legislative Assembly, *Official Report of Debates (Hansard)*, 38th Parl, 4th Sess, Vol 32, No 9 (8 May 2008) at 12183 (Bill Bennett).
Canada, House of Commons, Subcommittee on Solicitation Laws of the Standing Committee on Justice and Human Rights, Evidence, 37th Parl, 2nd Sess, No 3 (21 October 2003) at 1700 (Cherry Kingsley).
Canada, House of Commons, Subcommittee on Solicitation Laws of the Standing Committee on Justice, Human Rights, Public Safety and Emergency Preparedness, Evidence, 38th Parl, 1st Sess, No 5 (7 February 2005) at 20 (Yolande Geadah).
Canada, House of Commons, Subcommittee on Solicitation Laws of the Standing Committee on Justice, Human Rights, Public Safety and Emergency Preparedness, Evidence, 38th Parl, 1st Sess, No 6 (9 February 2005) at 13 (Art Hanger).
Canada, House of Commons, Subcommittee on Solicitation Laws of the Standing Committee on Justice, Human Rights, Public Safety and Emergency Preparedness, Evidence, 38th Parl, 1st Sess, No 6 (9 February 2005) at 13 (Lyne Kurtzman).
UK, HC, *Parliamentary Debates*, vol 183, col 302 (2 May 1866) (Mr Knatchbull-Hugessen).
UK, HC, *Parliamentary Debates*, vol 836, cols 409W-410W (11 May 1972) (Mr Maudling).
UK, HC, *Parliamentary Debates*, vol 77, col 24 (15 April 1985) (Norman Fowler).

UK, HC, *Parliamentary Debates*, vol 77, col 25 (15 April 1985) (Peter Bruinvels).
UK, HC, *Parliamentary Debates*, vol 77, col 27 (15 April 1985) (Mr Frank Field).
UK, HC, *Parliamentary Debates*, vol 77, col 28 (15 April 1985) (Norman Fowler).
UK, HC, *Parliamentary Debates*, vol 77, col 28 (15 April 1985) (Michael Meacher).
UK, HC, *Parliamentary Debates*, vol 77, col 32 (15 April 1985) (Sir Bernard Braine).
UK, HC, *Parliamentary Debates*, vol 77, col 37 (15 April 1985) (Anna McCurley).
UK, HC, *Parliamentary Debates*, vol 77, col 39 (15 April 1985) (Harry Cohen).
UK, HC, *Parliamentary Debates*, vol 77, col 40 (15 April 1985) (Harry Cohen).
UK, HC, *Parliamentary Debates*, vol 77, col 41 (15 April 1985) (John Butterfill).
UK, HC, *Parliamentary Debates*, vol 77, cols 46-47 (15 April 1985) (David Amess).
UK, HC, *Parliamentary Debates*, vol 122, col 785 (16 November 1987) (Douglas Hurd).
UK, HC, *Parliamentary Debates*, vol 122, col 826 (16 November 1987) (Anne Widdecombe).
UK, HC, *Parliamentary Debates*, vol 170, col 968 (2 April 1990) (D.N. Campbell-Savours).
UK, HC, *Parliamentary Debates*, vol 248, col 972 (26 October 1994) (Michael Jopling).
UK, HL, *Parliamentary Debates*, vol 305, col 1802 (24 May 1886) (Duke of Argyll).
UK, HL, *Parliamentary Debates*, vol 216, col 779 (9 June 1959) (Lord Stonham).
UK, HL, *Parliamentary Debates*, vol 216, col 784 (9 June 1959) (Lord Stonham).
UK, HL, *Parliamentary Debates*, vol 216, col 787 (9 June 1959) (Lord Archbishop of Canterbury).
UK, HL, *Parliamentary Debates*, vol 216, col 804 (9 June 1959) (Lord Chancellor).
UK, HL, *Parliamentary Debates*, vol 216, col 830 (9 June 1959) (Lord Denning).
UK, HL, *Parliamentary Debates*, vol 321, col 1218 (9 July 1971) (Lord Bishop of Lichfield).
UK, HL, *Parliamentary Debates*, vol 321, col 1223 (9 July 1971) (Lord Chancellor).
UK, HL, *Parliamentary Debates*, vol 464, col 1520 (14 June 1985) (Earl of Caithness).
UK, HL, *Parliamentary Debates*, vol 464, col 1532 (14 June 1985) (Viscount Sidmouth).
UK, HL, *Parliamentary Debates*, vol 464, col 1533 (14 June 1985) (Viscount Sidmouth).
UK, HL, *Parliamentary Debates*, vol 464, col 1534 (14 June 1985) (Viscount Brentford).
UK, HL, *Parliamentary Debates*, vol 464, col 1535 (14 June 1985) (Earl of Caithness).
UK, HL, *Parliamentary Debates*, vol 465, col 925 (28 June 1985) (Earl of Caithness).
UK, HL, *Parliamentary Debates*, vol 465, col 934 (28 June 1985) (Baroness Warnock).

UK, HL, *Parliamentary Debates*, vol 468, col 978 (28 November 1985) (Earl of Halsbury).
UK, HL, *Parliamentary Debates*, vol 491, col 1454 (15 January 1988) (Lord Skelmersdale).
UK, HL, *Parliamentary Debates*, vol 491, col 1471 (15 January 1988) (Duke of Norfolk).
UK, HL, *Parliamentary Debates*, vol 495, col 49 (21 March 1988) (Lord Renton).
UK, HL, *Parliamentary Debates*, vol 495, col 50 (21 March 1988) (Lord Bonham-Carter).
UK, HL, *Parliamentary Debates*, vol 513, col 21 (22 November 1989) (Lord Mackay of Clashfern).
UK, HL, *Parliamentary Debates*, vol 513, col 1003 (7 December 1989) (Lord Mackay of Clashfern).
UK, HL, *Parliamentary Debates*, vol 515, col 1283 (13 February 1990) (Baroness Hooper).
UK, HL, *Parliamentary Debates*, vol 558, col 626 (26 October 1994) (Lord Fraser of Carmyllie).
UK, HL, *Parliamentary Debates*, vol 648, col 181 (13 May 2003) (Lord Faulkner of Worcester).
UK, HL, *Parliamentary Debates*, vol 648, col 182 (13 May 2003) (Lord Faulkner of Worcester).
UK, HL, *Parliamentary Debates*, vol 648, col 183 (13 May 2003) (Baroness Blatch).
UK, HL, *Parliamentary Debates*, vol 648, col 184 (13 May 2003) (Lord Lucas).
UK, HL, *Parliamentary Debates*, vol 648, col 189 (13 May 2003) (Lord Lucas).
UK, HL, *Parliamentary Debates*, vol 654, col 1638 (13 November 2003) (Baroness Scotland of Ashthal).

Government Reports

Austl, Australian Capital Territory, Standing Committee on Justice and Community Safety, *Inquiry into the Prostitution Act 1992* (Report No 9) (2012).
Austl, Commonwealth, Governor-General of the Commonwealth of Australia, Press Release, *Multiculturalism Promotes National Unity*. [Online, 28 July 1997]. Available at: http://www.gg.gov.au/news.php/view/id/60/title/multiculturalism-promotes-national-unity [accessed: 27 October 2012].
Austl, Commonwealth, John Gardiner-Garden, *The Multiculturalism and Immigration Debate 1973-1993*, Background Paper No 8 (Canberra: Parliamentary Research Service, 1993).
Austl, Commonwealth, Joint Standing Committee on Migration, *Submission No 48 (name withheld)* (2011).
Austl, Commonwealth, Joint Standing Committee on Migration, *Submission No 205 (Endeavour Forum)* (7 April 2011).

Austl, Commonwealth, Joint Standing Committee on Migration, *Submission No 277 (B M)* (2011).
Austl, Commonwealth, Joint Standing Committee on Migration, *Submission No 299 (Family Council of Victoria)* (2011).
Austl, Commonwealth, Law Reform Commission, *The Recognition of Aboriginal Customary Laws* (Report No 31) (Canberra: Australian Government Publishing Service, 1986).
Austl, Commonwealth, Law Reform Commission, *Multiculturalism: Family Law* (Discussion Paper No 46) (Canberra: Australian Government Publishing Service, 1991).
Austl, Commonwealth, Law Reform Commission, *Multiculturalism and the Law* (Report No 57) (Canberrra: Australian Government Publishing Service, 1992).
Austl, Commonwealth, Standing Committee of Attorneys-General, *A Proposal for a National Model to Harmonise Regulation of Surrogacy* (Sydney: Attorney General's Department, 2009).
Austl, New South Wales, New South Wales Law Reform Commission, *Artificial Conception Report 3: Surrogate Motherhood* (Report No 60) (Sydney: New South Wales Law Reform Commission, 1988).
Austl, New South Wales, New South Wales Law Reform Commission, *Uniform Succession Laws: Intestacy* (Issues Paper No 26) (Sydney: New South Wales Law Reform Commission, 2005).
Austl, New South Wales, Parliamentary Library Research Service, Stewart Smith, *The Regulation of Prostitution: A Review of Recent Developments* (Briefing Paper No 21/99) (Sydney: New South Wales Parliamentary Research Service, 1999).
Austl, New South Wales, L. Roth, *Provocation and Self-Defence in Intimate Partner and Homophobic Homicides* (Briefing Paper No 3/07) (2007).
Austl, New South Wales, Standing Committee on Law and Justice, *Legislation on Altruistic Surrogacy in NSW* (Report No 38) (Sydney: Standing Committee on Law and Justice, 2009).
Austl, Queensland, *Investigation into Altruistic Surrogacy Committee: Report* (2008).
Austl, Queensland, Crime and Misconduct Commission, *Regulating Prostitution: A Follow-up Review of the Prostitution Act 1999* (Brisbane: Crime and Misconduct Commission, 2011).
Austl, Queensland, Prostitution Licensing Authority, *Submission to the Crime and Misconduct Commission Review of the Prostitution Act 1999* (Brisbane: Crime and Misconduct Commission, 2010).
Austl, Queensland, Taskforce on Women and the Criminal Code, *Women and the Criminal Code* (Brisbane: Office of Women's Policy, 2000).
Austl, Tasmania, *Community Development Committee Report on the Need for Legislative Regulation and Reform of the Sex Industry in Tasmania*, Report No 8 (1999).

Austl, Tasmania, Hon. Brian Wightman, MP, Attorney General and Minister for Justice, *Regulation of the Sex Industry in Tasmania (Discussion Paper)* (Hobart: Minister for Justice, 2012). [Online]. Available at: http://www.justice.tas.gov.au/__data/assets/pdf_file/0008/188738/Regulation_of_the_Sex_Industry_Discussion_Paper.pdf [accessed: 16 June 2013].

Austl, Victoria, Victorian Law Reform Commission, *A.R.T., Surrogacy and Legal Parentage: A Comparative Legislative Review* (Melbourne: Victorian Law Reform Commission, 2004).

Austl, Victoria, Victorian Law Reform Commission, *Assisted Reproductive Technology and Adoption: Final Report* (Melbourne: Victorian Government Printer, 2007).

Austl, Western Australia, *Prostitution Law Reform for Western Australia: Report of the Prostitution Law Reform Working Group* (Perth: Office of the Attorney General, 2007).

Austl, Western Australia, Reproductive Technology Council. *Surrogacy in Western Australia*. Available at: http://www.rtc.org.au/consumer/surrogacy_wa.html [accessed: 9 October 2012].

Canada, British Columbia, Anonymous, *Life in Bountiful: A Report in the Lifestyle of a Polygamous Community* (Committee on Polygamous Issues, 1993).

Canada, British Columbia, The Honourable Wally T. Oppal Q.C., Commissioner, *Forsaken: The Report of the Missing Women Commission of Inquiry* (Victoria: Ministry of the Attorney General, 2012).

Canada, British Columbia, R.C.C. Peck Q.C., *Report of the Special Prosecutor for Allegations of Misconduct Associated with Bountiful, BC: Summary of Conclusions* (Victoria: Criminal Justice Branch HQ, Ministry of Attorney General, 2007).

Canada, British Columbia, Sisterwatch Project of the Vancouver Police Department and Women's Memorial March Commitee, *The Tragedy of Missing and Murdered Aboriginal Women in Canada: We Can Do Better* (2011). [Online]. Available at: http://vancouver.ca/police/assets/pdf/reports-policies/missing-murdered-aboriginal-women-canada-report.pdf [accessed: 8 June 2013].

Canada, Criminal Justice Branch of the Ministry of the Attorney General of British Columbia, Media Release, 07-08, *Special Prosecutor Recommends Reference Question on Constitutionality of Polygamy Law* (1 August 2007). Available at: http://www.ag.gov.bc.ca/prosecution-service/media-statements/pdf/07-08_Bountiful-SpProsReport-1Aug2007.pdf [accessed: 11 November 2012].

Canada, Criminal Justice Branch of the Ministry of the Attorney General of British Columbia, Media Release, 08-10, *Leonard Doust, Q.C., Confirms Findings and Recommendations of Special Prosecutor* (7 April 2008). Available at: http://www.ag.gov.bc.ca/prosecution-service/media-statements/pdf/08-10_Bountiful-LDoustQC_ConfirmsSpProsRecomm-7Apr2008.pdf [accessed: 11 November 2012].

Canada, Criminal Justice Branch of the Ministry of the Attorney General of British Columbia, Media Release, 08-11, *Special Prosecutor Appointed in Bountiful* (2

June 2008). Available at: http://www.ag.gov.bc.ca/prosecution-service/media-statements/pdf/08-11_Bountiful-SpProsApptd-2Jun2008.pdf [accessed: 11 November 2012].

Canada, Department of Justice, *Pornography and Prostitution in Canada: Report of the Special Committee on Pornography and Prostitution*, vol 2 (Ottawa: Minister of Supply and Services Canada, 1985).

Canada, Department of Justice, *Street Prostitution: Assessing the Impact of the Law: Synthesis Report* (Ottawa: Department of Justice, 1989).

Canada, Department of Justice, R. Cook and L. Kelly, *Polygyny and Canada's Obligations under International Human Rights Law* (Ottawa: Department of Justice, 2006). Available at: http://www.justice.gc.ca/eng/dept-min/pub/poly/poly.pdf [accessed: 11 November 2012].

Canada, House of Commons, Standing Committee on Health, *Assisted Human Reproduction: Building Families* (December 2001) (Chair: Bonnie Brown).

Canada, Law Commission of Canada, *Beyond Conjugality: Recognizing and Supporting Close Personal Adult Relationships* (Ottawa: Law Commission of Canada, 2001).

Canada, Law Reform Commission of Canada, *Working Paper 42* (Ottawa: Law Reform Commission of Canada, 1985).

Canada, Law Reform Commission of Canada, *Working Paper 65* (Ottawa: Minister of Supply and Services Canada, 1992).

Canada, Ontario, *Raising Expectations: Recommendations of the Expert Panel on Infertility and Adoption* (Toronto: Ministry of Children and Youth Services, 2009).

Canada, Ontario, Marion Boyd, *Dispute Resolution in Family Law: Protecting Choice, Promoting Inclusion* (Toronto: Ministry of the Attorney General, 2004).

Canada, Ontario, Ontario Law Reform Commission, *Report on Human Artificial Reproduction and Related Matters* (Toronto: Ontario Law Reform Commission, 1985).

Canada, Parliament, "Indian Affairs, Annual Report" in *Sessional Papers*, No 6 (1882).

Canada, Parliament, "Transmitting Report of Royal Commission on Chinese Immigration" in *Sessional Papers*, No 54a (1885).

Canada, Parliamentary Information and Research Service, L. Barnett and J. Nicol, *Prostitution in Canada: International Obligations, Federal Law, and Provincial and Municipal Jurisdiction* (Ottawa: Library of Parliament, 2012).

Canada, Parliamentary Information and Research Service, J.R. Robertson, *Prostitution*, CIR 82-2E (Ottawa: Library of Parliament, 2003).

Canada, Quebec, Commission de l'éthique de la science et de la technologie, *Ethique et procréation assistée: des orientations pour le don de gametes et d'embryons, la gestation pour autrui et le diagnostic préimplantatoire* (Quebec: Commission de l'éthique de la science et de la technologie, 2009).

Canada, Royal Commission on New Reproductive Technologies, *Proceed with Care: Final Report of the Royal Commission on New Reproductive Technologies* (Ottawa: Minister of Government Services, 1993).

Edmonton Social Planning Council, *Street Prostitution in Edmonton* (Edmonton: Edmonton Social Planning Council, 1993).

Edwards, A., *Selling Sex; Regulating Prostitution in Queensland: A Report to the Prostitution Licensing Authority* (Brisbane: Prostitution Licensing Authority, 2009).

UK, *Report of the Committee on Homosexual Offences and Prostitution* (London: Her Majesty's Stationery Office, 1957).

UK, *Sexual Offences Act 2003 Explanatory Notes*. [Online]. Available at: http://www.legislation.gov.uk/ukpga/2003/42/notes/contents [accessed: 14 January 2013].

UK, HC, "Report of the Committee of Inquiry into Human Fertilisation and Embryology," Cm 9314 in *Sessional Papers* (1984) 1.

UK, HC, "Human Fertilisation and Embryology: A Framework for Legislation," Cm 259 (1987) 1.

UK, HC, "Review for Health Ministers of Current Arrangements for Payments and Regulation," Cm 4068 (1998) 1.

UK, HC/HL, Joint Committee on the Human Tissue and Embryos (Draft) Bill, "Human Tissues and Embryo (Draft) Bill," HL Paper 169-I/HC Paper 630-I, vol 1 (2007).

UK, Home Office, *Setting the Boundaries: Reforming the Law on Sex Offences*, vol 1 (London: Home Office, 2000).

UK, Home Office, *Paying the Price: A Consultation Paper on Prostitution* (London: Home Office, 2004).

UK, Home Office, *A Coordinated Prostitution Strategy and Summary of Responses to Paying the Price* (London: Home Office, 2006).

UK, Law Commission, *Murder, Manslaughter and Infanticide* (Law Com No 304) (London: UK Law Commission, 2006).

UK, Quality Protects Program, H. Cleaver et al., *Child Protection, Domestic Violence and Parental Substance Misuse: Family Experiences and Effective Practice – Executive Summary*. Available at: http://dera.ioe.ac.uk/8820/1/child-protection-domesticviolence-parentalsubstance-misuse-2.pdf [accessed: 8 June 2013].

Woodward, C. et al., *Selling Sex in Queensland 2003: A Study of Prostitution in Queensland* (Brisbane: Prostitution Licensing Authority, 2004).

Secondary Materials

Abrams, K. 1995. Sex Wars Redux: Agency and Coercion in Feminist Legal Theory. *Columbia Law Review*, 95(2), 304-376.

Acorn, A. 2005. Surviving the Battered Reader's Syndrome, or: A Critique of Linda G. Mills' Insult to Injury: Rethinking our Responses to Intimate Abuse. *UCLA Women's Law Journal*, 13(2), 335-374.

Al-Krenawi, A. 2001. Women from Polygamous and Monogamous Marriages in Out-Patients Psychiatric Clinic. *Transcultural Psychiatry*, 38(2), 187-199.

Al-Krenawi, A. and Graham, J.R. 2001. Polygamous Family Structure and Its Interaction with Gender: Effects on Children's Academic Achievements and Implication for Culturally Diverse Social Work Practice in Schools. *School Social Work Journal*, 25(3), 1-16.

Al-Krenawi, A. and Lev-Weisel, R. 2002. Wife Abuse Among Polygamous and Monogamous Bedouin-Arab Families. *Journal of Divorce and Remarriage*, 36(3/4), 151-165.

Al-Krenawi, A. et al. 2001. The Psychosocial Impact of Polygamous Marriages on Palestinian Women. *Women and Health*, 34(1), 1-16.

Alberta Civil Liberties Research Centre. 2005. Separate and Unequal: The Women and Children of Polygamy, in *Polygamy in Canada: Legal and Social Implications for Women and Children: A Collection of Policy Research Reports*. Ottawa: Status of Women Canada, 1-71.

Albiston, C. 2005. Anti-Essentialism and the Work/Family Dilemma. *Berkeley Journal of Gender Law & Justice*, 20, 30-49.

Alexandre, M. 2007. Big Love: Is Feminist Polygamy an Oxymoron or a True Possibility? *Hastings Women's Law Journal*, 18(1), 3-30.

Allman, D and Myers, T. 1999. Male Sex Work and HIV/AIDS in Canada, in *Men Who Sell Sex: International Perspectives on Male Prostitution and AIDS*, edited by P. Aggleton. Philadelphia, PA: Temple University Press, 61-82.

Allred Solomon, D. 2003. *Predator, Prey and Other Kinfolk: Growing up in Polygamy*. New York: W.W. Norton & Company.

Altman, I. 1993. Challenges and Opportunities of a Transactional World View: Case Study of Contemporary Mormon Polygynous Families. *American Journal of Community Psychology*, 21(2), 135-163.

Altman, I. and Ginat, J. 1996. *Polygamous Families in Contemporary Society*. Cambridge: Cambridge University Press.

Anderson, C.M. 2000. The Persistence of Polygyny as an Adaptive Response to Poverty and Oppression in Apartheid South Africa. *Cross-Cultural Research*, 34(2), 99-112.

Anderson, M.J. 2005. Negotiating Sex. *Southern California Law Review*, 78(6), 1401-1438.

Anderson, P. 2010. An Evaluation of Surrogacy Law and Its Potential Development in the UK: Is There a Clear Way Forward? *King's Student Law Review*, 2(2), 37-50.

Apold, V.J. 2005. *Commercial Surrogacy: Reconsidering Canada's Criminal Prohibition*. Master of Laws thesis, Dalhousie University [unpublished].

Avellar, S. and Smock, P.J. 2005. The Economic Consequences of the Dissolution of Cohabiting Unions. *Journal of Marriage and the Family*, 67(2), 315-327.

Baggish, M.A. 1989. Surrogate Parenting: What We Can Learn From Our British Counterparts. *Case Western Reserve Law Review*, 39(1), 217-271.

Bailey, M. et al. 2005. Expanding Recognition of Foreign Polygamous Marriages: Policy Implications for Canada, in *Polygamy in Canada: Legal and Social Implications for Women and Children: A Collection of Policy Research Reports*. Ottawa: Status of Women Canada, 1-56.

Baker, B.M. 1996. A Case for Permitting Altruistic Surrogacy. *Hypatia*, 11(2), 34-48.

Baker, K.K. 2001. Dialectics and Domestic Abuse. *Yale Law Journal*, 110(8), 1459-1491.

Baker, P. 1997. And I Went Back: Battered Women's Negotiation of Choice. *Journal of Contemporary Ethnography*, 26(1), 55-74.

Bakht, N. 2007. Religious Arbitration in Canada: Protecting Women by Protecting them from Religion. *Canadian Journal of Women and the Law*, 19(1), 119-144.

——. 2012. Veiled Objections: Facing Public Opposition to the Niqab, in *Reasonable Accommodation: Managing Religious Diversity*, edited by L.G. Beaman. Vancouver: UBC Press, 70-108.

Bala, N. 2009. Why Canada's Prohibition of Polygamy is Constitutionally Valid and Sound Social Policy. *Canadian Journal of Family Law*, 25(2), 165-221.

Bala, N. et al. 2005. An International Review of Polygamy: Legal and Policy Implications for Canada, in *Polygamy in Canada: Legal and Social Implications for Women and Children: A Collection of Policy Research Reports*. Ottawa: Status of Women Canada, 1-57.

Barnett, R.E. 2012. Contract is Not Promise; Contract is Consent. *Suffolk University Law Review*, 45(3), 647-665.

Barrett, B.J. and St. Pierre, M. 2011. Variations in Women's Help Seeking in Response to Intimate Partner Violence: Findings from a Canadian Population-Based Study. *Violence against Women*, 17(1), 47-70.

Bartlett, K.T. 1990. Feminist Legal Methods. *Harvard Law Review*, 103(4), 829-888.

Baslington, H. 2002. The Social Organization of Surrogacy: Relinquishing a Baby and the Role of Payment in the Psychological Detachment Process. *Journal of Health Psychology*, 7(1), 57-71.

Baudouin, J.-L. et al. 2005. *Les Obligations*. 6th edition. Cowansville: Yvon Blais.

Beaman, L.G. 2004. Church, State and the Legal Interpretation of Polygamy in Canada. *Nova Religio*, 8(1), 20-38.

Belkin, L. 2003. The Opt-Out Revolution. *New York Times Magazine*, 6, 42.

Bennion, J. 1998. *Women of Principle: Female Networking in Contemporary Mormon Polygamy*. New York: Oxford University Press.

——. 2008. *Evaluating the Effects of Polygamy on Women and Children in Four North American Mormon Fundamentalist Groups: An Anthropological Study*. Lewiston, NY: Edwin Mellen Press.

——. 2011. The Many Faces of Polygamy: An Analysis of the Variability in Modern Mormon Fundamentalism in the Intermountain West, in *Modern Polygamy in the United States: Historical, Cultural, and Legal Issues*, edited by C.K. Jacobson and L. Burton. New York: Oxford University Press.

Benoit, C. and Millar, A. 2001. *Dispelling Myths and Understanding Realities: Working Conditions, Health Status, and Exiting Experiences of Sex Workers*. Victoria: University of Victoria.

Benshushan, A. and Schenker, J.G. 1997. Legitimizing Surrogacy in Israel. *Human Reproduction*, 12(8), 1832-1834.

Berend, Z. 2010. Surrogate Losses: Understandings of Pregnancy Loss and Assisted Reproduction among Surrogate Mothers. *Medical Anthropology Quarterly*, 24(2), 240-262.

Bergelson, V. 2007. The Right to be Hurt: Testing the Boundaries of Consent. *George Washington Law Review*, 75(2), 165-236.

Biggs, H. 2007. Decision Making at the End of Life: The Choice is Yours, or is it?, in *Choice and Consent: Feminist Engagements with Law and Subjectivity*, edited by R. Hunter and S. Cowan. New York: Routledge-Cavendish, 142-157.

Bilardi, J.E. et al. 2011. The Job Satisfaction of Female Sex Workers Working in Licensed Brothels in Victoria, Australia. *Journal of Sexual Medicine*, 8, 116-122.

Billie, B.M. 2008. The "Lost Boys" of Polygamy: Is Emancipation the Answer? *Journal of Gender, Race & Justice*, 12(1), 127-152.

Bindman, J. and Doezema J. 1997. *Redefining Prostitution as Sex Work on the International Agenda*. [Online: Anti-Slavery International]. Available at: http://www.walnet.org/csis/papers/redefining.html [accessed: 26 November 2012].

Blyth, E. 1994. I Wanted to be Interesting. I Wanted to be Able to Say "I've Done Something Interesting with My Life": Interviews with Surrogate Mothers in Britain. *Journal of Reproductive and Infant Psychology*, 12(3), 189-198.

Boehmer, R. 2010. *The Experience of a Female Being Raised in an Isolated Polygamous Community in British Columbia: A Heuristic Study*. Doctor of Philosophy thesis, Capella University [unpublished].

Bograd, M. 1999. Strengthening Domestic Violence Theories: Intersections of Race, Class, Sexual Orientation and Gender. *Journal of Marital and Family Therapy*, 25(3), 275-289.

Boivin, S.P. 1984. *Soliciting for the Purpose of Prostitution: A Brief Presented before the Special Committee on Pornography and Prostitution*. Ottawa: National Association of Women and the Law.

Boyd, S. 1997. Challenging the Public/Private Divide: An Overview, in *Challenging the Public/Private Divide: Feminism, Law and Public Policy*, edited by S. Boyd. Toronto: University of Toronto Press, 3-33.

——. 2004. Legal Regulation of Families in Changing Societies, in *The Blackwell Companion to Law and Society*, edited by A. Sarat. Toronto: Oxford University Press, 255-270.

Boyle, F.M. et al. 1997. *The Sex Industry: A Survey of Sex Workers in Queensland, Australia*. Brookfield, VT: Ashgate Publishing.

Bradley Evans, M. 2011. The Past as Prologue: A Comparison of the Short Creek and Eldorado Polygamy Raids, in *Saints Under Siege: The Texas State Raid on the Fundamentalist Latter Day Saints*, edited by S.A. Wright and J.T. Richardson. New York: New York University Press, 25-50.

Bramham, D. 2008. *The Secret Lives of Saints: Child Brides and Lost Boys in Canada's Polygamous Mormon Sect*. Toronto: Random House.

Brett, N. 1998. Sexual Offences and Consent. *Canadian Journal of Law and Jurisprudence*, 11(1), 69-88.

Brewis, J. and Linstead, S. 2000. "The Worst Thing is the Screwing" (1): Consumption and the Management of Identity in Sex Work. *Gender, Work & Organization*, 7(2), 84-97.

Brown, D. et al. 2006. *Criminal Laws: Materials and Commentary on Criminal Law and Process of New South Wales*. 4th Edition. Leichhardt: The Federation Press.

Brown, J.R. 2010. How Could English Courts Recognize Sharia? *University of St. Thomas Law Journal*, 7(3), 411-435.

Bruckert, C. et al. 2003. *Erotic Service / Erotic Dance Establishments: Two Types of Marginalized Labour*. Ottawa: University of Ottawa.

Bungay, V. et al. 2011. Structure and Agency: Reflections from an Exploratory Study of Vancouver Indoor Sex Workers. *Culture, Health & Sexuality*, 31(1), 15-29.

Bunting, A. 1993. Theorizing Women's Cultural Diversity in Feminist International Human Rights Strategies. *Journal of Law and Society*, 20(1), 6-22.

Burpee, A.L. 2009. Momma Drama: A Study of How Canada's National Regulation of Surrogacy Compares to Australia's Independent State Regulation of Surrogacy. *Georgia Journal of International and Comparative Law*, 37(2), 305-338.

Burrows, C.L. 2011. *Deconstructing Motherhood: A Critique of the Legal Regulation of Surrogacy*. Master of Jurisprudence thesis, Durham University [unpublished].

Busby, K. and Vun, D. 2010. Revisiting the Handmaid's Tale: Feminist Theory Meets Empirical Research on Surrogate Mothers. *Canadian Journal of Family Law*, 26(1), 13-93.

Bushman, R.L. 2008. *Mormonism: A Very Short Introduction*. New York: Oxford University Press.

Campbell, A. 2002. A Place for Criminal Law in the Regulation of Reproductive Technologies. *Health Law Journal*, 10, 77-101.

——. 2005. How Have Policy Approaches to Polygamy Responded to Women's Experiences and Rights? An International, Comparative Analysis, in *Polygamy in Canada: Legal and Social Implications for Women and Children: A Collection of Policy Research Reports*. Ottawa: Status of Women Canada, 1-63.

——. 2006. Proceeding with "Care": Lessons to Be Learned from the Canadian Parental Leave and Québec Daycare Initiatives in Developing a National Childcare Policy. *Canadian Journal of Family Law*, 22, 171-222.

——. 2008. Wives' Tales: Reflecting on Research in Bountiful. *Canadian Journal of Law and Society*, 23(1), 121-141.

——. 2009a. Book Review: *The Importance of Being Monogamous: Marriage and Nation Building in Western Canada to 1915* by Sarah Carter, Edmonton, University of Alberta Press, 2008, pp 383. *Ottawa Law Review*, 41(1), 163-169.

——. 2009b. Bountiful Voices. *Osgoode Hall Law Journal*, 47(2), 183-234.

——. 2010. Bountiful's Plural Marriages. *International Journal of Law in Context*, 6(4), 343-361.

——. 2013a. *Plus ça change...?* Bountiful's Diverse and Durable Marriage Practices, in *Polygamy's Wrongs? The Social Family in the Culture of Rights*, edited by L. Beaman and G. Calder. Vancouver: UBC Press, 17-37.

——. 2013b. Religious Claims as Public Reason? Polygamy as a Case Study, in *Religious Revival in Post-Multicultural Societies*, edited by R. Provost (forthcoming).

——. 2013c. Representations of Women in Polygamy, in *Reference re: Section 293 of the Criminal Code of Canada. Annuaire Droit et Religion* (forthcoming).

Campbell, A. et al. 2011. Child Citizenship and Agency as Shaped by Legal Obligations. *Child and Family Law Quarterly*, 23(4), 489-512.

Campbell, M.K. 2001. Mr. Peay's Horses: The Federal Response to Mormon Polygamy, 1854-1887. *Yale Journal of Law and Feminism*, 13(1), 29-70.

Capp, B. 2009. Bigamous Marriage in Early Modern England. *The Historical Journal*, 52(3), 537-556.

Carline, A. 2012. Of Frames, Cons and Affects: Constructing and Responding to Prostitution and Trafficking for Sexual Exploitation. *Feminist Legal Studies*, 20(3), 207-225.

Carter, S. 2008. *The Importance of Being Monogamous: Marriage and Nation Building in Western Canada to 1915*. Edmonton: University of Alberta Press.

Caulfield, T. 2002. Politics, Prohibitions and the Lost Public Perspective: A Comment on Bill C-56: The *Assisted Human Reproduction Act*. *Alberta Law Review*, 40(2), 451-463.

Chambers, C. 2008. *Sex, Culture, and Justice: The Limits of Choice*. University Park, PA: Pennsylvania State University Press.

Chambers, D.L. 1997. Polygamy and Same-Sex Marriage. *Hofstra Law Review*, 26(1), 53-83.

Chan, M. 2011. Beyond Bountiful: Toward an Intersectional and Postcolonial Feminist Intervention in the British Columbia Polygamy Reference. *Appeal*, 16, 15-30.

Chapman, S. 2001. *Polygamy, Bigamy and Human Rights Law*. Philadelphia, PA: Xlibris.

Church, S. et al. 2001. Violence by Clients Towards Female Prostitutes in Different Work Settings: Questionnaire Survey. *British Medical Journal*, 322, 524-525.

Ciccarelli, J.C. 1997. *The Surrogate Mother: A Post-Birth Follow Up Study*. Los Angeles, CA: California School of Professional Psychology.

Ciccarelli, J.C. and Beckman, L.J. 2005. Navigating Rough Waters: An Overview of Psychological Aspects of Surrogacy. *Journal of Social Issues*, 61(1), 21-43.

Cler-Cunningham, L. and Christensen, C. 2001. *Violence against Women in Vancouver's Street Level Sex Trade and the Police Response*. Vancouver: Pace Society.

Connell, S. 2012. *Bringing in Finn: An Extraordinary Surrogacy Story*. Berkeley, CA: Seal Press.

Cooper, B.S. et al. 2004. Traumatic Stress in Prostitutes. *Journal of Trauma Practice*, 3(1), 51-70.

Cossman, B. 1990. A Matter of Difference: Domestic Contracts and Gender Equality. *Osgoode Hall Law Journal*, 28, 303-380.

——. 2009. The "Opt Out Revolution" and the Changing Narratives of Motherhood: Self Governing the Work/Family Conflict. *Utah Law Review*, 2, 455-474.

Cusick, L. and Hickman, M. 2005. "Trapping" in Drug Use and Sex Work Careers. *Drugs Education, Prevention and Policy*, 12, 369-379.

Dalton, C. et al. 2001. *Battered Women and the Law: Theory and Practice*. New York: Foundation Press.

Daunt, F. 1991. Exploitation or Empowerment? Debating Surrogate Motherhood. *Saskatchewan Law Review*, 55(2), 415-428.

Davies, J. et al. 1998. *Safety Planning with Battered Women: Complex Lives/Difficult Choices*. Thousand Oaks, CA: Sage Publications.

Davies, M. 2005. The Ethos of Pluralism. *Sydney Law Review*, 27, 87-112.

Day, S. 2008. *Prostitution: Violating the Human Rights of Poor Women* (Ottawa: Action ontarienne contre la violence fait aux femmes).

Daynes, K.M. 2001. *More Wives than One: Transformation of the Mormon Marriage System, 1840-1910*. Urbana,IL: University of Illinois Press.

Dingwall, R. 2010. Divorce Mediation: Should We Change Our Mind? *Journal of Social Welfare & Family Law*, 32(2), 107-117.

Dodson, J. and Smith, E. 2011. The Introduction of Surrogacy Law in New South Wales: The *Surrogacy Act 2010*. *Australian Health Law Bulletin*, 27.

Doezema, J. 1998. Forced to Choose: Beyond the Voluntary v Forced Prostitution Dichotomy, in *Global Sex Workers: Rights, Resistance, and Redefinition*, edited by K. Kempadoo and J. Dozema. London: Routledge, 34-50.

Drummond, S. 2009. Polygamy's Inscrutable Criminal Mischief. *Osgoode Hall Law Journal*, 47(2), 317-369.

Duncan, E.J. 2008. The Positive Effects of Legalizing Polygamy: "Love is a Many Splendored Thing." *Duke Journal of Gender Law and Policy*, 15(1), 315-337.

Dunn, J.L. and Powell-Williams, M. 2007. "Everybody Makes Choices": Victim Advocates and the Social Construction of Battered Women's Victimization and Agency. *Violence against Women*, 13(10), 977-1001.

Dworkin, A. 1983. *Right-Wing Women*. New York: Perigree Books.

——. 1987. *Intercourse*. New York: Free Press.

——. 1991. *Pornography: Men Possessing Women*. New York: Plume.

Edwards, S. 2009. Justice Devlin's Legacy: Duffy—A Battered Woman "Caught" in Time. *Criminal Law Review*, 12, 851-869.

Eichler, M. 1997. *Family Shifts: Families, Policies, and Gender Equality*. Toronto: Oxford University Press.

Eichner, M. 2009. Feminism, Queer Theory and Sexual Citizenship, in *Gender Equality: Dimensions of Women's Equal Citizenship*, edited by Linda C. McClain and Joanna L. Grossman. New York: Cambridge University Press, 307-326.

Einwohner, J. 1989. Who Becomes a Surrogate: Personality Characteristics, in *Gender in Transition: A New Frontier*, edited by J. Offerman-Zuckerberg. New York: Plenum, 123-133.

Elbedour, S. et al. 2002. The Effect of Polygamous Marital Structure on Behavioural, Emotional, and Academic Adjustment in Children: A Comprehensive Review of the Literature. *Clinical Child and Family Psychology Review*, 5(4), 255-271.

Embry, J.L. 1984. Effects of Polygamy on Mormon Women. *Frontiers*, 7(3), 56-61.

Ertman, M. 2010. Race Treason: The Untold Story of America's Ban on Polygamy. *Columbia Journal of Gender and Law*, 19(2), 287-366.

Esplugues, C. 1984. Legal Recognition of Polygamous Marriages. *Comparative and International Law Journal of Southern Africa*, 17, 302-321.

Farley, M. 2003. Prostitution and the Invisibility of Harm. *Women & Therapy*, 36, 247-280.

——. 2004. Bad for the Body, Bad for the Heart: Prostitution Harms Women even if Legalised or Decriminalised. *Violence against Women*, 10(10), 1087-1125.

Fehlberg, B. and Smyth, B. 2002. Binding Pre-Nuptial Agreements in Australia: The First Year. *International Journal of Law, Policy and the Family*, 16(1), 127-140.

Fineman, M. 2008. The Vulnerable Subject: Anchoring Equality in the Human Condition. *Yale Journal of Law & Feminism*, 20(1), 1-24.

——. 2010. The Vulnerable Subject and the Responsive State. *Emory Law Journal*, 60(1), 251-275.

Forbes, S. 2003. "Why Have Just One?": An Evaluation of the Anti-Polygamy Laws Under the Establishment Clause. *Houston Law Review*, 39(5), 1517-1547.

Fournier, P. 2001. The Erasure of Islamic Difference in Canadian and American Family Law Adjudication. *Journal of Law & Policy*, 10(1), 51-95.

——. 2012a. Calculating Claims: Jewish and Muslim Women Navigating Religion, Economics and Law in Canada. *International Journal of Law in Context*, 8(1), 47-72.

——. 2012b. *Halacha*, the Jewish State and the Canadian *Agunah*: Comparative Law and the Intersection of Religious and Secular Orders. *Journal of Legal Pluralism*, 65, 165-204.

Frances, R. 1994. The History of Female Prostitution in Australia, in *Sex Work and Sex Workers in Australia*, edited by R. Perkins et al. Sydney: University of New South Wales Press, 27-52.

Freeman, M. 1989. Is Surrogacy Exploitative?, in *Legal Issues in Human Reproduction*, edited by S. McLean. Aldershot: Darmouth, 164-184.

——. 1999. Does Surrogacy Have a Future after Brazier? *Medical Law Review*, 7(1), 1-20.

Frye, M. 1985. History and Responsibility. *Women's Studies International Forum*, 8(3), 215-217.

Gaffney, P. 2009. Why the "Widespread Agreement" is Wrong: Contesting the Non-Harm Arguments for the Prohibition of Full Commercial Surrogacy. *Journal of Law and Medicine*, 17(2), 280-296.

Gamble, N. 2009. Modern Surrogacy in the UK. *The Review*, 142, 58-59.

Gamble N. and Ghevaert, L. 2009a. The Chosen Middle Ground: England, Surrogacy Law and the International Arena. *International Family Law*, 223-227.

——. 2009b. The *Human Fertilisation and Embryology Act 2008*: Revolution or Evolution? *Family Law*, 730-733.

Gavigan, S.A.M. and Chunn, D.E. 2007. From Mothers' Allowance to Mothers Need Not Apply: Canadian Welfare Law as Liberal and Neo-Liberal Reforms. *Osgoode Hall Law Journal*, 45(4), 733-771.

Geertz, C. 1977. *The Interpretation of Cultures*. New York: Basic Books.

Gibson, M. 1994. Contract Motherhood: Social Practice in Social Context, in *Living with Contradictions: Controversies in Feminist Social Ethics*, edited by A.M. Jaggar. Boulder, CO: Westview Press, 402-419.

Gill, R.C. 2007. Critical Respect: The Difficulties and Dilemmas of Agency and "Choice" for Feminism. *European Journal of Women's Studies*, 14(1), 69-80.

Gilligan, C. 1982. *In a Different Voice: Psychological Theory and Women's Development*. Cambridge, MA: Harvard University Press.

Giroux, M. 1997. L'encadrement de la maternité de substitution au Québec et la protection de l'interet de l'enfant. *Revue générale de droit*, 28(4), 535-547.

——. 2011. Le recours controversé à l'adoption pour établir la filiation de l'enfant né d'une mère porteuse: entre ordre public contractuel et l'intérêt de l'enfant. *Revue du Barreau*, 70, 509-544.

Goldfarb, S. 2000. Violence against Women and the Persistance of Privacy. *Ohio State Law Journal*, 61(1), 1-88.

Goslinga-Roy, G.M. 2000. Body Boundaries, Fiction of the Female Self: An Ethnographic Perspective on Power, Feminism, and the Reproductive Technologies. *Feminist Studies*, 26(1), 113-140.

Gossop, M. et al. 1994. Sexual Behaviour and Its Relationship to Drug-Taking among Prostitutes in South London. *Addiction*, 89, 961-970.

Griffith, R. 2011. Payment for Surrogacy Arrangements Approved by the Courts. *British Journal of Midwifery*, 19(4), 257-258.

Grillo, T. 1991. The Mediation Alternative: Process Dangers for Women. *Yale Law Journal*, 100(6), 1545-1610.

Groves, J. et al. 2008. Sex Workers Working within a Legalised Industry: Their Side of the Story. *Sexually Transmitted Infections*, 84, 393-394.

Hadfield, G.K. 1995. The Dilemma of Choice: A Feminist Perspective on the Limits of Freedom of Contract. *Osgoode Hall Law Journal*, 33(2), 337-351.

——. 1997. Expressive Theory of Contract: From Feminist Dilemmas to a Reconceptualization of Rational Choice in Contract Law. *University of Pennsylvania Law Review*, 146(5), 1235-1285.

Halley, J. 2006. *Split Decisions: How and Why to Take a Break from Feminism*. Princeton, NJ: Princeton University Press.

Hallgrimsdottir, H.K. et al. 2006. Fallen Women and Rescued Girls: Social Stigma and Media Narratives of the Sex Industry in Victoria, B.C., from 1980 to 2005. *Canadian Review of Sociology*, 43(3), 265-280.

Hanna, C. 2009. The Ruth Bader Ginsburg Lecture: Beyond the Castle Walls: Balancing Privacy and Security in Domestic Violence Cases. *Thomas Jefferson Law Review*, 32(1), 65-86.

——. 2010. Rethinking Consent in a *Big Love* Way. *Michigan Journal of Gender & Law*, 17(1), 111-156.

Harcourt, C. and Donovan, B. 2005. The Many Faces of Sex Work. *Sexually Transmitted Infections*, 81(3), 201-206.

Harcourt C. et al. 2001. The Health and Welfare Needs of Female and Transgender Street Sex Workers in New South Wales. *Australian and New Zealand Journal of Public Health*, 25(1), 84-89.

Harding, L.M. 1987. The Debate on Surrogate Motherhood: The Current Situation, Some Arguments and Issues: Questions Facing Law and Policy. *Journal of Social Welfare and Family Law*, 9(1), 37-63.

Harding, S. 1987. Introduction: Is there a Feminist Method, in *Feminism and Methodology: Social Sciences Issues*, edited by S. Harding. Bloomington, IN: Indiana University Press, 1-14.

Haritaworn, J. et al. 2006. Poly/logue: A Critical Introduction to Polyamory. *Sexualities*, 9(5) 515-529.

Harris, M. et al. 2011. Risk and Risk Management for Australian Sex Workers. *Qualitative Health Research*, 21(3), 386-398.

Harvison Young, A. 2005. Let's Try Again … This Time with Feeling: Bill C-6 and New Reproductive Technologies. *UBC Law Review*, 38(1), 123-145.

Harvison Young, A. and Wasunna, A. 1998. Wrestling with the Limits of Law: Regulating New Reproductive Technologies. *Health Law Journal*, 6, 240-277.

Hassouneh-Phillips, D. 2001. Polygamy and Wife Abuse: A Qualitative Study of Muslim Women in America. *Health Care for Women International*, 22(8), 735-748.

Haviland, M. et al. 2001. *The Family Protection and Domestic Violence Intervention Act of 1995: Examining the Effects of Mandatory Arrest in New York City: A Report by The Family Violence Project of the Urban Justice Center*. New York: Center on Crime, Communities and Culture of The Open Society Institute.

Healy, K. 2006. *Last Best Gifts: Altruism and the Market for Human Blood and Organs*. Chicago, IL: University of Chicago Press.

Healy, P. 1995. Statutory Prohibitions and the Regulation of New Reproductive Technologies Under Federal Law in Canada. *McGill Law Journal*, 40(4), 905-946.

Heckathorn, D.D. 1997. Respondent-Driven Sampling: A New Approach to the Study of Hidden Populations. *Social Problems*, 44(2), 174-199.

Heise, M. 2002. The Past, Present, and Future of Empirical Legal Scholarship: Judicial Decision Making and the New Empiricism. *University of Illinois Law Review*, 2002(4), 819-850.

Higgins, T.E. 2000. Reviving the Public/Private Distinction in Feminist Theorizing. *Chicago-Kent Law Review*, 75(3), 847-867.

Hill Kay, H. 2003. Making Marriage and Divorce Safe for Women Revisited. *Hofstra Law Review*, 32(1), 71-92.

Hogg, P. 2012. *Constitutional Law of Canada*. 5th Edition: Supplemented. Toronto: Thomson Carswell.

Hohman, M.M. and Hagan, C.B. 2001. Satisfaction with Surrogate Mothering. *Journal of Human Behaviour in the Social Environment*, 4(1) 61-84.

Holden, K.C. 1991. The Economic Costs of Marital Dissolution: Why Do Women Bear a Disproportionate Cost? *Annual Review of Sociology*, 17, 51-78.

Holmes, C. and McRae-Williams, E. 2011. *"Captains" and "Selly-welly": Indigenous Women and the Role of Transactional Sex in Homelessness*. Canberra: Commonwealth Government of Australia, Department of Families and Housing, Community Services and Indigenous Affairs.

Horsey, K. 2010. Challenging Presumptions: Legal Parenthood and Surrogacy Arrangements. *Child and Family Law Quarterly*, 22(4), 449-474.

Horsey, K. and Sheldon, S. 2012. Still Hazy after All These Years: The Law Regulating Surrogacy. *Medical Law Review*, 20(1), 67-89.

Hunter, R. 2007. Consent in Violent Relationships, in *Choice and Consent: Feminist Engagements with Law and Subjectivity*, edited by R. Hunter and S. Cowan. New York: Routledge-Cavendish, 158-173.

Hunter, R. and Cowan, S. (eds). 2007. *Choice and Consent: Feminist Engagements with Law and Subjectivity*. New York: Routledge-Cavendish.

Hurd, H.M. 1996. The Moral Magic of Consent. *Legal Theory*, 2(2), 121-146.

Hurka, T. 1996. *Perfectionism*. Oxford: Oxford University Press.

Ince, S. 1994. Inside the Surrogate Industry, in *Living with Contradictions: Controversies in Feminist Social Ethics*, edited by A.M. Jaggar. Boulder, CO: Westview Press, 387-394.

Jackson, E. 2001. *Regulating Reproduction: Law, Technology and Autonomy*. Portland, OR: Hart Publishing.

Jackson, L.A. et al. 2005. Female Sex Trade Workers, Condoms, and the Public-Private Divide. *Journal of Psychology & Human Sexuality*, 17(1/2), 83-105.

Jackson, L.A. et al. 2007. Stress in the Sex Trade and Beyond: Women Working in the Sex Trade Talk about the Emotional Stressors in Their Working and Home Lives. *Critical Public Health*, 17(3), 257-271.

Jadva, V. et al. 2003. Surrogacy: The Experiences of Surrogate Mothers. *Human Reproduction*, 18(10), 2196-2204.

Jakobsen, J. and Perkins, R. 1994. Oral History of Sex Workers in Syndey, in *Sex Work and Sex Workers in Australia*, edited by R. Perkins, G. Prestage, R. Sharp and F. Lovejoy. Sydney: University of New South Wales Press, 53-66.

Jankowiak, W. and Allen, E. 1995. The Balance of Duty and Desire in an American Polygamous Community, in *Romantic Passion: A Universal Experience?*, edited by W. Jankowiak. New York: Columbia University Press, 277-295.

Jeal, N. et al. 2008. The Multiplicity and Interdependency of Factors Influencing the Health of Street-based Sex Workers: A Qualitative Study. *Sexually Transmitted Infections*, 84(5), 381.

Jeffrey, L.A. and MacDonald, G. 2006a. It's the Money Honey: The Economy of Sex Work in the Maritimes. *Canadian Review of Sociology and Anthropology*, 43(3), 313-327.

——. 2006b. *Sex Workers in the Maritimes Talk Back*. Vancouver: UBC Press.

Jeffrey, L.A. and Sullivan, B. 2009. Canadian Sex Work Policy for the 21st Century: Enhancing Rights and Safety, Lessons from Australia. *Canadian Political Science Review*, 3(1), 57-76.

Jessop, C. and Palmer, L. 2007. *Escape*. New York: Broadway Books.

Johnson, T. 2010. Queensland's Proposed Surrogacy Legislation: An Opportunity for National Reform. *Journal of Law and Medicine*, 17(4), 617-632.

Kaganas, F. and Murray, C. 1991. Law, Women, and the Family: The Question of Polygyny in a New South Africa. *Acta Juridica*, 116-134.

Kanefield, L. 1999. The Reparative Motive in Surrogate Mothers. *Adoption Quarterly*, 2(4), 5-19.

Kantola, J. and Squires, J. 2004. Discourses Surrounding Prostitution Policies in the UK. *European Journal of Women's Studies*, 11(1), 77-101.

Kashmeri, S. 2008. *Unravelling Surrogacy in Ontario, Canada: An Ethnographic Inquiry of the Influence of Canada's Assisted Human Reproduction Act (2004) on Surrogacy Contracts, Parentage Laws, and Gay Fatherhood*. Master of Arts thesis, Concordia University [unpublished].

Kaufman, A. 2004. Choice, Responsibility and Equality. *Political Studies*, 52(4), 819-836.

Kaufman, A.J. 2005. Polygamous Marriages in Canada. *Canadian Journal of Family Law*, 21(2), 315-344.

Keller, J. 1997. Autonomy, Relationality, and Feminist Ethics. *Hypatia*, 12(2), 152-164.

Kennedy, D. 1993. *Sexy Dressing, etc*. Cambridge, MA: Harvard University Press.

Kessler, B. 2009. Recruiting Wombs: Surrogates as the New Security Moms. *Women's Studies Quarterly*, 37(1), 167-182.

Kim, N. 1993. Toward a Feminist Theory of Human Rights: Straddling the Fence Between Western Imperialism and Uncritical Absolutism. *Columbia Human Rights Law Review*, 25, 49-106.

Kirkman, M. and Kirkman, A. 2002. Sister-to-Sister Gestational "Surrogacy" 13 Years On: A Narrative of Parenthood. *Journal of Reproductive and Infant Psychology*, 20(3), 135-147.

Kleinhans, M. and Macdonald, R.A. 1997. What is a Critical Legal Pluralism? *Canadian Journal of Law and Society*, 12(2), 25-46.

Kleinpeter, C.H. and Hohman, M.M. 2000. Surrogate Motherhood: Personality Traits and Satisfaction with Service Providers. *Psychological Reports*, 87(3), 957-970.

Klinger, K. 2003. Prostitution Humanism and a Woman's Choice. *The Humanist*, 63(1), 16-19.

Koken, J.A. 2010. The Meaning of the "Whore": How Feminist Theories on Prostitution Shape Research on Female Sex Workers, in *Sex Work Matters: Power and Intimacy in the Global Sex Industry*, edited by M. Ditmore et al. London: Zed Books, 26-84.

Koshan, J. 1997. Sounds of Silence: The Public/Private Dichotomy, Violence, and Aboriginal Women, in *Challenging the Public/Private Divide: Feminism, Law and Public Policy*, edited by S. Boyd. Toronto: University of Toronto Press, 87-109.

Kwiatkowski, C.F. and Booth, R.E. 2000. Differences in HIV Risk Behaviors among Women Who Exchange Sex for Money, or Both Drugs and Money. *AIDS and Behavior*, 4(3), 233-240.

Lacey, N. 1995. Feminist Legal Theory Beyond Neutrality. *Current Legal Problems*, 48(2), 1-38.

Langevin, L. 2009. Liberté contractuelle et relations conjugales: font-elles bon ménage? *Revue Nouvelles Questions Féministes*, 28(2), 24-35.

LaViolette, A.D. and Barnett, O.W. 2000. *It Could Happen to Anyone: Why Battered Women Stay*. 2nd edition. Thousand Oaks, CA: Sage Publications.

Leckey, R. 2007. Contracting Claims and Family Law Feuds. *University of Toronto Law Journal*, 57(1), 1-41.

——. 2008a. *Contextual Subjects: Family, State and Relational Theory*. Toronto: University of Toronto Press.

——. 2008b. What is Left of Pelech? *Supreme Court Law Review (2d)*, 41, 103-129.

——. 2009. A Common Law of the Family? Reflections on Rick v. Brandsema. *Canadian Journal of Family Law*, 25, 257-296.

——. 2011. Law Reform, Lesbian Parenting and the Reflective Claim. *Social and Legal Studies*, 20(3), 331-348.

Levine, H.B. 2003. Gestational Surrogacy: Nature and Culture in Kinship. *Ethnology*, 42(3), 173-185.

Levine, N.E. and Silk, J.B. 1997. Why Polyandry Fails. *Current Anthropology*, 38(3), 375-398.

Lewis, J. et al. 2005. Managing Risk and Safety on the Job: The Experiences of Canadian Sex Workers. *Journal of Psychology and Human Sexuality*, 17(1/2), 147-167.

Loke, T-L. 1997. Trapped in Domestic Violence: The Impact of United States Immigration Laws on Battered Immigrant Women. *Boston University Public Interest Law Journal*, 6(2), 589-614.

Lowman, J. 2000. Violence and the Outlaw Status of (Street) Prostitution. *Violence against Women*, 6(9), 987-1011.

MacCallum, F. et al. 2003. Surrogacy: The Experience of Commissioning Couples. *Human Reproduction*, 18(6), 1334-1342.

Macdonald, R.A. 2002. *Lessons of Everyday Law*. Montreal: McGill-Queen's Press for the School of Policy Studies, Queen's University.

Macdonald, R.A. and Kleinhans, M.M. 1997. What is a Critical Legal Pluralism? *Canadian Journal of Law and Society*, 12(2), 25-46.

Macfarlane, J. 2005. *The Emerging Phenomenon of Collaborative Family Law (CFL): A Qualitative Study of CFL Cases*. Ottawa: Ministry of the Attorney General of Canada. [Online: Justice Canada]. Available at: http://www.justice.gc.ca/eng/rp-pr/fl-lf/famil/2005_1/pdf/2005_1.pdf [accessed: 8 June 2013].

MacKinnon, C.A. 1985. Pornography, Civil Rights, and Speech. *Harvard Civil Rights-Civil Liberties Law Review*, 20(1), 1-70.

——. 1989. *Toward a Feminist Theory of the State*. Cambridge, MA: Harvard University Press.

Maclean, M. 2010. Family Mediation: Alternative or Additional Dispute Resolution? *Journal of Social Welfare & Family Law*, 32(2), 105-106.

Maguire Shultz, M. 1990. Reproductive Technology and Intent Based Parenthood: An Opportunity for Gender Neutrality. *Wisconsin Law Review*, 2, 297-398.

Majury, D. 2009. Women are Themselves to Blame: Choice as a Justification for Unequal Treatment, in *Making Equality Rights Real: Securing Substantive Equality Under the Charter*, edited by M. Denike, F. Faraday and M.K. Stephenson. Toronto: Irwin Law, 209-244.

Malik, M. 2006. "The Branch on which We Sit": Multiculturalism, Minority Women and Family Law, in *Feminist Perspectives on Family Law*, edited by A. Diduck and K. O'Donovan. New York: Routledge, 211-233.

Marasinghe, M.L. 1978. Polygamous Marriages and the Principle of Mutation in the Conflict of Laws. *McGill Law Journal*, 24(3), 395-421.

Martin, C. 1998. Unequal Shadows: Negotiation Theory and Spousal Support Under Canadian Divorce Law. *University of Toronto Faculty of Law Review*, 56(1), 135-159.

Martin, J. 1994. English Polygamy Law and the Danish Registered Partnership Act: A Case for the Consistent Treatment of Foreign Polygamous Marriages and Danish Same-Sex Marriages in England. *Cornell International Law Journal*, 27(2), 419-446.

Martinson, D. et al. 1991. A Forum on *Lavallee v. R.*: Women and Self-Defence. *UBC Law Review*, 25 23-68.

Matsuda, M.J. 1990. Pragmatism Modified and the False Consciousness Problem. *Southern California Law Review*, 63(6), 1763-1782.

McDonald, P.K., Bradley, L.M. and Guthrie, D. 2006. Challenging the Rhetoric of Choice in Maternal Labour-Force Participation: Preferred Versus Contracted Work Hours. *Gender, Work and Organization*, 13(5), 470-491.

McDonnell, K. 1984. *Not an Easy Choice: A Feminist Re-examines Abortion*. Cambridge, MA: South End Press.

McGillivray, A. and Comaskey, B. 1999. *Black Eyes All of the Time: Intimate Violence, Aboriginal Women, and the Justice System*. Toronto: University of Toronto Press.

McKeganey, N. and Barnard, M. 1996. *Sex Work on the Streets: Prostitutes and Their Clients*. Buckingham: Open University Press.

McLanahan, S. and Kelly, E. 2006. The Feminization of Poverty: Past and Future, in *Handbook of the Sociology of Gender*, edited by J.S. Chafetz. New York: Springer, 127-145.

McLaren, J.P.S. 1986. Chasing the Social Evil: Moral Fervour and the Evolution of Canada's Prostitution Laws, 1867-1917. *Canadian Journal of Law & Society*, 1, 125-166.

McRae, S. 2003. Constraints and Choices in Mothers' Employment Careers: A Consideration of Hakim's Preference Theory. *British Journal of Sociology*, 54(3), 317-338.

McVerry, S. and Lindop, E. 2005. Negotiating Risk: How Women Working in Massage Parlours Preserve Their Sexual and Psychological Health. *Health Care for Women International*, 26(2), 108-117.

Mead, F. and Bodkin, A.H. 1885. *The Criminal Law Amendment Act, 1885, with Introduction, Notes, and Index*. London: Shaw & Sons, Fetter Lane and Crane Court.

Menon, N. 2009. *Regulating Reproduction: Evaluating the Canadian Law on Surrogacy and Surrogate Motherhood*. Master of Laws thesis, University of Toronto [unpublished].

Miccio, G.K. 2005. Exiled from the Province of Care: Domestic Violence, Duty and Conceptions of State Accountability. *Rutgers Law Journal*, 37(1), 111-195.

Michelman, K. 2005. *With Liberty and Justice for All: A Life Spent Protecting the Right to Choose*. New York: Hudson Street Press.

Millbank, J. 2011. The New Surrogacy Parentage Laws in Australia: Cautious Regulations or "25 Brick Walls"? *Melbourne University Law Review*, 35(1), 1-44.

Minichiello, V. et al. 2001. Male Sex Workers in Three Australian Cities: Socio-Demographic and Sex Work Characteristics. *Journal of Homosexuality*, 42(1), 29-51.

Minow, M. 1990. *Making All the Difference: Inclusion, Exclusion and American Law*. Ithaca, NY: Cornell University Press.

——. 1992. Choices and Constraints: For Justice Thurgood Marshall. *Georgetown Law Journal*, 80, 2093-2108.

Minow, M. and Shanley, M.L. 1996. Relational Rights and Responsibilities: Revisioning the Family in Liberal Political Theory and Law, *Hypatia*, 11(1), 4-29.

Mir-Hosseini, Z. 2003. The Construction of Gender in Islamic Legal Thought and Strategies for Reform. *Hawwa: Journal of Women in the Middle East and the Islamic World*, 1(1), 1-28.

Morgan, D. 1986. Who to Be or Not to Be: The Surrogacy Story. *Modern Law Review*, 49(3), 358-368.

Moss, V.A. et al. 1997. The Experience of Terminating an Abusive Relationship from an Anglo and African American Perspective: A Qualitative Descriptive Study. *Issues in Mental Health Nursing*, 18(5), 433-454.

Mossman, M.J. 2004. Choices and Commitments for Women: Challenging the Supreme Court of Canada in the Context of Social Assistance. *Osgoode Hall Law Journal*, 42(4), 615-624.

Munro, V.E. and Scoular, J. 2012. Abusing Vulnerability? Contemporary Law and Policy Responses to Sex Work in the UK. *Feminist Legal Studies*, 20(3), 189-206.

Murphy, K. et al. 2009. Nurturing Regulatory Compliance: Is Procedural Justice Effective When People Question the Legitimacy of the Law. *Regulation & Governance*, 3(1), 1-26.

Musser, J.W. 1944. *Celestial or Plural Marriage: A Digest of the Mormon Marriage System as Established by God through the Prophet Joseph Smith*. Salt Lake City, UT: Joseph W. Musser.

Nadon, S.M. et al. 1998. Antecedents to Prostitution: Childhood Victimization. *Journal of Interpersonal Violence*, 13, 206-221.

Nedelsky, J. 1993. Reconceiving Rights as Relationship. *Review of Constitutional Studies*, 1(1), 1-26.

——. 2011. *Law's Relations: A Relational Theory of Self, Autonomy, and Law*. New York: Oxford University Press.

Newman, Dwight G. 2007. Exit, Voice, and "Exile": Rights to Exit and Rights to Reject. *University of Toronto Law Journal*, 57(1), 43-79.

Nixon, K. et al. 2002. The Everyday Occurrence: Violence in the Lives of Girls Exploited through Prostitution. *Violence against Women*, 8, 1016-1043.

O'Doherty, T. 2011a. Victimization in Off-Street Sex Industry Work. *Violence against Women*, 17(7), 944-963.

——. 2011b. Criminalization and Off-Street Sex Work in Canada. *Canadian Journal of Criminology and Criminal Justice*, 53(2), 217-245.

Palmer, D. and Perrin, D. 2004. *Keep Sweet: Children of Polygamy*. Lister: Dave's Press.

Pateman, C. 1988. *The Sexual Contract*. Stanford, CA: Stanford University Press.

——. 2002. Self-Ownership and Property in the Person. *Journal of Political Philosophy*, 10(1), 20-53.

Parker, P.J. 1983. Motivation of Surrogate Mothers: Initial Findings. *American Journal of Psychiatry*, 140(1), 117-118.

Parkinson, P. 1994. Taking Multiculturalism Seriously: Marriage Law and the Rights of Minorities. *Sydney Law Review*, 16(4), 473-505.

——. 1996. Multiculturalism and the Regulation of Marital Status in Australia, in *Families across Frontiers*, edited by N. Lowe and G. Douglas. The Hague: Kluwer Law International, 309-326.

Peaslee, R.J. 1902. Separation Agreements Under the English Law. *Harvard Law Review*, 15(8), 638-656.

Peled, E. et al. 2000. Choice and Empowerment for Battered Women Who Stay: Toward a Constructivist Model. *Social Work*, 45(1), 9-25.

Pelland, M-A. 2007. *Allégations d'entorse aux lois: Effets sur la réalité sociale d'un groupe de mormons polygames canadiens*. Doctor of Philosophy thesis, Université de Montréal [unpublished].

Pelland, M.-A. and Casoni, D. 2010. Vicissitudes de l'identité sociale et allégations d'entorses aux lois chez un groupe de mormons polygames canadiens. *Déviance et Société*, 34(1), 49-69.

Peters, F. 2004. Choice, Consent and the Legitimacy of Market Transactions. *Economics and Philosophy*, 20(1), 1-18.

Peters, M. 1994. *"Pearls before Swine": Secrecy in a Mormon Polygynous Colony*. Master of Arts thesis, University of Alberta [unpublished].

Petro, M. 2010. Selling Sex: Women's Participation in the Sex Industry, in *Sex Work Matters: Exploring Money, Power and Intimacy in the Sex Industry*, edited by M.H. Ditmore, A. Levy and A. Willman. New York: Zed Books, 155-170.

Phillips, A. 2011. It's My Body and I'll Do What I Like with It: Bodies as Objects and Property. *Political Theory*, 39(6), 724-748.

Pivot Legal Society Sex Work Subcommittee. 2004. *Voices for Dignity: A Call to End the Harms Caused by Canada's Sex Trade Laws*. Vancouver: Pivot Legal Society.

Poote, A.E. and van den Akker, O.B.A. 2009. British Women's Attitudes to Surrogacy. *Human Reproduction*, 24(1), 139-145.

Porter, J. and Bonilla, L. 2010. The Ecology of Street Prostitution, in *Sex for Sale: Prostitution, Pornography, and the Sex Industry*, edited by R. Weitzer. 2nd edition. New York: Routledge, 163-186.

Posner, R.A. 2002. Legal Scholarship Today. *Harvard Law Review*, 115(5), 1314-1326.

Post, D. 1997. Why Marriage Should be Abolished. *Women's Rights Law Reporter*, 18(3), 283-313.

Powell, A. and Murray, S. 2008. Children and Domestic Violence: Constructing a Policy Problem in Australia and New Zealand. *Social and Legal Studies*, 17(4), 453-474.

Pyett, P.M. and Warr, D.J. 1997. Vulnerability on the Streets: Female Sex Workers and HIV Risk. *AIDS Care*, 9(5), 539-547.

——. 1999. Women at Risk in Sex Work: Strategies for Survival. *Journal of Sociology*, 35, 183.

Rabinovitch, B. 2003. PEERS: The Prostitutes' Empowerment, Education and Resource Society, in *Prostitution, Trafficking and Traumatic Stress*, edited by M. Farley. New York: Routledge, 239-253.

Ragoné, H. 1994. *Surrogate Motherhood: Conception in the Heart*. Boulder, CO: Westview Press.

——. 1996. Chasing the Blood Tie: Surrogate Mothers, Adoptive Mothers and Fathers. *American Ethnologist*, 23(2), 352-365.

Raymond, J.G. 1990. Reproductive Gifts and Gift Giving: The Altruistic Woman. *The Hastings Center Report*, 20(6), 7-11.

Reame, N.E. et al. 1998. Long Term Outcomes of Surrogate Pregnancy: A Report of Surrogate Mother's Satisfaction, Life Events, and Moral Judgments Ten Years Later. *Fertility and Sterility*, 70(3), S28-29.

Reed, R. 1997. Roseanne: A "Killer Bitch" for Generation X, in *Third Wave Agenda: Being Feminist, Doing Feminism*, edited by L. Heywood and J. Drake. Minneapolis, MN: University of Minnesota Press, 122-133.

Reese, E. 2005. *Backlash against Welfare Mothers Past and Present*. Berkeley, CA: University of California Press.

Remple, V. et al. 2007. Conducting HIV/AIDS Research with Indoor Commercial Sex Workers: Reaching a Hidden Population. *Progress in Community Health Partnerships*, 1(2), 161-168.

Rengachary Smerdon, U. 2008. Crossing Bodies, Crossing Borders: International Surrogacy between the United States and India. *Cumberland Law Review*, 39(1), 15-85.

Rhoades, H. 2010. Mandatory Mediation of Family Disputes: Reflections from Australia. *Journal of Social Welfare & Family Law*, 32(2), 183-194.

Rhode, D.L. 2002. Legal Scholarship. *Harvard Law Review*, 115(5), 1327-1361.

Rogerson, C.J. 1991. Judicial Interpretation of the Spousal and Child Support Provisions of the *Divorce Act, 1985* (part I). *Canadian Family Law Quarterly*, 7, 155-269.

——. 2003. "They are Agreements Nonetheless" *Miglin v. Miglin*, 2003 SCC 24. *Canadian Journal of Family Law*, 20(1), 197-228.

Ruparelia, R. 2007. Giving Away the "Gift of Life": Surrogacy and the Canadian *Assisted Human Reproduction Act*. *Canadian Journal of Family Law*, 23(1), 11-54.

Ruttenberg, M.H. 1994. A Feminist Critique of Mandatory Arrest: An Analysis of Race and Gender in Domestic Violence Policy. *American University Journal of Gender and the Law*, 2, 171-199.

Ryan, R.K. 1991. And then there was One: An Analysis and Comparison of Polygamy among Jews and Mormons. *Jewish Law Annual*, 9, 205-231.

Sanders, T. 2004a. A Continuum of Risk? The Management of Health, Physical and Emotional Risks by Female Sex Workers. *Sociology of Health & Illness*, 26(5), 557-574.

——. 2004b. Controllable Laughter: Managing Sex Work through Humour. *Sociology*, 38(2), 273-291.

——. 2004c. The Risks of Street Prostitution: Punters, Police and Prostesters. *Urban Studies*, 41(9), 1703-1717.

——. 2005. It's Just Acting: Sex Workers' Strategies for Capitalising on Sexuality. *Gender, Work and Organisation*, 12(4), 319-342.

——. 2007. Becoming an Ex-Sex Worker: Making Transitions out of a Deviant Career. *Feminist Criminology*, 2, 74-95.

Sanders, T. and Campbell, R. 2007. Designing out Vulnerability, Building in Respect: Violence, Safety and Sex Work Policy. *British Journal of Sociology*, 58, 1-19.

Sanders, T. et al. 2009. *Prostitution: Sex Work, Policy and Politics*. London: Sage Publications.

Schloenhardt, A. and Human Trafficking Working Group. 2009. *Happy Birthday Brothels! Ten Years of Prostitution Regulation in Queensland*. [Online]. Available at: http://www.law.uq.edu.au/documents/humantraffic/reports-presentations/UQ-HTWG-Ten-Years-of-Prostitution-Regulation-in-Qld-Sep-2009.pdf [accessed: 28 November 2012].

Schneider, E.M. 1991. The Violence of Privacy. *Connecticut Law Review*, 23(4), 973-999.

Scott, J.W. 1991. The Evidence of Experience. *Critical Inquiry*, 17(4), 773-797.

Sen, A. 1999. *Development as Freedom*. Oxford: Oxford University Press.

Serratelli, A. 1993. Surrogate Motherhood Contracts: Should the British or Canadian Model Fill the U.S. Legislative Vacuum? *George Washington Journal of International Law & Economics*, 26(3), 633-674.

Seuffert, N. 2003. Shaping the Modern Nation: Colonial Marriage Law, Polygamy and Concubinage in Aotearoa New Zealand. *Law Text Culture*, 7(1), 186-220.

Shachar, A. 1999. The Paradox of Multicultural Vulnerability: Individual Rights, Identity Groups, and the State, in *Multicultural Questions*, edited by C. Joppke and S. Lukes. New York: Oxford University Pres, 87-129.

Shaffer, M. 1988. Divorce Mediation: A Feminist Perspective. *University of Toronto Faculty of Law Review*, 46(1), 162-200.

——. 1997. The Battered Woman Syndrome Revisited: Some Complicating Thoughts Five Years after *R. v. Lavallee*. *University of Toronto Law Journal*, 47(1), 1-33.

——. 2004. Domestic Contracts, Part II: The Supreme Court's Decision in *Hartshorne v. Hartshorne*. *Canadian Journal of Family Law*, 20(2), 261-289.

Shah, P.A. 2003. Attitudes to Polygamy in English Law. *International and Comparative Law Quarterly*, 52(2), 369-400.

Shaver, F.M. et al. 2011. Rising to the Challenge: Addressing the Concerns of People Working in the Sex Industry. *Canadian Review of Sociology*, 48(1), 47-65.

Shaw, R. 2008. Rethinking Reproductive Gifts as Body Projects. *Sociology*, 42(1), 11-28.

Sheppard, C. 1995. Uncomfortable Victories and Unanswered Questions: Lessons from *Moge*. *Canadian Journal of Family Law*, 12(2), 283-329.

Shewchuck, T.R. 1993. Regulation of Pre-Conception Agreements: A Synthesis of Individual Rights and Community Values. *Health Law Journal*, 1, 147-189.

Showden, C. 2011. *Choices Women Make: Agency in Domestic Violence, Assisted Reproduction, and Sex Work*. Minneapolis, MN: Minneapolis University Press.

Sigman, S.M. 2006. Everything Lawyers Know about Polygamy is Wrong. *Cornell Law Journal*, 16(1), 101-185.

Sloan, L. 2011. Women's Oppression or Choice? One American's View on Wearing the Hijab. *Affilia*, 26(3), 233-238.

Sloman, S. 1985. Surrogacy Arrangements Act 1985. *New Law Journal*, 135, 978-980.

Smyth, L. 2002. Feminism and Abortion Politics: Choice, Rights, and Reproductive Freedom. *Women's Studies International Forum*, 25(3), 335-345.

Snow, D. 2009. *From Commission to Conception: Commercial Surrogacy and Morality Policy in Canada*. Master of Arts thesis, University of Calgary [unpublished].

Snow, D. and Knopff, R. 2012. Assisted Reproduction Policy in Federal States: What Canada Should Learn from Australia. *School of Public Policy Research Papers*, 5(12), 1-28.

Sokoloff, N.J. and Dupont, I. 2005. Domestic Violence at the Intersections of Race, Class, and Gender: Challenges and Contributions to Understanding Violence against Marginalized Women in Diverse Communities. *Violence against Women*, 11(1), 38-64.

Starr, S. and Brilmayer, L. 2003. Family Separation as a Violation of International Law. *Berkeley Journal of International Law*, 21(2), 213-287.

Stoljar, N. 2000. Autonomoy and the Feminist Intuition, in *Relational Autonomy: Feminist Perspectives on Autonomy, Agency and the Social Self*, edited by C. Mackenzie and N. Stoljar. Oxford: Oxford University Press, 94-111.

Stone, A. 2007. On the Genealogy of Women: A Defence of Anti-Essentialism, in *Third Wave Feminism: A Critical Exploration*, edited by S. Gillis et al. 2nd edition. New York: Palgrave Macmillan, 16-29.

Stone, P. 2007. *Opting Out? Why Women Really Quit Careers and Head Home*. Berkeley, CA: University of California Press.

Stubbs, J. 2002. Domestic Violence and Women's Safety: Feminist Challenges to Restorative Justice, in *Restorative Justice and Family Violence*, edited by H. Strang and J. Braithwaite. New York: Cambridge University Press, 42-61.

Stuhmcke, A. 2004. Looking Backwards, Looking Forwards: Judicial and Legislative Trends in the Regulation of Surrogate Motherhood in the UK and Australia. *Australian Journal of Family Law*, 18(1), 1-28.

Suk, J. 2006. Criminal Law Comes Home. *Yale Law Journal*, 116(1), 2-70.

——. 2010. The Trajectory of Trauma: Bodies and Minds of Abortion Discourse. *Columbia Law Review*, 110(5), 1193-1252.

Sullivan, B. 1994. *The Politics of Sex: Prostitution and Pornography in Australia Since 1945*. Cambridge: Cambridge University Press.

——. 2008. Working in the Sex Industry: The Re-organization of Sex Work in Queensland, Australia in the Wake of Law Reform. *Labour and Industry*, 18, 73.

——. 2010. When (Some) Prostitution is Legal: The Impact of Law Reform on Sex Work in Australia. *Journal of Law and Society*, 37(1), 85-104.

TAMPEP. 2009. *Sex Work in Europe: A Mapping of the Prostitution Scene in 25 European Countries*. Amsterdam: TAMPEP International Foundation.

Teman, E. 2003. The Medicalization of "Nature" in the Artificial Body: Surrogate Motherhood in Israel. *Medical Anthropology Quarterly*, 17(1), 78-98.

——. 2008. The Social Construction of Surrogacy Research: An Anthropological Critique of the Psychosocial Scholarship on Surrogate Motherhood. *Social Science and Medicine*, 67(7), 1104-1112.

——. 2009. Embodying Surrogate Motherhood: Pregnancy as a Dyadic Body Project. *Body & Society*, 15(3), 47-69.

——. 2010. *Birthing a Mother: The Surrogate Body and the Pregnant Self*. Berkeley, CA: University of California Press.

Thapar-Björkert, S. and Morgan, K.J. 2010. "But Sometimes I Think ... They Put Themselves in the Situation": Exploring Blame and Responsibility in Interpersonal Violence. *Violence against Women*, 16(1), 32-59.

Theis, L. et al. 2009. *Re X and Y (Foreign Surrogacy)*: A Trek through a Thorn Forest. *Family Law*, 39, 239-243.

Thompson, S.E. 2000. Prostitution: A Choice Ignored. *Women's Rights Law Reporter*, 21(3), 217-247.

Thörnqvist, C. 2006. Family-Friendly Labour Market Policies and Careers in Sweden—and the Lack of Them. *British Journal of Guidance and Counselling*, 34(3), 309-326.

Tieu, M.M. 2009. Altruistic Surrogacy: The Necessary Objectification of Surrogate Mothers. *Journal of Medical Ethics*, 35(3), 171-175.

Timoshkina, N. and McDonald, L. 2009. *Building Parternships for Service Provision to Migrant Sex Workers*. Toronto: Wellesley Institute.

Tyldum, G. and Brunovskis, A. 2005. Describing the Unobserved: Methodological Challenges in Empirical Studies on Human Trafficking. *International Migration*, 43(1-2), 17-34.

Valcke, C. 2004. Comparative Law as Comparative Jurisprudence: The Comparability of Legal Systems. *American Journal of Comparative Law*, 52, 713-740.

Valverde, M. 2012. *Everyday Law on the Street: City Governance in an Age of Diversity*. Chicago, IL: University of Chicago Press.

van den Akker, O.B.A. 2003. Genetic and Gestational Surrogate Mothers' Experience of Surrogacy. *Journal of Reproductive and Infant Psychology*, 21(2), 145-161.

——. 2007. Psychosocial Aspects of Surrogate Motherhood. *Human Reproduction Update*, 13(1), 53-62.

——. 2010. Surrogate Mothers, in *Parenthood and Mental Health: A Bridge Between Infant and Adult Psychiatry*, edited by S. Tyano et al. New York: John Wiley & Sons, 39-49.

van Niekirk, A. and van Zyl, L. 1995. The Ethics of Surrogacy: Women's Reproductive Labour. *Journal of Medical Ethics*, 21(6), 345-349.

Van Praagh, S. 1996. The Chutzpah of Chasidism. *Canadian Journal of Law & Society*, 11(2), 193-215.

Vanwesenbeeck, I. 2001. Another Decade of Social Scientific Work on Sex Work: A Review of Research 1990-2000. *Annual Review of Sex Research*, 12, 242-289.

Waldfogel, J. 1998. Understanding the "Family Gap" in Pay for Women with Children. *Journal of Economic Perspectives*, 12(1), 137-156.

Waldron, J. 2002. Legal and Political Philosophy, in *The Oxford Handbook of Jurisprudence and Philosophy of Law*, edited by J. Coleman and S. Shapiro. Oxford: Oxford University Press, 352-381.

Ward, C.M. 2004. I Now Pronounce You Husband and Wives: *Lawrence v Texas* and the Practice of Polygamy in Modern America. *William and Mary Journal of Women and the Law*, 11(1), 131-151.

Webber, J. 2006. Legal Pluralism and Human Agency. *Osgoode Hall Law Journal*, 44(1) 167-198.

Weinrib, E.J. 1992. Corrective Justice. *Iowa Law Review*, 77(2), 403-425.

Weitzer, R. 2010. Sex Work: Paradigms and Policies, in *Sex for Sale: Prostitution, Pornography, and the Sex Industry*, edited by R. Weitzer. 2nd Edition. New York: Routledge, 1-43.

Weitzman, S. 2000. *"Not to People Like Us": Hidden Abuse in Upscale Marriage*. New York: Basic Books.

Weldon, J. 2010. Show Me the Money: A Sex Worker Reflects on Research into the Sex Industry, in *Sex Work Matters: Exploring Money, Power and Intimacy in the Sex Industry*, edited by M.H. Ditmore, A. Levy and A. Willman. New York: Zed Books, 147-154.

Welstead, M. 2010. Addicted to Motherhood: A Cautionary Tale. *Denning Law Journal*, 22, 209-218.

Wendell, S. 1990. Oppression and Victimization; Choice and Responsibility. *Hypatia*, 5(3), 15-46.

West, R.L. 1987. The Difference in Women's Hedonic Lives: A Phenomenological Critique of Feminist Legal Theory. *Wisconsin Women's Law Journal*, 3, 81-145.

——. 1995. Authority, Autonomy and Choice: The Role of Consent in the Moral and Political Visions of Franz Kafka and Richard Posner. *Harvard Law Review*, 99(2), 384-428.

Whelehan, I. 2007. Foreword, in *Third Wave Feminism: A Critical Exploration*, edited by S. Gillis, G. Howie, and R. Munford. 2nd Edition. Basingstoke: Palgrave Macmillan, xv-xx.

White, R. 2009. Two Sides of Polygamy. *Journal of Law and Family Studies*, 11(2), 447-454.

Wiegers, W.A. 1992. Economic Analysis of Law and "Private Ordering": A Feminist Critique. *University of Toronto Law Journal*, 42(2), 170-206.

Wiegers, W. and Keet, M. 2008. Collaborative Family Law and Gender Inequalities: Balancing Risks and Opportunities. *Osgoode Hall Law Journal*, 46(4), 733-772.

Williams, J. 1991. Gender Wars: Selfless Women in the Republic of Choice. *New York University Law Review*, 66(6), 1559-1634.

——. 1994. Is Coverture Dead? Beyond a New Theory of Alimony. *Georgetown Law Journal*, 82(7), 2227-2290.

——. 1996. Restructuring Work and Family Entitlements around Family Values. *Harvard Journal of Law & Public Policy*, 19(3), 753-757.

——. 2010. *Reshaping the Work-Family Debate: Why Men and Class Matter*. Cambridge, MA: Harvard University Press.

Willman, A. 2010. Let's Talk About Money, in *Sex Work Matters: Exploring Money, Power and Intimacy in the Sex Industry*, edited by M.H. Ditmore, A. Levy and A. Willman. New York: Zed Books, 143-146.

York, S.G. 1990. A Contractual Analysis of Surrogate Motherhood and a Proposed Solution. *Loyola of Los Angeles Law Review*, 24(2), 395-420.

Yuracko, K. 2003. *Perfectionism and Contemporary Feminist Values*. Indianapolis, IN: Indiana University Press.

Zeitzen, M.K. 2008. *Polygamy: A Cross-Cultural Analysis*. Oxford: Berg.

——. 2013. Claiming the Right to Polygamy: Fundamentalist Mormon Challenges to North American Legal Cultures, in *Contemporary Gender Relations and Changes in Legal Cultures*, edited by H. Petersen et al. Copenhagen: DJOEF Publishing.

Zylan, Y. 2012. Polygamy Reference: Comments. *LawFemme*, 11(1), 2, 10-11. [Online]. Available at: http://faculty.law.ubc.ca/cfls/files/LawFemme-February-2012.pdf [accessed: 29 October 2012].

Media Reports

Ali, L. 2008. The Curious Lives of Surrogates. *Newsweek*. [Online, 7 April]. Available at: http://www.newsweek.com/id/129594/page/1 [accessed: 3 October 2012].

Anonymous. 2005. B.C. Polygamists Want Age of Consent Raised. *CTV News Online*. [Online, 19 February]. Available at: http://www.angelfire.com/film/tmtv/BC_polygamists.html [accessed: 8 June 2013].

——. 2007. Paid Surrogacy Driven Underground in Canada: CBC Report. *CBC*. [Online, 1 May]. Available at: http://www.cbc.ca/news/health/story/2007/05/01/surrogates-pay.html [accessed: 3 October 2012].

——. 2008a. Gender Equality and Polygamy are not Compatible. *The Age*. [Online, 27 June]. Available at: http://www.theage.com.au/opinion/editorial/gender-equality-and-polygamy-are-not-compatible-20080626-2xf5.html [accessed: 27 October 2012].

——. 2008b. One Law Fits All. *The Australian*. [Online, 26 June]. Available at: http://www.theaustralian.com.au/news/one-law-fits-all/story-e6frg72f-1111116735656 [accessed: 27 October 2012].

——. 2008c. A Nine-Month Partnership. *National Post*, 26 April, FW5.

——. 2012a. Australia Muslim Women's Group Lashes Out at Polygamy Claims. *bikyamasr*. [Online, 15 July]. Available at: http://www.bikyamasr.com/72836/australia-muslim-womens-group-lashes-out-at-polygamy-claims/ [accessed: 17 October 2012].

——. 2012b. B.C. Special Prosecutor Given OK to Charge Polygamists. *CBC*. [Online, 26 March]. Available at: http://www.cbc.ca/news/canada/british-columbia/story/2012/03/26/bc-polygamy-charges-allowed.html [accessed: 26 October 2012].

——. 2012c. BBC on this Day: 1985: Inquiry Over "Baby-for-Cash" Deal. *BBC News*. [Online, 3 October]. Available at: http://news.bbc.co.uk/onthisday/hi/dates/stories/january/4/newsid_2495000/2495857.stm [accessed: 3 October 2012].

Avery, D. 2002. A Surrogate Replies. *The Globe and Mail*, 7 February, A18.

Blackwell, T. 2009. The Impotency of Canada's Fertility Laws. *National Post*. [Online, 17 February]. Available at: http://www.canada.com/Health/impotency+Canada+fertility+laws/1288389/story.html [accessed: 3 October 2012].

Bolt, A. 2008. Polygamy: The Right to Put Down Women. *Herald Sun*. [Online, 27 June]. Available at: http://www.heraldsun.com.au/news/polygamy-the-right-to-put-down-women/story-e6frf7jo-1111116747515 [accessed: 27 October 2012].

Crenshaw, K.W. 1994. *Mapping the Margins: Intersectionality, Identity Politics, and Violence against Women of Colour*. [Online]. Available at: http://www.peopleofcolororganize.com/wp-content/uploads/pdf/mapping-margins.pdf [accessed: 9 December 2011].

Drummond, S. 2008. Your Really Want Them All Charged? *The Globe and Mail*. [Online, 5 August]. Available at: http://www.theglobeandmail.com/commentary/you-really-want-them-all-charged/article715353/ [accessed: 31 October 2012].

Eccles, L. 2011. Couple are Ordered to Pay Surrogate Mother £568 a Month for the Baby They Will Never See. *DailyMail*. [Online, 12 April]. Available at: http://www.dailymail.co.uk/news/article-1375861/Child-custody-Couple-ordered-pay-surrogate-mother-monthly-baby-wont-meet.html#ixzz1JagE4cBP [accessed: 3 October 2012].

Ferretti, L. 2009. La polygamie pour tous ou pour personne. *Le Devoir*. [Online, 4 March]. Available at: http://www.ledevoir.com/societe/actualites-en-societe/237135/la-polygamie-pour-tous-ou-pour-personne [accessed: 27 October 2012].

Fraser, J. 2012. Polyamory: Exploring the Ins and Outs of Multiple Partners. *The Globe and Mail*. [Online, 21 September]. Available at: http://www.theglobeandmail.com/life/relationships/polyamory-exploring-the-ins-and-outs-of-multiple-partners/article4560587/?page=1 [accessed: 31 October 2012].

Gazze, M. 2007. Canada: Destination for Infertile Couples. *The Globe and Mail*, 26 June, A12.

Hirshman, L.R. 2005. *Homeward Bound*. [Online]. Available at: http://prospect.org/article/homeward-bound [accessed: December 9th 2011].

Javed, N. 2008. GTA's Secret World of Polygamy. *The Star*. [Online, 24 May]. Available at: http://www.thestar.com/news/gta/article/429490--gta-s-secret-world-of-polygamy [accessed: 17 October 2012].

Jeanes, T. 2005. British Man Convicted of Bigamy. *ABC*. [Online, 28 April]. Available at: http://www.abc.net.au/pm/content/2005/s1355850.htm [accessed: 27 October 2012].

Kennedy, D. 2007. 1,000 Men Living Legally with Multiple Wives Despite Fears Over Exploitation. *The Times*. [Online, 28 May]. Available at: Factiva [accessed: 27 October 2012].

Kuczynski, A. 2008. Her Body, My Baby. *NYT Magazine*. [Online, 28 November]. Available at: http://www.nytimes.com/2008/11/30/magazine/30Surrogate-t.html?pagewanted=all [accessed: 3 October 2012].

Mayeda, A. 2009. Tories Determined to Defend Polygamy Ban. *Calgary Herald*, 25 March, A5.

O'Malley, K. 2007. No Big Love Lost. *Macleans*. [Online, 25 June]. Available at: http://www.macleans.ca/article.jsp?content=20070625_124219_1740&source=srch [accessed: 27 October 2012].

Pearce, T. 2011. Surrogate Who Kept Baby Gets $785 a Month from Would-be Parents. *The Globe and Mail*. [Online, 14 April]. Available at: http://www.theglobeandmail.com/life/the-hot-button/surrogate-who-kept-baby-gets-785-a-month-from-would-be-parents/article1986311/ [accessed: 3 October 2012].

Serck, L. 2012. Polygamy in Islam: The Women Victims of Multiple Marriage. *BBC News*. [Online: 31 May]. Available at: http://www.bbc.co.uk/news/uk-england-berkshire-18252958 [accessed: 17 October 2012].

Stueck, W. 2012. Special Prosecutor Gets Go-Ahead to Weigh Polygamy Charges. *The Globe and Mail*. [Online, 26 March]. Available at: http://www.theglobeandmail.com/news/british-columbia/special-prosecutor-gets-go-ahead-to-weigh-polygamy-charges/article534383/ [accessed: 26 October 2012].

Index